For more than twenty years I wor
native language, making use of m<
helped me greatly in understandin

I started to read the commentary on Genesis 1-11 by Anwarul Azad and Ida
Glaser, I gained more than knowledge. My heart was filled with joy because
this book highlights the truth of the Bible from an Eastern perspective that I
can relate to. The authors have woven together biblical and cultural threads
into a beautiful, unique tapestry. I highly recommend this book to any person
who is seeking to find our Creator and his plan for humanity.

Nilufar Abdusatarova
Bible Society of Uzbekistan

This commentary on Genesis represents the fruit of deep conversation between
the Abrahamic faiths. Accessible to the reader without avoiding challenging
issues, it provides a fresh encounter with this foundational biblical text. This
work is sensitive to both ancient traditions and modern realities while keeping
the illumination of the text as its main focus. An engaging read for all.

Mark J. Boda, PhD
Professor of Old Testament,
McMaster Divinity College, Canada

This commentary is as exquisitely splendorous as a rainbow. Its bands of colour
come from Christian, Jewish and Islamic readings; from shining, evocative
Bangladeshi poetry; from everyday culture that illuminates the biblical text
for a regional reader and piques the interest of an international one; from local
anecdotes, glowing gem-like; from careful reflections on the text for today's
reader. What a radiantly different, biblically faithful and Christ-honouring
approach to understanding and applying Genesis 1–11!

Havilah Dharamraj, PhD
Head of the Department of Biblical Studies,
South Asia Institute of Advanced Christian Studies, Bangalore, India

This commentary authentically reflects Bangladesh with vivid local images
and ideas that are interesting, widely relevant and helpful beyond that cultural
locale. Strongly rooted in biblical exegesis, with larger theological connec-
tions enhancing, not distracting, from the focus on the biblical commentary
aspect. The focus is constructive, positive and practically encouraging for the

Christian life. The writing communicates a pastoral, pedagogical tone. I think this is a successful, valuable and distinctive contribution. I can't wait to have it in print and start using it.

Elisabeth Kennedy, PhD
Professor of Old Testament,
Assistant Professor in Comparative Religions,
The American University in Cairo, Egypt

This commentary gives us a perspective on Genesis as story of the ancestry of all humanity, and therefore especially how it can be heard by the Bengali Muslims who call themselves the "community of Ibrahim." It is keenly aware of the universal orientation of Genesis and its concern to place the worship of the true God in the midst of the nations and their gods. (It ends, significantly, at 12:3). It unfolds concepts from Genesis (such as blessing and grace) in dialogue with those of the Qur'an and has a respectful orientation towards those who treasure the Qur'an, and an awareness of the Qur'an's respect for the heritage of the Bible.

Gordon McConville, PhD
Professor Emeritus, Old Testament,
University of Gloucestershire, UK
Associate Professor, Old Testament, Trinity College Bristol, UK

Mr. Anwarul Azad worked hard to make God's words known to others, a task that he took as his God-given responsibility, a duty to both God and God's people. I count myself privileged to have come to know the content of the book from one of its authors, my friend Mr. Azad, even before its publication. I feel my friend's physical absence among us, but he will be with me and other readers through this book. This is a useful book not only for followers of Jesus the Messiah, but also for truth-seeking people of other faiths. This book is indeed a tool to be equipped with the truth! I am grateful to Dr. Ida Glaser and my friend, Mr. Azad for their hard work in writing a book that will help all its readers know the truth and conduct their lives in a way that is pleasing to God.

M. Shahidur Rahman
Learning for Living Educational Welfare Trust (SKT), Bangladesh

The subtitle of this inimitable commentary grabbed my attention before the authors did (one of whom I know well and the other from reputation). Genesis

1–11 is foundational for the interfaith contexts as has been demonstrated ably by others. What this work does is evident in its exceptional integrity, which reflects the authors. They come from disparate language and cultural backgrounds and, despite their differences, through their demonstrable dependence on God's revelation in the scriptures, offer the reader an exciting new journey through the first eleven chapters of Genesis. The primacy of the biblical narrative is scrupulously preserved throughout even as the authors highlight comparisons. Readers will find, as I did, a heartfelt and excitingly refreshing account through the merging of horizons for insights. I do not doubt it will generate much discussion making room for the Spirit to operate without obstacles.

David Singh, PhD
Research Tutor, Islamic Studies,
Oxford Centre for Mission Studies, UK

Windows on the Text

Genesis 1–11

Genesis 1–11

*Bud of Theology,
Grandmother of the Sciences,
Seedbed of the Holy Books*

Anwarul Azad and Ida Glaser

Series Editors: Ida Glaser and Martin Accad

Langham
GLOBAL LIBRARY

© 2022 Solomon Academic Trust

Published 2022 by Langham Global Library
An imprint of Langham Publishing
www.langhampublishing.org

Langham Publishing and its imprints are a ministry of Langham Partnership

Langham Partnership
PO Box 296, Carlisle, Cumbria, CA3 9WZ, UK
www.langham.org

ISBNs:
978-1-83973-585-1 Print
978-1-83973-668-1 ePub
978-1-83973-669-8 Mobi
978-1-83973-670-4 PDF

British Library Cataloguing-in-Publication Data
A catalogue record for this book is available from the British Library

ISBN: 978-1-83973-585-1

Cover & Book Design: projectluz.com

Contents

Preface

Anwarul Azad

One of my seminary teachers used to use the water buffalo as a parable of religious compromise. From the riverside, all we can see of the water buffalo is its two horns; since its whole body is under water, we do not see what it is really like. He told the story of a visit to a newly baptized believer in Jesus the Messiah. Her home was full of pictures – of Hindu deities, of Jesus the Messiah, and of al-Burāq, the celestial creature on which the Islamic Prophet Muhammad is said to have ridden to heaven. He taught the new believer that she no longer needed these pictures, and he was glad when he returned to see that she had removed them. She happily thanked him, but, as he was leaving, he looked and saw a picture of another god on the back of the front door, which he had not seen when he entered. The new believer explained that her mother was a devotee of this deity, so she had kept this picture to honour her mother. When a person hears about another new value without really understanding it, they often continue to live according to their previous values. We know that if we put new wine in an old bag, it will explode, and the bag will be ruined.

One of the things I love about Abraham is that he was not a water buffalo hiding under water. In his heart and mind, he no longer served the gods that his people had worshipped in the past. This is why he has become the father of the believers. In the Bible, God names him "the father of a multitude of nations" (Gen 17:5), and even calls him "my friend" (Isa 41:8; cf. 2 Chr 20:7; Jas 2:23). The Qur'an agrees, calling him the *imam* of the peoples (Sūra *al-Baqara* 2:124) and God's *khalil* (friend) (Sūra *an-Nisā'* 4:125). Although he was childless when he was called, today in this world, like the stars in the sky, like the sand on the shores of the sea, countless people are his biological and spiritual children. To this day, his most popular title in Bangladesh is *Khalil ullah* – the friend of God.

Most people in Bangladesh have heard stories of Abraham, and also of Adam and Eve, Abel and Cain, Seth, Enoch, Noah and Nimrod; but these stories often include many additions which are not found in either the Bible or the Qur'an. They are written in *Kasasul Ambiya* (Stories of the Prophets) and are still heard in religious gatherings that may last all night. They remain crowded into peoples' minds like cloud-covered stars. That is why, in this *tafsir* (commentary) book, we have explored some of the stories that we have heard over and over again, and we have helped the readers to distinguish between these traditional stories and the Qur'an. We have done this in the context of studying the first chapters of the *Kitabul Muqaddas* (Bible), which are the original revelation concerning all these stories. This book is written not only for the biological and spiritual descendants of Abraham's son Isaac, but also for their Ishmaelite siblings, so that all can learn about God's blessing and mercy.

It seems to me that the author of the book of Genesis, inspired by the Holy Spirit, worked to remove false preconceptions from the minds of God's people, so that they could get to know the One True God and live according to his will. Today, as in that ancient world, people have many stories and many gods, all very different from the real God who created everything. Genesis removes the weeds of idolatry from the minds of the readers and sows theological seeds in a unique way so that the seeds germinate into trees which grow buds, and later the buds blossom and spread the fragrance of their flowers all around. In addition, these trees provide oxygen by removing carbon dioxide from the surrounding wasteland, allowing their neighbours and others to survive. In Genesis, we have no record of Noah speaking to anyone in his corrupt world but the Apostle Peter could still call him "a herald of righteousness" (2 Pet 2:5). May God's people, like Noah, bear witness to the fragrance of the Messiah to their neighbours, not only in word but also in deed and life!

One of my favourite theology teachers said that theology teachers do not always answer students' questions. Rather, theological education should give students the opportunity to think about the questions for themselves. The author of Genesis, too, refrained from telling readers exactly what to do and to think. He talked about things known to the readers even as he highlighted his unique new message and provoked many questions. As God guided him, he selected some of the information on the creation and flood stories from the traditions of his time, even as he rejected the rest. In this way he was able to just drink the milk that had been mixed with water like a swan, and throw away the water. Every time I read the book of Genesis, I am fascinated by new discoveries and new insights. And that is why so many doctrines, so many theories, have been written as people have inquired about the author of this immortal literature. The author did not even mention his name in the book; he did not want to make himself famous by excluding God, like the people of Babel. He humbly glorified God by writing the word of God. Thousands of years later, I pay my respects to this anonymous author for his great efforts.

I would like to thank the Institute for Classical Languages (ICL) team in Bangladesh for their valuable help in writing this book. I would also like to express my sincere gratitude to the local and foreign teachers of theology at the Christian College of Theology Bangladesh, and the Holy Cross Major Seminary authorities in Bangladesh, for giving me the opportunity to use their rich libraries. I would like to express my sincere gratitude to the Centre for Muslim-Christian Studies and Bodleian Library in Oxford for their thoughtful advice and opportunity to use their facilities. I will never forget the advice and inspiration of the teachers of the Arab Baptist Theological Seminary (ABTS) and their president, Rev. Dr. Elie Haddad. I had the opportunity of using ABTS's huge library and benefitted from discussions with students from the Middle East and North Africa, as well as teachers from the Middle East, Europe and America, and even our Indian subcontinent. I would also like to express my sincere gratitude to Ida Glaser and Emad Botros, and to Langham Literature, for their part in producing this commentary. May God bless them for this good initiative!

Anwarul Azad
ICL Dhaka, Bangladesh
May 2020

Preface

Ida Glaser

A nwarul Azad entered his Sabbath rest on 6 June 2020 and is now enjoying the full beauty of the unfurled bloom of the glory of God. His gate to the presence of his Lord was a sudden stroke, almost certainly COVID-related, which left the rest of the team with the job of retrieving his penultimate Bangla manuscripts, and of translating, revising and completing the work without his advice. We are thankful to his wife and to the principal of the Institute for Classical Languages (ICL) Dhaka, Jalu Hussain, for their collaboration in these matters. Jalu, too, has gone to glory as a result of COVID and was buried on Easter Day 2021 in the sure and certain hope of new creation which pulses through this commentary. Anwarul left no physical children on this earth, but he did leave many spiritual children. He and his wife are a true example of a "barren couple" through whom God's blessing has come to their adopted daughter and to countless others in Bangladesh and around the world.

This commentary has been a true team effort. Anwarul was the lead writer, and I put in a great deal of work in basic research,[1] in developing concepts, and in shaping the material. But it was all done in the context of Anwarul's teaching in Bangladesh, fed by the questions of his students, and discussed at every stage with the staff of ICL Dhaka. Suraiyea Manju and Sujit Sarkar worked closely with him throughout, and, since his death, have worked with me on the revision and completion of the book. An important stage was the translation of the Bangla manuscript into English, which was done by John Thorpe with the assistance of Suraiyea, Sujit and Jalu. Throughout, the project has been ably facilitated by Dr. Emad Botros of the Arab Baptist Theological Seminary (ABTS) in Beirut who has contributed to our discussions and helped with editing as well as making sure that we all did what we needed to do. Emad also visited Dhaka and helped us to discern the interests and needs of

---

1. My journey into reading Genesis 1–11 in an Islamic context began with my doctoral thesis, "An Experiment in Contextualized Comparative Hermeneutics: Reading Genesis 1–11 in the Context of Parallel Qur'anic Material and Christian Mission amongst Muslims in Elswick, Newcastle upon Tyne," University of Durham, 1994.

ICL staff and students, and twice hosted Anwarul for studies in Genesis, the Qur'an and Arabic at ABTS.

Anwarul described himself as a Muslim-heritage believer in Jesus the Messiah. He loved to search his heritage for the light which he saw shining in the Bible, because he saw all that light as coming from the light of his beloved Messiah. I could describe myself as a Jewish-heritage believer in Jesus the Messiah, and I am fascinated by the way in which both the New Testament and the Qur'an enter into Jewish discussions of the Torah, often coming to different conclusions.

Anwarul and I shared a love of questions. We did not always come to the same conclusions about the answers, but we agreed on the importance of seeking the right questions. Both of our heritages encouraged us to search the texts, to savour the words, and to seek resonances throughout the scriptures. The Jewish heritage sees study of the Torah as itself a form of worship, a way of loving the Lord our God with all our minds; and we must never "close the text" by supposing that we have finished our study. We do not have to decide on a single answer to every question: on the contrary, if the text has several possible meanings, it is meant to be like that; and, if it raises questions which it does not answer, that, too, is intentional.

In Anwarul's Bangladeshi context, people like to discuss every detail of their scripture – whether the Bible or the Qur'an. Anwarul insisted that this commentary should not so much answer the questions as give people material for discussing them. When asked whether he really wanted the chapter on creation to take up such a large proportion of the book, he responded:

> Bengali people like to hear God's words the whole night, even in an open field in the cold winter weather. So we are very happy with the length of this chapter as it will tell them about God's good creation, call them to act as *khalīfa* in this world and help them to look at the perfect Khalīfah, 'Isa al-Masīḥ, who is the true image of God.

So . . . come, read, question, search, discuss . . . and worship!

Ida Glaser
Centre for Muslim-Christian Studies, Oxford, UK
September 2021

Anwarul, Emad, and Ida

1

Introduction

Beginnings and Blessings

The Bible (*Kitabul Muqaddas*[1]) begins with the Book of Beginning. The Hebrew title of this first book of the Torah (*Tawrat*) is *Bereshit*, which is the very first word of the book, usually translated "in the beginning": this is the very start of all things. In Greek, the word is translated *genesis* which means origin, source or genealogy. The book of Genesis recounts the origins of the heavens and the earth, of animals and humans, of human sin, and of the *Bani Isra'il*.[2]

The Qur'an (*Qur'an Sharīf*) begins with the sūra, "The Opening." The title in Arabic is *al-Fātiḥa*, denoting the opening of a door or of a book or a topic. In this "Opening" of the Qur'an, there is nothing about creation. Instead, the Qur'an opens with a prayer (*du'a*) which is now used in every unit (*rakah*) of prayer (*ṣalaḥ*). It speaks against the misguided path of idolatry and upholds the unity of God. It praises the One who is Lord of all creation (*rabb al-'alamīn*) and the King of Judgement Day (*malik yawm ad-dīn*). It pleads to God to guide worshippers on the true path (*ṣirāṭ al-mustaqīm*).

Genesis 1–11 also deals with idolatry, but in a very different way. Its historical context is the polytheistic ancient nations of Canaan, Babylon and Egypt. When we read their literature, we can see that Genesis contrasts their idolatry with the Hebrew belief in One God who created all things and who is

---

1. In Bangla, both the Bible and the Qur'an are always referred to with the honorific – *Kitabul Mokaddos* and *Qur'anul Sharif*. In this English version, we will simply refer to them as "the Bible" and "the Qur'an." The Bible was first translated into the Muslim language Bengali as *Kitabul Mokaddos*, published by Manjile Kitabul Mukaddos in 1982, and ICL Dhaka was founded for the study of this text and the original languages of the Holy Scriptures.

2. We retain the Arabic phrase, meaning "The Children of Israel," throughout this book. This is to make a clear distinction between the biblical people of Israel and the current State of Israel.

the judge of all nations. We also see that opposition to idolatry is not enough. In Genesis 2–3 we learn that, although Adam and Eve lived in a perfect garden in the presence of the One True God, they were unable and unwilling to follow his commands. The book of Genesis reveals how their disobedience was the beginning of all kinds of trouble and despair with which we human beings are faced today.

WHAT IS BLESSING AND WHO RECEIVES BLESSING?

"Blessing" (Ar. *baraka*; Heb. *berakah*) is of monumental importance. Humans are always seeking the blessing of Almighty God in all kinds of circumstances.

The Qur'an sees *baraka* as good things, both spiritual and material, given by God (e.g. Sūras *al-An'ām* 6:92, 155; *al-A'rāf* 7:96; *al-Mu'minūn* 23:29; *Qāf* 50:9). However, Sufi Muslims in Bangladesh also see it as a kind of spiritual power which can flow to the believer in different ways; for example, it can come through prayer or through going on the ḥajj pilgrimage. *Baraka* can also come through objects; for example, through drinking water from the Zam Zam well in Mecca, or through touching certain objects. Most frequently, people think that *baraka* comes from a *pir* (a holy person or spiritual guide). There are many ways of receiving the *baraka* of a *pir*, including attending his worship services and touching him or his garments. After a *pir* has died, people seek *baraka* by visiting his tomb.[1]

The meaning of *berakah* in Genesis can be found by reading the text and by seeing how the Genesis ideas then blossom in the rest of the Bible. From 1:28 onwards, Genesis tells us that the Almighty God desires to bless humanity. Elsewhere, we learn that we can only expect to receive that blessing by humbly seeking him and trusting in the promises that he has made (Prov 3:5–6; Jas 4:6; 1 Pet 5:5). This is because, as we will also learn in Genesis, we are sinful, and we do not deserve and cannot earn God's blessings – we can only receive them as his free gift to us. The New Testament uses the word *charis*, translated *rohomot* in Bangla and *grace* in English, to describe God's wonderful undeserved free gifts of blessing. In Genesis 1–11, we will see the grace of God demonstrated in the lives of Adam and Eve, Cain and Abel, Noah and his descendants, and in the life of Abraham and his family. But, when humans lack humility and think that they can somehow get blessings for themselves, how can they expect to receive his grace?

---

1. See also Schimmel, *Deciphering the Signs of God*, ch. 1.

The Beginning of Blessing

The Good News is that Genesis 1–11 does not only tell of the beginning of our troubles, but also of the beginning of God's blessing and grace. In spite of all the human failures, God gives us hope for the future by revealing the beginning of his great plan of salvation. God's loving promises of commitment to our world are written in this section of Genesis.

The root of the Hebrew word translated into English as "blessing" is *b-r-k*, which is cognate with the Arabic *b-r-k*. It appears six times in Genesis 1–11 (in 1:22; 1:28; 2:3; 5:2; 9:1 and 9:26). In the Bengali *Kitabul Muqaddas*, this word is translated *borokot* in Genesis 1, but is translated in different ways in the other verses. This is because the meaning of *borokot* in Bangla has some significant differences from the meaning of *berakah* in Genesis (see text box on page 2). It is important that we pay attention to the Hebrew word in order to understand this important concept in Genesis. We will not try to explain what it means here: we will let Genesis itself tell us what it means as we study.

Genesis 1–11 is leading up to Genesis 12:3, with which we will end this commentary. Here is possibly the most important verse in the Old Testament:[3]

> *Through you [Abraham] all the nations of the earth will be blessed.*
> *(Gen 12:3)*

The Apostle Paul explains this verse: "And the Scripture, foreseeing that God would justify the Gentiles by faith, preached the gospel beforehand to Abraham, saying, "In you shall all the nations be blessed" (Gal 3:8). He is explaining how this blessing (Gk. *eulogia*) of Abraham will be showered on all peoples through Jesus the Messiah and the Holy Spirit (Gal 3:14).

The two verses, Genesis 12:2 and 3, contain the root *b-r-k* no less than five times. It is used as a verb four times. The other time, it is a noun – *berakah*. At the end of verse 2, God says to Abraham, "You will be a *berakah*." We can see a pattern of how the root *b-r-k* appears in our chapters: the blessing is there in creation, in the people in the line of Seth, in God's covenant after the flood, and in the call of Abraham. In between the blessings come sad accounts of human sinfulness and its consequences.

There is another very important word which expresses God's loving purposes for humanity: the Hebrew word is *chen*, and it appears only once in our chapters, in Genesis 6:8:

> *But Noah found* chen *in the eyes of the LORD.*

---

3. "Old Testament" refers to the *Tawrat, Zabur* and *Writings* of the Prophets. It is the collection of the inspired books given by God to the *Bani Isra'il* before the time of Jesus the Messiah.

This verse introduces the central part of Genesis 1–11, which is the turning point of the whole account of beginnings (see chiastic structure, page 22). *Chen* is translated "grace" or "favour" in English, and *rohomot* in Bangla. It is one of the ways in which God describes himself in his awesome revelation to Moses on Mount Sinai:

> The LORD, the LORD, a God merciful [*rachum*] and gracious [*channun*], slow to anger, and abounding in steadfast love [*chesed*] and faithfulness [*emet*]. (Exod 34:6)

The reader will notice that the word translated into English as "merciful" is cognate with *rohomot*, which is used to translate *chen* in the *Kitabul Muqaddas*. Arabic readers will also notice that these words are cognate with *ar-Raḥmān* and *ar-Raḥīm* – the two names of God used at the beginning of every sūra of the Qur'an (except Sūra 9 *at-Tawbah*). Both the Hebrew and the Arabic roots *r-ch-m/r-h-m* express "womb," and therefore remind us of the mercy and compassion that a woman has for the children she has borne.[4]

We pray that all who read this commentary may receive blessing, mercy and grace!

The Beginning of History and Theology

Genesis plants the seed from which we can see everything blossom in Scripture. We consider it the seedbed for the holy books – the Torah (*Tawrāt*), Psalms (*Zabūr*), Gospel (*Injīl*) and other prophetic books. This is also confirmed by the Qur'an, which holds these books in high esteem and bears testimony to them as God's heavenly books (*as-samāwī kutub*) which were given to the People of the Book (*ahl al-kitab*) and in which light and guidance are found (Sūra al-Mā'ida 5:46). The Qur'an refers to many subjects and people about which we can find fuller information in Genesis, including creation, Adam and Eve, Cain and Abel, Enoch, Noah, Abraham and his wife, Ishmael and Isaac, Jacob, and Joseph and his brothers.

Genesis tells of the beginnings of all peoples and of a particular people. Genesis 1–11, which is the subject of this commentary, is about how the heavens and the earth were made and how humankind began. It is written in a way which leads to the rest of the book, which is the history of how the *Bani*

---

4. This is a very common interpretation, but readers should note here and elsewhere in this commentary that a shared root does not necessarily imply a similar meaning.

Isra'il began. The table below shows how Genesis 1–11 recounts four primary events, and Genesis 12–50 recounts four primary lives.

A. Human history (Gen 1–11:26)	B. The history of God's special people (Gen 11:27–50:26)
1. Creation (Gen 1–2)	1. Abraham (Gen 12–20)
2. Fall into sin (Gen 3–4)	2. Isaac (Gen 21–26)
3. The flood (Gen 5–9)	3. Jacob (Gen 27–36)
4. The nations (Gen 10–11)	4. Joseph (Gen 37–50)

Genesis tells of the beginning of God's covenants.[5] The word "covenant" (Heb. *berit*) appears for the first time in the central portion of Genesis 1–11, where we read about God's covenant with Noah and his descendants and all creation (Gen 6:18; 9:1–17). But we can see the beginning of the idea of covenant right at the start, where God pronounced blessings on all men and women made in his image (Gen 1:26–27). After this, humans, through their sin, became misguided and went astray (Gen 3). Yet, again and again, we see God showing mercy, leading to the explicit covenant commitment which implies that God will deal with all the evil that has been let into the world (Gen 9).

Genesis tells of the beginnings of human society, and of religious life and traditions. These include such matters as observance of the Sabbath, clean and unclean animals, the institution of marriage, and accounts of power struggles among humans. In each instance we can see two things. On the one hand, we see the goodness of God's creation and God's grace and blessings toward humankind; on the other hand, we read of sinful pride and of conflicts which bring grief to God and his curse on parts of his creation.

Our chapters finish with *the beginnings of the Bani Isra'il*, the community through which God will bless the world. Genesis 1–11 tells us how the patriarch Abraham was linked to Adam and his descendants, about the society out of which and for which the *Bani Isra'il* were selected, and about the place of the *Bani Isra'il* among the nations. Our commentary will finish with the first three verses of Genesis 12, in which God announces his covenant promises to

---

5. The word "covenant" describes commitments between God and humankind. The Hebrew word is *berit*, the Greek is *diatheke*, and in Arabic, it is *'ahd* or sometimes *mithaq*. The main biblical covenants are with Noah and all living things (Gen 9), with Abraham and his family (Gen 15), with Moses and the *Bani Isra'il* (Exod 24:4–8), and with David and his descendants (2 Sam 7:12–16, 1 Chr 17:11–15). All the covenants would come to fruition in the new covenant of the Messiah (Jer 31:31–34; Luke 22:19; Heb 8). The Qur'an speaks of some of these covenants, but gives few details (e.g. Sūra *al-Mā'ida* 5:7, 12–13).

Abraham. This is the beginning of God's great plan of salvation to which all the beginnings in Genesis 1–11 are pointing.

Genealogy or Toledoth

How does the writer of Genesis present the beginnings? Although he lived so long ago, he was like us in many ways – he asked who were the ancestors of his family and his people. He used many sources and divided his writing into eleven sections, each marked with the words "this is the *toledoth* . . ." (Gen 2:4; 5:1; 6:9; 10:1; 11:10; 11:27; 25:12; 25:19; 36:1; 36:9; 37:2). *Toledoth* is a Hebrew noun from the root *y-l-d*, to beget or give birth. It often identifies a list of descendants of the lead person of a clan. In English, it is translated genealogy, account, generations, family history or ancestral narrative. Genealogy is an important biblical way of doing history (see also 1 Chr 1–9; Matt 1:1–17; Luke 3:23–38).

We Bengalis proudly call ourselves *millate Ibrahim* – the community of Abraham – and our historian Dr. M. A. Hannan tells us that we are the physical descendants of Noah through his grandson, Bong.[6] Today, some of us can recite our family trees back for fourteen generations. The Genesis writer also sees his people – the *Bani Isra'il* – as part of Abraham's family: he uses genealogy to show the linkage between Adam, the ancestor of humankind, and the nations; between the nations and Abraham; and between Abraham and the *Bani Isra'il*. The writer of Genesis is signalling that the ancestors of all humankind have a share in this history, and that all humanity is included in the blessing that will come through him (Gen 12:1–3). So Genesis will help us to understand what it means to belong to the *millate Ibrahim*.

Looking forward from the blessings on Abraham, Genesis 12–50 will trace the line of Abraham through Isaac and Jacob to the *Bani Isra'il*. Looking back from that blessing, our chapters take us back to the forebears of Abraham – but they do more than that! We are only interested in our own ancestors, not in everyone else's ancestors. Genesis is interested in the ancestors of the whole human race. We cannot overemphasize the importance of this for our study. God plans to bless all the peoples through Abraham's family. The *millate Ibrahim* will not exist for its own sake, and it will not be just one ethnic group. All the peoples of the earth will be called to share in the blessing.

Genesis is not a book of only one beginning. The Hebrew word *toledoth* which begins each of its major sections signals a new beginning, and we see

---

6. Hannan, *Banglir Itihas*, 94. See also commentary on Genesis 10:6–20.

many things growing out of that beginning. The next section chooses one person or family, and follows their line. The first beginning is the beginning of everything – of the whole universe and probably of time itself. There is no *toledoth* formula here, as there was nothing from which a birth could come. The second section focuses on one part of the universe – on this small planet, earth, on a garden which God planted here, and on the first two human beings whom he places in the garden. The third section recounts the descendants of just one of their sons, Seth. The fourth section gives an account of just one of Seth's descendants and his children. And so on. It is as if we were looking at a tree, with huge roots and trunk, and then following just one major branch, and then one branch from that branch, and so on. Genesis 1–11 is leading us towards the branch of Abraham from whose seed the salvation plan of God unfolds and by which that blessing extends back to the whole tree.

How Shall We Read?

Genesis 1–11 is often called Primeval History because it tells us about the origins of everything – the time before history began. It is not the sort of history book that we might read in school today: it is a very ancient book. Neither is it the sort of science book that we might read today if we want to know the latest theories on the beginnings of the universe and the origins of humanity. As we shall see, Genesis 1–11 is not only a genealogy but also a story, and it uses various narrative and poetic forms which open its message to its readers. This means, for example, that we sometimes find repetitions, or material organized according to symbolic numbers: we will need to pay attention to these forms rather than simply looking for information in order to discern what they are teaching. We will find that Genesis 1–11 is more than a story: it is a record of human lives with a spiritual message and with metaphorical meanings.

Genesis 1–11 is different from our school books in another way. It is not a textbook about human discoveries: it is the beginning of the Torah, the first book of God. We will study hard to understand its genealogies, its stories and its poetry, but we will do this because it is God's word, and we want to hear his message more clearly. Genesis 1–11 will address our curiosity about where we come from, and how the world was made, and why it is like it is – but that is not its main purpose. It calls us to listen to God, to repent and turn to him, to know him better and to live for his glory with other people in his world. It opens the door to the whole Bible.

We will see that there are differences between Genesis 1–11 and the Qur'an even though twenty-first-century readers will see many similarities between the two books. The Qur'an and Genesis 1–11 refer to many of the same events, but there are both differences and similarities in how these are presented. For example, the Qur'an does not present them in chronological order. It is more like a collection of sermons that is based on the biblical accounts. For this reason, it is often necessary to read the biblical accounts in order to understand the qur'anic message. The Qur'an itself directs its readers to read the former Holy Books in order to have their doubts alleviated (Sūra *Yūnus* 10:94). In this way, a Muslim can have his or her doubts removed and can find the straight path of truth and life.

SCRIPTURE AND SCIENCE

We have said that Genesis 1–11 is not like current scientific books about the beginnings of the universe. It does not ask the same questions as current science, it does not have the same format as current science, and it does not have the same purpose as current science. Science is a human study of the world which God has made, while the Bible is inspired writing which records what God has done and which tells us things which we could not find out for ourselves. However, there are plenty of people who compare science and scripture, and who try to use science to either prove or disprove the truth of Holy Books – whether the Bible, the Qur'an or other scriptures. At several points in our commentary, we will see that the Qur'an's descriptions of creation raise many of the same questions that are raised in Genesis.

For those who believe that Genesis is God's inspired scripture, there are three main ways of thinking about how the Genesis account of creation relates to scientific accounts of the beginnings of the earth and of human history:

1. Separate Genesis and science. This method sees Genesis as a theological text that explains how God relates to the earth and human beings: Genesis 1–2 should be read as ancient literature that discusses theology with the Babylonian and Egyptian creation stories. It tells us that God was in control of whatever happened, but we have to go to the scientific disciplines to find out how it happened, when it happened, etc. In short, the Bible and science give us two different kinds of knowledge about two different subjects. Genesis does not tell us what science tells us, and science cannot tell us what Genesis tells us.

2. Use Genesis as the key to understanding scientific findings. This method sees Genesis as giving a literal account of what happened, and it interprets scientific observations as fitting into the Genesis account. For example, evidence of evolution is interpreted within the constraints of a six-day creation, and geological findings are interpreted within the constraints of the flood story.

3. See Genesis and science as complementary. That is, the account of origins in scripture and the insights on origins available through science are two views on the same subject. They do not contradict each other – rather they need each other. Not only will Genesis help us to understand science, science will help us to interpret Genesis. For example, geological findings must mean that the "days" of Genesis 1 are *not* periods of twenty-four hours.

The team writing this commentary represent all the above approaches. We will acknowledge the various possibilities, but try to focus on understanding the meaning and the message of Genesis.[1]

---

1. To readers who would like to consider further the relationship between science and faith, we recommend Berry, *Lion Handbook of Science and Christianity*; and Alexander, "Models for Relating Science and Religion."

So, then, we will read Genesis 1–11 as we would read no other book – we will read it as the word of God which will feed our souls and which we will follow and obey. However, we will also read it as ancient literature. We will study the ancient world in order to read Genesis in the context in which it was written, and only then will we ask how it applies to the twenty-first-century world in which we live. That is, we will consider three "worlds":

- *The world behind the text*: that is, the world in which Genesis was written, with its history, geography, cultures and ways of thinking.
- *The world of the text*: that is, the biblical text itself, with its literary form, its language and its logic. We read any particular passage remembering that it is part of a book, which is part of the whole Bible.

- *The world in front of the text*: that is, the world in which we live today, and in which we want to hear what God has to say to us.

We will look systematically at each of these "worlds," and will consider the similarities and the differences between our world and the ancient world. In Bangladesh, we are going to be particularly interested in how the Qur'an enters the discussion, as it refers to the Genesis 1–11 events in many places. Most importantly, we want to learn for our own lives and to obey God. So in each chapter, we will finish with a theological reflection and a "what about us?" section.

In the rest of this chapter, we will deal with introductory questions using this "world behind the text," "world of the text," "world in front of the text," "theological reflection," and "what about us?" framework.

The World Behind the Text

In order to understand what the text of Genesis 1–11 is saying for our place and time, we need to study the place and time of the Genesis 1–11 writer and its first readers. To whom was the book of Genesis written, and when? It is not always easy to find answers to these questions, but we will search for them.

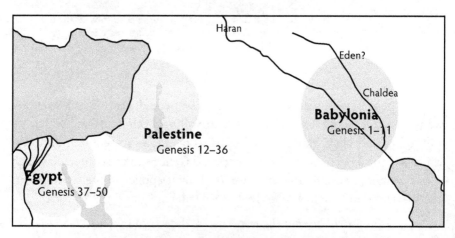

Figure 1: Main locations for events in Genesis
Three major geographical locations for incidents in Genesis

Geography

Genesis originates from what is now known as the Middle East. The main background for the first section (Gen 1–11) is Mesopotamia,[7] the land between the rivers Tigris and Euphrates, which is today's Iraq. The second part (Gen 12–36) is about events in Canaan, the Promised Land of God; and the third part (Gen 37–50) takes us to the ancient civilization of Egypt. The first part covers at least two thousand years of human history as well as pre-historic times. The remaining thirty-nine chapters span perhaps three hundred years.

The Qur'an mentions many Genesis characters, like Adam, the two sons of Adam, Seth, Enoch, Noah, and Abraham, some in detail and some only by name. While the Qur'an gives very few geographical details, Genesis names many places and gives us glimpses into culture as well as environment. Some places we can locate today, but some have disappeared, and scholars can only guess where they were. Genesis 1–11 mentions the rivers Euphrates and Tigris, the mountains of Ararat, and the ancient cities of Babylon and Ur of Kasideem. It also uses names like Ashur, Haran and Canaan, all of which can still be found in what, even in South Asia today, we call the Fertile Crescent, which archaeologists have called the "cradle of civilization." The main urban centres were in Mesopotamia and Egypt; elsewhere, people lived in smaller settlements or lived nomadic lives.

**Anwarul Azad near Sidon (mentioned in Gen 10:15)
during his study visit to Beirut**

---

7. The word "mesopotamia" means "between rivers" in Greek.

Religion and Mythology

The ancient world was a world of many gods. Each people group had its own gods, its own stories and its own religious observances. The *Bani Isra'il* believed in One God, but everyone else believed that there were many gods, and that one or two particular gods were "theirs" – that is, they were the god or gods of that particular group and of that particular place. There are very few references to those other gods in Genesis, and none at all in Genesis 1–11.[8] However, it is helpful to know something about these gods and the stories about beginnings that were told by ancient peoples. It will help us to understand that Genesis 1–11 is ancient writing, a bit like other ancient writings. It will also help us to see how different it is from those writings, and so to understand its revolutionary message.

We know about the ancient religions from statues and other artefacts, and also from written stories. We will consider the details of these stories in the relevant places in this commentary. The stories to which we will most often refer are *Enuma Elish* and *The Epic of Gilgamesh*, both of which come from Mesopotamia. *Enuma Elish* is a creation epic composed probably in the eighteenth-century BC (about 500 years before Moses). *The Epic of Gilgamesh* has a story of a great flood, and probably dates from about 200 years later.

It seems that, by about 2,000 BC, there were some ideas about the beginnings of the world which were shared by many of the peoples of Mesopotamia. There were stories about a time of creation, when the world and the animals and the human beings were made by supernatural beings; and there were stories about how something went wrong, and the supernatural beings sent a great flood which destroyed all the human beings except a few favoured ones. From the available evidence, it is not possible to be sure how these stories are related to Genesis and to each other, but, as we read Genesis, we will see how it affirms some of the ideas but, at the same time, has some crucial differences.

For example, *Enuma Elish* tells of the creation of many gods from two original beings, of fighting between the gods, of the victory of the young god Marduk, of his making the world and the human beings, of the building of his temple in Babylon, and of the feasting of the gods there. When we turn to Genesis after reading *Enuma Elish*, we will find that some of the things which appear as gods in *Enuma Elish* appear as God's creation in Genesis, and we will read about a great building which cannot reach the one creator God. The

---

8. Some people see the *bene ha-elohim* of Gen 6:2 as spiritual beings, so this could be a reference to gods. But see the discussion on p.187. Direct references to other gods can be found in Gen 31:30–35 and 41:50.

revolutionary message is clear: there is One True God, who is the God of all places and all peoples, and he is not like the other peoples' ideas of the gods.

When and By Whom Was Genesis Written?

Genesis is the first part of the Torah – the Scripture given by God to the *Bani Isra'il*. The Torah records that God gave to Moses stone tablets of written commandments and that God himself wrote this portion of the Torah. The Qur'an and Islamic literature also record this (Exod 24:12; 31:18; 32:15–16; cf. Sūra *al-Aʿrāf* 7:145; *Abi Daʾud*, Book 34 Hadith 3617, *Muslim Sharif*, Hadith 33.6409). But the original tablets were broken and Moses re-wrote them (Exod 32:19; 34:1–5; 34:27–29).

Many other laws which God revealed to Moses on Mount Sinai are recorded in Exodus to Deuteronomy, but there are also other things in the Torah, especially the many narratives and genealogies. Because there is so much in it about Moses, and because so many of the laws were given to Moses, the Torah became known as The Books of Moses, and people have traditionally seen it as written by him. So the Qur'an sees the Torah as a book that was given to Moses by God (Sūra *al-Baqara* 2:87) "as a guide and a light" (Sūra *al-Māʾida* 5:44).

However, the Old Testament does not say that the whole Torah was given to Moses. In fact, it does not refer to the authorship of Genesis (or to that of many other Old Testament books). We can conclude that it was not important to the *Bani Isra'il* to know the human author of a sacred book. The Torah was given to them by God, and they knew that God had spoken very directly to Moses and had come to dwell among them in his glory. There was no need to ascribe earthly authorship to the word of God. And so it is with us. We understand that if we believe that he has revealed his word to us, there is no urgent need for us to discover the human author(s) of Genesis.

Nevertheless, Western scholars have long been interested in investigating how Genesis came to be. They wonder how the Genesis stories and genealogies were transmitted from one generation to the next, and who wrote them down. We will spend some time considering these questions and how God's word may have come to us.

First, we need to understand that the Bible does not claim to be revealed by God in the same way as the Qur'an claims to have been revealed. With some exceptions, the Bible does not describe its words as having been directly dictated by God or by an angel. Rather, it teaches that God inspired humans to write his word through the power of the Holy Spirit (2 Tim 3:16; 2 Pet 1:21).

These human writers would record what they witnessed and what God showed them, and some would also carefully collect information from previously written tablets, manuscripts or oral traditions (Eccl 12:9; Luke 1:1–4). Under the direction of the Holy Spirit, they then wrote the words that would fulfil God's purpose. In this way it can be said that God, indeed, wrote his word, but also that he used humans with their own language, style and culture to write it. In short, God is the ultimate author, but there are also human authors. Rather than thinking that God gave a book to a prophet, we can say that God gave books to his people, and that he did it through inspiring a human process.

In the case of Genesis 1–11, we may imagine someone inspired by the Holy Spirit carefully gathering information from written tablets and scrolls and from oral traditions, and then selecting what would be needed to produce the book which would achieve God's purposes. But who was this person? Were there several different people involved at different times? When did they live? And what were the sources? We look briefly at traditional views and then at a well-known alternative.

Traditional Views Regarding the Authorship of Genesis

Deuteronomy states that Moses wrote a book of law (Heb. *torah*) in 31:9 and 31:24–26; and Exodus 17:14 and Numbers 33:2 specify that Moses wrote particular details, so traditional thinkers believe that God used Moses for writing much of or even the whole of the Torah. Other portions of the Old Testament as well as later Jewish literature ascribe authorship of the Torah to Moses. The orthodox Jewish understanding is that, on Mount Sinai, Moses received both the written Torah and the oral Torah which explained the 613 commandments which the Jews were to keep. This is not far from the Qur'an's testimony on the subject.

An important witness to the traditional view is the record that, by the time of Joshua, the Torah given to Moses was in written form (Josh 1:7–8; 8:31–22, 34; 22:5). There are many other Old Testament references to a written *torah* of Moses (1 Kgs 2:3; 2 Kgs 14:6; 2 Chr 23:18; 34:14; Ezra 6:18; Neh 8:1–8; 13:1; Dan 9:11, 13; Mal 4:4). However, while these references make it clear that the *Bani Isra'il* had the Torah in written form from the time of Moses, and that some of it was actually written by Moses, they do not tell us about all that it contained. They leave open the possibility that Moses did not write some portions, and that there was later editing of the texts. Suggestions are that Joshua wrote the account of Moses's death in Deuteronomy, that some editorial work was done during the time of the united monarchy, and that the final version was produced by Ezra.

What about the New Testament? It often refers to the Torah as the writings of Moses (Mark 10:3–5; 12:19; Luke 20:28; John 1:45; 5:46), and the law is described as what Moses gave or said (Matt 8:4; Mark 12:26; John 7:22; Acts 15:1; Rom 10:19; 1 Cor 9:10). Sometimes, "Moses" becomes a shorthand for the law or the Torah (Luke 16:29; 24:27, 44; 2 Cor 3:15). Some of these references come from Jesus the Messiah himself (Mark 12:26; Luke 16:29–31; 24:44; John 5:24; 7:19, 22).

Traditional views interpret this New Testament material as affirmation that Moses wrote the Torah. On the other hand, it could be that in the New Testament "Moses" is simply shorthand for "The Law" or "The Torah" because these were so closely identified with what Moses received on Sinai; this usage does not necessarily require that he was the author of every chapter and verse of the five books in their final form.

Even within traditional views, people may ask about the sources of Genesis. How far was the information directly given by God, how far was it passed down orally, and what written sources might there have been at the time of Moses? Writing was introduced in Canaan during the middle bronze age, the time when Abraham's family entered that land, but the Hebrew verb for writing (*katab*, used 262 times in the Old Testament) does not appear in Genesis. "Book" or "written record" (Heb. *sefer*) is first mentioned in Genesis 5:1, where we read, "this is the book of the generations of Adam." This is the only place where Genesis adds *sefer* to *toledoth*, and it could imply there was a written source for Genesis 5.[9] Elsewhere in the Torah, other written sources are mentioned. For example, the "Book of the Wars of the LORD" is mentioned in Numbers 21:14–15. All this implies that Genesis is based on a variety of sources which were carefully preserved by the *Bani Isra'il* and their ancestors.

Alternative Views Regarding the Authorship of Genesis

Mosaic authorship of the Torah has been questioned during the past three hundred years, usually on the grounds of content or literary style and vocabulary. Here are some of the issues which are discussed, along with some of our questions in response:

First, it is said that the Torah itself implies that Moses was not its author. For example, Genesis 12:6 and 13:7 speak of the Canaanites as "then" being in the land, which might mean that at the time of writing the Canaanites were no longer there. Another example is the account of Moses's death in Deuteronomy

---

9. Wiseman, *Ancient Records and Structure*, suggests that each *toledoth* was written on a clay tablet.

34 – how could a man write about his own death? But can we conclude from these observations that Genesis was written at a time when Canaanites and Perizzites were no longer living in the land? Why should it not mean that they were there both at the time of Abraham and at the time of the writing? And could Moses not have anticipated his own death or asked someone to write of it after he had died?

Second, there is material in the Torah that seems to relate to a later time in history. For example, Babel in Genesis 11:1–9 clearly alludes to the city of Babylon, which would be the heart of the later Babylonian empire, so would this not fit better into the time of exile? At that time, the *Bani Isra'il* would have been looking at the tall temple of the god Marduk in Babylon. Indeed, much of Genesis 1–11 can be read as a refutation of Babylonian views, which would strengthen the argument that it was written during the exile. On the other hand, the Babylonian creation story with its apex in the building of the Marduk temple existed long before the exile, so we could argue that the Holy Spirit led an earlier author to write something which would be relevant to the *Bani Isra'il* in the distress of exile. It is, after all, a characteristic of divine Scripture that it is relevant to believers of every epoch.

Third, scholars have analyzed the names of God and linguistic styles, and have proposed that the Genesis author used four different sources or that there were four groups of authors. This is called the Documentary Hypothesis or the JEDP Theory, after the initials J, E, D and P which are given to the four sources: the author who uses Jehovah or Yahweh for God's name is Yahwist or Jahwist (J); the author who uses Elohim for God is Elohist (E); the author who is interested in law is the Deuteronomist (D); and there is also a Priestly author who represents a Levitical priestly (P) source. The theory originated with the German Old Testament scholar Karl Heinrich Graf (1815–1869) and his student Julius Wellhausen (1844–1918), and its proponents think that most of the Torah was written after Moses's death.

Since that time, many questions have been raised about the JEDP hypothesis. There have been disagreements as to which passages originated with J, E, D and P; and some scholars have dismissed JEDP and offered different theories on when Genesis reached its present form. There are now so many theories about the origins of Genesis that John Goldingay, in his recent commentary, concludes, "We know virtually nothing about how Genesis came into existence."[10]

---

10. Goldingay, *Genesis*, 9.

Bangladeshi readers may find these discussions of authorship puzzling. We know that a single author can use different literary styles. We do not use the same style when we write a poem, a newspaper article and a financial report, so why should a biblical author use the same style when writing about history, law and the sacrificial system? Further, it is not only in Genesis that there are varying literary styles and different names for God: the Holy Qur'an also includes different styles and uses both the term *ar-Rabb* (the Lord) and the term *Allah* to designate God, but Muslims do not imagine that there were different authors of the Qur'an. As we shall see in our theological reflection at the end of this chapter, there can be good theological reasons for using different names for God in different places.

However, the discussions can be useful in helping us to think about God's word. First, they alert us to the relevance of Genesis 1–11 to the *Bani Isra'il* at different times in their history. Genesis itself does not tell us when it was written, but we can imagine how it would have spoken to different readers. What would it have meant during Moses's lifetime, when he was teaching the *Bani Isra'il* about the God of their ancestors who rescued them from slavery in Egypt? What would it have meant during the time of the Davidic dynasty, when temple worship was established? What would it have meant during the exile in Babylon and after the return to the promised land? And how did Jesus the Messiah and the writers of the New Testament understand it?

Second, we can learn a great deal from the scholarly discussions of those who have studied the history of Genesis from different perspectives and at different times. For example, the extensive *Genesis 1–11* commentary of Claus Westermann, who used the JEDP theory, supplies helpful observations on vocabulary, content and setting.

However, like the *Bani Isra'il* and many more recent scholars, we are much more interested in what Genesis says than in how it was produced, so we will study the text as a coherent whole. We do not have a set of documents from different periods, but a single document. The final author may have used different sources, but he put them together as they are for a particular purpose. As Goldingay points out, "One cannot base an understanding of Genesis on knowing the date of its stories or on seeing it as the expression of the ideology of a particular group or date in Israel's history."[11] We have learned much from

---

11. Goldingay, *Genesis*, 9.

Gordon Wenham's *Genesis 1–15* and *Rethinking Genesis 1–11*, which offer invaluable analyses of literary structures and their meanings.[12]

The main point is that, although we will read Genesis 1–11 as we read no other book, because it is the word of God, we will also read it as we would any other book, because it is human words. So all these questions about authorship and date can help us to appreciate the Torah, to which the Old Testament, the New Testament and Jesus the Messiah all bear witness as God's inspired word, given to the *Bani Isra'il* for the blessing of all humankind.

The World of the Text

In order to interpret the book of Genesis, we must study the text itself. It is not sufficient to read the words and assume that we know what they mean: we must consider the type (genre) of the writing, the structure of the writing, the language used, and other literary features common to the historical period in which the text was produced. We will consider these things in a section on "The World of the Text" in each chapter of this commentary. Here, we will consider some broader questions about the literary nature of Genesis 1–11 and the way in which it has been structured. This will also help us to identify some of its main themes and intentions.

The Literary Style of Genesis

Like Bengalis, the ancient Hebrews loved stories. Like Bengalis, they were interested in their family histories and loved to read works by their national poets. We see evidence of this love of story and genealogy and poetry in Genesis 1–11, but the styles of writing differ much between the *Bani Isra'il* and modern Bengali literature. Although Hebrew writing, like Bengali, sometimes uses rhyme, meter, and puns, Hebrew poetry also has its own characteristics. Although some of these characteristics are evident in translation, others are only understood through the original language.[13]

One of the easiest characteristics to spot is parallelism or similitude. This means that one idea is consecutively said in two ways: the second expression

---

12. We have also learned from the other writers listed in our bibliography. We will seldom indicate which insights we received from which book, as there is much common ground between commentaries. Westermann, Wenham and Goldingay all have extensive writings to which the reader can refer if they wish to dig deeper.

13. To read more about this, see Gillingham, *Poems and Psalms*.

of the idea enhances the first expression. Examples are found in Genesis 2:3; 2:24–25; 3:14–19; 4:23–24; and 9:24–27. For example, Genesis 4:23–24 uses three parallels:

> *Lamech said to his wives:*
> *"Adah and Zillah, hear my voice;*
> > *you wives of Lamech, listen to what I say:*
> *I have killed a man for wounding me,*
> > *a young man for striking me.*
> *If Cain's revenge is sevenfold,*
> > *then Lamech's is seventy-sevenfold."*

Even in translation, we can appreciate the poetic form through the word repetitions and patterns. But other characteristics of language are not so easy to translate. Hebrew poetry uses a very concise style, which may create emphasis, assist memory and produce a rhythmic meter. This poem has only twenty-one words in Hebrew. There are also word patterns which augment these effects. The final stanza of this poem is:

> *Ki shib'atayim yuqqam Qayin, wa-lemech shib'im wa-shib'ah*
> If sevenfold shall-be-avenged Cain, and-Lamech seven and-
> > seventy

Hebrew literature also makes use of puns or similar sounding words in order to suggest double meanings. Sometimes the sound of the words themselves help accent the meaning. Well-known examples are *tohu wa bohu* (Gen 1:2), describing the formlessness of things before creation, and the many "s" and "sh" sounds describing the seventh-day rest of Genesis 2:2–3.

Unlike English or Bangla poetry, rhyme and meter do not play large roles in Hebrew poems. If the text is not formatted as poetry by the publisher, it may be difficult to identify a passage as poetry. Because the Torah is written on parchment scrolls, there are no paragraph or sentence breaks in the manuscript and so translators need to make their own decisions regarding what is poetry and what is prose, and this is not always an easy task. Genesis 1–11 has so many repetitions, restatements, parallels and puns that, if the reader was actually aware of all of them, they might consider every section to be a poetic work.

There are similar considerations in reading the Qur'an. Some portions of the Qur'an are clearly poetry while others are clearly prose. But the prose style can suddenly be interrupted by rhyme and meter in an abrupt change of style from prose to poetry, and prose passages often display rhyme and rhythm.[14]

The Structure of Hebrew Writing

In today's world, we organize our writing in a way that expresses what we want to say. A newspaper report will not be organized in the same way as a historical study, or a textbook in the same way as a novel. The ancient Hebrews had their own ways of organizing their thoughts and their writings. Many paragraphs and portions of the Bible are written using a structural form known as chiasm (after the Greek letter *chi*, uppercase X, lowercase χ). Modern interpreters also see this structure in the Qur'an.[15] A paragraph, poem, section or even a whole book written in this format reveals a particular progression of thought. The best way to illustrate this is using letters, as shown here:

> **A.**
>> **B.**
>>> **C.**
>>>> **D.**
>>> **C'.**
>> **B'.**
> **A'.**

The beginning A bears a relationship to the end A', often marked by the repeated use of words. From the start (A), the passage moves toward a central thought (D) which marks the turning point and the central idea. It then follows a reverse pattern C' mirroring C, B' mirroring B, and A' mirroring A. Perhaps the most dramatic use of this form in Genesis 1–11 is the story of the flood in chapters 6–9 (see page 200-201). Other forms in Genesis 1–11 include a repeated pattern of ideas. For example, there is an A-B-C-A'-B'-C' pattern in Genesis 1:3–31 (see page 47).

---

14. Pioneering studies of the Qur'an as literature can be found in the works of Mustansir Mir. For example, see Mir, "Qur'an as Literature," 49–64. Many others have followed his example.

15. See Mir, "Qur'anic Story of Joseph," 1–15; Ernst, *How to Read the Qur'an*; and Cuypers, *Composition of the Qur'an*.

The Significance of Numbers

Hebrew writing often shows the significance of certain people or events by using numbers. Sometimes, even the number of words used in a phrase or sentence has meaning. In Lamech's poem, there are three stanzas, each with seven words. The numbers "three" and "seven" are important numbers in Hebrew thought, but this also emphasizes the "sevenfold" and "seventy-sevenfold" of the final stanza.

The study of numbers in Hebrew literature is called *gematria*,[16] and there are many significant uses of numbers in the Torah. For example:

1   is the number of wholeness. God is one!

3   is the number of completeness and stability. There are three patriarchs: Abraham, Isaac and Jacob.

7   is a very important number indicating blessedness and perfection. There are seven days of creation, and there is a sevenfold blessing on Abraham (Gen 12:1–3).

10   is another number of completion. There are ten generations in the genealogies of Genesis 5 and 11.

12   is used to show the completion of God's purposes. There are twelve tribes of the *Bani Isra'il.*

40   signifies the completion of a long period of time. The *Bani Isra'il* spent forty years in the wilderness at the time of Moses, and there were forty days and nights of rain at the time of Noah.

70   represents the whole world. There are seventy nations listed in Genesis 10.

We note that 70 = 7 x 10: the number of generations in two genealogies multiplied by the number of blessedness and perfection. We then recall the emphasis in Genesis 2:1–3 that God made the world in seven days. It amazes us that we can see, just from these numbers, that Genesis 1–11 is telling us that the world God made is blessed and complete, and that God is multiplying his blessings as the people multiply!

---

16. Readers should note that this study is sometimes taken to extremes, with questionable results. For example, letters of the alphabet are given numerical values and esoteric interpretations are developed on that basis. For further reading, see Carol, "Making Sense of the Numbers," 239–51.

The Structure of Genesis 1–11

Genesis 1–11 is carefully crafted and displays many interwoven themes and patterns, therefore different commentaries on Genesis 1–11 analyse its structure in different ways.[17] The most obvious structure is that of the *toledoths*, which divide the whole of the book of Genesis into sections headed, "These are the generations of . . ." (see page 6). We have used this structure as the main structure of this commentary. However, there is also a very important A-B-C-D pattern of creation, fall, punishment and hope which helps us to see the theology of Genesis 1–11, and we have learned much by looking for chiastic structures both within each *toledoth* section and in Genesis 1–11 as a whole.

Structure #1: *Toledoth*

The overall structure of this commentary follows the genealogical structure which we mentioned when we discussed the use of the Hebrew term *toledoth* to indicate a new section. These are the sections by which the writer of Genesis organized his work, and we have therefore followed them in organizing the commentary. The sections are as follows:

1.   Prologue: Creation of the Heaven and Earth (Gen 1:1–2:3)

2.   *Toledoth* of Heaven and Earth (Gen 2:4–4:26)

     Adam and Eve in the Eden garden, the fall and its consequences, escalation of sin outside Eden

3.   *Toledoth* of Adam (Gen 5:1–6:8)

     The line of Seth, escalation of sin before the flood

4.   *Toledoth* of Noah (Gen 6:9–9:29)

     Preparation for the flood, the flood and salvation, God's covenant with Noah, prophecies about Noah's sinful offspring

5.   *Toledoth* of the sons of Noah, Shem, Ham and Japheth (Gen 10:1–11:9)

     Table of nations, escalation of sin in Babylon

6.   *Toledoth* of Shem (Gen 11:10–26)

---

17. We have found Wenham, *Genesis 1–15*, to be very helpful in analyzing structures, although we have also used our own analyses.

7. Beginning of *Toledoth* of Terah (Gen 11:27–12:3)

    The call of Abraham

This structure emphasizes the continuity and relatedness of humankind. It also draws our attention to the narrowing down of the history, as each section focuses on one branch of what grew in the previous section. Later in Genesis, the focus will be on Isaac, then on Jacob and his children – the whole of Genesis is taking us towards the *Bani Isra'il*.

Structure #2: Creation, Fall, Punishment, Hope

Several times in Genesis 1–11, we see God creating and blessing, then human beings falling into sin, then God judging them but giving hope for future blessing. This pattern offers another way of seeing the structure of Genesis 1–11:

1. The First Humans
   A. Creation and blessing (Gen 1–2)
   B. Fall into sin (Gen 3:1–7)
   C. Punishment (Gen 3:8–24)
   D. Future hope and promise of provision (Gen 3:15, 21, 23)

2. The First Family
   A. The son of Adam blessed and his worthy sacrifice accepted (Gen 4:1–4)
   B. Cain's sin (Gen 4:5–9, 23–24)
   C. Punishment (Gen 4:10–16)
   D. Signs of hope: children are born, the devotion of Seth's descendants (Gen 4:17–22, 25–26)

3. A Budding Society
   A. The blessing of a growing population (Gen 5)
   B. The universal influence of sin (Gen 6:1–5)
   C. Punishment (Gen 6:6–7:24)
   D. Signs of hope: The salvation of Noah's family, a worthy sacrifice, the rainbow covenant (Gen 8:1–9:20)

4. The Budding of Nations
   A. The blessing of a growing population (Gen 10)
   B. The rise of the community's sinful power (Gen 9:20–29; 11:1–4)
   C. Punishment (Gen 11:5–9)
   D. Sign of hope: The call of Abraham (Gen 11:10–12:3)

This structure draws our attention to some of the key theological themes which are seeded in Genesis and which will grow throughout the Bible – God's love and blessing for his creatures, human sinfulness and its consequences, the judgement of a holy God, and God's promises and plan of salvation.

Structure #3: Chiasm

We can see clear chiasms in many places in Genesis 1–11. Profound examples are found in the *toledoth*s of the heavens and the earth (Gen 2:4–4:26) and of Noah (Gen 6:9–9:29). The centres of these two extended narratives give us keys to the Bible's views of humans and of God. At the heart of the first is the human disobedience which results in the "fall." At the heart of the second is God's faithful remembrance of Noah, which leads to the covenant.

We can also see a chiastic structure in the whole of Genesis chapters 1–11:

1. **A.** God creates the world and blesses humankind (1)
2.   **B.** Human origins, sin and expulsion from Eden (2–3)
3.   **C.** Violence, dispersion and the first city (4)
4.   **D.** Genealogy of Adam (5)
5.   **E.** The violent state of the earth (6:1–6)
6.   **F. Noah and the flood (6:7–8)**
7.   **E'.** The covenant with Noah (9)
8.   **D'.** Table of Nations (10)
9.   **C'.** The city, the tower and the dispersion (11:1–9)
10.   **B'.** *Bani Isra'il*'s forebears and Abram's call from sinful Ur (11:10–32)
11. **A'.** God's plan for the blessing the nations (12:1–3)

This is not a neat structure, and it does not account for everything in the text. However, it helps us to see the shape of Genesis 1–11 and some more of its basic themes. At A and A', we see again the major theme of God's desire to bless all peoples: he begins by blessing them, and the whole of Genesis 1–11 is introducing the plan of blessing through Abraham. In between, we see the sin which prevents blessing and separates people from God and from each other (B, C, B', C'), and we see the relatedness of all humanity, both as individuals, as families and as whole people groups (D and D'). At the centre, we see God's judgement and salvation (F), in the context of terrible violence on the one hand (E) and God's commitment to His creation on the other (E'). This, says Genesis 1–11, is our world; this is our human predicament; and this is our amazing God.

THE QUESTIONS WE WANT TO ASK

Genesis 1–11 makes people ask questions. This is because:

- Its stories are very powerful, so readers want to fill in the gaps in them.

- It has the seeds of many ideas which are not developed until later in the Torah and the rest of the Bible: readers want to know what those seeds will grow into.

- It deals with the beginnings of the world, so readers want to know how it fits into other accounts of the beginnings of the world.

- It deals with unfamiliar names and times and places, so readers want to know about them all.

In short, it is a text which provokes questions, but does not give the answers.

This commentary will have many boxes which discuss the questions which Bangladeshi readers ask. We will not always be able to answer the questions, but we will give material for further discussion. All of these questions have been asked by many people in history. We will briefly explore how Jews, Christians, Muslims and others have tried to answer them, but our concern every time will be, "How does this help us to understand Genesis?" Have we learned something through discussing the question? Why does Genesis not give us the answer? When we go back to Genesis, do we notice something new?

For example, what about the six days of creation in Genesis 1? For millenia, people have discussed whether these are six periods of twenty-four hours, whether they are long time periods, how there could be days before the creation of the sun, and how this might relate to other theories about how the world began. We can follow such discussions in Jewish and Christian thinking, and into the modern world of science. We can also note the mentions of six days in the Qur'an. We can relate all this back to Genesis in two ways. First, we note the extraordinary nature of the Genesis texts and how they differ from other sources. Second, we notice that there are not six days of creation, but seven. The first Genesis section does not finish at the end of the sixth day, but with the seventh day of 2:1–3. Were we to have missed these two points, we would have failed to provide readers with crucial understanding of Genesis's teaching about God's relationship with the world and with humanity.

The World in Front of the Text

We are reading the text of Genesis 1–11 in Bangladesh in the twenty-first century. This is "reading the text in today's world" or asking what it means for "the world in front of the text." This world contains all sorts of people: believers in God, unbelievers, non-religious, rich and poor, citizens and foreigners, scientists and artists, educated and illiterate. In this crowd there are also many who fit into none of these categories, and some who fit into more than one.

As we read Genesis 1–11, we need to consider our own cultures and ideas and how they shape our interpretation. We also need to consider the ways in which people have read the texts in their own "worlds in front of the text" through history, and how that relates to their faiths. This is important, because the scriptures of Christians and Muslims often refer to material in Genesis 1–11. In front of Genesis is the world of the Old Testament, and of Jewish readers of Genesis down the ages. In front of the Old Testament is the world of New Testament and of Christian readers of Genesis over the past 2,000 years. In front of the New Testament is the Qur'an, and of 1,400 years of Islamic tradition and commentary.

Genesis 1–11 and the New Testament

The New Testament is greatly influenced by the book of Genesis and indeed by the whole of the Old Testament. We will consider many of the detailed links in the appropriate places in our commentary. Here, we note the reason for these links: the New Testament is about Jesus the Messiah, who came into the world of the *Bani Isra'il* and who is the fulfilment of the former law and prophets.

Genesis 1–11 sets the scene for the whole history of God's interaction with human beings, and points us forward to this fulfilment. We read how humans were separated from God's presence by their sin, and how their fellowship with each other was disrupted. Yet the covenant God loved humans, and longed to see these relationships completely restored. The history of restoration began with the call of Abraham and his family (Gen 12:1–3). At one point in the story of Abraham, an alternate life was given as a sacrifice in order to save Abraham's son (Gen 22). Christians see this as pointing to the life of the Messiah which was laid down in order to save us from our sins. The first pointers towards this sacrifice are found in Genesis 1–11.[18]

In Genesis 3:24, the vivid picture of human separation from God is a closed path. Adam and Eve were not only expelled from Eden but also repelled from

---

18. See commentary on Genesis 3:15; 4:2–5; 8:20–22.

it; the way was closed and an angel with a flaming sword was put on guard outside. The gospel offers an open path. It gives us the hope of entering the kingdom of God through Jesus the Messiah, who promises salvation to those who trust in him when he says, "I am the way" and "I am the door" (John 14:6; 10:9). The closed path to Eden is now open! The New Testament also points us forward to the end of history, when heaven itself takes the path to earth, and the whole of creation is made new (Rev 21–22).

Genesis 1–11 and the Qur'an

The Qur'an holds the Torah in high esteem as the holy Book revealed to the Prophet Moses. It proclaims that, in the Torah, the Jews were given "light and guidance" (Sūra al-Māʾida 5:44). The Torah is mentioned eighteen times in the Qur'an, and Moses is mentioned 136 times. The Qur'an does not directly quote Genesis 1–11, but it has many references to its characters and events, which we will explore in the appropriate chapters of our commentary.

Despite the high esteem of the Qur'an for the Torah, many Muslims believe that the text we have today is corrupted. One theory is that the original Torah was destroyed during the time of the Babylonian exile, and that a corrupt priest Ezra (the Qur'an calls him ʿUzayr) wrote an altered version in league with other Jews. This, it is said, is why the Qur'an accuses Jews of distorting the Scriptures (Sūra an-Nisāʾ 4:46). However, most of the early classical commentaries would say that the distortion (taḥrīf) is not of words but of meaning: that is, the text of the Torah is pure, but the rabbis were interpreting it wrongly. It was only later that belief in the corruption of the text became prevalent.[19] The Torah (and the rest of the Bible) certainly existed in its present form long before the time of the Islamic Prophet Muhammad, so how could the Qur'an tell the Jews to abide by their book if the actual text was corrupted?

Muslims in Bangladesh learn about the characters and events described in the Torah not only from the Qur'an, but also from hadith, commentaries, and various books about prophets. These stories are taught to the people during night-time preaching and in teaching by imams, and they are taught to children

---

19. For a thorough study of Muslim views of the Torah, see Whittingham, *History of Muslim Views*.

by their parents. "Islamic literature" mentioned in this commentary generally refers to the most popular sources, as listed below:[20]

Tafsir (Commentary)	Hadith (Traditions)	Ta'rīkh and Qiṣaṣ al-Anbiyā' (History and stories of the prophets)
Tofsirul Baizawi	*Bokhari Sharif*	*Kasasul Ambiya* (Stories of the Prophets)
Tofsir Ibn Kasir	*Muslim Sharif*	Ibn Kathīr, *Stories of the Prophets*
Tofsir Jalalin	*Mishkat ul Maasabih*	Muhammad Ibn Jarīr at-Ṭabarī, *The History of At-Ṭabarī*
Ma'reful Kuran		
Boyanul Kuran		

There are very few Muslim writers who have written commentaries on the Bible. One exception is the well-known Indian scholar, Sir Syed Ahmad Khan, who wrote the *Mohammedan Commentary of the Bible* in1862 (*Tabyīn al-kalām fī tafsīr at-Tawrat wa'l-Injīl 'alā Millat-al-Islām*), to which we will occasionally refer.

Genesis 1–11 and Jewish Writings

We will often refer to Jewish views of Genesis 1–11. Jewish scholars pay very close attention to the texts, and sometimes point out things which Christian commentators have missed. They are often interested in aspects of the text which interest Muslims, so they can help us to think about the questions which we ask in our context. The most relevant text for our discussions is *Genesis Rabbah*, a collection of rabbinic discussions on Genesis which reached its present form in the fourth or fifth century AD. Some of the discussions would have been going on at the time of Jesus the Messiah; and the whole collection was in use at the time of the Islamic Prophet Muhammad. It is one of the books known as *Midrash*, or "inquiry/interpretation."

Often, the rabbis answer a question raised by the text by adding something to the Genesis story, and these additions are at times mentioned in the Qur'an. For example, Genesis 4 does not tell us how Abel's body was buried or who buried him. Few Christian readers are interested in this question, because

---

20. Details can be found in the bibliography. Note that these titles are transliterated from Bangla. In the body of this English text we will generally refer to them using direct transliterations from Arabic – Ibn Kathir, the Jalalyan, al-Baydāwī, etc... Other classical qur'anic commentaries and hadith collections exist in many editions, and will be referred to by their usual names, transliterated from Arabic, the references being to their comments on the verses being discussed.

they ask theological questions rather than practical questions, and they do not worry about whether early people knew the burial laws. The rabbis suggested a range of possible answers: the Qur'an chooses one of their answers and gives a clear picture of who buried Abel and of how he knew what to do. The New Testament also alludes to the burial of Abel, but in a very different way (Heb 12:24). We will explore all this further in the commentary on Genesis 4, and ask what we might learn from the fact that Genesis itself does not give us the answer to the question.

It is not unusual to find the Qur'an and the New Testament answering a Jewish question in different ways. Take for example the very first word: *bereshit*. It is translated, "in the beginning." In Bangla or in English this seems like a simple construction, but the rabbis of *Genesis Rabbah* noted two problems. First, the prefix *be* can have various meanings, but it is more often like the English "with" rather than "in." Second, *reshit* is a verbal noun which would normally have an object. That is, we would expect "the beginning of something" and not simply "the beginning." So the rabbis ask, "What is the *reshit*?" The main answer takes them to Proverbs 8:2–31, where wisdom is described as the *reshit* of God's work, which was there before the heavens and the earth and even before the "deep" (Heb. *tehom*) of Genesis 1:2. Wisdom, say the rabbis, is the Torah. So *bereshit* means "with the Torah" or maybe "for the sake of the Torah." That might mean that the Torah was God's blueprint for making the universe, or that the whole world was made so that the *Bani Isra'il* could receive the Torah and bless the nations.

We can see a similar idea in the Qur'an – the *lawḥ al-maḥfūẓ* or the *umm al-kitāb* from which all the books have been revealed, including the Torah (Sūras *al-Burūj* 85:22; *Āl 'Imrān* 3:7; *ar-Ra 'd* 13:39; *az-Zukhruf* 43:4). The Qur'an does not say that these books were instrumental in creation, but there is general agreement among Muslims that the Qur'an itself is eternal. Islamic traditions say that God wrote with a pen on the *lawḥ al-maḥfūẓ* his glorious plan of creation, and even that this pen also wrote of the 144,000 prophets yet to come.[21] A famous hadith tells us that God created the pen and told it to write, and it responded, "What shall I write?" God then said, "Write the decree (*al-qadr*) of all that will be until the hour is come" or "Write all that is in the heavens and the earth."[22]

---

21. *Kachachul Ambiya*, 17.

22. Versions of this hadith appear in a number of collections, for example, *al-Tirmidhī* #3537 and the *Mishkāt Sharīf* cited in Sir Syed Ahmad Khan, *The Mohammedan Commentary on the Holy Bible, Genesis 1–11*, 13. The idea of the divine pen can be found in Sūras *al-Qalam*

Scholars have long recognized that there is a difficulty here: if God is pure unity, how can the Qur'an also be eternal? Can there be two eternals? Could God have had a partner in creation? Islamic theology vehemently denies such a possibility, so this problem is solved by saying that the Qur'an existed eternally, but that it was not a part of God. Conservative Islamic scholars say that this subject is impossible to understand, so we should not even try. God knows everything!

The New Testament takes the rabbinic discussion in a different direction, identifying Jesus the Messiah as the eternal wisdom (1 Cor 1:24). He is described as God's word who was with God "in the beginning," and through whom everything was created (John 1:1–3). But the problem of two eternals is solved differently than in Islamic thought. John's gospel tells us that the word was not only with God, but was God, and that this word came into the world not as a book, but as a human being. Perhaps even the Qur'an hints at this by calling Jesus the Messiah *kalimat Allah*, that is, God's word (Sūras *Āl 'Imrān* 3:45; *an-Nisā'* 4:171; *Maryam* 19:34).

Theological Reflection

In each of our chapters, we will follow the verse-by-verse commentary with a "Theological Reflection" which will gather together some of the strands from our study of the text. In most cases, we will follow a three-fold structure: we will look at Genesis 1–11 as the "bud of theology," the "grandmother of the sciences," and the "seedbed of the Bible."

Bud of Theology

Genesis 1–11 is a *theological bud* ready to blossom – that is, it provides the beginning for understanding God. It contains the petals which will unfurl and blossom as we read on in the Bible. Here we can just see the beautiful colours of the edges of the petals, and we cannot yet get the glorious scent of the full blossom – the glory of God in the face of the Messiah (2 Cor 4:6). We cannot conceive of the fragrance yet to come, but, here in Genesis, we find indispensable hints in a garland of words.

For example, we have already noticed the beautiful word *chen* (grace or favour) which introduces the central portion of Genesis 1–11 in Genesis 6:8. When we come to comment on this verse, we will see that we can get only a hint

_____

68:1 and *al-'Alaq* 96:4.

of what it means from its context in Genesis. Later in the Torah (Exod 34:6), God will reveal that he is *channun* (gracious); so we realise that Genesis 6:8 is giving us a glimpse of an attribute which will unfurl throughout the history of the *Bani Isra'il* and blossom into the *charis* (grace) which spreads its aroma through the New Testament.

Another important glimpse comes through the words used for God. There are two Hebrew words used in Genesis 1–11: Elohim and YHWH, which we will translate "God" (Bangla, *Allah*) and "Lord" (Bangla, *mabud*) respectively. Genesis 1–11 sometimes uses one and sometimes the other, and sometimes both together. As we have seen, this is one of the features of Genesis 1–11 which led people to suggest that the different names indicated different sources, and led to the JEDP Theory. Instead, we want to ask what we can learn from the uses of these two names.

In Genesis 1, Elohim is used of the One God who created everything. The word is plural in form, and is used throughout the Old Testament for God. It is related etymologically to the Arabic *Allāh*, which Arabic-speaking Christians have always used to refer to the creator of the heavens and the earth. Here in Genesis, it tells us that there are not many different gods who are in charge of different parts of the universe: no! there is just one God, and he is more than all so-called "gods" put together. The Mesopotamians' gods were like human beings in their emotions and their motivations: the One God is not like them. He is high above them, and he is motivated by holiness and love. When we read "Elohim," we remember that God is the one transcendent creator of all things.

The name YHWH was revealed to Moses at the burning bush on Mount Sinai (Exod 3:2). The word *YHWH* is related to the word "being" and can be translated "I am who I am" or "I am that I am." It identifies YHWH as the One who determines who he is.[23] With this name, God established his covenant with the *Bani Isra'il*. With this name, God is revealed as faithful and full of unfailing love.

The name YHWH is so holy that, to this day, Jewish people will not pronounce it; instead, they substitute the word *adonai* (Lord) or *ha-Shem* (the Name). Therefore, since the Hebrew of the Torah is written without vowels, we do not know how it was pronounced. When we read this name, we remember who God is and how, by appearing to Moses, he came to dwell with the *Bani Isra'il*. In the same way today, God has come to dwell with us by his Holy Spirit given through Jesus the Messiah.

---

23. Compare the qur'anic name for God, *aṣ-Ṣamad*; Sūra al-Ikhlāṣ 112:2.

When the two names are combined as YHWH Elohim (as in, for example, Gen 2:4, 15), they remind us that the immanent, personal, covenant God is also the one transcendent creator. The one who created in Genesis 1 is also the one who walked in the garden in Genesis 3. The breathtaking wonder which we glimpse in the rest of Genesis 1–11 is that this powerful, good, beautiful God also wants to relate to sinful humanity in the ugliness of the fallen world outside the garden.

The Qur'an often refers to God as "Rabb," translated Lord or Protector. It may be that this word is referring to the name YHWH; but does Rabb carry the same meaning as YHWH in the book of Genesis? The Qur'an says:

> And We have already created man and know what his soul whispers to him, and We are closer to him than [his] jugular vein. (Sūra Qāf 50:16)

But what kind of closeness is this? Is it, as many orthodox Muslims believe, simply a closeness of the total knowledge of a transcendent being? Or does it imply, as the rationalist Muslim sect, the Mu'tazilites, assert, that God is immanent? Bangladeshi Sufis emphasize the relationship with God implied by this verse. Human beings cannot survive without the jugular vein; as the blood circulates from heart to brain through this vein, so, say the Sufis, we would die without relationship with God. The qur'anic verse itself does not tell us whether they are right, but we will glimpse the meaning of the closeness of God to humanity as we feast our eyes on the beautiful *theological bud* of Genesis 1–11.

Grandmother of the Sciences

"Science" comes from the Latin *scio*, to know; so "science" is knowledge about what God has made. Genesis 1–11 tells us how human beings relate to God, and therefore about why they can know about his creation. Moreover, it gives us the mandate to study and to manage the world. It is not surprising that Genesis 1–11 was part of what inspired the growth of the modern experimental sciences. We might say that it has provided some of the essential DNA out of which science has grown.[24]

---

24. See Mandelbrote and Bennet, *Garden, the Ark, the Tower*; Harrison, *Bible, Protestantism*; and the various papers in Killeen and Forshaw, *Word and the World*. See also Geisinger, "Sustainable Development and the Domination of Nature," 43–73.

First, Genesis 1–11 shows us that human beings are made in the image of God. This means that we are, in some ways, like God, and one of the outcomes is that we can learn from what he has made. Is it not amazing that pure mathematics, which is a product of our human minds, can be used so powerfully to describe and predict what goes on in the universe? The reason that our minds "match" the universe in this way is that it is God's "mind" which designed both our minds and the universe, and that something of God's mind is reflected in our minds.

More than that, our role in relation to the world that is the object of scientific study is having "dominion."[25] In Genesis 1–2 as well as in our everyday lives, we can see that we are different from the animals. We have language with which we can talk about the world, we have responsibility for looking after the world, and we have responsibility for looking after the animals. We can expect to be able to learn about this world, and to be able to find ways of controlling it – the development of science and technology is not a surprise to the reader of Genesis.

Second, Genesis 1–11 shows us that it is our human responsibility to find knowledge: we cannot expect God to simply give us all the knowledge that we need. In the Qur'an, God teaches Adam the names, and this knowledge equips him to do his work as khalīfa[26] and proves him superior to angels. In Genesis, Adam is even more honoured: God gives him the job of naming the animals.[27] This verse was one of the motivations for the development of modern science in Europe. People realized that they could, like Adam, look at the world for themselves and learn about it and "name" it – take authority over it. Again, we see that it is the nature of humanity to be able to do science.

So, in our commentary, we do not expect that God will tell us things in Genesis 1–2 that we can find out ourselves by observing his world. But neither do we expect science to be able to tell us all that we need to know about our Creator. Adam could have learned something about God by looking at the Garden and by studying the animals, but he also needed to hear what God had to say and to experience God "walking in the Garden" with him. That is why studying Genesis is vital for scientists as well as for everyone else.

---

25. See commentary on Genesis 1:26–27.

26. Sūra al-Baqara 2:31–32. For further discussion of this passage and its interpretation, see page 45.

27. See commentary on Genesis 2:19.

Seedbed[28] of the Bible

We have already noted that Genesis 1–11 provides the theological basis for the entire Bible – here are sown the seeds of many themes which will be transplanted to grow throughout the Bible. Creation and sin, punishment and covenant, sacrifice, human responsibility, God's Spirit, marriage and family, the Sabbath – all these subjects are introduced here. Other themes include fearful waters, beautiful rivers, sibling rivalry, and the tree of life. Readers can see the seedlings growing in the rest of the Torah and the Old Testament, bearing fruit in the New Testament and leading to a great harvest in the new Creation.

Genesis 1–11 also tells us about the soil which produces the Bible. This is important – the Bible is the product of human minds as well as divine inspiration, and Genesis 1–11 shows us how that is possible. It shows us that the One True God is not only transcendent but also immanent, and how he relates to the human beings who are made in his image. The various books of the Bible are a result of that relationship, and God uses them today to speak to all of us.

We can see from the Old Testament that God sometimes spoke directly to prophets and sometimes sent angels to speak to people, so he could have given people the exact words that he wanted them to write. The Qur'an describes itself in this way when it says that God revealed his word through dictation. It quite literally came down (*nazala*) from God. But this is not what the Bible says about how it was written (see page 13-14). The Bible was written by people who did their own thinking and wrote their own words under the inspiration of the Holy Spirit of God. We can understand this as a consequence of the divine-human relationship which is described in Genesis 1–11. If God is as he is revealed in these chapters, and if human beings are as they are revealed in these chapters, then a divine-human partnership is possible and it is to be expected. We may wonder how God can work so closely with humans who are finite and full of evil deeds. Genesis 1–11 will show us that God has always blessed the world by drawing near to us.

What About Us?

We will finish each chapter of this book by returning to our "world in front of the text" and thinking about some ways in which we can apply what we have learned in our own lives. This introductory chapter has dealt with some

---

28. The idea in Bangla is of the seedbed in which rice is planted and grows before being transplanted to the field.

of the questions which people ask about Genesis 1–11. The first "what about us?" section calls us to think about how and why we ask questions about God's Holy Word.

What sort of literature is the Bible? When and by whom was Genesis written? What does the Qur'an say about this book? How does the New Testament use Genesis? What is the relationship between this book and science? These are some of the questions we have raised. Why have we done that? We have done it because many people are asking these questions, but they do it for different reasons. Some want to challenge the Holy Book. They want to show that Genesis is just another version of similar ancient documents of the past, and hence that it is not really the word of God. We are not asking the questions for these reasons; rather, we want to know what God is saying to us through this book. We want to know God and to understand how to please him in our daily lives.

There is a personal challenge here for all of us. How will we read? What will we be looking for? What questions will we ask?

- Will we ask questions like the snake, who wanted to persuade Eve to disobey God's word? He asks, "Did God really say this?" (Gen 3:1) – the same question as those who want to say that Genesis is not God's word.
- Will we ask questions like Cain, who wanted to avoid his responsibilities? He asks, "Am I my brother's keeper?" (Gen 4:9) – this question actually challenges God as to whether his expectations of us are reasonable.
- Or will we be listening to the questions which God will ask us? "Where are you? Who told you? What have you done? Why are you angry? Where is your brother?" (Gen 3:9, 11, 13; 4:6, 9, 10). The challenges ring down the ages to us. But there is also the question which gives hope, "If you do well, will you not be accepted?" (4:7).

In short, will we read Genesis to undermine it and to challenge God, or will we read to understand and follow him? We all want to be blessed, but will we accept the blessing that God so freely offers us, or will we, like Eve and Adam, try to be better than God and grab whatever looks good to us?

2

In the Beginning, God Created – Genesis 1:1–2:3

Let them praise the name of the LORD!
>For he commanded and they were created. (Ps 148:5)

Know that the LORD, he is God!
>It is he who made us, and we are his;
>We are his people, and the sheep of his pasture. (Ps 100:3)

The Holy Scriptures declare that there is one God of the universe who has created the heavens and the earth. He alone rules over all things – all nations, all life, all plants and weather – and he is Lord over all things in heaven and earth. He is Lord. He is Lord of the worlds (*rabb al-ʿalamīn* – see Sūra *al-Fātiḥa* 1:2), ruler over everything in the earth, outside the earth, seen or unseen. For this reason, humankind is dependent on him for all things and is answerable only to him. God is the ruler, the overseer, and the provider of those who have lived in the past, live in the present or are yet to be born. He is the judge of all.

The Qur'an and the Bible agree that all creation points to this one God.

>Verily in the heavens and the earth are signs for those who believe. And in the creation of yourselves, and the fact that animals are scattered (through the earth), are signs for those of assuring faith. And in the alternation of night and day, and that fact that God sends down sustenance from the sky, and revives therewith the earth after its death, and in the change of the winds, are signs for those who are wise. (Sūra al-Jāthiya 45:3–5)

>The heavens declare the glory of God, and the sky above proclaims his handiwork. (Ps 19:1)

> For his invisible attributes, namely, his eternal power and divine
> nature, have been clearly perceived, ever since the creation of the
> world, in the things that have been made. (Rom 1:20)

In the world in which Genesis was written, people had many gods, and they
believed that created entities like the sun, moon and stars, and the birds and
the animals, were divine beings. Genesis 1 refutes this by revealing the One
God as creator of all.

We need this message in Bangladesh today! Muslims and Christians
alike acknowledge these truths, but do we live by them, or do we follow
local superstitions? People fear owls hooting, they use horoscopes, they see
particular times as auspicious, and they think that the planets govern their
fortunes. There are even superstitions about food – during exam times, some
Bangladeshi students avoid eggs and potatoes, because they think that eating
round things might get them a 0 mark in the exam.

Genesis 1:1–2:3 uses Elohim as the word for the One Creator God. Belief
in him is the foundation of the monotheistic faiths. Without it, neither the
Qur'an nor the Bible makes sense. Every passage of the Torah, the Prophets,
the Psalms, and the Gospels assumes it, even though they may not directly
refer to creation as frequently as does the Qur'an. We cannot understand the
meaning of the *Bani Isra'il* or of Jesus the Messiah without understanding that
the Lord created the whole earth and all its peoples and that it is these peoples
whom he will bless through Abraham's descendants.

However, while the creation is referred to in many places in the other
books, it is only here, in Genesis 1–2, that we find a coherent account of the
whole creation. The Psalms, the Prophets and the Qur'an have scattered verses
which mention different parts of the creation. Genesis tells us to what they
are referring.

Our passage has given rise to much controversy: the controversies are
similar for all the Abrahamic faiths, and we will need to explore some of them –
but let us not focus on controversy. Let us focus on what we learn from Genesis,
and on how this account of creation lays the foundation for all that will follow.

The Worlds Behind and in Front of the Text
The Ancient World and Today's World

All the peoples of the world have their stories about how the world began.
In today's world, one of the main stories is that of science; for example, the
Big Bang theory and theories of evolution. In the ancient world, the stories

had personalized beings (deities) who made and organized everything. The scientific stories and the ancient world's stories may seem very different, but they all try to make sense of the world. Why does anything exist? What drives the world? Why is it as it is? Does it have to be that way?

Science might answer that it is not possible to know *why* anything exists: the universe can only be observed. What drives it is the nature of matter and energy, and the forces which exist as a result of them. Why is it as it is? Because, little by little, over a long period of time, these forces have produced what we see now. It probably does not have to be the way it is, as there is a large measure of chance in the systems.

The ancient peoples might have answered that things exist because gods exist, and the gods made and organized the world. What drives it is those gods. It is as it is because of the actions of gods and of human beings. It could have been different had the gods acted differently, and human beings can change the way in which the gods act if they do the right things.

We will see that Genesis 1 agrees with both the scientific answers and the ancient answers in some ways, but that it also disagrees with the ancient answers in some very important ways. Does it disagree with the scientific answers? It may disagree with some details, but, on the whole, it does not disagree: rather, it answers some of the questions which scientists know that science cannot answer.

In order to understand how the first readers would have understood Genesis 1:1–2:3, we need to know about two aspects of their world: first, what they thought the universe was like and, second, more about the various creation accounts that were circulating during those times.

Understandings of the Universe in Ancient Times

The Old Testament uses three words to describe the parts of the universe: *erets* – the habitable earth; *shamayim* – the heavens above; and *sheol* – an underworld or the world of the dead. There was also the vast, watery "ocean" (e.g. Neh 9:6; Pss 24:2; 136:6). For example, we get the picture of the three parts when the Ten Commandments tell us not to worship "*anything that is in heaven above, or that is on the earth beneath, or that is in the water under the earth*" (Deut 5:8).

Sometimes, the sky seems to be like an inverted bowl, and the earth is described as having "ends" (e.g. Ps 65:5; Deut 13:7; 1 Sam 2:10) – the picture is of a flat disc with a dome-like roof. Other vivid descriptions of the world include rain falling from "the windows of heaven" (e.g. Gen 7:11) and the "pillars" holding the earth firm (e.g. Ps 75:3). Putting all the references together, people have constructed a picture of how the ancient Hebrews seem to have imagined the world. See fig 2. However, all this can also be read as poetic description, or as description of how the world looked to people at that time. We do not need to insist that the Bible teaches us that these are scientific facts that we must believe.[1]

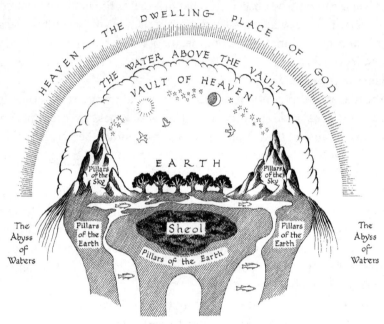

Figure 2[2]

Genesis 1:1–2:3 and Ancient Mesopotamian Texts

As Table 1 shows, there are huge differences between Genesis 1 and *Enuma Elish* and other ancient creation stories; however, there are parts of the Genesis narrative which seem to relate to those stories. In *Enuma Elish*, the young God Marduk fights with the goddess Tiamat, who represents the seas. All kinds of chaos have already resulted from the raging battles among the gods and goddesses. Eventually, Marduk kills Tiamat, splits her body in two, and from it makes the earth and the sky and adorns the sky with lights. He then creates human beings to serve the deities, using the flesh and blood of a dead deity. We can see parallels as well as differences; and that helps us to understand how the Genesis creation account refutes the polytheism of its time.

---

1. See the text boxes on Genesis and science, pages 8–9, and on evolution, page 63.

2. Image by Horace Knowles © The British and Foreign Bible Society 1954, 1967, 1972. Additions and amendments are by Louise Bass © The British and Foreign Bible Society 1994.

Subject	Bible	*Enuma Elish*
Regarding the nature of God	Monotheism (*tawḥīd*) – one God, the only God, without a consort or partner, source of all things.	Many gods and goddesses consorting with each other.
Creation	God creates light, the cosmos, earth, humankind, and all things.	Different gods create light, the cosmos, the earth, humankind and all things.
The universe	A three-tiered universe	A three-tiered universe
The waters	Creation begins with *tohu wa bohu* and a deep sea.	History begins with the fighting of two water-gods, Apsu and Tiamat
Timing	Everything created in six days	Creation not set in any chronological order.
Heavenly lights	Sun, moon and stars created	Moon and stars created. No mention of the creation of the sun.
Creation	Everything created by God's word.	Creation by the hands of the gods, out of pre-existing elements.
Purpose of humankind	Humans to work in and oversee creation.	Humans to serve the gods and decrease their workload.
Nature of humankind	Created from the earth and given God's breath (Gen 2:7).	Marduk created mankind by mixing the earth with the slain blood of a goddess.

The New Testament (Injil Sharif)

The worldview presented in Genesis 1:1–2:3 is so basic to the Bible that we can see it reflected in more places than we can enumerate. In the New Testament, we not only look back to the creation at the beginning: we rejoice in the new creation that is now available to believers in Messiah right now, and we joyfully await the new heavens and the new earth which are the goal of all history.

Looking back: the New Testament sees Jesus the Messiah as having been involved in creation as the Word of God (John 1:1–4). It also shows that he is Lord of creation. He commands the chaotic waters (Matt 8:23–27; Mark 4:37–41; Luke 8:22–25; cf. Gen 1:2); he is the Light of the world (John 8:12; cf. Gen 1:3–4); he walks on water (Matt 14:22–33; Mark 6:45–51; cf. Gen 1:9); he is the incomparably pure image of God (Col 1:15–16; cf. Gen 1:26); and he is the Lord of the Sabbath (Matt 12:1–8; Mark 2:23–28; Luke 6:1–5; cf. Gen 2:3).

Right now: the New Testament has many ways of describing the new life in the Messiah. It is a new birth (John 3:1–7); it is dying to an old life and being raised to a new life (Rom 6:4; Gal 2:20); it is taking off old, dirty clothes and putting on new, clean clothes (Col 3:9–10). It is a new creation (Eph 2:10; 2 Cor 5:17). In short, through Jesus the Messiah, sinful human beings can have a new start and become the people that God created them to be. This also involves the activity of the Holy Spirit: just as the Spirit of God hovers over the dark chaos in Genesis 1:2, the new creation requires the Spirit (John 3:8). The giving of the Holy Spirit is now the present sign and foretaste for believers of what is to come (Rom 8:19–23).

Looking forward: Romans 8 speaks of a coming day when the whole creation will be freed from the effects of sin. Revelation, the New Testament book which has the most allusions to Genesis 1–11, is also the book which describes the coming new heavens and new earth. The new earth has the jewels and the rivers which remind us of the Eden Garden (Rev 21:18–21; 22:2; cf. Gen 2:10–18), and the moon, sun and stars that were created in Genesis 1 will no longer be necessary because God will replace all darkness with the light of his presence (Rev 21:23; 22:5; cf. Gen 1:3–4).

The Qur'an

The Qur'an's view of the physical world is remarkably similar to that of Genesis. It seems that the seventh-century Arabs had much in common with the Hebrews living 2,000 years previously. The basic idea of a sky above, an earth beneath and a living space in between is the same (e.g. Sūras *al-Mā'ida* 5:18; *al-Ḥijr* 15:85; *Maryam* 19:65; *al-Anbiyā'* 21:16; *al-Furqān* 25:59). The biblical dimension of "under the earth" is mentioned but not emphasized (Sūra *Ṭā Hā* 20:6). A difference is that the Qur'an speaks of seven heavens that are in layers (Sūras *al-Baqara* 2:29; *al-Isrā'* 17:44; *al-Mu'minūn* 23:86; *Fuṣṣilat* 41:12; *at-Ṭalāq* 65:12; *al-Mulk* 67:3; *Nūḥ* 71:15). One verse suggests that the earth also has seven layers (Sūra *at-Ṭalāq* 65:12). It is surrounded by waters, which God has separated by a barrier, *barzakh* (Sūras *ar-Raḥmān* 55:19–20; *al-Furqān* 25:53).[3] Above all this stands God's throne (Sūras *al-Baqara* 2:255; *al-A'rāf* 7:54;

---

3. These references are literally to two seas and have been variously interpreted. At-Ṭabarī sees them as the oceans which surround the earth and the waters in the heavens, but most see them as referring to different earthly bodies of water as in a Ptolemaic worldview.

at-Tawba 9:129; *ar-Ra'd* 13:2; *Ṭā Hā* 20:4–6; *al-Furqān* 25:59; *as-Sajda* 32:4; *al-Ḥadīd* 57:4). In one place, the throne is described as resting on water (*Hūd* 11:7). The sky is described as a canopy or roof, *saqf* (*al-Anbiyā'* 21:32; *at-Ṭūr* 52:5), which shields the world and was built by God's hands (*al-Dhāriyāt* 51:47; *at-Ṭūr* 52:5; *an-Nāzi'āt* 79:26–7; *ash-Shams* 91:5), the mountains are "pegs" (*an-Naba'* 78:7) which keep the earth stable, and the earth has pillars, although these are invisible (*ar-Ra'd* 13:2). As most followers of Jesus the Messiah see parallel Old Testament passages as poetic metaphor, so most Muslims today read these qur'anic references as poetic or as descriptions of the world as it appeared to people in seventh-century Arabia.

Like Genesis, the Qur'an insists that one God made all of this, but it uses a different strategy. Genesis mentions no other spiritual beings than God, and so presents God's supreme power as Creator over against all other cultural narratives about gods and goddesses. The Qur'an has no single creation narrative, but frequently refers to aspects of creation as signs of the one God and as refuting polytheism (for example, Sūra *Yūnus* 10:5–6). Many of its references echo Genesis 1–2. For example, Genesis repeats that the creation was good, and the Qur'an agrees that it was flawless (Sūra *al-Mulk* 67:3–4). Genesis has a lot about water, and the Qur'an has every living being created from water (Sūras *al-Anbiyā'* 21:30; *an-Nūr* 24:45; *al-Furqān* 25:54) and more than twenty references to the place of water in the creation.

The Genesis account and the viewpoint of the Qur'an are in such harmony that if anyone wanted to understand the relationship of the creation accounts with science, they could look to both books for the answers. However, because the Qur'an's presentations of creation are scattered, we do note some differences. For example, the Qur'an recounts creation in six days – the days of creation are mentioned in Sūras *al-A'rāf* 7:54; *Yūnus* 10:3; *al-Furqān* 25:59; *as-Sajda* 32:4; *Fuṣṣilat* 41:9–12; *Qāf* 50:38; and *al-Ḥadīd* 57:4. All except the passage in Sūra *Fuṣṣilat* 41 refer to six days, but Sūra 41 mentions two days, four days and then two days. This means that commentators have to reconcile this with the other references, so they see these times as overlapping to give the same total of six. The Qur'an mentions the Jewish Sabbath, but it does not include the seventh day in its creation accounts.

It is not the Qur'an but the Hadith that give details about what was created on which day, although these differ significantly from Genesis and there are differing versions. For example, one Hadith says that God created the earth on Monday, unpleasant things on Tuesday, light on Wednesday, beasts on Thursday, and Adam after the time of afternoon prayers on Friday (*Mishkāt Sharīf* 24, C, i. pt.3). Another says:

The Messenger of God said: "God, glorified, created the earth on Saturday, the mountains on Sunday, the trees on Monday, the things entailing labour on Tuesday, light on Wednesday, he scattered the animals in it on Thursday, and he created Adam, peace upon him, after 'asr on Friday, the last of creation in the last hour of Friday, between 'asr (afternoon) and nightfall." (Sahīh Muslim, Hadith 7054)

Questions about the order of creation also arise from the Qur'an itself. Sūra al-Baqara 2:29 has the earth created first, and then the heavens: "He made for you all that lies within the earth, then turning to the firmament He proportioned several skies." But Sūra an-Nāziʿāt 79:27 has the heavens created before the earth: "He built (the heavens), raised it on high, proportioned it, gave darkness to its night and brightness to its day; and afterwards spread out the earth." Reconciling these two verses is not easy. One way is to translate the "then" in al-Baqara 2:29 as "in addition" – that is, the verse is not giving the order of creation, but saying that God made both the earth and the heavens. Another is to see these passages as poetic, therefore not meant to give a chronological description of creation.

Trying to discover a chronological order from the Qur'an's various references to creation is much like trying to do the same from the Psalms or the other prophetic writings. Their various references are like parts of a jigsaw puzzle, and they may leave us unable to reconcile all the "pieces." Genesis 1–11 is like the picture on the front of the puzzle box – it helps us to see where the pieces fit!

An Important Difference

There is an important difference between Genesis 1:26–27 and the Qur'an regarding the creation of humankind. The Qur'an does not designate humans as created "in the image of God" as found in Genesis 1:26. Rather, the Qur'an uses the word khalīfa, usually translated as "vicegerent." The word literally means "someone who stands in the place of another," and, as we will see, it has been variously interpreted. Nearest to the biblical understanding of humanity is the common interpretation that the human being is to act as God's representative or steward on earth.[4] A similar idea is expressed in Sūra al-Ahzāb 33:72, the amana verse or the verse of the "trust," in which God offers the amana to the

---

4. For a thorough discussion of the interpretation of khalīfa and of amana, see Johnson, *Earth, Empire and Sacred Text.*

heavens and the earth and the mountains, but all refuse it. Eventually, the humans accept it and take on the responsibility. Many modern commentators, and Sufis such as Shah Wali Ullah Deholvir (AD 1303–62), link the *amana* with the *khalīfa*: it is something needed for the humans to carry out their job. The *amana* is sometimes interpreted as a seed of faith (*iman*) or of mystic light, sometimes as moral and legal responsibility, and sometimes as the free will to choose good or evil. The *amana* verse goes on to say that the human beings were unjust (*ẓālim*) and ignorant (*jahal*). As Genesis 3 will agree, whatever the *amana* was, we have failed!

In these ways, the Qur'an shares the important idea that humans have God-given responsibilities in creation. The main difference is that the Qur'an does not imply that the human being is like God although, as we shall see, the Adam in the Qur'an shares some of the god-like characteristics of the Adam in Genesis, for example, speech and knowledge.

The key qur'anic passage for comparison with Genesis 1:26–27 is Sūra *al-Baqara* 2:30–34:

> And [mention, O Muhammad], when your Lord said to the angels, "Indeed, I will make upon the earth a successive authority." They said, "Will You place upon it one who causes corruption therein and sheds blood, while we declare Your praise and sanctify You?" God said, "Indeed, I know that which you do not know." (2:30)

> And He taught Adam the names – all of them. Then He showed them to the angels and said, "Inform Me of the names of these, if you are truthful." (2:31)

> They said, "Exalted are You; we have no knowledge except what You have taught us. Indeed, it is You who is the Knowing, the Wise." (2:32)

> He said, "O Adam, inform them of their names." And when he had informed them of their names, He said, "Did I not tell you that I know the unseen [aspects] of the heavens and the earth? And I know what you reveal and what you have concealed." (2:33)

> And [mention] when We said to the angels, "Prostrate before Adam"; so they prostrated, except for Iblīs. He refused and was arrogant and became of the disbelievers. (2:34)

At first glance, only verse 30 seems to be parallel to Genesis 1:26–27, the rest being more like the naming of the animals in Genesis 2:19–20. But here is part of the *Genesis Rabbah* Midrash which discussed the plural "Let us create" of Genesis 1:26:

> When the Holy One, blessed be he, proposed to create the first man, he took counsel with the ministering angels. He said to them, "Shall we make man?" They said to him, "What will be his character?" (*Gen Rab*, VIII:2, trans. Neusner)

God then tells the angels that the man will have righteous descendants, but does not tell them about the wicked descendants. The next discussion begins:

> When the Holy One, blessed be he, came to create the first man, the ministering angels formed parties and sects. Some of them said, "Let him be created," and some of them said, "Let him not be created." (*Gen Rab*, VIII:3, trans. Neusner)

There follows a reference to the discussion between mercy, truth, righteousness and peace in Psalm 85:11. Mercy and righteousness want humans to be created, because they will do acts of mercy and righteousness. Truth and peace are not of the same mind, because the humans will lie and fight. There is then rabbinic agreement that God's creation of the human was "very good" (Gen 1:31). God created the humans while the angels were still arguing! Another discussion of the "image of God" in Genesis 1:26 has the angels mistaking the human being for God and wanting to worship him. It is only when the man sleeps that the angels realise their mistake (*Gen Rab*, VIII:10). We see that the Qur'an deals with the same questions as the Midrash and that it does so in a similar way, by envisaging a heavenly discussion about the effects of freewill.[5]

The Quran confirms the high status of humanity even though it does not use the term "image of God": God declared, "We moulded man in the most noble image" (Sūra *at-Tīn* 95:4). Many Muslims dislike the term "image of God" because they think that it implies that God has a body; but the Hadith report that the Islamic Prophet Muhammad said that humans were made "in God's image" or "in the image of the Most Merciful" and directed, "If any one

---

5. Related elaborations on the Genesis text can be found in other pre-Islamic Jewish and Christian texts. Particularly relevant to the study of the Qur'an is the Syriac *The Cave of Treasures*, which is often attributed to Ephrem the Syrian (4th century AD, but probably dating from the 6th century AD in its present form). A translation can be found online at http://www.sacred-texts.com/chr/bct/bct04.htm.

of you strikes (another), he should avoid the face, for God created Adam in his image."[6] In Bangladesh, Sufis love the idea of the image of God (see box on page 76).

The World of the Text
Structure and Genre

This section has many repetitions and patterns. The overall pattern is:

> **A.** God and the disorder at beginning (1:1–2)
>> **B.** Day 1: Light and darkness (1:3–5)
>>> **C.** Day 2: Waters and sky (1:6–8)
>>>> **D.** Day 3: The dry land and the plants (1:9–13)
>> **B'.** Day 4: The heaven is filled with the lights (1:14–19)
>>> **C'.** Day 5: The waters and the skies are filled with sea creatures and birds (1:20–23)
>>>> **D'.** Day 6: The land is filled with humans and animals (1:24–31)
>> **A'.** Day 7: God and the completed creation (2:1–3)

From this structure we see that God's creation followed a beautiful plan. From the beginning A to the final A', this passage brims with encouragement as God brings creation from a fearful state of *tohu wa bohu* and dark waters to the ordered peace of the final seventh day.

The number seven, which symbolizes completeness and perfection, is very important in this *toledoth*. "And God saw that it was good" and "and it was so" both occur seven times; the word "God" occurs thirty-five times, "earth" twenty-one times, and "heaven" twenty-one times. In Hebrew, Genesis 1:1 has seven words, 1:2 has fourteen words, and 2:1–3, which describes the seventh day, has thirty-five words. Yet the pattern is not quite the same for each day, since there are eight acts of creation signalled by God's decree that something should happen (vv. 3, 6, 9, 11, 14, 20, 24, 26), and these eight acts are distributed across six days. We also see slight variations in the word patterns. For example, we have "and God saw that it was good" six times, and the seventh time has "*very* good" (v. 31). We have eight times when "and God said" (*wa-yomer Elohim*) is followed by a decree that something should happen, and then a

---

6. Bukhārī, Vol. 8, Book 74, Hadith 246; Muslim, Book 32, Hadith 6325; *Musnad* 11, 244, 251, 315, 323, 434, 463, 519. *Mishkāt*, 16:72.

ninth time when it is followed by a word to the newly created humans: "Look at what I have given to you!" (v. 29).

The genre of this text has been much discussed. It is easier to say what it is not than to say what it is. It is not myth like the ancient Mesopotamian creation stories, but neither is it history like modern history, nor science like modern science. It is not the same sort of narrative as we find elsewhere in Genesis, but neither is it poetry like we find in the Psalms. There are poetic elements in its careful structures, repetitions and rhythms; but the patterns are broken as some days are described in more detail than others, and a short poem is inserted at 2:27. Genesis 2:2–3 has long been used in Jewish liturgy, and its repetitions and structure suggest that it may have been so used from the beginning.

In short, Genesis 1:1–2:3 is a unique piece of literature, beautifully organized and wonderfully structured, yet with a variety of different elements and irregularities which may surprise the reader. We might say that, in these ways, it reflects the creation which it describes. So as we go on to detailed commentary, let us keep in mind the b
igger picture painted by the structure.

COMMENTARY
A. Genesis 1:1–2 God and the Chaos Found at the Beginning of Creation

In the beginning, God created the heavens and the earth.

בְּרֵאשִׁית בָּרָא אֱלֹהִים אֵת הַשָּׁמַיִם וְאֵת הָאָרֶץ

Bereshit bara Elohim et ha-shamayim wa-et ha-arets.

In Hebrew, the opening verse of Genesis has seven words. Each word and each phrase has been discussed over the centuries, and we will discuss them one by one.

In the beginning, *bereshit*
The introduction has already mentioned discussions about the unusual grammatical form of this very first word (page 29). Some translations solve the grammatical problem as "When God began to create the heavens and the earth." Either way, we have the clear teaching that there was a beginning. Although the One Creator God existed eternally, the universe – his creation – did not exist from eternity.

Created, *bara*

The verb translated "create" (Heb. *bara*) is used many times in the Old Testament, but only three times in Genesis 1 (vv. 1, 21, 27). This form of the verb is used only of God and refers to his sovereign creative acts. In some forms and contexts, it means "cut" or "slash" – a sharp, decisive action, for example, in making something by cutting it out.

Bara is not a synonym of the verb translated "made" (Heb. *'asah*), which is used in verses 7, 11, 12, 16, 25, 26, 31. *'Asah* usually means bringing something new into existence by using something that existed previously. In this sense, humans, who are made in the image of God, can also "make" things, but only God can create. The use of *bara* here and in verses 21 and 27 captivates the reader's mind with God's sovereign creative power.

God, *Elohim*

"God" here, and elsewhere in Genesis 1–11, translates the Hebrew "Elohim" using the plural form with the singular meaning discussed in the introduction (page 38). This Elohim existed before creation. God existing in eternity prompts the philosophical question of time and eternity. Did time begin with the beginning of creation? What do we mean by "time"? The book of Genesis does not answer these questions, but it does clearly state that the Creator God has existed before all time and that the heavens and the earth were not always in existence.

The heavens and the earth, *et ha-shamayim wa-et ha-arets*

This is a set phrase meaning "everything," that is, the entire universe. It is frequently used in the Qur'an with a similar meaning. The Bible begins with the most basic fact: all existence is due to the sovereign creative activity of the one God. This main message forms the foundation for all understanding of God, humanity and the world.

The word translated "heavens" (*shamayim*) does not describe the abode of God, but the great expanse above us in which we see birds fly, clouds float, and the orbiting of the planets, stars and sun. The Old Testament refers to the heavens in three ways: first, there is the lower heaven, the place of the clouds and the birds from which rain descends (Gen 1:20; 7:11; 8:2; 27:28; 2 Sam 21:10; Ps 147:8; Lam 4:19); second, there is the heaven where we see the starry host of planets and stars (Gen 1:14–17; Ezek 32:7–8); and third, there is a spiritual and unfathomable heaven where God and his angels dwell. This place is above all and beyond all. For this reason, we should not see this third heaven as a physical place, but as something existing beyond our natural boundaries of time and space (Gen 28:12; 1 Kgs 8:27).

At least from the mid-first century AD, some Jewish and Christian traditions have divided the heavens into seven strata,[7] and the Qur'an similarly tells readers that God created seven heavens, one upon another. God beautifully adorned the closest of these heavens as a canopy of light and, when the *Shayṭāns* attack the earth, they are pelted with hurling lights which humans see as shooting stars (Sūras *al-Ḥijr* 15:16–18; *aṣ-Ṣāffāt* 37:6–10; *al-Mulk* 67:3–5; *Nūḥ* 71:15–16; *al-Jinn* 72:8–9). However, these ideas are not found in the Bible.

> *The earth was without form and darkness was over the face of the deep.*
> *(Gen 1:2)*

Tohu wa bohu, translated here as "without form," is an onomatopoeic (sounding like what it is describing) phrase describing something which is empty and shapeless. *Tohu* is used elsewhere in the Old Testament to describe waste places, futility and devastation, and is sometimes translated "confusion" (e.g. Deut 32:10; Job 12:24; Isa 24:10; 59:4). So the pre-creation environment is variously described as formless, empty, confused, dark and watery. No wonder people have often called this chaos!

The phrase *tohu wa bohu* is used in Jeremiah 4:23 and Isaiah 34:11 to describe the chaos resulting from God's judgement of human sin. However, here in Genesis 1:2 it does not describe moral or spiritual chaos but rather the natural world. This is a physical formlessness and not a spiritual one. Neither is this a chaos due to fighting gods, as in *Enuma Elish*. Genesis does not present the darkness and emptiness as some personified antagonistic being.

The Psalms often portray God as controlling and overthrowing the powers of the waters (Pss 74:13–17; 89:9–10; 104:7–9). Here, however, the empty deep indicates that God has not yet done his creative work. He did not create the earth to be barren and empty, but to be inhabited (Isa 45:18); and so he began the work of establishing order out of the chaos from the very beginning.

There has been a great deal of speculation on this sentence over the centuries. We explore three questions here.

First, does the darkness before creation and the light after it imply that there are two equal competing forces, one bad and one good, in the world (this idea is called "dualism")? The answer to this question is clearly, "No." First, this

---

7. For example, the apocryphal book 2 Enoch describes Enoch ascending through seven heavens.

WHEN WAS THE BEGINNING?

There has been an on-going debate among both theologians and scientists about the age of the earth. Scientists who accept the Big Bang theory would say that our universe began 10–20 billion years ago. Readers of the Scripture known as Gap Creationists would agree that this is a possibility. Their theory is that there is a gap between Genesis 1:1 and Genesis 1:2. In verse 1, God created the heavens and the earth; in the gap, everything was or became disorganized, and, in verse 2, he began to re-order it.

At the other extreme, some traditional calendars have used the dates in Genesis literally to calculate the exact date of creation. Even today, the Jewish calendar counts its years from the creation of the world as calculated by the medieval scholar Maimonides – 6 October 3761 BC. From the same evidence, others have calculated different exact dates, one of the most famous being Archbishop James Usher (AD 1581–1656), who held that the creation of the earth took place at 6 p.m., 22 October 4004 BC. Such calculations deliberately ignore the natural history, geology and palaeontology of the earth. In fact, there is clear evidence of human civilization as early as 5,000 BC in, for example, the Harappa-Mohenjo-Daro civilization of the Indus valley.

Actually, Genesis does not tell us the specific time of creation. The beginning of creation is hidden in the abyss of eternity. Genesis is not meant to be a modern scientific textbook: the narrators were eager to inform their readers *about* the Creator of the universe, not *when* the creation came into being.[1]

---

1. For further reading, we recommend Robert S. White, "The Age of the Earth," Faraday Paper no. 8, available at www.faraday.cam.ac.uk/resources/faraday-papers/.

is actually countering the ancient story of dualistic powers of good and evil warring against each other. Darkness and light are not opposing forces vying for control of the world. The Scripture says that God is Lord of both light and darkness (Ps 104:20; Isa 45:7). No spiritual darkness can overcome the light of truth and holiness: rather the light wins victory over the darkness (John 1:5). Second, physical darkness is not evil: God does not reject the darkness (Ps 139:11–12). He is even said to dwell in the darkness (1 Kgs 8:12; Pss 18:11; 97:2; etc.).

Many people in south Asia live in remote mountainous areas where electricity and electric lights are scarce or non-existent and they view the darkness as beautiful as the light. The poet Satyendranath Dutta writes in his poem "Hope":

> Seeing clouds, you fill with fear,
> the sun in hiding laughs;
> The absent sun, the mislaid light
> from darkness shines again.

The writer Sharat Chandra Chatyopadhyay writes of the beauty of darkness in his novel *Srikanto*:

> Suddenly, a beauteous vision rolled over me. I think, "What liars there be who have taught me about the nature of light and the nature of deep darkness. How could they have deceived me so?"[8]

Second, does *tohu wa bohu* describe something or nothing? Is this primeval matter, or is it a complete void being described as chaotic? Scholars have differed on the matter over the centuries, but many think that verses like Psalm 33:6; John 1:3; Romans 4:17; 1 Corinthians 1:28; and Hebrews 11:3 imply that creation was *ex nihilo* – that there was nothing physically in existence before God created the world.

Third, is there a time gap between verse 1 and verse 2? What is known as the Gap Creationist theory sees verse 1 as describing God's creation of a perfect world from nothing, and verse 2 as describing that world becoming chaotic.[9] Verses 3 and following describe its restoration or recreation. This idea is used to explain the age of the universe and the findings of fossils and geological history, and then to interpret the six days of restoration as six literal days. The textual evidence cited is the use of *bara* in verse 1 as compared to the use of *'asah* in verses 3 and following, and the possibility that the word translated "was" could mean "became."[10] However, this is a very slender foundation for a theory which finds no support elsewhere in Scripture.

███   *. . . and the Spirit of God moved over the waters. (Gen 1:2b)*

The Spirit of God (*Ruach Elohim*) was moving over the chaos. The Hebrew term *rûach* has several meanings: the metaphysical Spirit, the physical "breath," or

---

8. Sharat Rochona Samagra, *Srikanto* (Dhaka: Nouroj Shahitya Shamsad, 1998).

9. Some suggest that this could have been because of Shayṭān's rebellion against God, implied by Isaiah 14:12 and Luke 10:18 (for more on this, see pages 95-96).

10. The Hebrew word *haythah* (הָיְתָה) is usually translated as "was." However, insofar as Hebrew past tense does not designate time so much as it does perfect and imperfect action, the translation can read "became."

the meteorological "wind." The *Bani Isra'il* understood God's Spirit as God's power, and not as an entity different from God. Elsewhere in the Bible, we read of the storm-wind as God's *ruach* (Ps 18:16) and Psalm 104 associates the *ruach* with the wonders of creation (vv. 3, 30). The mighty wind of God returns in the flood account in Genesis as the means by which God restores the earth (Gen 8:1). Many Christian interpreters see *ruach* here as the Holy Spirit, the third person of the Trinity: certainly, the *Ruach Elohim* here is describing God's presence and action from the beginning of creation.

In its creation references, the Qur'an does not have God's Spirit hovering over the earth, but God's throne resting on the water (Sūra *Hūd* 11:7). God's throne is mentioned several times in the Qur'an's references to creation (e.g. Sūras *Yūnus* 10:3; *al-Furqān* 25:59; *as-Sajda* 32:4) and it is the subject of the famous *Ayat al-Kursī* (*Verse of the Throne*) in Sūra *al-Baqara* 2:255. God is the owner of this throne, which existed before the heavens and the earth (*Ghāfir* 40:15). He is and always has been the ruler of all.

The renowned Bangladeshi philosopher, sage and Baul[11] saint, Fakir Lalon Shah (1772–1890), expressed this in a song[12] about his great neighbour (Bn. *porshi*):

> This porshi lives near my abode; there is a wondrous city of Mirror
> (Bn. *Arshinogor*).

The *porshi* sits next door in a great house: the author explained this as referring to the throne[13] of God. He considered God his great neighbour! But, as God is invisible, the poet also expressed his deep anguish that he never sees him. He further wrote, *Khonek Thake Shunner upor, Khonek Vase neere* (Sometimes he is on the throne, sometimes on the waters). This song reflects the tension in the qur'anic concept of God's presence. He is here, because he is omnipresent, but he is hidden. Sufis solve this by saying that the believer's heart is (or, at least, it should be) the throne of God (Ar. *qalb mu'min 'arsh Allāh*).

---

11. The Bauls are a mainly Bengali religious group, well-known for their songs and poems. Their beliefs and practices include elements from Buddhism and Hinduism as well as from Sufi Islam.

12. See *Baul Ganer Nondontotto*, p 53.

13. Arabic *'arsh*. *Kursi*, used in the "throne verse," more literally means a chair.

SPIRIT AND SPIRITS IN THE QUR'AN AND POPULAR BANGLADESHI THOUGHT

The mystery of the Spirit. The Qur'an tells us that the Islamic Prophet Muhammad was asked about the Spirit, and God instructed him to reply that because humans have such little understanding, God did not wish to explain this – it remains a mystery (Sūra *al-Isrā'* 17:41). So although the Holy Spirit (*Rūḥ al-Qudus*) is mentioned three times in the Qur'an (*al-Baqara* 2:81, 254; *al-Mā'ida* 5:109), most Muslims interpret this as referring to the Angel Gabriel, who brought the Qur'an to the Prophet (*al-Baqara* 2:97). However, according to al-Bayḍāwī, some understand it to refer to the spirit of Jesus and others to the gospel of Jesus, while some think it is the *Ism al-'Ajam*, or the exalted name of God whereby Jesus the Messiah raised the dead (*Tofsirul Baizawi*, 65; Sūra *an-Naḥl* 16:102). The Qur'an also acknowledges Jesus as Spirit of God (*Rūḥ Allāh*; Sūras *an-Nisā'* 4:171; *al-Anbiyā'* 21:91; *at-Taḥrīm* 66:12). This is the special *kālima* or title of Jesus.

Spiritual beings and creation. The Qur'an says much about the spiritual world. It puts the creation of jinn and angels before the creation of humans (*al-Ḥijr* 15:27; *al-Baqara* 2:30), and tradition has jinn dwelling on earth before humanity. Adam's title, *khalīfa* (one who stands in another's place, *al-Baqara* 2:30), is then understood to mean that the human beings took the jinn's place. The jinn, it is said, caused mischief, shedding blood and killing one another, so God sent angels to destroy them and replaced them with humankind. Similarly, Jewish tradition has supernatural beings called *shedim* living on earth until humans replaced them.

Many Bangladeshi people believe in jinn and hear about them in popular TV shows as well as in Islamic stories. They also believe in ghosts, fairies, and other non-bodied spirits which have the power to do them good or harm. In the novel by Abu Ishak, *Surjo Dighol Bari*, set in the context of a Bengali village, the people believe in the power of these disembodied spirits. The people there follow the teaching of the Bible in order to overcome this. They discover that these spirits, purported to live in the trees, the sea and various animals, do not really exist.

Genesis 1 shows us that belief in the One True Creator God means we can cast aside any thoughts of jinn, ghosts, bad spirits or superstitions ruling our lives. The New Testament clearly teaches that while there are such things as idols and evil spirits, Jesus the Messiah has power over them all (Matt 8:28–34; Mark 5:1–20; Luke 8:26–33). The Bible makes no mention of jinn and Genesis 1 speaks only of the Spirit of God, not of any other ruling spirit.

B–D'. Genesis 1:3–31 The Six Days of Creation

Unlike the Holy Qur'an (see page 43), the Bible clearly describes each day of creation. As can be seen in the box below, there is much discussion about just what is meant by a "day" (Heb, *yom*). Here, we note three things:

First, looking at ancient times and various creation accounts, we find variation among different cultures regarding how a "day" is defined. Second, we do not always know how the ancient Hebrews counted time. Looking at the lifespans recorded in Genesis 5–11, we wonder what sort of time calculations were being used, and we see that some times have symbolic meanings. Third, God's view of time vastly differs from human understanding, since he dwells in eternity. So, we need to accept that our understanding is limited, and to see what we can learn from the text. Rather than being frustrated because we cannot answer our twenty-first-century questions, we can read with great joy and satisfaction the story that they *do* tell – of the power and goodness of God's creation.

WHAT IS A "DAY"?

In Genesis 1, the word "day" is used six times (vv. 5, 8, 13, 19, 23, 31). Many people view the recurring words "and there was evening and there was morning" as a twenty-four-hour period of time set according to the sun. However, others point out that there was no sun until the fourth day, and that Psalm 90:4 and 2 Peter 3:8 teach that God has a different view of time than we do. For him, a thousand years is like a day. Elsewhere, the Old Testament sometimes uses the word "day" to indicate significant times which are clearly more than 24 hours long (e.g. Gen 2:4; Is 22:5; Zeph 1:14–16).

Of verse 5, people ask whether the words day (*yom*) and night (*laylah*) signify periods of twelve hours, or simply periods of light and darkness? There could have been light without the sun, but how could there have been 24-hour periods of light and darkness before the sun existed? Even with the most literal interpretation, we could argue that the use of "evening and morning" and "day" in this verse proves that all the "days" of Genesis 1 could not have been 24-hour periods.

There is a parallel discussion among Muslims. Some, with the classical writings like the *Tafsīr al-Jalālayn*, see the six days of Sūras *al-A'rāf* 7:54; *Yūnus* 10:3; *Hūd* 11:7; *al-Furqān* 25:59; *as-Sajda* 32:4; *Qāf* 50:38; and *al-Ḥadīd* 57:4 as literal periods of twenty-four hours, but others quote Sūras *al-Ḥajj* 22:47 and *as-Sajda* 32:5 which, like Psalm

90 and 2 Peter 3, teach that a thousand years is like a day for God. For both Christians and Muslims, the difference in interpretation of the "day" goes with different beliefs about how scripture relates to science. The literal interpretation usually goes with a denial of the evolutionary theory, whereas an understanding of the days as epochs usually goes with belief in some form of theistic evolution.

Genesis describes the day as "evening and morning": even now, Jews count days from sunset to sunset, following Leviticus 23:32. This is also how the Qur'an counts days. In contrast, the Egyptians, like today's Europeans, counted days from midnight to midnight, and the Babylonian day began at sunrise. The latter is what we follow in Bangladesh. We divide the day into daytime starting at sunrise, and nighttime, starting at sunset. Traditionally, the daytime was counted in eight periods (Bn, *prohor*), which were marked by a guard's drum (Bn, *prohori*), and women would light lamps to mark the commencement of the second part of the day. We also have different ways of counting months and years – the Islamic lunar calendar, the Western solar calendar, and the Hindu calendars, which use both the sun and the moon. We see that, even in Bangladesh today, there are different ways of counting time.

So, as we read Genesis 1–11, we should examine what it is saying in its own terms. We will find that the unfolding of the eternal God's creation of time and in time is glorious!

The text divides the six days of creation into two parallel accounts of three days each, using a beautiful balance of poetic language and repeated words and phrases. Here are some of the repeated patterns which we need to note:

The process of "separating." God separates the light from the darkness, he separates the day from the night, he separates the waters, and he marks a boundary between them (Gen 1:4, 6–7, 9–10, 14, 18).

"God spoke . . . and it was so" (vv. 3, 7, 9, 11, 15, 24, 30) – that is, by means of God's command, all things came into being. Creation takes place in a simple and straightforward way. At each step, that which God says, happens. Elsewhere, the Bible confirms that God's creation was through his word (Heb. *dabar*; Gk. *logos*, e.g. Ps 33:9; Heb 11:3). This contrasts with other ancient creation myths in which multiple gods use magic powers or mould pre-existing materials. God does not create in this way in the Genesis story. God simply says, "Let there be." The Qur'an agrees: God simply says "Be and it is," *kun fa-yakūn* (*al-Baqara* 2:117; *an-Naḥl* 16:40; *Yā Sīn* 36:82).

The New Testament calls Jesus the Word of God (John 1:1–14). The Bible reveals that each person of the Godhead is active in creation. The one God (1 Cor 8:6), Jesus the Word (John 1:3), and his Spirit (Gen 1:2; Isa 40:12–13), all three persons of the Trinity in one Godhead were involved (see also Prov 8:27; John 1:10; Eph 3:9; Heb 1:2; Job 26:13; John 1:3; Col 1:16).

In stark contrast, most Muslims would insist that the Qur'an denies the possibility that Jesus, as the Word of God and the Spirit of God, was present in the work of creation. They point out that, although he is the word of God (*kalimat Allāh*), he was a created human being like Adam (Sūra *Āl ʿImrān* 3:59). However, although the biblical idea that "everything was created for Jesus and through Jesus" might be denied, many would confess that the Qur'an does indirectly imply that Jesus the Messiah is Creator (*khāliq*). In the same way in which God created (*khalaqa*) man from clay and breathed life into him (Sūra *Ṣād* 38:71–72), so the Qur'an claims that Jesus the Messiah created (*khalaqa*) birds from clay, and by his breath gave them life (Sūras *Āl ʿImrān* 3:49; *al-Māʾida* 5:110).

And God saw that it was good (vv. 4, 10, 12, 18, 21, 25, 31). Much pagan thought sees the physical world and the spiritual world as being in opposition: the spirit is good, but the material is evil. Genesis refutes this idea. All the universe which God has created – spiritual and physical – is good, and there is no need for holy water to cleanse it. Many Hindus believe that this physical world is illusory (*maya*, not what it seems to be), but this idea is contrary to the shared belief of Jewish people, followers of Jesus the Messiah, and Muslims, that everything in heaven and earth is not only real but good.

The Qur'an agrees that God created the various creatures in a beautiful form and from a good substance (*as-Sajda* 32:7–9). The eminent Muʿtazila[14] theologian az-Zamakhsharī (AD 1075–1144), emphasizes this in his commentary on this verse by saying, "All creatures are (created) well, even though they show variation with regard to the good and the better."

God names his creation (vv. 5, 8, 10). In the ancient world and in Hebrew thinking, naming was very important. Names had meanings, and they were given by authoritative persons. A king could display his authority over his

---

14. At the beginning of the second century AH (early eighth century AD), during the Umayyad rule, Muʿtazila theology and ethics were developed based on Greek logic and Buddhism in dialogue with proto-Shiʿite beliefs based on the Qur'an and Hadith. Muʿtazila leaders believed that God was eternal, but that the Qur'an was not. In the year AD 827, the Abbasid caliph al-Maʾmūn declared that the Qur'an was not the actual word of God. The Muʿtazila scholars maintained that God created everything, including the Qur'an (*khāliq Qurʾān*), and as a result, traditional theologians considered this group to be in error.

subjects by naming them (see Gen 17:15; 41:45; 2 Kgs 23:34; 24:17; Dan 1:7). Thus, God's naming of his creation signifies that he owns it, that he is in control of it, and that he knows all about it. We note that God names only the day and the night (v. 5), heaven (v. 8) and the earth and the seas (v. 8). The sun, moon and stars are not named, perhaps because they were given such prominence in ancient worship.[15] The living creatures are also un-named: that is because it will be Adam's job to give them names (Gen 2:19–20).

B. Genesis 1 The First Day (Gen 1:3–5)

And God said, "Let there be light," and there was light. And God saw that the light was good. And God separated the light from the darkness. God called the light Day, and the darkness he called Night. And there was evening and there was morning, the first day.

Light of mine; indeed light,
Light that fills the earth and skies
Light that cleanses all my sight,
Steal my heart away.
    (*Rabindranath Tagore*, Rabindra Sangeet)

Light! We need light. At nighttime in the village when the electricity goes off, we must rely on lanterns or light from the stars and moon to get us through. Only in such ways can we imagine what life before creation was like. Only as we experience a dark state can we understand how good (Heb. *tov* – see vv. 10, 12, 18, 21, 25) and beautiful light is in God's sight.

These short verses have universal impact. The Qur'an agrees that God made the darkness and the light (*al-An'ām* 6:1), and light in the darkness is an important theme throughout both the Bible and the Qur'an.[16] In both, it comes to mean spiritual as well as physical light. Light is also important in science – it is a form of energy, of the electromagnetic radiation which is so fundamental to the universe. A description of the world as beginning with water and with light is certainly not contrary to a scientific worldview.

---

15. See commentary on Genesis 1:16.

16. "From the darkness into the light" (*min al ẓulma īlā an-nūr*) appears seven times in the Qur'an (Sūras *al-Baqara* 2:257; *al-Mā'ida* 5:16; *Ibrāhīm* 14:1; *al-Aḥzāb* 33:43; *al-Ḥadīd* 57:9; *at-Ṭalāq* 65:11). The idea also occurs frequently in the Bible (e.g. 2 Sam 22:29; Job 12:22; Ps 112:4; Isa 9:2; Acts 26:18; 2 Cor 4:6).

Verse 3 has the first of the sevenfold "God said" phrases (Heb. *Elohim yomer*). Sir Syed Ahmad Khan says that it also means "God has willed," as in the 1811 Arabic translation of the Bible. He goes on to write,

> We Mahomedans accept it as rightly applied in this sense. It is to be remembered that we and Christians are here shown quite to agree in explaining the meaning of this word.[17]

In verse 5, the naming of the light and the darkness begins the pattern of naming which will be repeated in verses 8 and 10. Naming is an act of authority – God has full authority over the light and the darkness.

It is sometimes asked how there can have been light and days before the sun and stars. In response, we must remember that though the lights in the galaxy and the sun serve the earth as sources of light, they are not the sources of light for the whole universe. God himself is the source of all light and the creator of these light sources. Several Old Testament texts speak of light independently of the sun (Job 38:19, 20; Isa 30:26). Isaiah 60:19 asserts that:

> The sun shall be no more
>   your light by day,
> nor for brightness shall the moon
>   give you light;
> but the LORD will be your everlasting light,
>   and your God will be your glory.

Our wisdom is limited, so we may be unable to conceive of how light existed before the sun, but from a theological perspective there is no need of the sun for God to light up the world. From a scientific perspective, there are many different sources of the different kinds of electromagnetic radiation, and the cosmos may have begun with energy even before the stars came into being.

As Genesis has light apart from the sun and the moon at the beginning, so Revelation has light without sun or moon at the end. When Jesus the Messiah returns to earth, there will be a new heaven and new earth; and God himself will illuminate them. In biblical poetic imagery, the presence of God means the presence of light.

> And night will be no more. They will need no light of lamp or sun, for the Lord God will be their light, and they will reign forever and ever. (Rev 22:5)

---

17. Khan, *Mohammedan Commentary on the Holy Bible, Genesis 1–11*, 74.

The Bible goes further than this and proclaims that God *is* light (1 John 1:5). Muslims would agree: *an-Nūr* (the Light) is one of the ninety-nine names of God, and eventually, "the earth will shine with the light of its Lord" (Sūra *az-Zumar* 39:69). The Qur'an has a whole sūra called *an-Nūr* (the Light), which contains the famous "Light Verse" which proclaims that only God is the light (*an-Nūr* 24:35). The light, says this verse, is in a lamp in a niche, a common interpretation being that the prophets are like the lamps which bring the revelation of God's light. We can compare this with John 1:4–8, which teaches that John the Baptist was a witness to the Light, but he was not the Light. So the qur'anic idea is that God is the Light, and that the prophets show the Light but are not themselves the Light.

However, Sufi teachers such as Sahl al-Tustarī (d. AD 898), came to see the Light Verse as a reference to the pre-existent light of the Islamic Prophet Muhammad (*nūr Muhammad*). As a result of Tustarī's teaching, many believe that the Prophet was made from light and therefore cast no shadow! This opinion has been refuted by scholars who note that the Prophet had a body of flesh like everyone else and that he too bled when he was struck. The Qur'an teaches that he was a man like other men (*Fuṣṣilat* 41:6).

There is a verse which describes the Islamic Prophet Muhammad as a light-giving lamp (*sirājām munīrān*; *al-Aḥzāb* 33:46) – that is, like John the Baptist, he is the lamp which holds the light but is not the Light itself. In contrast, John 1 declares that Jesus the Messiah is the source of life and light, and this is in a passage which clearly teaches that he was the pre-existent Word of God. In John 8:12, Jesus the Messiah declares himself as the Light of the World.

C. Genesis 1:6–8 The Second Day: Water and Sky

> And God said, "Let there be an expanse in the midst of the waters, and let it separate the waters from the waters." And God made the expanse and separated the waters that were under the expanse from the waters that were above the expanse. And it was so. And God called the expanse Heaven. And there was evening and there was morning, the second day.

Human beings need water to live, but they also need air – a space between the waters. On the second day of creation, God takes control of the frightening chaotic waters of verse 2. He separates them into what we would call the seas and lakes and subterranean waters, and the clouds and atmospheric waters. This reminds us of the *Enuma Elish* story of how Marduk divided the dead body of Tiamat, who represents the seas, and from it made the earth and the heavens. The Genesis message is clear: the world was not made from the body of a dead goddess! The whole world is God's creation, and he is Lord over all the waters. When Marduk killed Tiamat, he speared her belly and her heart and crushed her skull before cutting her body in half. In complete contrast, Genesis tells us that the One Creator God simply speaks, and the waters are divided.

The idea of the earth being divided in two is implicitly stated in the Qur'an Sūra al-Anbiyā' 21:30. Some readers see this qur'anic verse and these Genesis verses as supporting the Big Bang theory. However, we have a major caveat: Genesis is not a scientific textbook, and neither is the Qur'an. Moreover, both clearly teach that God created the world with deliberate intent, and thus refute any idea that it came into being by chance.

The overall message of the second day is clear, but there are some questions about its detail. How did the first readers understand the waters above and below? And exactly what is meant by the words translated "firmament" (raqi'a) and "heaven" (shamayim)? The latter is the same word used for "heavens" in verse 1. The word "firmament" (raqi'a) derives from a verb which means "spread abroad," "expand" or "enlarge" and seems here to mean the watery area which holds the clouds. It conveys the same sense as the Bangla term, bitan.

There are three major ways of understanding these images. The first way is to see the verses as describing the ancient idea of the universe described above (page 39-40). The second is to read the language as poetic, describing what was perceived in terms of what people saw in their everyday lives (e.g. the rain as coming down as through an open window). The third is to read the verses as describing the world as we understand it today. An interesting example of the latter comes from the Muslim commentator, as he sought for common ground between the Bible and the Qur'an and the science of his day. He comments,

> This verse (v. 6) points to the event of the creation of air, since the heat of light caused the production of mists in the waters which effected expansion between them, and thus separated waters from waters, in the same manner as a bubble is seen to be divided in its upper and lower waters by the air between them.[18]

D. Genesis 1:9–10 The Third Day: Dry Land

And God said, "Let the waters under the heavens be gathered together into one place, and let the dry land appear." And it was so. God called the dry land Earth, and the waters that were gathered together he called Seas. And God saw that it was good.

---

18. Khan, *Mohammedan Commentary on the Holy Bible, Genesis 1–11*, vol. 2, 70.

> *And God said, "Let the earth sprout vegetation, plants yielding seed, and fruit trees bearing fruit in which is their seed, each according to its kind, on the earth." And it was so. The earth brought forth vegetation, plants yielding seed according to their own kinds, and trees bearing fruit in which is their seed, each according to its kind. And God saw that it was good. And there was evening and there was morning, the third day.*

The third day is the next stage in the ordering of the universe. As on the second day, we begin with a separation of what was already in existence. The waters are gathered together into oceans and lakes and rivers, and dry land appears. God further establishes his authority over the earth and the sea by naming them.

Elsewhere in the Bible, God repeatedly shows his care by placing boundaries between the water and the dry land. The gracious power of God's hand and his faithfulness keeps the water from passing beyond its limits, and this third day of creation builds a foundation for humans to praise God and to wonder at his goodness (Prov 8:29; Ps 104:6–8; Job 38:8–11; Eccl 1:7).

The soil and water necessary for the growth of plants are now available so, by God's command, seed-bearing plants and fruit-bearing trees appear. These plants in their turn will provide food and oxygen (through photosynthesis) for the animals and humans. The creation is wonderfully ordered, and the plants are created in wonderful diversity and in many kinds: no wonder the psalmist pictures the watered earth with its abundant grain as singing with joy (Ps 65:9–13)!

The word "kind" (repeated three times in verses 11 and 12) might be the equivalent of our word "species" or biological "phylum." God gave the plants reproductive power for producing their own kind. A plant bears seeds, and those seeds grow new plants. Thus, the agricultural system began. And it was good. Genesis expresses God's joy and satisfaction in his work.

We note that the earth itself cannot produce anything without the commandment of God. There is no hint of the pagan notion of the earth as a type of divine mother. There is also an implied refutation of fertility worship, which was prevalent in Ancient Near Eastern cultures, and still remains in the Indian subcontinent. Since the Genesis account is quite unlike any modern evolutionary theory, some people think that it also refutes science. We address this question in the text box on the next page.

GENESIS AND THE THEORY OF EVOLUTION

In Genesis, God made animals "according to their kinds" (1:21–25), and human beings were made by a separate divine decree (1:26–27). In the Qur'an, too, humans are described as a special creation (*an-Nisā'* 4:1; *al-Ḥijr* 15:26–29; *as-Sajda* 32:7–9). There are also places where stages are described (e.g. *al-Ḥajj* 22:5; *al-Mu'minūn* 23:13–14; *Ghāfir* 40:67), but these are usually taken as describing the gestation of a baby in the womb.

The theory of evolution sees all life, including humanity, as having evolved by natural processes of adaptation over millions of years. The theory raises many questions, and there are variations on detailed theories of origins and processes. However, a measure of evolution is observable in some short-lived species, and the theory has provided a powerful way of organising observations of our complex world, so it is widely accepted today. Both Muslims and Christians ask how this theory relates to their creation accounts.

As with other questions about Genesis and science, believers in the One Creator God reach varying conclusions. At one extreme, evolution is seen as incompatible with creation: people reject the theory of evolution and let Genesis direct their science, which they may call "creation science." At the other extreme, people believe that God created everything, but that we can find out how he did it only through science. Darwin himself did not think that his theory excluded God. Such theories are called "theistic evolution" or "intelligent design."

In between are those who accept some of the evolutionary theory, but who believe that there were special acts of creation at various points in the process. In particular, human beings were produced by a creative act. In Genesis 2, humans are both made of the earth and enlivened by the breath of God. So, physically, humanity shares in the nature of the rest of creation, but there is also an extra dimension whereby humanity relates to God. So it is possible that, when the first human body evolved, God created the human soul in it.

Muslim discussions are remarkably similar, with conclusions ranging from theistic evolution to creationism. Debates centre on the meaning of "day" (*yawm*) and include discussion of what it means that humans beings were created "in perfect form" (Sūra *at-Taghābun* 64:3). As far back as the fourteenth century, Ibn Khaldun believed in a gradual creation process, and such important nineteenth century scholars as Jamaluddin al-Afghani and his Shi'ite contemporary, Hussayn al-Jisr, set the pattern for seeing evolution as compatible with the Qur'an. In stark contrast, the so-called Islamic State, set up in the Mosul area in 2014, banned the teaching of evolution in its schools. This has been echoed in the demands of the radical *Hefajote Islam* group that the teaching of evolution should be banned in Bangladeshi schools.

The problem is that some people see evolution as a universal process which replaces God. The various mechanisms which are proposed, such as natural selection, can be regarded as what determines the world and human beings. We therefore lose the idea that humans are responsible to someone greater than themselves. Further, in the nineteenth century, evolution was believed to be from lower to higher forms, so it was believed that humans and societies were always improving. Some believed that black people were a lower form than white people. Religion was also seen as part of the evolutionary process, with polytheism being a lower form, monotheism higher and Christianity highest. But many thought that the next stage would be evolution beyond religion to rationalism.

It is not the scientific theory of evolution which is completely incompatible with Genesis, but these sorts of atheistic ideas which may accompany it. However they view science, believers are agreed that Genesis gives us the authoritative account of how God relates to his creation, and therefore of how the parts of creation are to relate to each other.[1]

---

1. For further reading from different perspectives, we recommend Moreland et al. *Theistic Evolution*; Berry, "Creation and Evolution, Not Creation or Evolution;" and Institute of Medicine, et al. *Science, Evolution, and Creationism: A View from the National Academy of Sciences and the Institute of Medicine*, National Academies Press, 2008.)

B′. Genesis 1:14–19 The Fourth Day: The Upper Atmosphere Is Filled with Light

And God said, "Let there be lights in the expanse of the heavens to separate the day from the night. And let them be for signs and for seasons, and for days and years, and let them be lights in the expanse of the heavens to give light upon the earth." And it was so. And God made the two great lights – the greater light to rule the day and the lesser light to rule the night – and the stars. And God set them in the expanse of the heavens to give light on the earth, to rule over the day and over the night, and to separate the light from the darkness. And God saw that it was good. And there was evening and there was morning, the fourth day.

It is not until the fourth day that the luminaries appear. They are less important than the earth and the light which were created first, and than the human beings who were created last. They are only "made" (*'asah*) and not "created" (*bara*). From this we understand that, in God's sight, humanity stands as the most important part of creation, more important than the world and all that is in it. God's glory is revealed in these light-giving constellations which give light and set the times and seasons for the inhabitants of the earth – both humans and animals.

It is significant that the sun and the moon are not named, but only called a "greater and lesser light," and that the stars are described in only two words. In Hebrew, verse 16 ends, "and the stars," as if they were an afterthought.

Again, Genesis reminds us that God's creation is good. The Bible, the Qur'an and the great poets all testify to the glory of the heavens, and astronomy and space science lead us to a greater awe. Here, indeed, the majesty of creation points towards the majestic Creator. Our galaxy, the Milky Way (Bn. *Akash Gonga*), is not only a wonderful sight, it is also an amazing grouping of millions of stars. Yet it is only a small galaxy among billions of others.

Galaxy M-87-A has about 2.7 trillion stars (one thousand billion equals one trillion). It would take about 3,000 years to count them at the rate of one per second! Perhaps for this reason, God asked Abraham to count the stars in the heavens if he could (Gen 15:5). Even now, it is impossible for human beings to count all the galaxies, let alone all the stars, but the Almighty Creator God made all those stars, and he can count them.

As the Psalmist writes:

> He determines the number of the stars;
> > he gives to all of them their names.
> Great is our Lord, and abundant in power;
> > his understanding is beyond measure.
> > > (Ps 147:4–5. cf. Q. 29:62)

And he marvels:

> When I look at your heavens, the work of your fingers,
> > the moon and the stars, which you have set in place,
> what is man that you are mindful of him,
> > and the son of man that you care for him? (Ps 8:3–4)

As Lord of the heavenly lights, God even used them to announce the birth of Jesus the Messiah. Astronomers from the East learned the good news about the birth of the King of the Jews in advance through observing a star and they came to find him (Matt 2:1–12). This was the star known as "the star of Bethlehem."

Why, then, does Genesis 1 mention the creation of the stars in only two words, and why does it down-play the sun and the moon? The answer is that these heavenly bodies were worshipped in the ancient world, and that the stars were thought to direct peoples' destinies. For example, the Egyptian deities included the sun god *Ra* and the moon god *Thot*. Genesis refutes these ideas. The heavenly bodies are only God's creation, and cannot shine without his permission (Job 9:7–9).

Worship of celestial lights has continued throughout history, and in Bangladesh today some people view the stars and planets as having power to control their lives and fortunes. Despite God's warnings (Deut 4:19), even the *Bani Isra'il* copied their pagan neighbours and provoked God's anger by worshipping the "queen of heaven" (Jer 44:17–22). The Bible is particularly strong in its prohibition of sun worship, of astrology and of reading omens (Deut 17:2–5; 18:11–12). Genesis tells us that the sun, moon, and even planets merely mark the passing of days, months and seasons, which means that they do not control them. The notion that observing these lights in the heavens will help control our fate is dismissed, because these things are controlled by God alone (Ps 19:1–6; Neh 9:6).

Genesis 1:17–18 tells us that, ruling under the authority of the Creator, these lights have been given three tasks: (1) they illuminate the world, (2) they mark times and seasons, and (3) they separate the light of day from the darkness of night. The Qur'an, too, sees the celestial bodies as God's good creation, which point towards their Creator (*al-An'ām* 6:96–97). It also mentions three different purposes of the creation of stars in the lowest heaven (*al-buruj*): (1) as an ornament to the heavens (*al-Mulk* 67:5); (2) to prevent jinns and devils from entering heaven (*aṣ-Ṣāffāt* 37:6–10) – if they try to do so, then a *shihāb* (comet) chases them away (*al-Ḥijr* 15:18; *al-Mulk* 67:5; *al-Jinn* 72:9);[19] and (3) to direct travellers (*al-Ḥijr* 15:16).

The Qur'an also forbids all worship of the sun, moon and stars, although God himself takes oaths on them (*al-Wāqi'a* 56:75; *al-Ma'ārij* 70:40). This was very relevant in Mecca where there were many idols, which, according to Islamic tradition, were used for divination about the future; and some people

---

19. Az-Zamakhsharī wrote of *ar-Rajīm* (accursed Satan) as one who would be stoned with shooting stars (*shuhūb*). He adds, however, that it cannot be the stars themselves which are thrown, but only a sort of firebrand (*qabs*) from them.

think that they included sun and moon deities.[20] A key passage is the story of Abraham's discovery of monotheism. It is through the moon's waning and the sun's setting that he realises that the heavenly lights are only creations of the One True God (Sūra al-Anʿām 6:77–78). Elsewhere, the prohibition of sun and moon worship is explicit:

> And of His signs are the night and the daytime, and the sun and the moon. Do not prostrate yourselves to the sun, nor to the moon; and prostrate yourselves to God, Who created them, in case Him (alone) you do worship. (Sūra Fuṣṣilat 41:37)

According to orthodox Islamic views, astronomy is permitted as a science (Sūra ar-Raḥmān 55:5), but astrology is ḥarām (forbidden), as it is trying to find knowledge of the future which is known only by God (see ar-Raḥmān 55:5; al-Māʾida 5:3; and Mishkāat ul-Maasabih, Book 23, Hadith 87). On the other hand, some Sufis consider astrology to be permissible. They consider Idrīs (Enoch) to be the founder of the science of the stars (ʿilm al-nujūm), and interpret this as including astrology.

It is interesting, then, to note the importance of a particular heavenly body in Islamic worship. Shooting stars, which we know as meteorites, have been venerated by many people. For example, the book of Acts mentions the image of the Ephesians' goddess Artemis which fell from heaven (Acts 19:35–36), and this was probably a meteorite. Similarly, the Black Stone in the Kaʿba could well have been a meteorite.[21] It too is said to have fallen from heaven, and Muslims believe that it was given as a guide to help Adam and Eve build an altar. Today, Muslims try to kiss it, emulating the Islamic Prophet Muhammad when he performed the ḥajj. There is even a tradition that this holy black stone can wipe away sin; and that is why it changed its original colour from white to black (Jamiʾ at-Tirmidhi, Vol. 4, Book 2, Hadith 877, Musnad: 1/307, 329). Many believe that kissing this black stone brings forgiveness of all sins, others say that it brings forgiveness only of small sins, yet others disagree that the stone has any power at all. In a Sahih Hadith, Abbās bin Rabīʿa reported:

> Umar came near the black stone and kissed it and said "No doubt, I know that you are a stone and can neither benefit anyone nor

---

20. The idols and some such practices are listed by Ibn Ishaq. See Guillaume (trans), *Ibn Ishaq's Sirāt Rasūl Allāh*, 35–39, 66–67. Today, many people say that Hubal, the chief deity in the Kaʿba, was himself a moon god, but there is no evidence for this in the early traditions.

21. As argued by Burke, *Cosmic Debris*, 221–23. See also Elliott, *Your Door to Arabia*.

harm anyone. Had I not seen God's messenger kissing you I would not have kissed you." (Bukhārī, Vol. 2, Book 26, Hadith 667)

Umar understood that it is not a stone which came down from the heavens that can forgive us. No! Both the Bible and the Qur'an make it clear that only God can do that. In the New Testament, we read that the Savior Jesus the Messiah is the one who came down from heaven and that it is through him, the living cornerstone, that we can be cleansed from our sins – big and small (Eph 2:20).

C. Genesis 1:20–23 The Fifth Day: The Water and Sky Are Filled with Fish and Birds

> *And God said, "Let the waters swarm with swarms of living creatures, and let birds fly above the earth across the expanse of the heavens." So God created the great sea creatures and every living creature that moves, with which the waters swarm, according to their kinds, and every winged bird according to its kind. And God saw that it was good. And God blessed them, saying, "Be fruitful and multiply and fill the waters in the seas, and let birds multiply on the earth." And there was evening and there was morning, the fifth day.*

The fifth day has the first appearance of the root word meaning "blessing" (Heb. *b-r-k*, v. 22) in the Bible. God fills the sky and the seas which appeared on the second day, and blesses the creatures he has made. Here, too, is the second use of the verb "create" (Heb. *bara*), which has not been used since verse 1. These two words will be used again when we reach verses 27 and 28 where God creates human beings. The creation and the blessing signal something very significant on this day.

What is so significant? Why is the beginning of animal life different from the beginning of plant life? One answer is that animals possess consciousness, signalled by the Hebrew word *nefesh*, translated here "creature," but more often translated "soul." In verses 20 and 21, the animals are described as *nefesh chayyah* – living beings. The phrase will also appear in 1:24, 2:7, and 9:10, 12, 15 and 16. The living beings have special value in God's creation. Everything created up to this time prepares a place for them.

The living beings include all sorts of sea and air creatures: God is Lord of all these lives. The water monsters (Heb. *tanînim*) are particularly significant and include Leviathon and Behemoth over which God claims control in Job 40–41. Such monsters could be beasts such as the crocodile and the hippopotamus, but some see them as dinosaurs or as mythical beings. In Canaanite as well as Mesopotamian myths, the seas are personified as monstrous beings, like Tiamat in *Enuma Elish*, and there are mighty battles between these chaos monsters and the hero god. The verb *bara* used here emphasizes that there is no second, chaotic power – the One God created all things, and all are under his sovereignty.

All the living creatures are declared "good" (v. 21), all have special functions in God's world, and all receive God's blessing (v. 22). With the words, "be fruitful and multiply," he has given these living creatures the power to reproduce.

As with the previous days, the fifth day's creations cause wonder and prayer elsewhere in the Bible (e.g. Job 41; Ps 69:34; 104:12, 24–26); and Jesus the Messiah tells us to learn from God's care for the birds (e.g. Matt 6:26; 10:29–31). The Qur'an also speaks of the birds and the fish. It has many references to birds and points to them as signs which glorify the Creator God: *"Do they not see the birds controlled in the atmosphere of the sky? None holds them up except God. Indeed in that are signs for a people who believe"* (Sūras *an-Naḥl* 16:79; cf. *an-Nūr* 24:41; *al-Mulk* 67:19). The fish which appear in the Qur'an are all extraordinary and mysterious (*al-Aʻrāf* 7:163; *al-Kahf* 18:61–63; *aṣ-Ṣāffāt* 37:142).

A WORD ABOUT BIRDS

Every culture has traditions about animals and birds. In South Asia people have various superstitions regarding crows, owls and parrots. In Genesis 1:21, all the birds that God creates are declared "good," so we have no reason to fear birds. They have no power over humans, nor can they control our fates, so there is no need for superstitions.

Owls
In many places, owls are regarded as wise, but in South Asian villages people have many superstitions about them. First, they are connected with death. People believe that if an owl is heard in the darkness at the time of the new moon, a witch is near and someone in the house will die; so they try to keep owls from nesting near their homes.

Another belief is that, because owls have big eyes which enable them to see at night, eating owls' eyes will improve eyesight. Hence, a huge number of owls are killed every year in Bangladesh and beyond, thus making the owl an endangered bird.

Genesis teaches us that all birds are good and have their place in God's creation. Owls are helpful because they control the populations of mice, voles, moles, snakes, rats and insects and thus help humankind to preserve nature. We should not scare them or kill them, but treat them as friends.

Crows

In South Asia, crows or ravens are negatively perceived and deemed a nuisance due to their shrill cries, while cukoos are hailed positively for their pretty songs. But crows are very intelligent birds, with a useful role in God's creation. They eat some of the pests which damage crops, and they are scavengers, helping to rid the earth of dead and rotting matter. The Qur'an also recognizes the usefulness of crows: it teaches that a crow taught humankind the proper burial method for dead bodies (al-Mā'ida 5:30–31). During the time of the great flood, we read in Genesis that Noah sought news about the height of the water through a raven (a kind of crow). As he gave the animals shelter and took responsibility for their survival, so today, we should lovingly care for the well-being of animals.

Parrots

Parrot astrology is popular in Bangladesh, as in many other parts of South Asia. Parrot astrologers typically sit under a leafy banyan tree at a marketplace or roadside, and frustrated, unemployed and unhappy people come to them. They use parrots as fortune tellers, but the astrologers cheat the poor. As Genesis teaches us, parrots, like other birds, are simply God's creatures. They have no power to predict the future. As the Qur'an agrees, only the all-knowing God knows the fortune of his creatures, because he holds the keys to the unseen things of the world (al-An'ām 6:59; az-Zumar 39:46). According to the Qur'an, no human, not even the Prophet, can tell the future (al-An'ām 6:50), although Sūra Āl 'Imrān 3:49 states that Jesus the Messiah knew what was stored in peoples' houses and what they had eaten.

D'. Genesis 1:24–31 The Sixth Day: The Land Is Filled with Humans and Living Animals

And God said, "Let the earth bring forth living creatures according to their kinds – livestock and creeping things and beasts of the earth according to their kinds." And it was so. And God made the beasts of the earth according to their kinds and the livestock according to their kinds, and everything that creeps on the ground according to its kind. And God saw that it was good. (1:24–25)

On the sixth day, God fills the dry land which appeared on the third day. As on the fifth day, we have the words of creation (*bara*) and blessing (*b-r-k*); but these are not found until verses 27–28 – the special creation of the human being in God's image and likeness. As our attention was drawn to the first appearance of the *nefesh chayyah*, so our attention is drawn to the even more important appearance of humanity in God's world.

The living creatures of verse 24 are *nefesh chayyah*, like the air and sea creatures of the fifth day. They include the whole animal kingdom: cattle, reptiles, insects and wild beasts, etc. As on previous days, the creatures appear simply at the sovereign word of God.

Having begun with the foundations of creation, now, at last, we reach its apex: the creation of humankind. We note that "man" is not the only product of the sixth day of creation, but that he/she was created along with the other animals. From this we learn that, though "man" is God's greatest creation, he/she shares a relationship with the animal world. Here the Hebrew word translated "man" is *adam*, "human," and is to be understood as the man and woman together making up humanity. *Ish*, used in Genesis 2:23, refers to the male human.

> *Then God said, "Let us make man in our image, after our likeness. And let them have dominion over the fish of the sea and over the birds of the heavens and over the livestock and over all the earth and over every creeping thing that creeps on the earth."*

> *So God created man in his own image,*
> *in the image of God he created him;*
> *male and female he created them. (1:26–27)*

The creation of humankind takes up seven of the thirty-one verses of Genesis 1. It is not only this length which draws our attention, but also several unique features. First, there have been seven occurrences of the phrase "let there be . . ., and it was so," but here God announces his intention before he creates. Second, God uses first person plural pronouns: "Let **us** make man in **our** image (Heb. *na'aseh adam be-tselmenu*), according to **our** likeness (Heb. *ki-dmutenu*)." Third, God not only blesses the human beings but speaks to them. The previous day, God blessed the air and water creatures but did not speak directly to them (compare v. 22 and v. 28). Fourth, the day ends with God seeing that what he has made is not only "good" but "very good."

It is not surprising that these verses have given rise to much discussion over the centuries. They take us to the very heart of understanding human beings and their relationship with God. We will explore three key questions before going on to consider God's blessing in verse 28.

First, the question about God: Why does he speak in the plural?

Since the early church fathers, many Christians have seen this as the first reference to the Trinity[22] – God speaks of himself in plurality to reveal that, in one God, multiple persons are present (see also Ps 2:7; Isa 48:16). God was, they say, speaking to Jesus the Messiah, or this was a conference between the three persons of the Trinity. But we remind ourselves that the concept of the Holy Triune God is here an unopened bud, a mystery for us. The New Testament will begin to unfold the bud for us (e.g. Matt 3:16–17; 28:18–20; Mark 1:9–11), but it will not be fully opened until we see our Lord in glory (1 Cor 13:11–12).

Another possibility is that "us" is simply a plural of majesty, as occasionally occurs elsewhere in the Scripture (e.g. Gen 3:22; 11:7; Isa 6:8). In the Qur'an, God often speaks in the first-person plural, and commentators agree that this indicates majesty and not numerical plurality. The Qur'an denies the idea of the Trinity, and Muslim scholars agree that "We" is used to convey the greatness of God.

Whatever we conclude about this use of the plural, it is important to note that this is God himself speaking about what he intends to do. It is the first of six places in Genesis 1–11 where we read about the thoughts of God (see also Gen 2:18; 3:22; 6:6; 8:21; 11:7), and three of them use the first-person plural. So this verse signals that God is beginning a key part of his plan for creation.

Jewish tradition, including Philo and the Midrash, offers several different interpretations: the most common, and the most relevant to our context, is that God is addressing his heavenly court. The Jewish commentators use this idea as an opportunity to discuss the problem of human free will – how can a good and omnipotent God create a being who can and will choose to do evil? *Genesis Rabbah* has the angels involved in the discussion of this question (see page 46). The Qur'an concurs with this Jewish interpretation (*al-Baqara* 2:30–32, quoted on page 45). When God announces to the angels his intention to create humankind, they question why he would create a being who is going to cause trouble, and God replies first by declaring his omniscience and second by demonstrating that humans will be superior to the angels in some ways. We will explore this important story further in our commentary on Genesis 2:19–20. Here, we note that it explores similar questions to those raised by the ancient Jewish rabbis.

---

22. For example, Justin Martyr (100–165), Irenaeus, Tertullian, Augustine, *Cave of Treasures*.

The Ancient Near Eastern cultures believed in divine assemblies made up of the chief gods of the pantheon, and there is some support for the idea of a heavenly court in the Old Testament (cf. Isa 6; Job 1; 1 Kgs 22:14; Deut 33; Exod 15:11). However, Christian commentators generally reject the idea that Genesis 1:26 might be alluding to such ideas. As far back as Irenaeus (d. 202) and Tertullian (d. 240), they have argued that the omnipotent God has no need to consult with anyone (Isa 40:14). Saying that God sought advice from the angels is completely against the teaching of the Bible. These writers also refute the possibility that "our image" might refer to the image of angels. Genesis 1:27 uses the singular (that is *his*, not *their*) image and likeness, and repeats that this is the image of God himself. Some Christians would say that humanity is created in the image of the second person of the Trinity, Jesus the Messiah.

Second, the question about humanity: What is the meaning of "the Image of God?"

Genesis 1:26 is a case of Hebrew parallelism, that is "image" and "likeness" are virtually synonymous and are used to describe human nature in relation to God. These concepts are not found in the Qur'an; rather, the qur'anic story[23] of God's announcing the creation of Adam to the angelic council uses the term *khalīfa* – someone who does the work of a representative or caretaker on behalf of another. We have already noted the idea that the *khalīfa* was to replace the jinn on the earth, but a more common view is that Adam will somehow be the representative of God himself. This idea clearly reflects at least part of the idea of the "image of God" here in Genesis.

THE TITLE *KHALĪFA*

Many people read the term *khalīfa* in Sūra *al-Baqara* 2:31 as meaning that God appointed Adam as a representative of his rule on earth, and they see this as being confirmed by the command to the angels to bow down to him. Although Muslims regard Adam as a prophet, many extend the title and responsibility of *khalīfa* to all human beings. However, *khalīfa* has also been used as a title for Muslim leaders, starting with Abu Bakr, who took the place of the Islamic Prophet Muhammad in leading the Muslim community.

---

23. Sūra *al-Baqara* 2; see page 45.

The Qur'an also uses the term "*khalīfa* on the earth" for David the king (*Ṣād* 38:26). The context is God's giving David the responsibility of judging people. The use of the title for successive Muslim leaders is not, then, surprising. There have been many *khalīfa*s in history, each claiming to be the rightful leader of the worldwide *umma*. There are *hadith*s which can be interpreted as meaning that the *khalīfa* should be from the Quraysh tribe to which the Islamic Prophet Muhammad belonged. Most Sunnis did not interpret them in this way; and Shi'ites believe that only someone from *ahl al-bayt* (the Prophet's family) was worthy to inherit the title.

Historically, the authority of a *khalīfa* has usually been based on the affirmation of believers. In South Asia, some Muslims saw the Mughal rulers as the legitimate *khalīfa*, but others endorse the Ottoman line of rule. A major reason for the dispute is the belief that there cannot be two *khalīfa*s at the same time. Since the fall of the Ottoman empire at the beginning of the twentieth century, many Muslims have been dreaming of a new Caliphate ruled by righteousness and peace. Examples of claimants of the title include the Ahmadiyya leader Mirja Ahmed, and the Islamic State leader Abu Bakr al-Baghdadi. Before it was banned in Bangladesh, the international organization *Ḥizb ut-Taḥrir* (Party of Liberation) led a campaign to overthrow the democratic tradition and replace it with its own Caliphate.

In summary, it can be said that, amongst Muslims, the term *khalīfa* has mostly been used for a special, usually political, class of people. Not everyone is *khalīfa*, and even the Islamic Prophet Muhammad did not claim that title. If ordinary Muslims in Bangladesh apply the title to themselves, they understand it as meaning that they are God's slaves (Bn. *Allahar Banda*, Ar. *'abd Allāh*) rather than his representatives. In popular Bangla, *khalīfa* does not refer to an Islamic ruler, but to a skilled artisan, even a good tailor.

Some Muslims suppose that the Genesis phrase "image of God" implies that human beings look like God, and therefore that God has a physical body, which would be blasphemous. It is true that some biblical interpreters have suggested a physical meaning for the image (Gen 5:3 may be seen as using the phrase in this way), but the fact that God is Spirit (John 4:24) makes this interpretation unlikely. The early Christian writer, Origen (AD c. 182–253), comments:

> If anyone suppose that, because this man who is made according
> to the image and likeness of God is made of flesh, he will appear

to represent God himself as made of flesh and in human form. It is most clearly impious to think this about God.[24]

The Qur'an as well as the Bible has references to parts of God's body (e.g. his face, Gen 32:30; compare *al-Baqara* 2:272; *al-An'ām* 6:52), but interpreters of the Qur'an see these as metaphorical rather than literal descriptions. The Abrahamic faiths may disagree about the details, but all agree that God has no body and that we cannot and must not make statues or other idols to represent him (Lev 4:15–31; cf. Sūra *Luqmān* 31:13).

Probably the best way of understanding the "image and likeness of God" is to ask what it means in its Genesis 1 context. First, consider human speech. God, by his speech, brought everything into creation. By means of God's spoken command, humans are given food (Gen 1:29–30). Looking at the similarities and differences between God's speech and human speech, we understand both the potential and the limitations of each person. We cannot command creation, but we can communicate with each other, and, amazingly, we can communicate with God. Speech is one of the main things which makes humans different from animals, and speech enables us to relate to God.

Second, consider dominion. Because humans have been given dominion over the animals, we have an important task (v. 28). The peoples of the ancient world regarded the sun and moon as gods: Genesis denies this, saying that they rule only over the "day" and "night" (1:17).[25] But humankind, made in the image of God, is given authority to rule over all the animals of the world. That is, we are not only created to relate to God, but to work with God in ruling his world. The phrase "image of God" describes our relationship not only to God but to all of living creation (see also Ps 8:5–8).

In both Genesis and the Qur'an, there will be a link between language and dominion. We could say that it is language which equips the human beings for their role. In Genesis, God gives Adam the responsibility of naming the animals (Gen 2:19–20). In the Qur'an, God teaches Adam the names (*al-Baqara* 2:31). In both cases, the knowledge of the names is a mark of the human ability to exercise authority within the creation.

Ancient Near Eastern stories such as the Egyptian and Assyrian creation epics speak of kings being made in the image of God, so it is these special people who rule. In Genesis, Adam is simply the first human being, and it is clear that the responsibility of living as God's "image" is for everyone. We might

---

24. Origen, *Homilies on Genesis and Exodus*, 63.

25. The Hebrew word is different (*memshalah* in 1:17 and *r-d-h* in 1:26–28), but the meaning is similar.

SUFIS AND THE IMAGE OF GOD

In Bangladesh, Sufis love the idea of "the image of God." They have a saying, "as many men as many gods." That is, God has somehow hidden himself in every human being. The implication is that if we serve human beings, we serve God within them.

A few years ago during the Bengali month of *Kartik*, I (Anwarul) attended the full moon festival held by disciples in the Chistiya Sufi community. After the special dinner, a magical atmosphere was created and a sense of peace and happiness captivated my mind. With great emotion, the *murshid* (teacher) shared this story:

> Before the creation of humankind, God commanded the angels to make a body of Adam from the clay. The angels modelled him in the shape of familiar creatures – birds, animals, and other living beings. Then God told them to look at him and to make Adam according to his own shape!

Then taking his *ektara* (musical instrument), he sang this song of the Fakir Lalon Shah.

> In compassion He, Adam, in His own image made –
> Did He not bid the angels bow down?
> Perplexing as a sinner like Azazel,
> The mind spins in seeing this.
> See Adam and Adam you see
> Can animals know his heart?
> Lalon says, religion is in knowing Adam.

Finishing the song and putting down his *ektara*, he related the hadith, "God made Adam in his own image."

After bidding the disciples farewell, I thought to myself that Bauls also seek the *moner manush* – the ideal being or "human of the heart," perhaps best translated into English as the "divine beloved." The *moner manush* is not to be found on earth or in heaven but rather within themselves. In the communities of both Bauls and fakirs, people believe that human love is the path to divine love. The Bible will differ, because Genesis's picture of humanity is not only that we are wonderfully made in God's loving image, but also that we are terribly flawed because of the fall.

say that God has given us all the status of kings in creation. God has granted even ordinary people value, equality and honour.

Finally, consider free will. Likeness to God has a moral dimension. By nature, all human beings are like God in that they are personal beings with self-consciousness and intellect, and, as we shall see in Genesis 2 and 3, they also have choice. They can choose whether to obey God and to be the image of God's goodness.

The creation of humans in the image of God provides an essential basis for God's eternal son coming in human flesh. The Bible will reveal an indispensable need for a human perfectly "in God's image and likeness" (2 Cor 4:4; Col 1:15). This need was met in the person of Jesus the Messiah, *rūḥ-ullah* (the "spirit of God," as in Sūra *an-Nisā'* 4:171). In him, God bore the form of humanity – of his own image. Jesus the Messiah is not merely the perfect *khalīfa* – God's pure representative – but God himself, standing with us in our place.

Third, the question about gender: What is the significance of "male and female"?
The animals must all have been both male and female, but it is only in the case of human beings that "male and female" are mentioned (v. 27); and it seems that "male and female" is a poetic parallel to the "image of God." Why might this be?

Commentators down the ages have returned to this verse as they have tried to understand the relationship between men and women in their own times and cultures and elsewhere in the Bible.[26] It is the necessary foundation for, and the lens through which we should look at, understandings of gender: both the male and the female are equally in the image of God. God created what we might call today an "egalitarian society," with all humankind equal in status and God as their king. Together, male and female were to live out their blessed responsibilities of fruitfulness and dominion. They were equal partners in bringing forth children, and they had equal responsibility to care for the world.

It is because this partnership went terribly wrong (see Gen 3) that we need Genesis 1:27. The repercussions of the fall have so affected our minds that we need to emphasize it again. *Men and women are together, equally, made in the image of God*. History and our own observation underline it again: men and women must work together so that society can flourish. We need men and women working side by side as a basis for both family and social life. The national poet of Bangladesh, Kaji Najrul Islam (1899–1976), writes thus in his poem, "Nari" (Women):

---

26. A New Testament passage which has often been interpreted as teaching that women are inferior to men is 1 Cor 11:2–16. Since this passage has a reference to the "image of God," even the most patriarchal of commentators has had to acknowledge the essential equality of women and men in Genesis 1:27. Famous examples include St. Augustine, *De Trinitate*, 12:7; Thomas Aquinas, *Summa Theologica* 1:93; John Calvin, *Commentary on the Epistles of the Apostle Paul to the Corinthians*, 357.

I sing the song of equality;
In my view gender difference is essentially a triviality.
Everything that is great in the world,
all the works, beneficial and good,
half must be credited to woman, and to man half only we should.
All the vice or bad in the world,
and the pain or flowing tear,
for half, man should be blamed,
the other half only woman should bear.[27]

> *And God blessed them. And God said to them, "Be fruitful and multiply and fill the earth and subdue it, and have dominion over the fish of the sea and over the birds of the heavens and over every living thing that moves on the earth." (1:28)*

God's very first word to human beings is a blessing! This is the second God-given "blessing" of Genesis, and a comparison with verse 22 stresses that God is speaking to the male and female he has just called into being. But the blessing is not only a gift – it is also a responsibility. They have a two-fold commission: procreation and dominion.

Procreation: Be fruitful and multiply

Fruitfulness, or reproduction, is a blessing from God alone. It cannot be received from any religious observance, or from a saint or *pir* or guru or even from a Christian pastor. God wants the earth to thrive through being filled with human beings. Here is yet another contrast with other ancient texts, which consider human overpopulation a problem. For example, the Babylonian *Atrahasis Epic*[28] says that overpopulation made humanity too noisy, and that was the cause of the great flood.

Genesis sees multiplication as a blessing: God likes people more than we like ourselves! A few years ago, overpopulation was considered a hindrance to the development of Bangladesh. Now, it is a blessing rather than a problem. The trained population plays an important role in the country's economic development. We even export key thinkers and workers to other countries, and their activity both serves the world and helps the country's economy. God

---

27. Translation from https://www.poemhunter.com/poem/woman-121/ accessed 7 April 2021.

28. See https://www.ancient.eu/article/227/the-atrahasis-epic-the-great-flood--the-meaning-of/.

loves children, and he commanded us to procreate. Jesus the Messiah has taken fatherless children and adopted them with the words, "whoever accepts one of these little children in my name, accepts me" (Matt 18:5).

The name that Jesus the Messiah told us to use for God is "Father" (Matt 6:9). We can see here in Genesis God's intention to be father for what he created. The humans were to build a family with whom God wished to live – not only a few people in the small Eden garden, but many people in the whole earth.

Children can be spiritual as well as biological. Still today, God's desire is that through his anointed servant Jesus (Messiah means "anointed") he should be our Father. Ephesians 1:3–10 tells us that God is the Father of all who are re-created through the Messiah. Even before the world was created, he chose us as adopted children through his unique son, Jesus (vv. 4–5). This is the blessing of God's grace (v. 6). God is making a family to fill the whole world to his glory.

MUST ALL HUMAN BEINGS PROCREATE?

Some married couples are unable to bear children, but does the commandment to be fruitful mean that all human beings should get married and have children if they can? The biblical teaching is that, although marriage is the norm, God calls some people to refrain from marriage in order to serve him (see 1 Cor 7). The greatest example is Jesus the Messiah, who was unmarried. So Christianity developed a great tradition of unmarried people who have served God and others, including missionaries, priests, monks and nuns.

Islam has no monks. Indeed, a famous hadith says that man fulfils half his religion when he marries (*Al-Muj'am Al-Awsat* 992), and having children is seen as very important. Although the Qur'an appreciates some of the Christian monks, it clearly rejects monasticism.[1]

In contrast, some Bauls are ascetic and do not beget children. They practice sexual intercourse with seminal retention. When Anwarul asked a Guru about the matter, the response was that they consider semen as the *nūr* (light) which should not be given to a partner during cosmic sex. The female desires to get the *nūr*, and the male partner tries to retain it. If he fails, it means that he fails in his mystic inward journey. Believers from the ascetic Baul heritage may be reluctant to marry or to rear children. This is contrary to the teaching of the Bible. As Muslims also know, God himself is the *nūr*, and Jesus the Messiah is the *nūr* come to us. Some Bauls get married and have children only with their guru's permission. Believers in the Messiah do not need to get such permission, because God has already commanded us to be fruitful and multiply (Gen 1:28) and we know that children are a good gift from God (Ps 127:3).

---

1. *"Lā rahbāniyya fī al Islām,"* *Musnad* Aḥmad Ibn Hanbal; cf. Sūra *al-Ḥadīd* 57:27.

Dominion: Rule over all living beings

Dominion implies responsibility. God commissioned humanity to subdue (Heb. *kabash*) and to rule (Heb. *radah*, also used in v. 26) creation: that is, they are to bring it under control and then to govern it. It is important that we heed both words – *kabash* alone could make us think that the creation should be our servant, but *radah* reminds us that God's image has responsibility on the earth under God and as his representative. God cares for his world by putting us into it to care for the earth and its creatures, and in that sense, we are creation's servants (1:26; 2:15; Ps 8:6–8). The qur'anic term *khalīfa* (*al-Baqara* 2:30) affirms this idea of humanity as the stewards of God's world.

Since the fall, in this sinful and broken world, stewardship is a great challenge. Our temptation is to focus on subduing the earth, selfishly using its resources, ruining creation, destroying its rich bio-diversity, and ignoring our commission as the "image of God." As his children, believers have special responsibility to "rule" by working for the good of all creation, and not just for themselves. Those who exploit God's creation and ruin the natural environment are not fulfilling the blessing.

Putting together the twofold commission, we see that it is God's intention that humankind should live in community and care for the environment which he created. It is not surprising, then, that Genesis is organized according to *toledoth* – to the fruitfulness of humankind – and that it focuses on family. The story that begins with the blessing of fruitfulness for the first couple is leading to the calling of a barren couple (Gen 11:30) from whom will come a blessed and fruitful family (Gen 49:1–28).

And God said, "Behold, I have given you every plant yielding seed that is on the face of all the earth, and every tree with seed in its fruit. You shall have them for food. And to every beast of the earth and to every bird of the heavens and to everything that creeps on the earth, everything that has the breath of life, I have given every green plant for food." And it was so.

> *And God saw everything that he had made, and behold, it was very good.*
> *And there was evening and there was morning, the sixth day. (1:29–31)*

As a father, God provided food for his children. The *Enuma Elish* has human beings created to feed the gods (A. I. 190–191; U 6:35–37). The Bible and the Qur'an both refute such a concept. God needs nothing: it is he who provides everything that we need, and not the other way around (see also Acts 17:25). In Islam, one of God's ninety-nine names is *ar-Razzāq*, the Provider. God even provides food for the animals (Sūra *Hūd* 11:6; cf. Gen 1:30; Job 38:41).

From these verses, it seems that humans and animals were originally vegetarian. The new generation after the flood is given permission to eat meat (Gen 9:3–4). The Qur'an affirms God's provision:

> And it is He who subjected the sea for you to eat from it tender meat and to extract from it ornaments which you wear. And you see the ships plowing through it, and [He subjected it] that you may seek of His bounty; and perhaps you will be grateful. (Sūra an-Naḥl 16:14)

A' Genesis 2:1–3 Day 7: God and the Completed Creation

> *Thus the heavens and the earth were finished, and all the host*
>   *of them.*
>   *And on the seventh day God finished his work that he had done,*
>   *and he rested on the seventh day from all his work that*
>   *he had done.*
>   *So God blessed the seventh day and made it holy,*
>   *because on it God rested from all his work that he had done in*
>   *creation.*

This section of Genesis (1:1–2:3) began with the Spirit of God hovering over the *tohu wa bohu* – the deep dark chaos at the beginning of time (Gen 1:2). It ends with creation completed, and with God enjoying the beautiful order of what he has made. The six active days are not complete without the seventh day of perfect peace; it is a picture of the final perfection of the new creation in the Messiah (Heb 4:4–9).

The Qur'an frequently mentions that God created the heaven and the earth in six days (*al-A'rāf* 7:54; *Yūnus* 10:3; *Hūd* 11:7; *al-Furqān* 25:59) and then that God "settled himself upon the throne" (*al-Ḥadīd* 57:4). However, it does not discuss the seventh day, which is so special here. Genesis insists that creation was not completed in six days, but in seven days. This is underlined by the sevenfold word patterns of Genesis 1:1–2:3 (see page 59), by the threefold repetition of "seventh," and by the fact that 2:1–3 has thirty-five (5x7) words in Hebrew.

Even in translation, we can see the poetic character of these three verses, with their pattern of ideas and their word repetitions. In Hebrew, we particularly note:

- The threefold use of *kl* in verses 1 and 2 – "and were finished" (*waykulu*), "and all" (*wekal*) and "and finished" (*waykal*) – emphasizing the perfect completion of creation.
- The similarity between the word translated "seventh" (*shabi'i*) and the word translated "rested" (v. 2 *yishbot*, v. 3 *shabat*), which indicates the origins of the word "Sabbath."
- The frequent use of the letter *shin* (with the sound s or sh) – it appears once in verse 1, but then twelve times in verses 2 and 3.

These three verses have been recited every seventh day through the millennia, the poetic form aiding the memory, and the sibilant sounds soothing the soul as it prepares for rest.

The word translated "rest" (*shabat*) certainly does not mean that God took a rest because he was tired. The Genesis author could have used a word which would suggest the need for rest and refreshment (*nuach*), but he knew that God does not get tired (e.g. Isa 40:28; see also Sūras *al-Baqara* 2:255; *Qāf* 50:38). In contrast, the *Enuma Elish* and other ancient epics have humans being created in order to serve the gods when they are weary. *Shabat* might better be translated "ceased": that is, after dealing with the *tohu wa bohu*, the chaos and darkness of the opening verses, God now dwells in the peace of his finished work. God blesses and sanctifies this day for future generations.

This seventh day is not an empty day of doing nothing, but a day of special blessings. It is "holy" (Heb. *qadosh*). This is the only appearance of the very important root, *q-d-sh*, in Genesis 1–11. Its literal meaning is something that is set aside, separated from common things, and it comes to describe the very special purity of God. When the seventh day[29] is made holy, it is set aside by God and for God. In due course, the commandment would be given to the *Bani Isra'il* that all their families and the people who served them and lived

---

29. The Hebrews did not have names for the days of the week, like the Bangla names which are based on celestial bodies – *Shoni* (Saturn), *Robi* (a solar deity), *Shom* (a lunar deity), *Mongol* (Mars), *Budh* (Mercury), *Brihospoti* (Jupiter) and *Shukro* (Venus). They simply refered to the first day, the second day, etc.

with them and even their animals should keep this day special by stopping their normal work and worshipping God (Exod 20:8–11; Deut 5:12–15). This is part of God's blessing to his world. He has made human beings in such a way that they function best if they have a day's refreshment every week.

The observance of the seventh day by the *Bani Isra'il* created a lifestyle which marked them as different from other nations. Other nations, such as the Babylonians, had special days which were inauspicious for particular activities. The Israelites did not consider the Sabbath "inauspicious," but as a sign of their special relationship to God (compare Exod 31:12–17 to Ezek 20:12–20). This sign is extended to the followers of Jesus the Messiah because, through God's salvation, they will also participate in a final Sabbath rest (Heb 4:4, 9).

The Qur'an affirms the Sabbath as a holy day for the *Bani Isra'il*, but it does not command a weekly rest day for Muslims. It recognizes the seriousness for the *Bani Isra'il* of breaking the Sabbath, saying that God cursed Sabbath violators, and that they became "despised apes" (*al-Baqara* 2:65) or "pigs and monkeys" (*al-Mā'ida* 5:60). There is disagreement as to whether these descriptions are literal or metaphorical,[30] but it is clear that the Sabbath is one of the most important laws for the *Bani Isra'il*.

For Muslims, Friday is a special day and a day of prayer, but it is not a day of rest. According to some Islamic traditions, Friday is the best day on which the sun rises; the day on which Adam was taken into paradise and turned out of it, and the day on which he died; and it will be the day of the resurrection. It is the best day for human beings to die.

Theological Reflection

Surely Genesis 1:1–2:3 is the *theological bud* from which the rest of the Bible is going to blossom. In the midst of the daily struggles we face, we are called into the seventh day rest – to contemplate the glory of the creation and of the Creator who made and ordered it all. Herein is a glimpse of our loving Creator – he was present at the very beginning with his Spirit and by his word created all things. He is the one Creator God and has all authority. Even the first bud for understanding the wondrous idea of the Trinity is visible in these opening chapters.

As we contemplate the creation, we see that this One God is also good, and that everything that he makes is good and beautiful. And we human beings

---

30. For example, at-Ṭabarī sees them as metaphorical, while az-Zamakhsharī sees them as literal. For more details, see Reynolds, *Qur'an and Its Biblical Subtext*, 107.

are the highest wonder of creation! So much was made for us and given to us. How good is our loving Father God!

> Every good and perfect gift is from above, coming down from the Father of the heavenly lights, who does not change like shifting shadows. (Jas 1:17)

The Qur'an also calls people to contemplate the creation as a sign of God's mercy (e.g. *an-Naḥl* 16:79; *al-Jāthiya* 45:3–5). Again and again, it calls us to consider the care that the Creator God shows us, and urges us to remember all his blessings and to give him thanks (see especially Sūra *ar-Raḥmān* 55).

Genesis 1:1–2:3 calls us further: the Sabbath is not only a call to contemplate the Creator and to give thanks to him, but a call to share in something which the Creator does. He enjoys the Sabbath, and we are to enjoy it with him. How can this be? The clue is in the very nature of human beings – that mysterious "image and likeness of God" which distinguishes humanity from all other creatures. We are not only *khalīfa*, to steward creation on behalf of the Creator, we are also, in a way that is not yet revealed, somehow like the Creator.

The single idea that we are in some way like God is *the "grandmother" of what makes us scientists* – from this human clay will come the scientist who has been made to relate to God. It is also *the soil* which can produce a Scripture which is both human and divine, and *the seed* out of which the whole story of human sin and divine redemption will grow. It is because we are, in some way, like God that we can study his world and that our minds can produce the mathematics and logic which so powerfully describe it and predict what can happen in it. It is because we are in the image of God that we are given the job of ruling the earth and that we need scientific knowledge to do it effectively. It is because we are in the image of God that the Holy Spirit can partner with human writers to produce Scripture. But it is also because we are in the image of God that we have the moral choice which enables us to sin.

We might recall Jewish reflection on *bereshit* (in the beginning), which notes that wisdom is called the *reshit*, the beginning, in Proverbs 8 (see page 29). Jews are likely to see this wisdom as the Torah, and this is not far from the Islamic idea of the Qur'an as pre-existent and uncreated. But followers of Jesus the Messiah would see the pre-existent wisdom as the Logos, the eternal Word of God who came in Jesus the Messiah. It is because human beings are made in the image of God that his Word can come to us in human flesh, and not only in human words.

In Proverbs, Wisdom says,

> When he (God) established the heavens, I was there; . . .
> when he marked out the foundations of the earth,
>   then I was beside him, like a master workman,
> and I was daily his delight,
>   rejoicing before him always,
> rejoicing in his inhabited world,
>   and delighting in the children of man. (Prov 8:27, 29–31)

Here, the emphasis is not only on a shared mastery of creation, but on joy. Remarkably, the focus is not the beauteous wonder of creation, but the delight showered over humans as the crown of God's creation. Before we read about the entrance of sin in chapter 3, we are called to remember that God's creation of humanity is good. God's love and provision for us spring out of joy and not out of compulsion. We are made to be part of the beautiful, orderly world of the blessed and holy seventh day, in total contrast to the *tohu wa bohu* of the empty and chaotic time before the light began to shine.

What About Us?

We are God's joy; but as Genesis 3–11 will show us, we sin and cause him pain.[31] Sometimes, it seems as if human beings are trying to re-create *tohu wa bohu*! How should we be living in order to be part of the Creator's joyful world and not contributing to the chaos and emptiness caused by human sin? Genesis 1:1–2:3 calls us to live as God's creatures in his world, to recognize the image of God in all humanity, and to trust the One True God and him alone.

Living as God's Creatures in God's World

> O Human, dwell gratefully in God's earth
>   Profuse with fruits, sweet rivers flow,
>   Your God is gracious! (Nuzrul Islam, *Bangla Ghazal*)

The poet reminds us of God's provision for us and for the animals through the plants which he created (see also Pss 104:21; 145:15; 147:9). Before he created the animals and humans, God created an eco-system for their welfare. This was the blessing that was necessary for the other blessings: it is within this system that people and animals can be fruitful, and it is over this system that the humans are to exercise stewardship.

---

31. See commentary on Genesis 6:6.

If we expect to eat, we need to save by gathering the seeds, to invest by planting them in the ground, and to work to care for the plants and their environment. This is God's investment policy for humankind, and if we follow it, the plants will multiply and so will the animals and humans who depend on them. But if we do not care for the whole eco-system, the good environment is ruined and all the creatures suffer – and we will be the cause of their destruction.

In Bangladesh, we are suffering from the results of deforestation and greenhouse gases, which contribute to the tsunamis, floods and droughts which cause so much suffering. Many of these problems are caused by human actions outside Bangladesh, but we also have our own responsibilities. Due to our negligence, species are becoming extinct in Bangladesh. There are fifty-four native freshwater fish species which have been declared threatened in the Chalan Bill[32] areas. Twelve are critically endangered. Thirteen species of mammals out of eighty-nine species are already extinct from Bangladesh, including nilgai rhinoceros, Indian wolf, gaur, swamp deer, and wild water buffalo. Genesis 1:1–2:3 challenges us to look after all these creatures in our motherland of Bangladesh that God has entrusted to us.

Recognizing the Image of God in All People

One day, Mr. Faruk was travelling with a missionary in rural Bangladesh. The bus was crowded, so a beggar was compelled to lean on the missionary's seat. As this is considered improper in Bangladeshi culture, Mr. Faruk told the beggar to stand further away. After they got off the bus, the missionary took Mr. Faruk aside and said, "You have treated that beggar badly. God has made this brother and myself both in his image. James taught us in the Injīl that we are to make no distinction between a rich person and poor person or to show bias against a person on the basis of how well dressed they are [Jas 2:8–9]. Showing favor to a rich person is a sin." Hearing that, Mr. Faruq searched out the beggar and asked his forgiveness for treating him badly and

---

32. Chalan Bill is a big wasteland in Bangladesh. Forty-seven rivers and waterways flow into the Chalan Bill, so it is rich in flora and fauna. However, gradually, commercial overfishing and excessive use of pesticides have harmed the fish population and other life. Due to deposited silt, the area has shrunk from 1,085 to only 26 square kilometers.

they ended up becoming friends. The beggar was amazed
at such honour, so he wanted to know more and accepted
the Messiah as his Lord and Saviour.

God created all human beings in his image and likeness, and that means that
believers should associate with and respect every person. Elsewhere, the Bible
specifies the importance of equal treatment of people of all backgrounds and
of all statuses – Jew and Gentile, slave and free, rich and poor, male and female
(Gal 3:28; Jas 1:9–11).

We have a good practice in our culture: when someone accidentally
touches someone with his foot, he immediately seeks pardon and offers them
a greeting of peace. Our society is demonstrating a respect for all human
beings. However, there are also superstitions and cultural taboos which can
lead us to avoid people or to treat people as inferior or superior. Sometimes,
men treat women as inferiors. Often, despite the Islamic teaching about one
umma (people), people follow something more like the Hindu caste system,
whereby upper-class Brahmins will not associate with or even touch the lower-
class Dalits.[33]

Because the caste system is such a part of Indian culture, Hindus who
became Muslims after the arrival of Islam in the twelfth century AD brought
aspects of it into their Islamic life, and many of these persist. In the same way
that Dalits are treated as untouchable, Muslims have their lower-class members
whom they term "*Atraf*". The *Ashraf* (honourable) families and clans of the
Sayed, Bhuya, Pathans, and Talukdar, though seeing themselves as Muslims,
regard weavers, boatmen, fishermen, potters, transgender people, folk artists,
singers, the Bauls and sex workers all with the same low estimation as the Dalit
untouchables. As in the Hindu caste system, the lower classes are not permitted
to eat with or marry into these upper classes. Although Muslims are to make
no distinction of class as they say their prayers side by side in the mosque,
marriages are not arranged outside of a person's social class. A union of an
upper-class girl with a lower-class boy might even warrant an "honour killing".[34]

Such social values are against biblical values. The *Bani Isra'il* were given
food and marriage laws to keep them from falling into idolatry, but they were

---

33. Recently, in Uttarkhand, India, a low-caste Hindu was taken out and beaten to death
for eating at the table at a wedding party. See https://www.bbc.com/bengali/news-48334923.

34. Honour killing is a practice found among countries from South Asia to Africa and
is done to protect an offended family from shame. Honor killing is against the law in many of
these countries, but girls are often forced into suicide. Religion and culture together play a role
in the practice.

forbidden to consider any family group as inferior.[35] Jesus the Messiah rejected the inequalities of his day. He associated with Samaritans, he chose fisherman as some of his disciples, and he ate with those who were considered sinners by the religious people, thereby setting an example for his followers. Genesis 1:1–2:3 tells us why he acted thus – all people are precious to God, because all are made in his image.

Trusting the One True God

Genesis 1:1–2:3 wipes out all our fears of created things in the universe, and teaches us that we can trust in the Creator. All are under God's control, and God is good. All that he made is good, and he blesses his creatures and provides for them.

The stars cannot guide our fortunes. We should not be afraid of jinn, or of fairies, or any other spirits associated with created things like trees and seas and animals, because these spirits do not even exist. The Bible does acknowledge the existence of evil spirits, but it also shows us that they will flee at the very name of Jesus the Messiah (Mark 9:38; Acts 16:18). Genesis 1 wipes out all our idolatry, all our superstition and all our fear, and calls us to trust in the One True God and in him alone.

The Qur'an agrees that we should seek no helper other than our Creator (two words are used: *wali* – protector or guardian; and *anṣar* – helper; e.g. Sūras *al-Baqara* 2:107; *al-'Ankabūt* 29:22). However, many Sufi Muslims in Bangladesh seek help from their *pirs* (leaders). They do not regard them as ordinary men but, as many Hindus see their gurus as the very presence of Vaishnava, *pirs* are regarded as intermediaries between their disciples and God. Even if the *pir* forbids the practice, disciples of the *pir* will prostrate before him, and even worship at his grave after his death.[36] So we hear people crying out to the *pir* Bador from the river amidst the monsoon storms when, as on the sea of Galilee, a sudden afternoon storm whips up the waves and their boats begin to sink. Many trucks and buses, their passengers hoping for safe travel across rivers, have a prayer to a Sufi *pir* or a Brahman guru written on their sides.

---

35. Deut 7:3–4; 14:20–31; cf. Deut 10:17–20. On sharing food with people of other faiths, see also Glaser, *Bible and Other Faiths*, 174–85.

36. They justify this worship by pointing out that the Qur'an speaks of the angels being called to worship Adam in no less than seven sūras (*al-Baqara* 2:34; *al-A'rāf* 7:11–12; *al-Qiṣaṣ* 28:33; *al-Isrā'* 17:61–62; *al-Kahf* 18:50; *Ṭā Hā* 20:115–16; *Ṣād* 38:71–78).

Readers of Genesis 1 know that the Creator of the seas is the one who calms the *tohu wa bohu* of all our storms (see also Ps 107:29). As God commanded the waters in Genesis 1:8, so Jesus the Messiah calmed the waters of the sea of Galilee with a word (Matt 8:23–27; Mark 4:35–41; Luke 8:22–25). There is no need for believers to call for help from any human being other than the Messiah.

The Sabbath Is a Part of Our Trust in God

We do not have to work all the time but can trust that, if we follow the Sabbath ordinance, God will surely bless us. The Sabbath is not an onerous burden, but a good gift from God. We need not fear that halting our work will halt our income. God blessed this day, so if we follow his command, he will surely provide for us.

Observing the Sabbath is part of being in the image of God. He stopped work, and so must we. The commandments in Exodus 20:8–11 and Deuteronomy 5:12–15 emphasize that the whole household, including servants and animals, *Ashraf* and *Atraf*, should rest. This is a communal commandment because we are all together made in his image.

The Sabbath also reminds us that we are creatures, needing to live according to the nature which God has given us. We need to take regular rests to keep healthy and to do our work in God's creation. Rabindranath Tagore wrote in his poem, "Rest":

> Rest is the part of work, closing
> Like the eyelid belongs to the eye

Practically speaking, which day should we observe as Sabbath? The Jews observe Saturday, the seventh day, but followers of Jesus the Messiah observe Sunday because Jesus the Messiah rose from death to life on the first day of the week. In Bangladesh, it is difficult to observe the Sabbath on Saturday or Sunday because Friday is our "day off." However, Genesis says only "the seventh day," and there were different ways of counting days in the ancient world, so we need not think that we have to observe the Sabbath on a particular day. Anyway, it is impossible for everyone to observe the same day at the same time, because the earth is rotating. In practice, followers of Jesus the Messiah around the world observe their Sabbaths on Friday, Saturday or Sunday, depending on their contexts.

As loyal Bangladeshi citizens, we need to follow the weekly pattern of Friday as holiday, but we can also remember our Lord's resurrection on Sunday.

Most importantly, we need to keep in mind that the Sabbath institution is not a restrictive law, but a gift from God. As Jesus the Messiah taught us, "The Sabbath was made for the man, not man for the Sabbath" (Mark 2:27). In sum, which day is not important, but we should take rest once a week.

So if we do not work on the Sabbath, what are we to do? Jesus the Messiah's teaching that it was created for the welfare of humans means that we can do good works on that day (Mark 3:4). But, above all, it is a day to worship God for his goodness and steadfast love (Ps 135:1–9).

God himself has shown us how to keep the Sabbath. Before the universe was created, the Spirit of God was there hovering over the chaos (Gen 1:2). For six days, God worked to bring order out of the chaos, and on the seventh day, he declared all his work "good!" and blessed it and made it holy. Today, we are living in a world stained by sin and the fall. We can never measure up to God's creative purity, but we can go about our work of bringing the light of God's order into our world's moral and spiritual *tohu wa bohu*. On the Sabbath, we can take time to contemplate God's holiness and to let him make us holy. We can join the creator in rejoicing over the perfection of his creation, we can meditate on how that creation reflects the perfection of its maker, we can look forward to the time when we and all creation will be renewed, and we can prepare ourselves to return to the *tohu wa bohu* of the world to serve him, not only as his *khalifa*, but as his image.

3

The Beginnings of Human Life and Sin – Genesis 2:4–4:26

The *Toledoth* of the Heavens and the Earth

In Genesis 1, we learned how the heavens and earth were created. What came out of the heavens and the earth? This first *toledoth* covers three very important chapters. Chapter 2 tells of the creation of human beings, male and female, and of a special place for them to live in. Chapter 3 tells of the first disobedience to God and of its terrible consequences. Chapter 4 tells of the two sons of Adam and Eve, of the murder of the younger brother, and of the descendants of the older brother.

The focus throughout is on the relationship between human beings and God, and this is emphasized by the introduction of God's personal covenant name, YHWH (Eng. LORD; Bn. *mabud*). It is frequently used together with the Genesis 1 word, Elohim, which we translate as God (Eng.) or *Allah* (Bn.), in the compound title, YHWH Elohim, "Lord God." This signals that the almighty Creator God of Genesis 1 is also the personal Covenant God who will be revealed as the *bud of theology* opens later in the Torah.

There are so many fascinating ideas in this *toledoth* that we will consider each chapter separately. However, there is an overall structure to the *toledoth*. On the one hand, it presents a continuous narrative which we will follow in the commentary – each part of the narrative is carefully crafted. On the other hand, there are repeated themes throughout and a chiasmic structure for the whole.

A. Creation of the first man (2:4–7)

B. Blessed life in Eden (2:8–14)

C. The man placed in Eden (2:15)

D. Prohibiting the tree of the knowledge of good and evil (2:16–17)

E. Man, animals, woman: naming and nakedness (2:18–25)

F. Snake, woman and man: temptation (3:1–5)

G. Disobedience and calling to account (3:6–13)

F'. Consequences for snake, woman and man (3:14–19)

E'. The woman and the man: naming and clothing (3:20–21)

D'. Barring from the tree of life (3:22)

C'. The man driven out of Eden (3:23–24)

B'. Violent life outside Eden (4:1–24)

A'. Birth of Seth (4:25–26)

We can see several things from this structure. First, at the centre of this account stands the story of the origin of human disobedience, which is often known as the fall. Second, this is not only about the broken relationship between humans and God, but also about the broken relationships within humanity and between humanity and the animal world. Third, we learn that not only humans have changed as a result of this disobedience – the whole world has changed – and we live in a different world because of the fall. It will be remarkable to compare the fallen world we read of in Genesis 4 (B') with the pristine world of the Eden garden in chapter 2 (B').

Finally, we see the themes here that continue throughout the whole narrative: creation, blessing, good and evil, life and death, men and women, animals and the exile from Eden. Themes found here will be repeated throughout the Genesis account; for example, the interest in the ground (*adamah*) and the earth (*erets*) appears in 2:4, 5, 6, 7, 9, 19, then in 3:17–19 and 4:2, 3, 10, 12, 14. The good relationship that humans have with the earth in chapter 2 will be starkly contrasted with the cursing of the ground in chapter 4. A less obvious example is the metals in the ground: 2:12 describes the precious jewels and metals in Eden, and 4:22 mentions the beginnings of metalwork and of the making of tools – perhaps to till the ground, but perhaps weapons for killing people. Even such details remind us of the potential for evil as well as for good as human beings use God's creation.

Genesis 2:4–25 The Garden, the Humans and the Animals:

Our land of Bangladesh is beautiful, fertile and well-watered, but can it produce enough rice, fruit and vegetables to feed everyone in our huge population? How far can agricultural developments take us and how much do human beings around the world need to work together to feed all their peoples? Genesis 2:4–25 introduces us to a newly created fertile land. Adam had been given this land that would produce fruit and crops by cultivation and he was given a perfect partner to help him. No wonder the garden of Eden has caught the imagination of people through the centuries! No wonder people are always asking whether or not we can get back to that garden state!

> *These are the generations*
> *of the heavens and the earth when they were created,*
> *in the day that the Lord God made the earth and the heavens. (2:4)*

Scholars ask whether this introduces a second and different account of creation, or whether it introduces a new part of a single account. We have already noted that the term *toledoth* means that one generation proceeds from a previous generation. Therefore, it can be said that Genesis 2 is a continuation of chapter 1. Genesis 1 gives a cosmic perspective telling the readers about the creation of the heaven and the earth and the general place of humans in the universe. Genesis 2 then focuses on the humans in their environment and on their relationship with God, with the soil, with animals and with each other. The second description of creation (Gen 2:4–25) does not say anything contrary to the first description (Gen 1:1–2:3): rather, the two narratives are complementary.

The Worlds Behind and in Front of the Text

Various cultures and nations have had their own stories of the origins of creation. These stories describe the nature of human beings and how they depend on the world and how the world depends on them. In today's world, we have physiology, psychology, religious studies and sociology to study the physical, mental, spiritual and communal dimensions of humanity; Genesis 2 will introduce all these dimensions in its own way. We also have the physical, agricultural and environmental sciences to study how humans relate to the natural world; likewise, Genesis 2 will begin to address this question.

As in Genesis 1, the method of Genesis 2 is to use ideas which were common in the ancient world, but to use them in very different ways. By this we can see evidence of God's inspiration of the scripture writers. As Genesis 1 and 2 challenged some of the ideas of the ancient world, so too some of our own ideas will be challenged as we read this section.

The Babylonian *Atrahasis Epic* has the gods digging irrigation canals, then the humans created to work for them. Genesis has the rivers around the garden of Eden given by God alone, but the humans will have the work of tilling the ground. Today, how do we see the relationship between what God has given us and our own human responsibilities? The *Atrahasis Epic* has seven couples made from clay and the blood of a god. Genesis has just one couple enlivened by the breath or spirit of God, with no concept of God having physical blood which can be shed. Today, do we recognize both our spiritual and our physical natures, and the implications for our relationship with each other and with the One True God?

The creation of humans from dust enlivened by God's breath also has parallels in the Egyptian creation myth, where the ram-headed fertility god, Khnum, creates humans and animals on his potter's wheel using clay from the river Nile. His consort, Heket, the frog-headed goddess of child birth and fertility, then gives the breath of life to the creatures.[1] As we have seen again and again, Genesis 2's telling of creation rejects such polytheistic ideas. The Lord God needs no partner in his creation work!

The New Testament

The New Testament alludes to Genesis 2:4–25 to teach believers what God created them to be like, and to picture what the new creation will be like after final judgement has removed all sin. It also uses the warning that sin leads to death (Jas 1:15; cf. Gen 2:17). As a Bangladeshi proverb says, "Sin will not forgive its father."

The view of marriage and gender in Genesis 2 underlies the Bible's dealing with male-female relationships. Jesus the Messiah quotes Genesis 2:24 to teach about the nature and permanence of marriage as God intended (Matt 19:5; Mark 10:7), and the Apostle Paul uses it to warn against sexual union outside marriage (1 Cor 6:16). His teachings on husband-wife relationships (Eph 5:21–33) and on men and women in church (1 Cor 11:3–15) are also based on Genesis 2.

---

1. For information regarding Khnum and Heket, see Armour, *Gods and Myths of Ancient Egypt*, 182, and Seawright, "Khnum, Potter God," online.

Marriage is also used in the Bible as a picture of the relationship between God and believers. The *Bani Isra'il* are described as God's bride (Jer 2:2), but sadly, she is an unfaithful wife (e.g. Jer 2:32; Hos 1:2; Ezek 16; 23). The triumphant vision of the new creation in Revelation 21 has the believing community as the bride of Jesus the Messiah, prepared by him for everlasting fellowship (Rev 21:2, 9). The bride is pictured as a city – the new Jerusalem – which is described in terms which remind us of the Eden garden. There are rare jewels (Rev 21:11, 19–21), the light of God himself (21:22–23), and abundant waters (22:1). The best news is that people will again see the face of God (Rev 22:4), and that this is permanent. The tree of life is no longer inaccessible, but is freely available for all peoples (Rev 22:2). This is the final blessing for which Genesis 1–11 provides the hope.

The Qur'an

The Qur'an has plenty to tell us about Adam and his wife, the first human beings, and, as we are coming to expect, there are both similarities and differences with Genesis. The story is referred to in numerous places, the main accounts being in Sūras *al-Baqara* 2 and *al-A'rāf* 7. In each case, a different aspect of the story is used to develop the Qur'an's argument, and interpreters have to work to put all the references together if they want to produce a continuous narrative.

As to the creation of the man and the woman, we read only that God made them out of some kind of earth (it is described differently in different places) and breathed his spirit (*rūḥ*) into him (Sūras al-*Ḥijr* 15:29; *as-Sajda* 32:9), and that God made the couple from one being (*nafs*) (*an-Nisā'* 4:1). There is no mention of the wife's name, and often we only know that she is active because the verbs are in the dual form (Arabic has not only singular and plural, but also dual, which means that two are involved in an action). However, Islamic tradition, both *tafsīr* and *hadith*, supplies details which are similar to the Genesis account, including the idea that the woman (named *Hawwa*) was made from the man's rib.

As we saw in our commentary on Genesis 1:26–7, the Qur'an describes Adam as a *khalīfa* in the Earth; that is, the representative or vice-regent of God (Sūra *al-Baqara* 2:30). The story in Sūra *al-Baqara* (see page 45) indicates Adam's superior status through the story of God asking the angels to bow to him. When they refused, God taught Adam some names, and this superior knowledge persuaded them to bow. This incident is linked with the rebellion of Satan (*Iblis* or *Shayṭān*). Satan refuses to bow, asserting his superiority over humans, and this is seen as the point at which Satan falls, and as the beginning of an enmity with human beings which will last until the final judgement. This enmity is, in its turn, the cause of the first temptation, as God puts the man and his wife into the garden of Eden and forbids them to touch one tree, and Satan persuades them to disobey. God then reminds them of the ban on the tree, and they repent and are forgiven. The story ends with God sending all three – Adam, Eve and Satan, down to earth, where Adam and Eve and their descendants will receive guidance which they should follow, and Satan is their sworn enemy who will try to stop them from following the guidance.

There are obvious similarities and differences between this and Genesis, and we will explore their significance in the appropriate places in the commentary. We will also consider the various interpretative questions and additional details from the other sūras as we go along.

Other material appears in the Qur'an and Islamic tradition which cannot be found in the Bible. Tradition gives Adam the title *Safiy Allāh*, "chosen of God." It is believed that he built a place of worship on the site where Abraham would later build the Ka'ba (Sūra *al-Baqara* 2:125–127); the black stone is said to date from that time. Although the Qur'an does not call him a prophet (*nabī*) or messenger (*rasūl*), commentators since at-Ṭabarī have considered him the first prophet, and there is a tradition that he received ten *ṣuḥuf* or pages of scripture. Thus, although the qur'anic Adam is the first human being, he is also, as a prophet, in a different class than other human beings. So he does not necessarily symbolize all of humanity in the way that the biblical Adam does. Nevertheless, the comparison between the biblical and qur'anic Adam stories indicates some of the deep differences between biblical and qur'anic views of human nature as well as the common ground.

The World of the Text
Structure and Genre

Genesis 2:4–25 spans the first five elements of the chiasm of this *toledoth*:

> A Creation of the first human (2:4–7)
> > B The beauty and blessing of Eden (2:8–14)
> > > C The man placed in Eden (2:15)
> > > > D Prohibiting the tree of the knowledge of good and evil (2:16–17)
> > > > > E Man, animals and woman: naming and nakedness (2:18–25)

We note that elements A–D twice describes waters, the placement of human beings on the earth, and the tree of the knowledge of good and evil. This is one of the many narrative patterns which shows how carefully the author structured his work:[2]

    P. (2:4b–6) A mist waters the ground

        Q. (2:7–8) God placed the man in Eden

            R (2:9) The tree of the knowledge of good and evil

    P'. (2:10–14) Rivers water the Garden

        Q'. (2:15) God settled the man in Eden

            R'. (2:16–17) The tree of the knowledge of good and evil

The genre is mainly prose narrative. It is divided into a number of short sections which flow together into a continuous story, which will be continued into chapters 3 and 4.

COMMENTARY

A. Genesis 2:4–7 The Creation of the First Human

> *These are the generations*
> *of the heavens and the earth*
> *when they were created,*
> *in the day that the LORD God made*
> *the earth and the heavens.*
>
> *When no bush of the field was yet in the land and no small plant of the field had yet sprung up – for the LORD God had not caused it to rain on the land, and there was no man to work the ground, and a mist was going up from the land and was watering the whole face of the ground – then the LORD God formed the man of dust from the ground and breathed into his nostrils the breath of life, and the man became a living creature.*

---

2. For further discussion of narrative patterns in Gen 2–4, see Wenham, *Genesis 1–15* on these chapters and *Rethinking Genesis 1–11*, 18–34.

Genesis 2:4 is a short poem, structured as a chiasm.

> **A.** the heavens
>> **B.** and the earth
>>> **C.** when they were created
>>> **C'.** on the day the Lord God made
>> **B'.** the earth
> **A'.** and the heavens[3]

This is the first occurrence of Genesis's eleven *toledoths*[4] – the word translated as "generations." As we have said, this word begins a new section. It reminds us of what has been in the previous section, and it tells us what comes out of it. The poem points back to the creation of the heavens and the earth, and emphasizes that it was the Lord God who made them. This is not a genealogy of how a male and a female deity gave birth to the world. It is an account of the One God creating by His word. Genesis 2:4 is also the first use of the term Lord God, YHWH Elohim (see page 91 for the significance of this).

Genesis 2:5–6 describes an early environment, that is, the pre-cultivation stage of the earth. Two things are needed for the earth to be fruitful: water and human beings. In verse 6, God provides the water. At this first stage, there was no rain, but the mist from the earth wet the land. Perhaps it was like the winter season in Bangladesh, when a deep mist covers everything at or near the surface of the earth and blankets the ground with moisture. We have read that, on the third day, God created the green plants (Gen 1:11–12). Here, the narrator tells of plants which require human cultivation. We note a remarkable partnership: the earth and all that is on it depends on the provision which only the Creator can supply, but it also depends on humans to play their role.

God created the human in two steps. First, he formed (Heb. verb *yatsar*) the man (*ha-adam*) from the dust of the ground (*adamah*). *Yatsar* is the word used for a potter moulding clay. Second, God breathed life into his body so that Adam became a living being (*nefesh chayyah*), a key phrase used many times throughout Genesis 1–11. A similar picture is used in 1 Corinthians 15:45–52 when it describes Jesus the Messiah as the second Adam who became not only a living being but a life-giving Spirit.

Verse 7 has several significant words. *Nefesh*, translated "creature," is traditionally translated "soul." However, *nefesh* usually refers to the life of a

---

3. Greenwood, *Scripture*, 111.
4. Genesis 2:4; 5:1; 6:9; 10:1; 11:10, 27; 25:12, 19; 36:1, 9; 37:2.

person or to the person himself. The word translated "man" is *adam*: it does not mean "male man" but "human being," although in Genesis it is also used as the proper name of the first human being, who happens to be male. The word *adam* is related to the word *adamah*, the "ground" from which he was made.

Although the human body is made from the same elements as the ground (this is literally true: most of the chemical elements in the ground can be found in the human body), the life which makes us human comes from God. In Genesis 1 we read that the difference between humans and animals is that only humankind was created in the image and likeness of God (1:26). Here in Genesis 2, the uniqueness of humanity is described in terms of God's breath. Elsewhere, the image of breath is used to show that we continually and uniquely depend on God for our lives (Job 27:3). If God takes the breath away from a person (or an animal), they die (Ps 104:29–30).

BODY AND SOUL

One way of thinking about the two-stage creation of human beings is to say that God made the body first as the dwelling place for the soul. Some distinguish further, between "soul" and "spirit." Some have considered that the "soul" or the "spirit" is good and the "body" is either bad or does not matter. Others are more interested in caring for the body than for the soul. From Genesis 2:7, we cannot say that the body is unclean and the soul or spirit is clean, and it is not even easy to separate the soul from the body. The two together make the living being. However, we read elsewhere in the Bible that the human body is temporary (although we will have new bodies at the resurrection) and that what we might call "the soul" will continue after the physical body dies. The Apostle Paul describes this by saying that the body is like a "tent" in which "the real we" lives (2 Cor 5:1).

The Hebrew *nefesh* is translated *psuche* in Greek and *nafs* in Arabic. There is much discussion of the *nafs* in Islamic literature, not least because the Qur'an seems to speak of three different kinds of human *nafs* (*Yūsuf* 12:3; *Ghāfir* 40:1–2; *al-Fajr* 89:22–23). We will explore this further in our comments on Genesis 4.

Sufis often quote Hazrat Ali, the last of the rightly guided caliphs of Islam, who says, "*Man a'rafa, nafsahu, faqad a'rafa Rabbahu*" (Whoever know his *nafs*, knows his Lord)! They liken the *nafs* in the body to a bird captive in a cage. The great eleventh-century Sufi Imam al-Ghazali wrote a famous poem which was found beneath his head after he died.

> *I am a bird, this body my cage*
> *But I have flown leaving it as my memoir.*

A hadith also compares the *nafs* to a bird. When asked about the qur'anic verse "the Martyrs are alive with their Lord" (Sūra Āl 'Imrān 3:169), the Isalmic Prophet Muhammad explained, "The souls of the martyrs live in the bodies of green birds who have their nests in chandeliers hung from the throne of the Almighty. They eat the fruits of Paradise from wherever they like and then nestle in these chandeliers" (*Ṣaḥīḥ Muslim*, 1887).

The Baul sect in Bangladesh takes the idea in a different direction, thinking that the divine beloved (god) can be found housed in the human body. The body, they say, is a microcosm of the universe, mystically containing the whole universe. At death, the soul leaves the body and becomes like a bird. The prominent Baul poet, Lalon Shah (1774–1890 AD), symbolized his soul as an "unknown bird" and wanted to keep it forever in the cage of his body and thus become immortal.

> *"Khachar vitor Achin pakhi komne ase jai"?*
> *Ami Dorte Parle Mono Beri Ditam Pakhir Pai?"*
>
> *(The unknown bird in the cage – how does it fly in and out?*
> *Catch it, I would, if I could – and put my mind's chain*
> *on its feet.)*

Genesis does not portray the soul as imprisoned in a vile body; instead, God created the body and it is therefore good. In contrast to the Greek Gnosticism of his time, the Apostle Paul speaks about the resurrection of the body and not of the escape of the soul from the body, and he even calls our bodies temples, where God lives by his Spirit (1 Cor 6:19–20).

The Qur'an and Islamic tradition agree that God made Adam from the ground and then breathed life into him. However, the idea that we are made "in the image of God" is not found, except in Sufi thinking.[5]

---

5. See commentary on Genesis 1:26–27 above.

B. Genesis 2:8–14 The Beauty and Blessing of Eden

> And the LORD God planted a garden in Eden, in the east, and there he put the man whom he had formed. And out of the ground the LORD God made to spring up every tree that is pleasant to the sight and good for food. The tree of life was in the midst of the garden, and the tree of the knowledge of good and evil. (2:8–9)

God was the first gardener! We can imagine him as a heavenly Father, planting a garden – not merely by his divine command but with much care and attention – and then lovingly placing his child (cf. Luke 3:38) Adam there!

"Eden" is clearly a locality, made of dust on the dusty earth which God has just created. The word *eden* means "plain" or "steppe" in Assyrian, so may describe a flat land. In Hebrew, it means "delight" or "pleasure," so the name reminds us how beautiful it was. "In Eden, in the east," could mean that Eden was in the east of the region, or that the garden was in the easterly part of Eden. The garden seems to have had plenty of water, unlike the ancient land of Canaan, where people had to laboriously dig wells and haul water for themselves and their animals.

The Arabic word for garden is *jannat*, and the Bangla word is *began*, both of which resemble the Hebrew word used in these verses: *gan*. In the ancient Greek translation, the Septuagint, Eden is called *paradise*. This word is translated "paradise" in English translations of the New Testament (Luke 23:43; 2 Cor 12:4). The Bangla *Kitabul Muqaddas* has *paramdesh*, "the place of blessings." The word originates from the ancient Persian, *ferdous*, which denotes a royal park or an enclosed garden, which was often divided into four parts.

The garden was full of beautiful plants and there was plenty to eat. At the centre, there were two special trees. As yet, we know nothing but their names: later, we will find that the tree of life signifies life without death[6] (Gen 3:22; cf. Rev 2:7; 22:2, 14), and that the tree of the knowledge of good and evil signifies something which leads to death (vv. 3:3, 17). However, the knowledge of evil is not the same as evil. There was a possibility of evil; but evil was not yet present in the Eden garden. On the contrary, these trees confirm the excellence of God's original creation: they are "good" (cf. Gen 1:4, 10, 12, 18, 21, 25, 31).

The Qur'an, too, tells of God putting the first human beings in a garden (Sūras al-Baqara 2:35; al-A'rāf 7:19; Ṭā Hā 20:117). Here, the garden is called simply *al-janna* – literally, "the garden." Only one tree is specifically named in

---

6. The tree of life appears in many other ancient traditions.

the garden, the tree of immortality, *shajarat al-khuld* (*Ṭā Hā* 20:120), which God forbade to Adam and his wife. There is no mention of the tree of good and evil in the Qur'an.

The phrase *jannat 'adan* appears only once in the Qur'an, in Sūra *at-Tawba* 9:72, where it describes a beautiful, well-watered place promised to believing men and women. According to al-Bayḍāwī, *'adan* means "fixed abode." There are several other terms for the heavenly garden in the Qur'an, and some scholars say that they describe different levels of heaven rather than being different descriptions of the same place. In this scheme, *jannat 'adan* is in the fourth heaven. Sūra *al-Furqān* 25:15 mentions *jannat al-khulidīn*, "the eternal garden," promised to the *muttaqīn* (righteous). Sūra *al-An'ām* 6:127 has *dār as-salām*, a "home of peace," in the presence of *rabbihīm* (their Lord), the idea of "home" being repeated in Sūra *as-Sajda* 32:19, where the righteous will live in *jannat al-māwā*, "the garden of refuge." Sūra *al-Kahf* 18:107 mentions *jannat al-firdūs*, "the garden of paradise." Who would not long to enter such a garden?

The location of Eden is a much-debated question in Bangladesh. We want to know about Paradise, because we want to go there, and we want to know how to get there. Genesis makes it clear that Eden was on earth, but the Qur'an does not mention its location, and qur'anic commentators do not even agree on whether it was on earth or in heaven. Most would agree with Maulana Faridpuri that it was outside the earth, and that the humans were sent down from it to the earth (Sūra *al-Baqara* 2:36).[7] Another argument is that there will be no heat from the sun there (*Ṭā Hā* 20:118–19), and we know how much humans suffer under the heat of the sun on this earth. In contrast, Maulana Akram Khan says that the name *paradise* implies that the garden was on earth.[8] He adds that Adam was appointed to be *khalīfa* for this earth, and that the Arabic word translated "go down" (*habaṭa*) can also mean "to go, to be expelled, to go from one place to another" as well as going down from heaven to earth. The Qur'an speaks of *ihbiṭu miṣrān* – "going down to Egypt" (Sūra *al-Baqara* 2:61) – but this does not mean that Egypt was in heaven.

> A river flowed out of Eden to water the garden, and there it divided and became four rivers. The name of the first is the Pishon. It is the one that flowed around the whole land of Havilah, where there is gold. And the gold of that land is good; bdellium and onyx stone are there. The name of the second river is the Gihon. It is the one

---

7. See, for example, *Tafsirul Baizabi* on this verse.
8. Khan, *Qur'an Sharif*, vol. 1, 85; also http://bn.wikisource.org/wiki/, pdf/102.

that flowed around the whole land of Cush. And the name of the third river is the Tigris, which flows east of Assyria. And the fourth river is the Euphrates. (2:10–14)

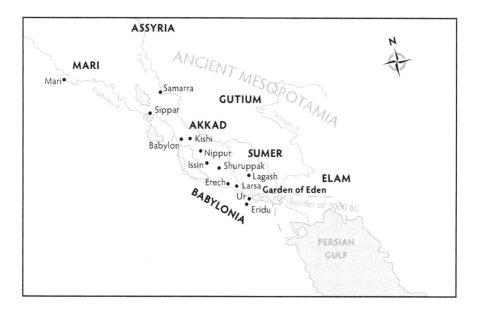

Figure 3 Supposed Location of the Garden of Eden

The beautiful garden is rich with precious stones and metals, and it is also well supplied with water. Here, the narrator first uses the term "river" (Heb. *nahar*). The ground water from the earth made four rivers! This brings to mind the four quarters of the ancient Persian walled gardens, which were watered by four branches from a central water source; but the geographical details imply that this was a real, and not a mythical, place.

The rivers should help in locating the Eden garden, but, although the Tigris and the Euphrates are well known, the names Pishon and Gihon complicate matters. Pishon is not mentioned elsewhere in the Old Testament. Havilah, the place which it supplies with water, means "sand region." Elsewhere in the Bible, Havilah is a part of Southeastern Arabia (Gen 10:7, 29; 25:18; 1 Sam 15:7; 1 Chr 1:9, 23), so the Pishon could have been in Arabia. But some have thought it was in India – Josephus thought that it was the Ganges. Gihon was a spring in Jerusalem (1 Kgs 1:44; 2 Chr 32:30), but the Jews did not occupy Jerusalem until the time of David, so it is unlikely to be the river of Genesis 2. Cush in the Old Testament usually refers to Ethiopia (e.g. Isa 20:3; Jer 46:9), but Genesis 10:8 makes Cush the father of Nimrod, who built Nineveh. So the Gihon could be the Nile, but it could also have been in Assyria.

The Pishon and Gihon may have disappeared, perhaps becoming the dry riverbeds which can be identified in satellite pictures, or perhaps disappearing during geological disturbances. We can see similar changes in the rivers of Bangladesh. At one time, Bangladesh was a country of more than seven hundred rivers. However, most of the rivers are no more, largely due to the effects of climate change caused by humans, unplanned dam building, and silt deposits in riverbeds. Following a 7.5 magnitude earthquake on AD 2 April 1762, the tectonic uplift of the *Modhupur* tract in Bangladesh caused the *Brahmaputra*, a major river of Central and South Asia, to change its course.

All we can say is that Genesis locates Eden somewhere in Mesopotamia, but its boundaries are not clear. It could have been limited to an area near the Persian Gulf, or it could have stretched from the Ganges to the Nile. It is interesting here to note that both the Ganges and the Nile have been considered sacred, and thousands of Hindus try to wash off their sins in the Ganges even today. Once again, Genesis refutes such worship: rivers, like everything else, are God's creation. It is not a particular source of water which can give us healing and forgiveness – only the God who made both us and the rivers can do that (see 2 Kgs 5:9–15; John 5:1–5; 9:1–12; Acts 22:16; Eph 5:26).

C. Genesis 2:15 The Human Placed in Eden

The LORD God took the man and put him in the garden of Eden to work it and keep it.

The scene is set: the earth is watered, the human being is made, the garden is prepared, and we have been given notice of the two trees which will be important in the coming story. Now we return to the event of verse 8, and focus on the human being who has been placed in this perfect environment. God created his spiritual child to live in blessed fellowship with God and to enjoy the manifold riches of the garden! But he was not created to sit idly and munch and laugh and play. The responsibility revealed in verse 5 is repeated and explained in verse 15. Jewish tradition notes that the *adam* was given work even before he was given food. The fruits of the garden did not fall from the tree into his mouth. He ate according to his work. Genesis breaks the false idea that work is a curse and God's punishment because of sin (cf. 3:16–19) – there was work before the fall. In contrast, the Quran has no mention of work in its garden, and that is one reason for thinking that it is not on the earth.

Verse 15 expands on the blessings of dominion and food of 1:28–31, and underlines the environmental responsibilities implied. Adam's two obligations are, in Hebrew, 'abad and shamar. The literal meaning of 'abad is "to work" or "to serve" – it has the same root as "servant" or "slave" (Ar. 'abd). Many Muslims have names beginning 'abd al-, "servant/slave of the . . .," and the second part of the name is a name of God. So, for example, 'Abd ar-Raḥmān is the servant/slave of the Merciful. Here, the human being is the servant of the earth. Shamar is the verb translated "keep" in the many biblical injunctions to keep God's commandments. Its basic meaning is "to guard" or "to protect." What might be the danger in such a perfect garden, we wonder? Is this about pruning and weeding the plants, or perhaps about making sure that the animals don't eat all the produce? We are not told, but it is clear that there is a responsibility to look after the earth, and that Adam has to keep alert and watch for anything that might go wrong.

These obligations may also be symbolic. The Torah tells us in three places that these two works are related to the work of the Levites in the tabernacle (Num 3:7–8; 8:26; 18:5–6). The Levites are to "serve" and "guard" the high priest and other priests and Levites, and to "guard" everything in the tabernacle and all the people who come to the tabernacle. This is not only about physical safety, but also about making sure that the holiness laws are properly kept. In the tabernacle, God is giving people a new opportunity to succeed where Adam failed – to serve and to guard in a beautiful place where they meet with God. Coming back to Genesis 2, we realise that it is because the adam is first the servant of God that he is also the servant of the earth; and, to protect the earth, he must keep God's commandments. When he serves anyone other than God, and when he breaks a commandment, he is not the only one who suffers; he loses the Eden garden, and the whole earth suffers.

D. Genesis 2:16–17 The Tree of the Knowledge of Good and Evil

> The Lord God took the man and put him in the garden of Eden to work it and keep it. And the Lord God commanded the man, saying, "You may surely eat of every tree of the garden, but of the tree of the knowledge of good and evil you shall not eat, for in the day that you eat of it you shall surely die."

This is God's first command to the adam. But what type of command is this? First, God tells him to eat to his heart's content; but then we find that this freedom comes with a condition, and to disobey it leads to death. It reminds us of when Jesus the Messiah said that God's commandment is eternal life, implying that rejection of it means death (John 12:50).

Only one tree is forbidden: the tree of the knowledge of good and evil. The Qur'an has a similar condition, but it is the tree of eternity or of everlasting life, *shajarat ul-khuld* (Sūras *al-A'rāf* 7:20; *Ṭā Hā* 20:120) which is forbidden, and the penalty for disobedience is not death. Rather, they will become *ẓālimūn*, unjust, or evil-doers (Sūra *al-A'rāf* 7:19).

The Qur'an sees death as inevitable and as part of God's original plan (Sūras *Āl 'Imrān* 3:185; *al-Anbiyā'* 21:35; *al-'Ankabūt* 29:57–58). It does not link sin and death as Genesis does, but tells readers that God created death and life as a test (Sūras *al-Mulk* 67:2). As we shall see, most Islamic interpretations of the Qur'an do not accept that Adam's disobedience had any drastic effects on the world or on future generations. In Genesis, disobedience will have terrible consequences. Genesis will gradually reveal that separation from God means death. This will be shown first as spiritual death, when Adam and Eve are exiled from the garden and barred from the tree of life. Physical death will come later.

Even though this prohibition of the tree of life may appear to be a lack of the heavenly Father's love, it is actually a mark of that love. Soon we will see how he sets in course his plan for the new creation, when "the one who conquers" will "eat of the tree of life" (Rev 2:7; 22:2, 14). God wants life for his children. No parent wants their children to die. The heaviest burden one can carry in this world is the dead body of one's child! So as we warn our children of danger, God warned his child not to eat. There is always danger alongside good things. For instance, electricity and nuclear power are good for the growth of civilization, but their wrong use is fatal. If Adam and Eve had stayed conscious of their heavenly Father's love, then surely they would have obeyed him!

E. Genesis 2:18–25 The Man, the Woman and the Animals: Naming and Nakedness

The text now moves on to what seems to be a new subject. We have read about the abundant provision and the solemn warning, but we do not immediately find out anything more about the trees. First, God will provide the man with something which he needs just as much as he needs food.

> Then the Lord God said, "It is not good that the man should be alone; I will make him a helper fit for him." Now out of the ground the Lord God had formed every beast of the field and every bird of the heavens and brought them to the man to see what he would call them. And whatever the man

> *called every living creature, that was its name. The man gave names to all*
> *livestock and to the birds of the heavens and to every beast of the field. But*
> *for Adam there was not found a helper fit for him. (2:18–20)*

The blessing of fruitful multiplication in Genesis 1:28 is about to be fulfilled; but first we need a couple and a heterosexual marriage. Genesis 1 repeats that the creation was good, and even *very* good. In striking contrast, God here states that it is "not good" to live alone. This is Genesis's second glimpse into God's thoughts: the heavenly Father's intention is that humankind should live in community (Ar. *ummah*). The loving Father sees that his child needs a helper, and that creation needs women!

Suitable helper (Heb. *'ezer neged*) suggests a person who is different from the *adam* but who can work in partnership with him. As in 1:27, there is no suggestion of inferior status: on the contrary, the word *'ezer* is elsewhere used for God himself as the helper of his people (e.g. Ps 121:2). In the search for this helper, God showed the *adam* the animals and birds. Like the man, the living beings are moulded (Heb. *yatsar*) from the dust (Heb. *adamah*; v. 7), but the Lord is not said to breathe into them the breath of life. There is a certain likeness between humans and animals, but no animal can be the partner which Adam needs. Today, people find some companionship with pets, but they can never replace human beings in our lives. Genesis portrays this vividly – as the animals are brought to Adam and he is given the job of naming them, not one is found who will be the suitable helper.

This account is not merely making a negative point and therefore preparing the way for the creation of the woman. The naming of the animals is highly significant in itself. In the Bible, as in many parts of the world today, naming indicates authority. In a Bangladeshi Muslim family, only a senior person such as a parent or a grandparent can arrange the *'aqiqa*[9] and invite people to the naming of a child. So the naming here is the *adam*'s first act of ruling the animals. It is also the first record of humans producing language. The insight and wisdom necessary for naming the animals are part of what it means to be made in the "image of God." We recall that, in chapter 1, God named parts of his creation (1:5, 8, 10), but he did not name the stars, the plants or the animals. That was the human beings' part in God's ordering of his world!

Jewish and Christian interpreters have given a lot of attention to the naming of the animals, seeing in it a key to understanding human dignity,

---

9. *'Aqiqa* is the ceremony sacrificing an animal and naming a child, usually seven days after the child's birth.

and even as implying that the *adam* had not only God-given abilities but also a God-like nature. By the time of the Islamic Prophet Muhammad, Adam was being described in Christian writings as a huge and glorious being, pointing to the greater glory of Jesus the Messiah, the "second Adam."[10] In contrast, the Qur'an states that God taught Adam the names (*al-Baqara* 2:33). It is Adam's knowledge of the names which convinces the angels that they should prostrate to him, and commentators agree that the knowledge of the names equips Adam for his job as *khalīfa*.

Verse 20 is the first occurrence of "Adam" without the definite article. We are moving from "the *adam*" as humanity in general to the proper name of Adam, the first male human.

> So the Lord God caused a deep sleep to fall upon the man, and while he slept took one of his ribs and closed up its place with flesh. And the rib that the Lord God had taken from the man he made into a woman and brought her to the man. Then the man said,
>
> "This at last is bone of my bones
>   and flesh of my flesh;
> she shall be called Woman,
>   because she was taken out of Man." (2:21–23)

To make a suitable partner for Adam, God put him into a deep sleep (Heb. *tardemah*) or, perhaps, a trance. (The same word will be used of Abraham in Genesis 15:12.) Next, he took parts from the man's side, or rib, not from the dust, from which God created both the man and animals. So the partner was actually made from part of Adam. There is a long tradition of seeing this as an important indication of the equality and mutuality of man and woman.[11] It is often said that since Eve was made from Adam's side rather than from his toe or his head, the man does not have dominion over the woman, nor she over him.

The Qur'an does not give details of the woman's creation, saying only, "Your Lord created you from a single person (*nafs*), and created from her (*nafs* is feminine) her mate" (*an-Nisā'* 4:1). As current feminist writers insist, there is no indication of whether the woman was created from the man or the man was created from the woman, so this verse can be read as teaching male/female

---

10. See, for example, the Syriac *Cave of Treasures*.

11. There is also a long tradition of the use of this text to prove the opposite. See "What About Us?" on page 115.

equality.[12] However, Islamic tradition, including many commentaries, usually follows the idea that Eve was made from Adam's rib, and draws some important conclusions from this. In the hadith, the Islamic Prophet Muhammad says: "Treat women nicely, because woman was created from a rib." A longer version indicates that this has to do with the marriage relationship:

> A woman is like a rib. The woman is created from a rib, a curved rib. If you try to straighten it, it will break; its break is divorce. (Muslim, Book 8, Hadith 3467, cf. Bukhārī Vol. 4, Book 55, Hadith 548; ; Tirmidhī, Vol. 2, Book 8, Hadith 118)

In Genesis 2, God presents Adam with the wonderful gift of a helper; this gift came out of Adam, for whom she had been made (v. 22). The heavenly Father presents a bride to his spiritual son, and thus institutes the marriage system for humanity.

When Adam awoke, he recognized her as what he had been looking for in a short poem, saying that at last, here was someone just like him: *bone of bones-my, flesh of flesh-my* (2:23). The last word of each part of the line ends with the suffix -*i* ("my") emphasising the likeness to Adam. The Hebrew for bone can signify not only a body part but also "essence" or "self" (e.g. Judg 9:2; 1 Chr 11:1). Thus equality between the two sexes is far more than biological – the woman is a complementary partner and a fellow-creature corresponding to Adam, because she, too, is made in the image of God.

Adam says "she shall be called" *woman* (Heb. *ishshah*), because she was "taken from a man (Heb. *ish*)." This is different from the naming of the animals. First, the text does not say that he is giving her a name, as the animals were given names in verses 19–20. There is a difference between her "being called" and "being named." Second, what he calls her is simply a feminine form of what he calls himself. The chiastic order of the seven words indicates that the man and the woman are like mirror images of each other: "This-one shall-be-called *ishshah* because out-of-*ish* was-taken this." Later, he will give her a name (Gen 3:20).

All this implies that, here in chapter 2, the man is recognising the woman as the same sort of being as himself. It is not until after the fall that he takes the authoritative position of giving her a name.

The Qur'an does not have anything like Adam's poem of recognition in verse 23, but it does make the point that male and female are of a similar nature, and that they are made to live together:

---

12. For example, Wadud, *Qur'an and Women*, 17–20.

It is who created you from a single person, and made his mate of like
nature, in order that he might dwell with her. (Sūra al-Aʻrāf 7:189)

The word translated "that he may dwell" (Ar. *yaskun*) implies resting or living
at peace. The Bible and the Qur'an agree that male and female are of the same
kind, equal in God's sight, and created to live together in his world.

> *Therefore a man shall leave his father and his mother and hold fast to his*
> *wife, and they shall become one flesh. (2:24)*

Genesis goes on to specify what living together looks like. This is the Bible's
basic definition of marriage. Of course, Adam and Eve had no parents, so this
verse is looking towards the future, but its situation here in the creation account
is very important. As Jesus the Messiah taught, it shows that marriage is not
a human institution which can be broken at will: it reflects our very nature as
God created us (Matt 19:4–6; Mark 10:5–9). There are plenty of laws about
marriage and sex elsewhere in the Torah, which indicate how these matters
should be regulated and what should happen when things go wrong. Here, we
have the description of what the marriage relationship should be.

Marriage is described in three parts: leaving parents, being joined together,
and becoming one flesh. Leaving does not necessarily mean literally leaving
the parental home, but it does mean that a new family unit takes priority
over the old family unit. The man's first duty is no longer to his parents, but
to his wife (cf. 1 Cor 7:2–5). Being joined together means clinging onto each
other or even being joined to each other. This union is permanent, and the
couple needs to hold on to each other (see also Prov 5:18). Becoming one flesh
includes sexual union, but the unity of husband and wife is more than that:
they are to be united in purpose and to belong together as the different parts
of a human body belong together. In the New Testament, this relationship is
vividly described in Ephesians 5:21–33.

It is grievous that our present-day society does not maintain this view of
marriage given to us in Genesis. Many definitions of marriage do not reflect
the following foundational principles:

First, marriage is monogamous. Although several important biblical figures,
such as Abraham, Jacob, David and Solomon, had more than one wife, this is
not the biblical norm. Indeed, the biblical stories of all these marriages show
how many problems are likely to arise in a polygamous household. The New
Testament specifies that church leaders must be monogamous (1 Tim 3:2). In
contrast, the Qur'an gives conditional permission for up to four wives, with
additional permission for sexual union with slave concubines (Sūra *an-Nisā'*

4:3–13; 2:187). In Bangladesh, some believers have more than one wife before they become believers. In those cases, we have agreed that the husband need not divorce the wives, but must continue to care for them; however, they should not be pastors or deacons (1 Tim 3:1, 12).

Second, marriage is heterosexual and between human beings. The Bible sees all sexual union outside heterosexual marriage as sinful (Lev 18:22; 20:13). Rape, prostitution, adultery (pre- or post-marital sexual union), and homosexual union are ruled out in the believer's life. Here, Islam agrees, although, as among Christians, there are people who are reconsidering the traditional understanding, especially with regard to homosexuality. There are important questions to be asked about how we deal with sexuality in our fallen world, but Genesis 2:24 enables us to distinguish between how we were created and what we may have become in this world-gone-wrong. No human court can change the way that God created us to be.

Third, marriage is permanent. Although the Bible recognizes that marriages may break down and has laws to deal with such situations (Deut 24:1), it does not see marriage as a contract which can be terminated but as a lifetime union. God hates divorce (Matt 19:8; Mal 2:16). Islamic tradition agrees, as the famous hadith states:

> The most detestable of all permissible deeds to God is divorce.
> (Sunan Abi Dawud, 2170–2171)

So Islamic law discourages divorce, but it does treat marriage as a contract which may be terminated by the husband,[13] and it specifies conditions for divorce. In Twelver Shi'a Islam, there is also an institution called *nikāḥ muta'a* (temporary marriage), whereby a marriage can be contracted for a set period of time, even as short as one day. Sunni Muslims consider this type of marriage adultery, a lustful act in religious cover, and it is therefore forbidden according to their jurisprudence.

Fourth, there is unity at every level. Husband and wife are not only to procreate, but to worship and work together in fulfilling their jobs in the world. In both the Old and the New Testaments, believers are told to marry other believers so that they can worship God together (see 1 Kgs 11:4; 2 Cor 6:14). But what happens when someone believes in Jesus the Messiah but their spouse does not? There are many people among the Muslim-heritage believers in Bangladesh whose spouse is not a believer. In this context, the Apostle Paul

---

13. In Islamic family law, it is also possible for the wife to ask a court to direct her husband to divorce her.

advises that if the unbelieving spouse agrees to continue the marriage, they should not divorce – the unbelieving spouse may come to faith through the believer's witness (1 Cor 7:12–15). The situation may be uncomfortable, and the unbelieving partner may not be a good helper, but we should lovingly bear that pain in marriage.

Fifth, the marriage relationship takes precedence over other family relationships. In the Indian subcontinent, men are often expected to give priority to their mothers over their wives, this sometimes being based on the famous hadith:

> A man came to the Prophet and asked, "O Messenger of God! Who among the people is the most worthy of my good companionship?" The Prophet said: "Your mother." The man said, "Then who?" The Prophet said: "Then your mother." The man further asked, "Then who?" The Prophet said: "Then your mother." The man asked ·again, "Then who?" The Prophet said: "Then your father." (Abi Dawud, Book 42, Hadith 5120; Bukhārī Vol. 8, Book 73, Hadith 2; Muslim, Book 32, Hadith 6180)

From Genesis 2:24, we can see this as a wrong priority after marriage, but we should note that the text cannot mean that parents should be completely forsaken, because the Bible commands honour toward parents (Exod 20:12; Lev 19:3), and believers are told to care for their parents in their old age (Mark 7:9–13; 1 Tim 5:3–8). In Bangladesh, it is common for a couple to live with the husband's family, but there are also matriarchal groups, in which the couple lives with the wife's family. Does the text teach that the latter is the correct model? In the light of the many patriarchal marriages that are found in Genesis, this seems unlikely. In some cases, it may be necessary to move out of the parental home in order to keep the focus on the marriage, but Genesis 2:24 is more about relationships than it is about living arrangements.

We should note that this description of marriage does not imply that everyone should marry. Jesus the Messiah never married, and he taught that some are given a gift of celibacy in order to better serve God (Matt 19:11–12). In contrast, the Islamic Prophet Muhammad condemned celibacy by saying, *Lā rahbānīya* ("not monasticism" or "not celibacy"), and Sūra *al-Ḥadīd* 57:27 is often read as implying that what the Christian monks invented which was not from God was celibacy. Most Muslims therefore see marriage as *farḍ* (obligatory) for those who are eligible and can afford to support a wife. However, some Sufi orders, perhaps under Christian influence, have practiced celibacy (see also page 79).

The first human couple lived in harmony with each other, with animals and with the Creator.

> *And the man and his wife were both naked and were not ashamed. (2:25)*

The word for naked in Hebrew is *'arom*. It is a word play on Genesis 3:1 where the serpent is described as *'arum* ("sly" or "crafty"). Adam and Eve were not crafty in Genesis 2. Before eating the fruit of good and evil, they knew only good, so they felt no shame before one another. Perhaps it was a childlike innocence and they were unaware of their sexuality or, more likely, they only knew the beauty and transparency of marriage as God intended it. This is the climax of the description of the first humans, and this is also the first thing that will change after the fall when, as the Qur'an agrees, nakedness will be seen as shameful (Gen 3:7; cf. Gen 9:22–23; Exod 20:26; Sūra Ṭā Hā 20:121).

Theological Reflection

The *bud of theology* begins to unfurl, showing us a God who not only provides for humanity and gives us a task, but also gives a warning and a prohibition. The human, who was made in the image of God, has choice. Unlike the other creatures, we have the potential to know, and even to produce, evil, as well as to appreciate the goodness of creation. Therefore, although God blesses, we can see the possibility of losing the blessing and inheriting death (v. 17) and shame (v. 25). This is fundamental to the biblical worldview – human beings are answerable to God. They can bring shame and death into his beautiful world, and he will judge them. Yet this chapter refers to God as YHWH Elohim, the Lord God, reminding us of the special relation with God which will appear more explicitly in the coming covenants (Gen 9; Gen 15; Exod 3). Although human beings are merely creatures, the covenant Lord wants to have fellowship with them.

This chapter has also been an important *grandmother of the sciences*. Adam's naming of the animals is an important piece of the DNA which led to early modern science. In the medieval period, European Christians believed that they could learn about God from the "book of his words" as well as from the "book of his works." That is, they could learn from nature as well as from the Bible. Because Adam named the animals, they were eager to collect information about animals, and beautifully illustrated "bestiaries" (books about animals) were shelved next to Bibles in monastery libraries. These books often gave the names of the animals in different languages. Why? Because people knew that many of the difficulties they had in agriculture and in relating to animals were due to the fall, and they wanted to return to Eden. They thought that if they could find the original names which Adam gave, it would return to them the dominion over creation which Adam had. They also collected and named plants, and arranged them in botanical gardens built on the pattern of the Persian "paradise" gardens, sometimes saying explicitly that they were "rebuilding Eden."[14]

At the time of the Reformation in Europe, as people began to read the Bible more literally, they realised that it was not possible to get back to the pre-fall state and language. The story of Babel (Gen 11:1–11), it was said, showed that the language had been lost. However, people who had been redeemed by Jesus the Messiah were, it was believed, being recreated in the image of God, so they could do the equivalent of naming the animals for themselves. That is, they could study the world and give it names – classifications, descriptions and explanations. Even the invention of observational instruments such as microscopes and telescopes was part of these Reformation ideas – it was thought that Adam had perfect vision and so microscopes and telescopes would help people to see what Adam saw. In such ways, the story of Adam's naming of the animals contributed to the beginnings of zoology, botany and physics.

The narrative of Adam and the names also contains one of the most significance differences between Genesis and the Qur'an. Did God teach Adam the names, as in the Qur'an, or did God give Adam the job of naming the animals, as in Genesis? Is knowledge something which humans need to be given, or is it something which they can find for themselves? We could follow this into the developments of science, philosophy and theology in Islam and in Christianity, but that would take us a long way from the Genesis text. Here, we note that this difference builds *the seedbed of the Scriptures*. We can see one answer as the soil which gives rise to the qur'anic idea of scripture, and the other as the soil which gives rise to the biblical idea of scripture. The qur'anic idea is that God sent an angel to teach the Islamic Prophet Muhammad the Qur'an, whereas the biblical idea is that God gave selected humans the job of producing scripture under his guidance.

The significant *seed ideas which will grow* as we read on include the beginnings of agriculture, of God-given law, and of the importance of human community. The latter focuses on the fundamental institution of marriage, which will become a key building block for all human societies. In Genesis 3, we will see how matters go wrong in all of these areas.

---

14. See Harrison, *Fall of Man*.

What About Us?

Genesis 2 shows us something of how God wanted the world to be and of our role in this world as "made in the image of God." In the previous "what about us?" section, we thought about our relationship with the created world and with all other human beings (ch. 2, pages 85-90). Here, we learn more about our relationship to God and about male-female relationships, especially in marriage.

Communion with God. Genesis 2 speaks of the first human being carefully formed and given life by the breath of the Lord God. This is the Almighty Creator who also wants covenant fellowship, creating his spiritual child, preparing a beautiful home, and placing him there. He speaks directly to the human, gives him a responsibility, and gives him a necessary warning. He then encourages him to use his talents, and finally presents him with an ideal partner. This is the sort of relationship with God for which we should long – we taste it through the Messiah, and we look forward to it in eternity.

The male-female relationship. In Genesis 1:26–27, male and female have equal status: together they were created in the image and likeness of God. In the new creation in Christ, there is also equality (Gal 3:28). The Bible refutes the concept that the women are *choron dasi*[15] of their husband or their gurus. They are equal with their gurus and their husbands, because all are created in the image of God.

But how does this relate to Genesis 2's account of the separate creation of the first woman from the side of the first man, and as his helper? There is a long history of people using this story to argue that women are inferior. They would disagree with our reading of Genesis 2:21–25. The man was made first, they say, so he is more important. The woman was made from the man, they say, so he is the original human being and she is just a derivative being. We say, "No. They were made together male and female, and Genesis 2 gives us details of that." She is his helper, they say, so she should do what he tells her to do. We say, "No. The 'helper' is not an inferior, but someone just like the man." He named her, they say, and that proves that he has authority over her. We say, "No. Here he recognized her – it was after the fall that he named her." In fact, we will see that all the ideas about women being inferior have their roots in the consequences of the fall, so it is not surprising that, in our fallen

---

15. *Choron dasi* denotes an "escort of the Baul," who serves her male counterpart Baul for achieving his divine fullness. It also denotes the devoted wife of a Muslim who believes according to hadith that there is heaven under her husband's feet.

world, people misinterpret Scripture in this way.[16] In our marriages, we expect the Holy Spirit to lead us towards the pre-fall joyful recognition of each other as equal partners.

The Qur'an gives no details of the separate creation of the man and the woman. It only says that one was made from the other – that could mean that the man was made from the woman or vice versa. Some Muslim writers therefore say that the Bible oppresses women, but the Qur'an gives them equal status. However, Islamic law does not give equal status to the woman in such areas as witness in the court, the law of inheritance, and divorce.[17] The daughter gets half the inheritance of a son. One female witness is not enough to prove a case: at least two are needed. According to *shari'a*, the right to divorce is primarily given to the husband not the wife. Why is this? One reason is that this qur'anic legislation was given in seventh-century Arabia, where the post-fall patterns of women's inequality were very strong, even to the point of people killing girl babies. The Qur'an forbade such terrible inequality (Sūra an-Naḥl 16:58–59), and improved the seventh-century situation, but we would want to say that that is not enough. We need to build our views of the value and status of humans on what God intended in creation: that is, the full equality which is described in Genesis 1 and 2 and is hinted at in the Qur'an's brief reports of the creation of man and woman. It is not the inequality which is implied by qur'anic legislation.[18]

It is very important that we distinguish between the "what we ought to be" of Genesis 2 and the "what we have become because of the fall" in Genesis 3–4. Believers in Jesus the Messiah remember that they are living in the world-after-the-fall, but that they are also being re-created in the image of Jesus the Messiah, who is the true image of God. Therefore, the perfect state of Genesis 2 is what we long for and are growing into, but we need to live with the facts that we are not yet in that perfect state and that the world around us sees the "fallen" state as normal.

---

16. See also Glaser and John, *Partners or Prisoners*, ch. 4.

17. The main qur'anic roots of these laws can be found in Sūras *al-Baqara* 2:226–37, 282; *an-Nisā'* 4:7–13; *aṭ-Ṭalāq* 65:1–7.

18. There is a substantial movement among Muslims today that interprets the legislative verses through the verses about equality in creation. See, for example, Ali, *Sexual Ethics and Islam*.

Genesis 3:1–24 The Fall of Humanity

God created the world perfect. There was good fellowship between the heavenly Father and humankind, his spiritual children. They lived in harmony with each other and with the animals, with plenty of food in a beautiful pollution-free environment. But the world we see today is not like that! Genesis 3 tells us why. It diagnoses our human problems, and it tells us that our sickness is fatal. The perfect situation was to come to a sudden end, not by God's command, but because humans ended it. The earth and everything in it would never be the same again.

God commissioned human beings to rule over the whole creation. Instead, they listened to one of the creatures – the serpent – and disobeyed God's command. It is attention-grabbing that the narrator does not use the term "sin" (Heb. *chattah*) until 4:7, and that the result of disobedience is described as "death." As we read on into chapter 5, we will find that the sinful condition infects offspring, and that all but one die. Here, in Genesis 3, we have another beginning: it is the beginning of rebellion against God, in what theologians have called "the fall."

The consequences of the fall are vividly described in verses 14–19. They help us to understand many of the problems in this world. Human abhorrence of snakes, women's pain in childbirth, male domination over women, the growth of weeds in crop fields, the production of grain with toil (Gen 3:17–19): all are the results of sin. But, in the midst of it all, we will see hopeful signs of God's grace to his disobedient children.

The Worlds Behind and in Front of the Text

The sin of Adam and Eve is an important basis for the Bible's theology of what has gone wrong with the world and how it can be put right. In the New Testament, the story of Genesis 3 is used to teach us that humans are "dead in sin" (Eph 2:1–9), which implies that we cannot save ourselves, and that we need a redeemer.[19] Jesus the Messiah is described as the second Adam, who took upon himself our death because we are "in Adam" – he gives resurrection life in himself to all who accept him (John 5:24–25).

---

19. Jewish and Christian traditions have various ways of describing what went wrong in Eden. For example, Jews would not call it a "fall," but would see Adam and Eve's sin as teaching about the "evil inclination" which strives inside all of us, resulting in the sad situation described in verses 14–19. See Patmore, Aitken, and Rosen-Zvi, eds., *Evil Inclination*.

The ancient world, like today's world, had rather different ideas about what has gone wrong with the world. Today, it is popular to blame politicians and colonial powers and the rich people for all the troubles of the poor. In the context of the ancient world, their stories gave very different reasons for the problems in the world. Problems were caused mostly by competition between different gods or by the human beings not doing the right rituals to satisfy the gods. Among Bangladeshi Muslims, many problems are seen as part of *kismet* (fate), or life simply under God's control. Other problems are caused by Satan or by jinn, or perhaps as God's punishment for human disobedience.

All these perceptions have in common the idea that human beings are struggling in a world of unseen powers. In Genesis 3, we see these in the snake and in the cherubim – the tempter of humankind and the servants of God who guard humankind. We need to know more of these symbols and how they relate to the Islamic worldview of angels, jinn and Satan.

Satan and the Serpent

Bangladeshi Christians and Muslims know about Satan, but at the time that Genesis was written, the idea of Satan had not yet been revealed to the *Bani Isra'il*. There are few references in the Old Testament to evil spiritual powers. There is plenty about Satan in the New Testament – Revelation 12:9 and 20:2 refers to him as the "ancient serpent," so the serpent of Genesis 3 has long been seen as a symbol or vehicle of Satan.[20] It is not surprising that, by the time the Qur'an tells the story of the first temptation, the serpent has been completely replaced by Satan. Islamic literature adds various stories about how Satan entered the garden; for example, he took on the form of a serpent, or he disguised himself as an angel and tempted a peacock to carry him into the garden, promising him eternal life.[21] We are reminded of the New Testament idea that Satan masquerades as an angel of light (2 Cor 11:14).

In the Ancient Near East, people associated serpents with wisdom, fertility, and death, so they worshipped them. Serpent worship existed in Asia, Egypt, Canaan and Mesopotamia. Genesis portrays the serpent as being attractive and as having a certain wisdom, but it is also dangerous and listening to it leads to

---

20. Snakes also appear in Numbers 21, where the children of Israel (*Bani Isra'il*) are punished by a plague of snakes, and rescued by looking at a bronze snake made by Moses. This in turn becomes a symbol for Jesus the Messiah on the cross (John 3:14).

21. *Kasasul Ambiya*, 43.

death. It seems that the Genesis writer was using the most appropriate symbol for the archetypal tempter that was available in his world.[22]

We continue to find snake worship on the Indian subcontinent today. The snake goddess *Manasa Devi* is popular in Bengal and Assam, and devotees bring offerings of milk to the snakes in her temple. A well-known Bangla classic epic, *Manasa Mangal* (Biprodas Pipalai AD 1545), honours her. She is a fertility goddess and is worshipped to avert snake bites during the rainy season, when snakes are most active.

At a popular level, many Bangladeshis share some of the superstitions about snakes; for example, they think that they can get rich by finding a jewel hidden in a snake, and that the snake's jewel will improve their marriages and protect them from snake bites. Genesis's treatment of the serpent as an animal under God's control and under God's judgement is as relevant to us as it was to the ancient world: it puts snakes in their place and tells us that we should neither worship them nor put them to death.[23]

Satan, Angels and Humans

The Qur'an uses the terms *Shayṭān* and *Iblis* to refer to the spiritual enemy of humankind, probably from the Hebrew *satan* and the Greek *diabolos* respectively. *Shayṭān* is a fallen jinn, originally made of fire (Sūras *al-Aʿrāf* 7:12; *al-Ḥijr* 15:26). As we have seen, he is among the angels whom God instructs to bow before Adam, and he refuses. God judges this original rebellion, and *Shayṭān* becomes a sworn enemy to God and to humankind. God permits him to stay on the earth to test human beings. This story is an important part of the qur'anic worldview, and it is repeated many times in the Qur'an (Sūras *al-Baqara* 2:34; *al-Aʿrāf* 7:11; *al-Ḥijr* 15:29; *al-Isrāʾ* 17:61; *al-Kahf* 18:50; *Ṭā Hā* 20:116; *Ṣād* 38:71–85). However, this story is not in the Bible at all, and Genesis 3 has no hint of it. We need a little history to understand this.

The Hebrew term *satan* means "enemy," and it is used of human enemies in, for example, Numbers 22:22. In Job 1 and 2, we meet "the Satan" – a special enemy – who appears among the heavenly hosts. In Job, he does not seem to be particularly evil, and is clearly subject to God's commands. He appears

---

22. Some have proposed that a snake which appears in the *Epic of Gilgamesh* and eats the plant of life and so prevents Gilgamesh from achieving immortality, is the model for the snake of Genesis 3. This is possible, but the two stories are very different (see Goldingay, *Genesis*, 74; Wenham, *Genesis 1–15*, 72–3).

23. Bangladeshi Muslims kill snakes whereas some Hindus worship them.

again in 1 Chronicles 21:1 and Zechariah 3:1–2. None of this gives us any clue as to who he is. However, there are two prophetic passages which are often interpreted as being about his "fall" – the poems about the king of Tyre in Ezekiel 28:11–19 and about the "Day Star" (Latin *Lucifer*), a name given to the king of Babylon in Isaiah 14:12. Both describe a character who had a very high position but was thrown down to the depths. In their contexts, both refer to actual earthly rulers; however, there are aspects of both passages which have been interpreted as alluding to the fall of Adam or of a spiritual being. During the intertestamental period, these passages contributed to the growth of many traditions about Satan, along with stories about other spiritual beings, both angelic and demonic.[24]

The New Testament sees Satan/the Devil as the spiritual enemy of God and of humanity, who was defeated by the death and resurrection of Jesus the Messiah and will be judged on the last day. Meanwhile, there is a spiritual war against him in which believers must play their part (e.g. Matt 4:1–11; John 8:44; Eph 2:2; 1 Pet 5:8–9; 1 John 3:8–10; Rev 12:7–12; 20:1–10). However, the New Testament says remarkably little about Satan's origin or how he relates to the angels. Angels fight Satan in Jude 9 and Revelation 12:7, and there are references to rebellious angels in 2 Peter 2:4 and Jude 6, but there is no equation made between Satan and the fallen angels.

We believe that the Bible tells us all that we need to know about these spiritual powers and that there are some things about them which we do not need to know. The warnings about spending time on myths and superstitions in 1 Timothy 4:1, 7; 2 Timothy 4:3–4; and Titus 1:14 suggest that it might even be dangerous for us to discuss them.

However, humans are curious. As time went on, Christian tradition further developed all these ideas and re-told the story of Adam and Eve in view of Jesus the Messiah being the "second Adam." The Syriac *Cave of Treasures* 2:1–3:2, and the Armenian *Life of Adam and Eve*, 12:1–14:3[25] tell the story of the angels being commanded to bow to Adam, and of Satan's refusal to bow, either because he was made before Adam or because Satan was made from fire and spirit while Adam was made from dust. This is the story to which the Qur'an refers

---

24. For more on the history of these stories, see Carman, "Falling Star and the Rising Son," 221–31; and Patmore, *Adam, Satan, and the King of Tyre*.

25. This text probably originated in the first century AD, and versions exist in several languages. For an analysis of relevant aspects, see Anderson, "Exaltation of Adam and the Fall of Satan," 105–34.

when it introduces its account of Adam, the angels and Iblis with '*wa idh*, "and when . . ." (Sūra *al-Baqara* 2:34).

Cherubim and Winged Mounts

In Genesis 3:24, we read of "Cherubim" (Heb. *kerubim*, sing. *kerub*) which are to guard the Eden garden and prevent the humans from returning there. We learn elsewhere in the Bible that these are winged beings, part of the heavenly hosts created and controlled by God and described in Ezekiel 1:10–11. Winged beings appear frequently in the Mesopotamian world "behind the text," and huge stone winged bulls and lions which guarded the entrances to temples and palaces in Babylonia and Assyria can still be seen.

The Cherubim are not called angels in the Old Testament, but in traditional Christian theology they have been seen as the second highest order of a ninefold heavenly hierarchy, and this sort of idea continues into Islamic thinking.

The Arabic *karūbīm* is not used of angels in the Qur'an, but al-Bayḍāwī uses it for the highest ranking angels, including those around the throne of God in *Ghāfir* 40:7 and *al-Ḥāqqa* 69:17–18. Similarly, the Cherubim in Ezekiel's vision surround and support God's throne (Ezek 1:5–28).

Figure 4 *al-Burāq*[26]

Some Quranic commentators view *al-Burāq*, a winged creature with a human face and a body like a horse, as a *karīb*. This creature is said to have

---

26. Reproduction of 17th century Indian (Mughal) miniature.

carried the Islamic Prophet Muhammad during the *mirāj* (the night journey from Jerusalem into the heavens; see *al-Isrā'* 17:1). In South Asia, pictures of *al-Burāq* are very popular.

The World of the Text
Structure and Genre

This chapter forms the central section of the chiasm of the *toledoth* of the heavens and the earth (see page 92):

> C. The man is placed in Eden (2:15)
>> D. The tree of the knowledge of good and evil is prohibited (2:16–17)
>>> E. Man, animals, woman: naming and nakedness (2:18–25)
>>>> F. The snake, woman and man: temptation (3:1–5)
>>>>> G. Disobedience and calling to account (3:6–13)
>>>> F'. Consequences for snake, woman and man (3:14–19)
>>> E'. The woman and the man: naming and clothing (3:20–21)
>> D'. The tree of life is prohibited (3:22)
> C'. The man is driven out of Eden (3:23–24)

From this structure, we can immediately see that Genesis 3 is all about the Eden garden, and why humanity no longer lives in that beautiful and safe place.

In element E, we see the completion of the order of creation – God over all, the man and the woman working under him and enjoying his creation, and caring for the animals under them. Male and female are partners, with no shame and no need to hide even their private parts from one another or from God. The central portion, F to F', will reverse that order, as an animal takes the first place, the woman listens to him, the man eats, and only after that does God come back into the story. Male and female cover their private parts, hide from God and from each other, and then start blaming each other. The last part of the chapter (elements E', D' and C') develop the consequences of this reversal: the changed relationship between man and woman, the loss of the tree of life, and, finally, the loss of Eden. The turning point, the focus of the whole chiasm, is the human disobedience of verses 6–13, and at the centre of these verses is God's call to his frightened, hiding children: "Where are you?" (v. 9)

COMMENTARY
F. Genesis 3:1–5 The Snake, the Woman and the Man: Temptation

> Now the serpent was more crafty than any other beast of the field that the
> LORD God had made. He said to the woman, "Did God actually say, 'You
> shall not eat of any tree in the garden'?" (3:1)

In Genesis the serpent (Heb. *nachash*) is not Satan, but a crafty or shrewd
(Heb. *'arum*) creature. It was only an animal created by God, but with speaking
power. The important point is that the human beings were to rule over the
animals, but, instead of rebuking the serpent, Eve listened to him, and Adam
simply looked on.

The basic mistake that Eve made was to get into conversation with the
serpent. She could have avoided the temptation by immediately leaving
that place. This was not a temptation from a powerful spiritual being or an
irresistible deception. The serpent could not force them to eat the *haram*
(forbidden) fruit, and he cannot force us to sin today. Their blessed nature in
the image of God gave them the power to obey God, but they chose not to.
The account of trust and obedience between God and humankind of Genesis
2 is becoming an account of disobedience and punishment.

By asking the woman, "Did God really say . . .?" the serpent sowed
confusion in the woman's mind regarding the word of God. The serpent implied
that God was not taking care of them properly and said that if they ate the
fruit, they would become like God. The woman thought that maybe God had
mistreated them and not told them the truth.

The Qur'an gives few details of the temptation and it does not separate the
roles of Adam and his wife. Most commentators say that *Shayṭān* whispered
words to both of them.[27]

> And the woman said to the serpent, "We may eat of the fruit of the trees
> in the garden, but God said, 'You shall not eat of the fruit of the tree that
> is in the midst of the garden, neither shall you touch it, lest you die.'" But
> the serpent said to the woman, "You will not surely die. For God knows
> that when you eat of it your eyes will be opened, and you will be like God,
> knowing good and evil." (3:2–5)

The woman focused only on the forbidden tree, and not on all the delicious
fruit that God had given, and she expanded upon God's command by saying

---

27. Early examples are 'Abd Allāh Ibn Mas'ūd, one of the companions of the Prophet (AD
594–653) and the classical commentator Ibn Abbās (AD 619–687).

that God forbade them even to touch it. Then the serpent created doubt. He assured her that she would not die, but become like God – he claimed to know better than the word of God. This was a wicked deception. They would experience evil, not the knowledge of God. God had already created them in his own image and likeness, and, in the most important ways, disobeying him would make them and their offspring less like him and not more like him.

As we read on, we will find that they did not immediately die physically (Gen 5:5), so we might ask whether the serpent was right. But we will see that they were immediately sent out of Eden, that is, they were separated from God and from fellowship with God, and this set them on a path toward death. Separation from God is spiritual or real death. They spiritually died, though their bodies remained alive for a time. If we obey someone, we become their slave (cf. Rom 6:16). If we listen to the tempter, we become enslaved to our own sinful desires and to the tempter himself.

Who will the woman obey? She has to decide whether she will accept God's word or the serpent's word. The serpent says that she could know good and evil (3:5). As in Genesis 4:1–2, where the word is used of the relationship between husband and wife, "knowing" is not just theory. So "knowing good and evil" means to get experience. She could be "like God." What a temptation!

G. Genesis 3:6–13 Disobedience and Calling to Account

> So when the woman saw that the tree was good for food, and that it was a delight to the eyes, and that the tree was to be desired to make one wise, she took of its fruit and ate, and she also gave some to her husband who was with her, and he ate. (3:6)

Now, we find out what was going on in Eve's mind: the tree appealed to her physical appetite for food, to her love of beauty, and to her desire for god-like knowledge. What a powerful combination! It parallels the "desires of the flesh and the desires of the eyes and pride of life" which the apostle John warns us against in 1 John 2:16.

So she decided. She took the fruit and ate it.

But what about her husband? Where was he? He was "with her" – not very far away. The Lord did not step in and warn her when she was tempted – that was her husband's responsibility. Not only did he fail in that job: he ate the fruit himself! It is foolish to lean on the self-centred notion that, when we are tempted, God should remind us and warn us. He has already made plain what we are to do and not to do; the responsibility for our failures is our own.

The Qur'an agrees that the tempter enticed the couple and they ate, but there are two important differences. First, although the Muslim commentators say that it was Eve who was approached by Satan, the Qur'an treats Adam and Eve together in Sūra *al-Baqara* 2 and Sūra *al-A'rāf* 7; Sūra *Ṭā Hā* 20:120 implies that it was Adam who was tempted. There has been an on-going debate among qur'anic commentators about this. At-Ṭabarī (d. AD 923) and al-Qurṭubī (d. AD 1230) interpret Sūra *al-Baqara* 2:35–36 as meaning that Eve ate first, but the modern commentator at-Ṭāhir ibn 'Ashūr interprets the same passage as teaching that Adam ate first. This discussion affects beliefs about gender relationships.

Second, the tempter's argument is different in the two books. In Genesis, the serpent questions God's truthfulness and goodness. In the Qur'an, Satan assures them that eating the fruit will enable them to live forever, and that he is a good advisor (Sūras *al-A'rāf* 7:20–22; *Ṭā Hā* 20:120). Islamic commentators suggest that the temptation was not rebellion against God, but an enticement for them to live forever in paradise without having to go through the test of earthly life. Satan persuaded them that this would please God. In short, they did not deliberately disobey God, but were deceived into thinking that they were doing something good. This difference has consequences for how we understand human nature.

WHAT WAS THE FORBIDDEN FRUIT?

The forbidden fruit is not identified in either Genesis or the Qur'an, but commentators on both books have, throughout history, been curious about it. While Genesis mentions two trees (the tree of the knowledge of good and evil and the tree of life), the Qur'an mentions only one – the tree of immortality (*shajara al-khuld*), and it is this that was forbidden (Ar. *shajara al-mamnu'*). There is also the mysterious *sidrah al-muntahā* ("lote" tree of the farthest boundary) of Sūra *an-Najm* 53:14, at which the Islamic Prophet Muhammad is said to have met the angel Gabriel during the *mirāj* (night journey). It is located near the garden, and no one can come near it. There are many interpretations of this tree. The closest to the "tree of the knowledge of good and evil" is that it marks the boundaries of human knowledge (Yusuf Ali), but the Qur'an does not link this tree to the story of Adam and Eve.

The forbidden tree appears three times in the Qur'an (Sūras *al-Baqara* 2:35–38; *al-A'rāf* 7:19–23; *Ṭā Hā* 20:120–22), but neither

Genesis nor the Qur'an tells us what kind of tree it was. (Neither do we know what the *lote* tree was. It appears as a mystical tree in ancient legends, and is identified with different trees in different countries.)

Most Christians follow the tradition that the forbidden fruit was an apple, but there is no scriptural basis for this. Other suggestions include pomegranate, carob, pear and mushroom. The Talmud[1] suggests grapes, wheat and figs. The latter is based on the fact that the fig tree is mentioned in Genesis 3:7. An argument for wheat (Heb. *khitah*) is that it is similar to the word *chattah*, meaning "sin" (cf. Ar. *khatah*). In popular Bangladeshi Islamic literature, the forbidden fruit is traditionally called *gondhom*, a Persian loan word meaning "wheat," much mentioned by both Sufi and orthodox Sunni teachers in their religious sermons. Wheat is shaped like the female genital organ and so some Sufis hold that it was after sexual engagement that the couple were sent out from the garden. Heaven, they say, is not a place for enjoying sexual lust but for living in close fellowship with God, their beloved lover. This resembles the biblical statement by Jesus the Messiah to the Sadducees, that, in the afterlife, people will live as angels (Luke 20:34–36). The difference is that the Sufi interpretation sees the garden as heaven, whereas the Genesis Eden garden is on earth, where the humans had been given the blessing of procreation. Genesis makes no suggestion that the original sin was a sexual act.

As interesting as these speculations may be, Genesis simply does not give the botanical identity of the fruit, so we must conclude that it does not matter. Eating the forbidden fruit does not symbolize any particular kind of sinful action; rather, it symbolizes just what Genesis says that it symbolizes. It stands for the God-given choice which led to the experience of discerning good and evil when human beings put their own pride and pleasure above the love of God, and decided that they wanted to replace his lordship with their own lordship.

---

1. *Berachos* 40a; *Sanhedrin* 70a

> *Then the eyes of both were opened, and they knew that they were naked. And they sewed fig leaves together and made themselves loincloths. (3:7)*

The serpent ('*arum*) told the woman that their eyes would be opened and they would be like God (Gen 3:1–5). He did not tell her that out of this knowledge would come fear (*yare*) and shame. After eating the forbidden fruit, their eyes indeed were opened. They came to understand something that they had not seen before. Rather than seeing the glory of God, they saw their own nakedness (*'erom*). They "knew" evil through their own experience with all of its attending guilt, sorrow, shame and misery.

The first consequence of sin was hiding from each other

Because of the shame of their nakedness, they sewed aprons of fig leaves to cover themselves. This was a very temporary dress, so God, out of his love for his children and desire to cover their shame, would later cover them with clothes of animal skins, a far better protection from the adverse environment outside the Eden garden (Gen 3:21).

The Qur'an agrees that the couple's nakedness became apparent, that they covered themselves with fig leaves, and that God later gave them clothing (Sūra al-A'rāf 7:22–26). Interpretations include the ideas that their nakedness was a result of losing the heavenly raiment that they had previously worn,[28] and that the nakedness implies not only a physical nakedness but a moral deviation.[29]

The second consequence of sin was fear

> And they heard the sound of the LORD God walking in the garden in the cool of the day, and the man and his wife hid themselves from the presence of the LORD God among the trees of the garden. But the LORD God called to the man and said to him, "Where are you?" And he said, "I heard the sound of you in the garden, and I was afraid, because I was naked, and I hid myself." He said, "Who told you that you were naked? Have you eaten of the tree of which I commanded you not to eat?" The man said, "The woman whom you gave to be with me, she gave me fruit of the tree, and I ate." Then the LORD God said to the woman, "What is this that you have done?" The woman said, "The serpent deceived me, and I ate." (3:8–13)

God's loving presence was there in the garden, even after they had sinned, but now they were afraid. God did not make them robots or puppets, or even slaves – they could play like children in the garden. They could make their own decisions. But they were afraid, and that is why they hid.

Yet God was still there. There is no suggestion that this "walking of God" in the garden was unusual. God's presence (Heb. *fane*, meaning "face") had been among human beings from the very beginning in the Eden garden, and it is an important theme throughout the Old Testament,[30] leading up to God's special presence in Jesus the Messiah and in the Holy Spirit in the New Testament.

---

28. Ashraf Ali Thanvi, *Boyanul Qur'an.*
29. Ibn Abbās, see *The Encyclopaedia of the Qur'an*, 548.
30. See for example, Gen 18:1; Exod 24:10; 33:11; 33:19–23; Isa 6:1; Amos 7:7.

God was not only present – he spoke to his disobedient children. Here we notice his genuine love for the sinners. He gave them an opportunity to repent and to keeping living in his presence. But they did not repent.

The third consequence of sin was hiding from God

In chapter 2, Adam gladly talked with God. Now, the joyful fellowship with God had broken, so he tried to avoid contact with God – a sure sign of spiritual death. Of course, it is impossible to hide from God. God knew where they were and called to them.

The scene becomes like a courtroom, with God as the righteous judge. He knows exactly what happened and why, but he questions the accused and gives them the opportunity for truth and repentance. "Where are you?" rings down through the ages to all of us, as we try to hide the things of which we are ashamed from others, from God and even from ourselves.

Adam, as the first created, is addressed first. He admits to hiding because he is ashamed and naked, and he admits that he has eaten from the forbidden tree, but he misses the chance to confess his sin to the loving judge. Previously, Adam considered Eve his partner, "bone of bone and flesh of flesh" (2:23). Now he blames his wife for what he has done and also blames God for creating her as his helper (3:12). God then addresses Eve and, like Adam, she admits to having eaten the fruit but does not accept responsibility. She blames the serpent – one of the animals over whom they should together have had dominion.

Here, the Qur'an is significantly different from Genesis. In both Sūra *al-Baqara* 2 and Sūra *al-A'rāf* 7, God does not so much call them to account for their sin as remind them that they should not have eaten from that tree. It is as if Satan has caused them to forget God's instructions, or has really convinced them that they were doing something good and right in eating the fruit. We can conclude that Adam and his wife made a serious mistake, but that they did not really want to disobey God – it was Satan who was really wicked. Adam and his wife do not hide, and they do not blame each other. As soon as God reminds them, they repent and seek forgiveness. God then gives them words that enable them to pray for forgiveness (Sūras *al-Baqara* 2:37; *al-A'rāf* 7:23); and he forgives them.

Of course, the picture in the Qur'an is how we ought to act when we realise our sin. We ought to want to obey God, to be devastated when we realise that Satan has led us astray, to repent and to seek forgiveness. But do we? Genesis tells us a different story: we want to have our own way, we really are to blame when we sin, and we don't want to repent. That is why guidance will never be enough – we need God to remake us and to restore us to relationship with him.

WHOSE FAULT WAS IT?

The man alone received the prohibition; the woman alone faced the tempter; the woman and the man both ate; but whose fault was it? Interpreters have long seen the woman as the problem, not only giving in to the tempter, but also in tempting the man herself. So women have been seen as weak, dangerous and easily deceived. The Qur'an deals with Adam and his wife together: it is Adam to whom God gives the prohibition, but, after that, there is no hint of separate roles through temptation and disobedience. Yet qur'anic commentators, too, have traditionally used aspects of the biblical version of the story to blame the woman.

The real question is, what does the text say? In Genesis 3:12, Adam's first response to God's indictment is to blame the woman, and then, of course, the woman blames the serpent. God is not impressed by either excuse and calls both of them to account for their own sin. Both the man and the woman are at fault.

In the New Testament, in a passage which forbids women from taking wrong authority[1] over men, 1 Timothy 2:13–14 points out that Adam was created first, and that it was Eve who was deceived, and not Adam. Eve is also said to have been deceived in 2 Corinthians 11:3. But does this make women more blameworthy and liable to error and to sin than men? Elsewhere, the Apostle Paul asserts that it is "in Adam" – because of his sin – that all humans die spiritually (1 Cor 15:22), and Romans has a long explanation of the effects of Adam's sin on all humanity (Rom 5:12–19). We see that the New Testament recognizes the different roles played by Adam and Eve, but it also recognizes that both of them were to blame. We could even argue that Eve was less to blame than Adam, because she was deceived, while he ate in full knowledge that what he was doing was wrong.

As we return to the text to hear God's opinion on the matter, let us remember that God made the man and the woman together, as equal but different partners. The woman was to help the man, and not to hinder him, and the man was to leave everything to become one with his wife, and not to hide from her. The very desire to make one better or worse than the other is going against God's plan for humanity.

---

1. The Greek word *authentein* is used only here in the New Testament. It is usually translated "have authority," but it is not the more common *exousia*, which is translated "authority" elsewhere. It probably means "domineer" – hence, "to take wrong authority"

F.' Genesis 3:14–19 Consequences for the Man, the Woman and the Snake

Because of Adam's sin, a curse came down upon the land and all of creation was affected. Adam and Eve's rebellion against the authority and benevolence of the creator God not only affected their spiritual relationship with him and their personal and social relationships with each other, but also their economic and material environment (see also Jer 12:4; Rom 8:20).

The snake

> The LORD God said to the serpent:
>
> "Because you have done this,
>   cursed are you above all livestock
>   and above all beasts of the field;
> on your belly you shall go,
>   and dust you shall eat
>   all the days of your life.
> I will put enmity between you and the woman,
>   and between your offspring and her offspring;
> he shall bruise your head,
>   and you shall bruise his heel." (3:14–15)

From being the most beautiful of creatures, the serpent became a loathsome reptile slithering on the ground. At this point, the question arises: did the serpent originally have legs and walk upright? As with so many of our questions, there is no answer in the text. We learn only about the serpent's punishment, not about what it was originally like.

"Eating dust" is a symbol of humiliation (Mic 7:17; Isa 65:25), but dust is also a symbol of death, since, after death, the body will return to the dust (Gen 3:19). Dust is not actually the food of the serpent, although doubtless dust gets into its mouth as it crawls along the ground. The curse on the serpent foreshadows the eventual fate of *Shayṭān* himself (Rev 20:10; Ezek 28:18–19).

Genesis 3:15 has long been interpreted as a messianic hope in Christian literature. From the dust of the curse emerges a dazzling *theological bud* – the promise of eventual victory for the woman's seed. But who is this "seed"? The pronouns are singular, clearly referring to an individual. Reading on, we might notice how often the Genesis genealogies mention un-named "daughters," and that much attention is given to the choice of mothers for the Abrahamic line. Yet none of their "seeds," not even Joseph, will manage to resist all temptation, let alone defeat the tempter!

In Bangladesh, we see that the name of a son or daughter is usually associated with their father's name. The Bible also identifies people through their father's line rather than their mother's line. So the key question is, "Who would be identified through their mother?" There would be only one person who would have a mother and no father – Jesus the Messiah, whom the Qur'an calls 'Isa ibn Maryam, Jesus son of Mary (Sūra Maryam 19:34). The New Testament underlines this, as it tells of his virgin birth that fulfils the prophecy of Isaiah 7:14 (Matt 1:18–25; Luke 1:26–2:7; cf. Sūras Āl 'Imrān 3:45–47 and Maryam 19:16–33), and of his birth as the seed of a woman (Gal 4:4).

So many Christian commentators call this promise the "proto-evangelium," the first announcement of the gospel. The salvation story, they say, begins in Genesis 3:15. Jesus the Messiah was the one who would defeat Shayṭān, sin and death on the cross (Luke 10:17–20; Col 1:13; 1 John 3:8; Rev 17:7–12).

We remember that the Qur'an also portrays Shayṭān as the enemy of humankind (Sūra al-Baqara 2:36 and many other places). According to the teaching of the New Testament, Shayṭān is under God's ultimate control and will eventually be defeated after the second coming of Jesus the Messiah. At the final judgement, he will be thrown into hell. The Qur'an agrees that Shayṭān is under God's ultimate control and will eventually be defeated, but it does not say how, and it has no redeemer who can bear our sins (Sūras al-An'ām 6:164; al-Isrā' 17:13–15).

The woman

> To the woman he said,
>
> "I will surely multiply your pain in childbearing;
>   in pain you shall bring forth children.
> Your desire shall be for your husband,
>   and he shall rule over you." (3:16)

Unlike the serpent, neither the man nor the woman is cursed. But, unlike other female animals, women will now suffer pain in giving birth (3:16; cf. 1 Tim 2:15). The Hebrew root used here ('-ts-b) can express not only physical pain but also mental anguish, perhaps referring to the anguish of both child-bearing and child-rearing.

We should note here the grace in the midst of the judgement: despite their sin, and the coming of death, the human race will continue. The woman will still desire (teshuqah) her husband, although we wonder how good this is given that natural desire has often turned into something more sinister. One good desire is for motherhood, but this desire cannot be fulfilled without the man's cooperation. We remember that, in chapter 2, the man needed the woman; here in chapter 3, the woman needs the man. Sadly, whereas the original relationship was of equal partnership, the result of sin is a power imbalance. Throughout the ages, wives will be ruled by their husbands, not only in sexual matters but also in other areas of life.

This word "desire" will appear only twice more in the Old Testament. In Genesis 4:7, it is sin's desire for Cain, but in Song of Songs 7:10 it is the man's desire for the woman he loves. This suggests that the "desire" in Genesis 3:16 includes the conflicting longings that so many women experience in a male-dominated society. The desire to be married and bear children, the feelings of inferiority and dependence on males, the wish to dominate and control those males, the inability to escape from abusive relationships . . . all these can distort the beautiful male-female relationship which God created, and women can be as sinful in seeking their desires as can men in exerting their power.

The idea of the woman as the "crop field of her husband" who must play a passive role in fulfilling her husband's sexual desire and reluctantly bear his children is evidence of the spiritual death that followed the fall. Sadly, this is how many Muslim husbands interpret Sūra al-Baqara 2:223. The human rights worker Nadia Murad, a Nobel prize winner, complained that the Islamic State prisoner camps used women as sex-slaves and raped them regularly.[31] The incident reminds us of the events before the flood when men took any of the women they chose (Gen 6:2). This behaviour is totally against Islamic laws regarding prisoners of war, and it is totally against the teaching of the Bible. Not even in marriage should women ever be treated like this. Those who have new life in the Messiah will maintain equality with their wives and treat all women with respect, as made in the image of God.

The man

> And to Adam he said,
>
> "Because you have listened to the voice of your wife
>   and have eaten of the tree
> of which I commanded you,
>   'You shall not eat of it,'
> cursed is the ground because of you;
>   in pain you shall eat of it all the days of your life;

---

31. https://www.theguardian.com/world/2018/oct/05/denis-mukwege-nadia-murad-nobel-peace-prize-2018.

> *thorns and thistles it shall bring forth for you;*
> *   and you shall eat the plants of the field.*
> *By the sweat of your face*
> *   you shall eat bread,*
> *till you return to the ground,*
> *   for out of it you were taken;*
> *for you are dust,*
> *   and to dust you shall return." (3:17–19)*

The earth was cursed because of human sin. Consequently, the man will now eat only "through painful toil," and prickly weeds will grow as well as food. Here again, we find judgement and grace together. Adam will have to work hard and long, but God's gracious provision continues, as the food will still grow.

Eventually, Adam and Eve and all their descendants will see the result of sin: physical death. The body which was made of the earth (2:7) will return to the earth. The origin of the man's body and the source of his food has become a symbol of his death. The Qur'an recognizes death as the destiny of all humankind, but it does not have the close link between sin and death that is developed in the Bible (Sūra Āl 'Imrān 3:185).

The Bible is clear that the results of sin described in Genesis 3:14–19 continue today. Broken relationships continue between God and humanity, between humanity and the animals, between men and women, and between humans and the very earth from which they derive their food. As the New Testament summarizes, "for as in Adam all die" (1 Cor 15:22; cf. Rom 5:12). The wages of sin are death (Rom 6:23) and the death sentence is passed on to all humankind.

E. Genesis 3:20–21 The Woman and the Man: Naming and Clothing

> *The man called his wife's name Eve, because she was the mother of all living. (3:20)*

Here is a subject that grabs our attention: the sentence of death is followed by an expectation of life. Adam called his mate, Chawwah ("Eve"), a name similar to the verb "to live" (Heb. *chaya*), as she was to become the mother of all the living (*kal-chay*). The name indicates that the woman and the man together comprise humanity: "Adam" reminds us of the ground (*adamah*) from which he was made, and "Chawwah" reminds us of the breath of life (*nishmat chayyim*) which made him a living being (2:7). Yet this is also an indication of his taking authority over her, as implied in Genesis 3:16. Eve is a good name, but we can also read it as a name by which the man defines her role and asserts his authority over her. What a contrast to the joyful recognition of her as an equal partner in Genesis 2:23!

The Qur'an does not mention the name of Adam's mate, but her Arabic name, *Hawwa*, is well known in the hadith and in other parts of Islamic literature. The Qur'an names only one of its female characters: Mary, the mother of Jesus the Messiah. Sūra 19 is named *Maryam* after her.

> *And the LORD God made for Adam and for his wife garments of skins and clothed them. (3:21)*

Although the humans are unable to hide their sin or to cover their shame, their loving Father makes garments of skins and clothes the sinful pair. The Quran follows this same sequence: Adam and Eve realise their nakedness and make clothing of heavenly leaves. Then they are sent out of the garden and God provides them with extraordinary new clothing (Sūra *al-A'rāf* 7:22–26). The main lesson that the Qur'an draws from this is that people should cover themselves. The following verses (27–31) are interpreted to mean that some of the Meccans worshipped naked, and that the Muslims should never do so. Similarly, in some places in the ancient world, priests worshipped naked. In the Torah, the Lord required his priests to dress properly in the tabernacle, including undergarments to cover them when they ascended stairs (Exod 28).

The Qur'an does not tell us what the clothing was, or from where it came. Genesis, by specifying that it was skins, implies that God killed an animal. In the Torah, it was not enough that the priests should wear the right clothes: they also had to be purified (made holy) through the blood of sacrifices (Exod 29).

So we can read this verse as describing the first shedding of blood as a covering for the impurity and shame that results from sin. It foreshadows not only the sacrifices of the Torah but also the perfect sacrifice of Jesus the Messiah on the cross. To restore fellowship with God, there is a need for sacrifice. Humankind cannot cover their sin with their good deeds or merit: there must be an atonement to cover their sin, and only God can do it. The Apostle Paul urges believers in Christ to clothe themselves with the Lord Jesus the Messiah (Rom 13:14). Believers have God-given clothes of righteousness which allow them to live in the presence of God (Isa 61:10).

D'. Genesis 3:22 The Tree of Life Prohibited

> *Then the LORD God said, "Behold, the man has become like one of us in knowing good and evil. Now, lest he reach out his hand and take also of the tree of life and eat, and live forever—"*

God speaks again in the first-person plural.[32] Again, we are given a glimpse of his divine thoughts. This time, God's speech to himself[33] shows us the reason for the judgement which is about to come. Verses 14–19 announced the punishment for sin, but the expulsion from Eden is different: its purpose is to prevent access to the tree of life and therefore to immortality on earth. The problem is that the humans have become "like God." They were already made in the image of God, but they tried to snatch extra freedom from their creator and so lost the freedom which he had already given them.

In Genesis 6:1–7 God limits lifespans, and in Genesis 11:5–9 he limits communication: in both cases, God is limiting the evil which humans can perpetrate. This suggests the reason for barring access to the tree of life: the experiential knowledge of evil has given humans a wrong power which will endanger creation, and this power had to be limited.

C'. Genesis 3:23–24 The Man Driven Out of Eden

> *Therefore the LORD God sent him out from the garden of Eden to work the ground from which he was taken. (3:23)*

Before the fall, Adam was to care for and tend a beautiful and pleasant garden (2:5, 15). After the fall, he has the same job. The difference outside Eden is that the work will be difficult (3:17–19). As in 2:5 and 15, the word for "till" means "work" or "serve" (Heb. '-v-d, like the Arabic '-b-d). Human beings were made to serve.

> *He drove out the man, and at the east of the garden of Eden he placed the cherubim and a flaming sword that turned every way to guard the way to the tree of life. (v. 24)*

The tree of life was the symbol of their former blessedness. Humankind was now cut off from the close presence of God and thus cut off from life. On the

---

32. See commentary on Genesis 1:26–27.

33. Another possibility is that "us" includes the cherubim of verse 24. "Like us" would then imply the immortality which is shared by God and the angels.

other hand, being cut off from the tree of life could be interpreted as a mercy: they would not live forever in their sinful condition.

The cherubim, the guardians of the holy places, were put in place to prevent re-entry (cf. Exod 37:7–9; 1 Kgs 6:33–37; Ezek 1:4–16; 10:5). Together with the flaming sword, they prevent access to the tree of life. Previously, it was the human's duty to keep the garden (Gen 2:15): ironically, after the fall, the same word for "keeping" (translated "guard" by the ESV) is used of the cherubim. The humans were the evil-doers against whom the garden had to be guarded! The cherubim guards are the sign and seal of the spiritual death the human couple experienced on the day they ate from the forbidden tree.

Genesis says nothing here about the serpent; we do not know whether or not he was banished from the garden. He simply disappears from the story. In contrast, the Qur'an states that God banished *Shayṭān* along with humanity[34] (Sūras *al-Aʿrāf* 7:13–24; *al-Ḥijr* 15:35–37; *Ṣād* 38:77–81). This is seen as a reprieve requested by *Shayṭān*, which defers his final judgement. During that reprieve, God will permit him to tempt human beings. *Shayṭān*'s role in creation is to be the enemy of humankind, and he will not be permitted to return to the paradise garden (Sūras *al-Baqara* 2:36–39; *Ṭā Hā* 20:123).

It is notable that in the Qur'an, *Shayṭān* is twice "cast down" – once after refusing to bow to Adam, and again when he is sent to earth with Adam and Eve (Sūra *al-Baqara* 2:38; cf. Sūra *al-Aʿrāf* 7:13, 24). This emphasizes that *Shayṭān* has fallen from his status among the jinn as well as from his location in the heavens. In contrast to the Bible, the qur'anic Adam and Eve repented and were forgiven (Sūras *al-Baqara* 2:37; *al-Aʿrāf* 7:23; *Ṭā Hā* 20:122), so their "sending down" is not a fall in status but, according to most commentators, the execution of God's original plan to place them on the earth.

Theological Reflection

Genesis 3 is usually understood as teaching about human nature, but it also unfurls a little more of *the bud of revelation* about God. We see a God who allows temptation and allows humans to face it. He does not force us to obey

---

34. There are several Islamic legends about how and where humans came to earth. A popular version has Adam alighting on "Adam's Peak" on the Island *Sarandib* (Sri-Lanka) and his wife arriving near Jeddah, the port near Mecca. Adam remained in *Sarandib* for 200 years, separated from his wife and doing penance, and then the angel Gabriel brought them both to Mount Arafat, near Mecca, whence they returned to *Sarandib*. There are also stories about the expulsion from heaven of the snake and the peacock who assisted Satan in his tempting of Adam and Eve. See *Kasasul Ambiya*, 49–51.

him, but presents us with a choice. We see a God who comes seeking humans like a shepherd searching for his lost sheep, and then calling them to account. He does not leave us in our sin, but challenges us with his questions: "Where are you?" "What have you done?" We observe a God who sees right through their excuses and their attempts to avoid responsibility. He insists that we take responsibility, since we are made in his image, to choose to do what we should do. We see a God who pronounces the consequences of disobedience: he limits the evil humans can do, and he lets us experience the consequences of it. Yet we also begin to glimpse a God who will find a way of blessing us despite our sinful wrong choices: somehow, the woman's seed will triumph, and God clothes his naked children before he sends them outside the garden.

This chapter also gives us a glimpse of *the problems with which the sciences have been trying to deal* since their beginning. All the blessings of fruitfulness will be painful. Agriculture is no longer easy: it needs tools to deal with the thorns and thistles and rocky, infertile ground. There will be great pain in work and in childbearing, so people will seek ways of dealing with that pain. There will be enmity between humans and some of the animals, so people will seek ways of taming and using the animals. The peace and beauty and control of Eden has been lost, so people will try to control the material world in order to recover it. Yet Genesis 3 also holds the warning that science (remember that the word "science" literally means "knowledge") can never, by itself, achieve such an aim, because the root cause of the problem is not the material world. Not until human sin has been dealt with can we expect to solve the problems of enmity, pain and fruitlessness.

This chapter is one of the most important in establishing the soil and the seeds for the rest of the Bible. The soil is the sombre fact of the need for revelation. Inside Eden, human beings were in direct contact with God and needed no intermediary prophet or scripture, as they knew him personally. Outside Eden, that fellowship has been broken, and something needs to be done so that people can know God.

The main seed theme is the truth of human sinfulness. Exactly how sin is passed down through the ages has been much debated by both Jews and Christians through the centuries, but all agree that Genesis 3 indicates a fundamental human problem. The good, innocent humanity that was God's original creation has used its freedom to disobey its Maker, and the result has been tragic. At first, the temptation came from outside, but humans let rebellious thoughts into their inner lives. Unlike the Qur'an, Genesis gives a sharp analysis of the workings of our rebellious minds as it describes Eve's progression from seeing the forbidden fruit, to enjoying its appearance, desiring its effects, choosing to eat it, and giving it to her husband (3:6). Ever since then, sin has been, as Genesis 4:7 describes it, right at the door of our beings. In short, we are "fallen." This is the root story for what has grown into the Christian doctrine of "original sin."[35]

As we read on in Genesis 1–11, we will see the escalation of sin as this fallenness takes effect. Genesis 12 then inaugurates God's plan for dealing with the fallenness, and this is the major theme for the rest of the Bible. Muslims generally believe that the qur'anic Adam's disobedience did not lead to a "fall" of humanity: Adam and Eve repented and were forgiven, and so their sin could not affect their offspring. The Qur'an emphasizes the role of *Shaytān* – it is he who is "fallen," and it is he who is responsible for the disobedience. Most Muslim commentators believe that prophets cannot sin (*dhanb*) and that Adam was a prophet, so they describe Adam's action as a small error – *zallatu Adam* or the "slip" of Adam.

This difference is one of the most significant disagreements between Muslims and Christians. If we are not fallen, redemption is not possible. That is, if we are not fallen, then we have nowhere to which we can be raised back. If we are not spiritually dead, but simply weak and ignorant, then how can we be made spiritually alive? And Genesis 3 does contain a seed of hope of redemption and of spiritual life: the seed of promise in verse 15, which is known as the *proto-evangelium*, the beginning of the gospel.

Although Islam has no doctrine of original sin and the fall, there are plenty of indications of the sinfulness of humanity in the Qur'an and Islamic literature. In the hadith of *al-Tirmidhī Ḥasan*, it is said that every child of Adam is a sinner and would do well to repent. We all see the truth of this. The Bengali poet Kazi Nazrul Islam writes in his poem, "*Pap*" (Sin):

> We are all sinners: measure the sin of others with the weight of your sin.

A particularly interesting story, which some associate with Sūra *al-Anʿām* 6:125, tells of the angels doing two open-heart operations[36] on the Islamic Prophet Muhammad, one before his mystical journey into the heavens and the

---

35. The theory of original sin is that every human born as a descendant of Adam has a sinful nature. Consequently, this theory says that we are not sinners only because we sin, but we are sinners according to our sinful nature from birth.

36. Muslim scholars debate the number of times that the Prophet had to be cleansed. They have identified four possible times: at age four at the house of his suckling mother Halima, at age ten in Mecca, at age forty in the cave in Hira, and during the *mirāj*, night-journey.

other when he was six years old. A black piece of flesh was cut off[37] and his heart was washed with Zam Zam water and then restored to its original position, full of faith and wisdom.[38] This would seem to indicate that even the greatest prophets need their hearts divinely cleansed from sin. This is not far from the biblical idea that all human beings have hearts which have been spoilt by sin, and that we therefore need to be cleansed with the blood of the Messiah. A big difference is that the angelic operation seems only to have been available to the prophet, while the blood of the Messiah is available to all who believe.

There is also a seed of hope. Down the millenia, human beings have been trying to find ways back into the garden – to the blessings of life with God. We have seen some hints of hope, especially in the promise that the serpent's head will be crushed (3:15), and in God's fatherly clothing of his disobedient children (3:21). Yet we do not know whether Adam and Eve will later repent, or whether humanity might be given a second chance.

From this seed question, in different ways, both the Qur'an and the Bible will come to see Jesus the Messiah as a second Adam, who was humble where Adam was proud, and who was obedient where Adam was disobedient. The Qur'an boldly speaks of Jesus the Messiah's miraculous birth through God's direct creative word, which is similar to Adam's creation (Sūra Āl 'Imrān 3:47). The New Testament shows Jesus the Messiah, in obedient service, leaving his position with God for the sake of humanity, then dying and rising again into glory. As Adam's disobedience led to death for all, so the Messiah's obedience opens the way to life for all (Phil 2:5–11; Rom 5:12–21; 1 Cor 15:21–22, 45).

What About Us?

The way was guarded. They could not get back. Their children could not get back. If we are not yet convinced that we cannot get back, then the Noah story will underline the message, as the world is un-made and re-made because of sin. Even if we receive new spiritual life through the Messiah, we have to live with the effects of the fall, in our work on the earth and in our male-female relationships. And the serpent's temptations are always before us.

---

37. Ibn Ḥajar, *Fatḥ al- Bari.* Sunni theologian Taqī ad-Dīn Subkī (AD 1284–1355) wrote that God creates a piece of flesh in every man's heart which receives everything that *Shayṭān* brings near to him. This flesh was cut out of the prophet's heart so that, after the operation, he would not receive *Shayṭān's* evil thinking.

38. See *Bukhārī* Vol. 5, Book 58, Hadith 227; *Muslim* Book 1, Hadiths 310–11.

Living with Sin, Shame and Temptation

How do we deal with our own sin and shame? Do we try to cover our shame with useless fig leaves, to hide from God and each other, and refuse to face the blame for our own part of the problem? Do we convince ourselves that we are not really sinful, but that we are trying to please God all the time? Or do we truly repent? If so, how can we know if God has forgiven us? And what makes us think that he should forgive us? Genesis 3 and the comparison with the Qur'an challenges us with all these questions. It is important that we take them into our study of Genesis 4–11, but also that we ask them regularly as we live in this world outside Eden.

In this world, we will always have temptation. Frequently in the Bible, we see the *Bani Isra'il* being tempted and, too often, giving way and breaking God's covenant. Because of this disobedience, God punishes them many times and eventually banishes them to a foreign land. Like them, even as believers, we will be tempted. How can we resist temptation if Adam and Eve in their perfect environment could not resist it?

First, temptation is not sin. Jesus the Messiah himself was tempted by *Shayṭān* (Matt 4:1–11; Mark 1:12–13; Luke 4:1–13), but he did not sin. As the second Adam, he did not give way to the tempter as the first Adam and Eve did. If we are in him, we have the power of the Holy Spirit to help us to fight against *Shayṭān*.

Second, we are not helpless. The serpent could not force them to eat the *haram* fruit, neither can *Shayṭān* force us to commit sin. A popular Bangladeshi song says, *Jemne nachai, temni nachi potulerki Dush* (we are like puppets, in the hand of the puppeteer, so we dance according to his will), implying that we should not be blamed for our actions. This follows a solution to an early Islamic debate about free will which was later rejected by more orthodox Muslims. The opposing groups were called Jabariyya (*jabar* means "compulsion") and Qādiriyya (*qadr* means "will" or "power"). The Jabariyya so emphasized God's power that they argued that all actions come from God, so that we are not responsible for what we do. The Qādiriyya argued that since humans are judged by their actions, we must have some responsibility for them. Historically, the latter group won, but the fatalism of the Jabariyya has by no means disappeared from popular thinking. When Muslims recite the "*amanu bi-llāhi*" *kalimat* ("I believe in God" creed), they understand the clause, "and in his *qadr* over all things good and bad," in different ways.

Genesis agrees that God as creator has great power, but also affirms that humans have free will, being made in the image of God. It is God's desire that we are able to choose good, which means that we can also choose evil. We are not puppets. We can commit sin or we can abstain from sin. Adam blamed Eve and Eve blamed the serpent, and both were wrong. We cannot blame each other or *Shayṭān* for our sin; and we certainly cannot blame God for it. Human beings are responsible for their sins!

Third, like Eve, we have the opportunity of walking away and not listening to the serpent. In the New Testament, James writes, "Resist the devil, and he will flee from you" (Jas 4:7). If we do not listen to the tempter, and we refuse to do what he says, he will run away. The key to this, says James, is humility and submission to God. If we are proud and think that we know better than God, we will, like Eve, be easy targets for the tempter. If we do not want to submit to God, then we will find ourselves submitting to *Shayṭān* instead.

One reason why these things are important is that they affect the way we bring up our children. Orthodox Sunni Muslims believe that people are born sinless, and that children should not be held responsible for their actions until the age of 6. The Bible teaches that we are all born outside Eden and share in the results of the first sin, and that we are all responsible to God from the beginning of our lives. We need to check whether we are following the mindset of our society or the mindset of the Bible. We need to remember that our children are made in the image of God, so that they can choose how to act; but also that they are part of the fallen world, so they need salvation. The sinful nature is latent even at the earliest stage in every child. This does not mean that we should not love our children. On the contrary, we should love them as Jesus the Messiah loves children (Matt 19:14; Luke 18:16); but the love will include discipline as well as teaching and nurture.

Living as Male and Female

Due to the fall, the perfect partnership and gender equity between man and woman has been spoiled. They hide from each other and they blame each other. The work they should share gets assigned: women take the role of child-bearers and men the role of providers. The balance of power also shifts, with women being dependent on men while men dominate women and take authority over them. The Bible offers us many narratives about women and men that help us to understand the problems and to see some hopeful ways forward.[39] The Torah also has laws about marriage, rape and divorce that protect people from the worst results of the fall (e.g. Exod 20:14; Lev 20:10–21; Deut 22:15–30;

---

39. Useful books which explore this include Evans, *Women in the Bible*, and Glaser and John, *Partners or Prisoners?*

24:1–3). But if, as Muslims believe, there has been no fall, then at least some of the role imbalance and male domination must be what God made, and we can only regulate it so that the domination is responsible. Good and bad examples should be sufficient to show people what to do.

The Bible shows us that examples and laws are not enough. We are fallen: what we need is redemption. The good news is that redemption is available. Jesus the Messiah again and again challenged the role divisions and blaming of the women of his days (e.g. Luke 7:36–50; 8:42–48; 10:36–42; 21:1–4; John 4:4–27; 8:1–11), and it is he whose death and resurrection opens the way to changed hearts.

In the "new creation" that takes place through union with the Messiah, vying for dominion over each other is done away with. A biblically based marriage is one that is in balance, with Jesus the Messiah as the head of the man and the wife together. The husband should fulfil his wife's sexual needs, and the wife also should fulfil her husband's needs (1 Cor 7:3). But in this fallen world, we fail to meet each other's expectations so quarrels arise. If quarrels continue, children are hurt and neighbours will not listen to any good news coming from that home. The Apostle Paul gives good advice: if we become angry, we should avoid sin by dealing with the problem before nightfall (Eph 4:26). If not, we will not agree in our prayer requests, and God will not accept our prayers (Matt 18:19).

There is a beautiful illustration in The Apostle Paul's letter to the Ephesians (5:21–33) – husband and wife are like head and body, so they cannot survive without each other and have to put each other's interests first (v. 21). It is important to note that although God is the head of Jesus the Messiah (1 Cor 11:3), we know that Jesus the Messiah and God are equal in status. Similarly, although the husband is the head of the wife, they have equal status. Ephesians is not prescribing differences in values or roles for the husband and wife – it is accepting the cultural pattern of the time, but transforming the relationship from the fallen state of dominion to the new-creation pattern of love. Jesus the Messiah and his body are one, and he sacrificed his life for the body of believers. Likewise, we may follow some of the patterns of our own culture, but, even within that, a husband should love his wife as his own body and be ready to sacrifice for her.

Living outside Eden

Over the centuries, people have tried to return to Eden. The accounts of the garden of Eden remind us of the symmetric design of Persian paradise gardens, often walled and divided into four segments. In the Abbasid period, Muslim leaders built Eden-like gardens in the area between the Tigris and Euphrates rivers. The original city of Baghdad of the Caliph al-Mansur, founded in AD 762, was known as the *Madina al-Salam*, the City of Peace, a reference to the description of paradise in Sūras *al-Anʿām* 6:127 and *at-Tawba* 9:72. The agriculture and parks around it were watered by an extensive irrigation system, also a reminder of the rivers of Eden. All this was devastated during the Mongol invasion of 1256–1258.

The Qur'an describes paradise as a place under which rivers flow, and mentions four rivers (of water, milk, honey and wine) (*Muḥammad* 47:15) and four gardens (Sūra *ar-Raḥmān* 55:46, 62). Baghdad was divided into four segments, and Islamic rulers have continued to build earthly paradises. On the Indian subcontinent, these were called *char bag* (four gardens) and include the *Humayun Tomb* in Delhi, the *Taj Mahal* in Agra, *Baghe Babur* in Kabul, and the *Shalimar Bagh* and the gardens of Jahangir Tombs in Lahore. Another famous garden is *Shaharbag* in Isfahan, Iran, built by Shah Abbas the Great in AD 1596. During a similar time period, European Christians were also seeking Eden. In their attempts to follow Adam's example of naming the animals,[40] they built gardens in the *char bagh* style to house their scientific collections. The botanical garden in Oxford was one of the first, and an early catalogue is titled *Adam in Eden, or Nature's Paradise*.[41]

Today, many firms and ecological projects use the name "Eden" in their titles, either trying to return the earth to its unspoiled state, or to convince their customers that their products will give them a taste of paradise. We try to find better ways to till the ground, so that we can produce food with as little toil and as few weeds as possible.

As we saw in our study of Genesis 1, it is right that we should do everything that we can to care for the earth, and from Genesis 2 we learned the importance of our role as farmers. However, the Bible gives us no hope that we will ever be able to remove the pain of hard toil and the reality of the weeds in our fields. Although we work to find ways around the reality of the hard toil, we can end up creating more problems; for example, chemical attempts to remove the weeds have often resulted in damage to the environment and to our health. Through Jesus the Messiah, the New Testament offers us victory over *Shayṭān* and renewed human relationships right now, but the hope for the complete

---

40. See theological reflection on Genesis 2 page 113.

41. William Coles, *Adam in Eden, or Nature's Paradise* (London: Printed by J. Streater for Nathaniel Brooke, 1657).

renewal of the environment is something the whole creation waits for (Rom 8:22–23).

As we read longingly of the beauty of Eden, we can look forward to the new heavens and the new earth at the end of time, where all will be good again (Rev 21–22). But as we look at this earth, we share God's pain as we consider the damage that human sin has produced.[42] If Eden was in Mesopotamia, it has certainly been lost! This area has been under strife between rival forces for ages, and today its natural beauty is devastated through war. Thus, the Bengali poet Kazi Nazrul Islam writes in "Shat-il-Arab":

> For ever glorious, for ever holy,
> Your sacred beaches, Shat-el-Arab,
> Are bathed in gore, the blood of fighters
> Of many races, and diverse colours.
> Strewn on these sands lie the bones of Arab,
> Egyptian and Turk and Greek and Bedouin,
> Also of women, bold and daring,
> Who sobbed as they battled, reckless of danger.[43]

The recent war between the Islamic State and its opposing forces to take possession of those areas, brings this poem, which was written nearly a century ago, vividly to mind. How tragic that some of the fighters have been deluded into believing that killing and being killed is the way to Paradise! Let us pray for the Creator to be honoured in the damaged land of the Eden story, and in all our outside-Eden world!

Genesis 4 Adam and Eve's Sons: Cain, Abel and Seth

The gate has been shut and is guarded by awesome winged beings and a flaming sword: there is no way back. What will happen now, outside that beautiful Eden garden? Genesis 4 shows us the continuing care and blessing of God, but it also shows us the development of the consequences of the sin of Genesis 3. The narrative in Genesis 4 begins with hope: the creation blessing of fruitfulness has not been lost. Children are born, and they acknowledge their Creator by bringing sacrifices. One of the sacrifices is accepted by God. Outside Eden,

---

42. See comment on Genesis 6:6.

43. Kazi Nazrul Islam, "Shat-el-Arab," trans. Syed Sajjad Husain, https://www.icnazrul.com/index.php/nazrul-s-work/poems/36-poetry-lyrics/47-shat-il-arab.

there is a new beginning, an opportunity for the humans to serve God and to have fellowship with him in their new environment.

But we are going to be disappointed. Sin is going to increase, and it will be judged. The first use of the word "sin" (Heb. *chattah*) in the Bible appears in verse 7 of this chapter. Adam's sin has opened the way for the sin of his first-born son. The first murder quickly follows the sacrifices and it is the terrible murder of a brother. It foreshadows the struggles between siblings down the ages – Isaac against Ishmael (21:8–21); Jacob against Esau (cf. 25:19–34; 27:1–45); the rivalry of Rachel and Leah (29–30); and the oppression of Joseph by his brothers (37:1–35) – all taking place in the book of Genesis. We are reminded of the struggle for succession between the fifth Mughal Emperor, Shahjahan (AD 1628–58) and his four sons. Eventually, the third son, Aurangzeb, killed his brothers and declared himself emperor.

The structure of the *toledoth* of the heavens and the earth (see ch. 3, page 92) invites us to compare life outside Eden with the life in Eden described in Genesis 2.

- Genesis 2 was concerned with the placing of the first human beings on the earth.

   Genesis 4 is concerned with the first human births. It is the very first genealogy, but, up to the last two verses, it is a sad genealogy, because it is of a line which will be completely wiped out in the flood.

- Genesis 2 described the perfect environment of the Eden garden, with its fruitful earth, its trees, its animals and its rich minerals.

   Genesis 4 describes human use and abuse of the earth and its fruits, animals and minerals outside of Eden.

- Genesis 2 narrated the institution of the first marriage, with the male and female as perfectly complementary and unashamed.

   Genesis 4 will portray a polygamous marriage and increasing violence in human relationships.

- Genesis 2 has the warning that sin will bring death.

   Genesis 4 has the first death as well as the first births.

The chapter begins with Adam (v. 1) and finishes with Enosh (v. 26), whose name also means "mortal man." There are other places in the Old Testament where the two terms (*adam* and *enosh*) are used in parallel (e.g. Ps 8:4). Together, the names emphasize that this life outside Eden is the fallen human condition. A striking feature is that, until verse 26, the chapter uses YHWH for God throughout, drawing our attention to his covenant commitment to sinful humanity.

The Worlds Behind and in Front of the Text

Birth, sacrifice, jealousy, murder, exile, revenge and the building of families, cities and civilizations – all these concerns of Genesis 4 characterized the ancient world, and we find them in today's world, including Bangladesh.

Births are important, but, as in Old Testament times, so in Bangladesh, there are many barren women longing for children. Barren women from all walks of life visit the tombs of Sufi saints to pray for live children through the mediation of dead saints. We can compare this to the Old Testament's portraits of barren women. In Genesis, Sarah was barren until God gave her the promised child, Isaac. Later, Jacob's wife Rachel saw that she was not bearing children and told Jacob "give me children, or I shall die!" (Gen 30:1). Jacob naturally became angry and admitted his helplessness, saying, "Am I in the place of God, who has withheld from you the fruit of the womb?" (30:2). Samuel's mother, Hannah, shows vividly the feeling of a barren woman as she begs God for a child (1 Sam 1:11–16). She did not ask the priest Eli, but God himself, because she knew that, as the psalmist wrote, only God can give children (Pss 113:9; 127:3–5). This is so relevant to today. Believing barren woman must rely on God and resist the temptation of praying to any living or dead holy man, just as believing women long ago had to resist the temptation of praying to the ancient fertility gods.

Sacrifices, in the ancient world behind the text, were offered by people to their gods, so it is not surprising that one of the first things people did outside Eden was to offer a sacrifice. From the time of Moses, Jews maintained fellowship with God through animal sacrifices, described in much detail in the Torah. In today's world, devotees of different faiths sacrifice many animals to seek reconciliation with God. Muslims sacrifice animals every year, remembering the sacrifice of Abraham, the father of the *ummah*. However, the Qur'an clearly states that it is not meat which reaches God, but piety, *taqwā* (Sūra *al-Ḥajj* 22:37). In a sense, the Old Testament agrees – sacrifices without a right heart do not please God (Hos 6:6).

The New Testament reveals the meaning of all these animal sacrifices by showing us the true sacrifice which will give and maintain fellowship with God. It agrees that animal blood cannot wash away sin (Heb 10:4), and demonstrates that all acceptable sacrifices point to the one sacrifice of the Messiah on the cross. It is because of this that believers have a reconciled relationship with God. They do not need to pay money to make animal sacrifices – their loving heavenly Father has paid the full price in Jesus the Messiah.

Murder. In Bangla we say, *Edeshe nun ar khun sosta* (in our country, salt and blood are cheap). Every day we read in the newspapers of murders in south Asia and all over the world. As the Indian writer and philosopher Rabindranath Tagore said, "The earth is crazed with violence – in constant conflict."

In 1971 Bangladesh experienced a horrible genocide at the hands of the Pakistan army, and political attacks have continued. We remember well the assassination of Bangabandhu (the father of the nation) Sheikh Mujibur Rahman in 1975. Further back in history is the Mughal Emperor Aurangzeb's killing of his brothers – a family genocide for political gain.

Today, we have wives being killed by their husbands, girl foetuses being killed in the womb, and jihadist groups trying to murder opponents. Like Cain, such murderers think they are justified in their actions, so they show no repentance. Some, like Lamech, are proud of their violent behaviour and want to take revenge on their adversaries seventy-sevenfold! We realise that this tragic situation reflects the same state as in the days of Noah. Genesis 4 diagnoses the problem of violence in the world outside Eden. Jesus the Messiah gives us hope that his coming will put an end to this sin (Matt 24:27).

The New Testament

As we shall see in God's covenant with Noah's descendants in Genesis 9:5–6, murder is seen as a terrible crime throughout the Bible (e.g. Exod 20:13; 21:12–14; Num 35:6–34; Jas 5:6; Rev 21:8). God hates violence, especially murder in the name of religion, race or caste. In the New Testament, Jesus the Messiah goes to the real root of the matter, explaining that murder, as well as other sins, comes from the heart. Anger, he says, is a road that leads to murder – the two are the same road (Matt 5:21–26). This reminds us of God's question to Cain, "Why are you angry?" (Gen 4:6). We can also find the answer to Cain's question to God, "Am I my brother's keeper?," in Jesus the Messiah's answer to the religious expert's question "Who is my neighbour?" (Luke 10:25–37). The parable of the Good Samaritan tells us that we are not only to care for our brothers, but also for those whom we count as our enemies.

The New Testament refers explicitly to Cain and Abel in several places. Cain, in 1 John 3:12–13, is an example of what believers ought not to be. It says he was "of the evil one," and killed his brother because his own deeds were evil while his brother's deeds were righteous. Hebrews 11:4 uses Abel as an example of what believers ought to be. He offered his sacrifice through faith, and therefore pleased God and was counted as righteous. He was killed, but his faith still speaks to us; we remember his blood crying from the ground after his death (Gen 4:10).

We might think from 1 John 3:12–13 and Hebrews 11:4 that the world is divided into those who are like Cain and those who are like Abel, but the New Testament also has allusions to the Cain and Abel story which challenge this view of humanity. Jesus the Messiah's parable of the obedient and disobedient sons (Matt 21:28–32), and his most famous parable, of the prodigal son, the waiting father and the elder brother (Luke 15:11–32), do not let us label one son as "good" and the other as "bad." In each case, the one who starts out "bad" eventually does what his father wants, whereas the one who seems to be "good" eventually brings shame on his father. All of us are like Cain in some ways, and we need forgiveness and redemption if we are to become like Abel. The writer of Hebrews remembers Abel's blood, and uses it to illustrate the power of the shed blood of Jesus the Messiah, which opens the way back into God's presence for all (Heb 12:24).

The Qur'an

Sūra *al-Māʾida* 5:27–32 has the only qurʾanic account of the "two sons of Adam."

> Recite to them the truth of the story of the two sons of Adam. Behold! They each presented a sacrifice (to God). It was accepted from one, but not from the other. Said the latter: "Be sure I will slay thee." "Surely," said the former, "(God) doth accept of the sacrifice of those who are righteous.
>
> "If thou dost stretch thy hand against me, to slay me, it is not for me to stretch my hand against thee to slay thee: for I do fear God, the cherisher of the worlds.
>
> "For me, I intend to let thee draw on thyself my sin as well as thine, for thou wilt be among the companions of the fire, and that is the reward of those who do wrong."
>
> The (selfish) soul of the other led him to the murder of his brother: he murdered him, and became (himself) one of the lost ones.
>
> Then God sent a raven, who scratched the ground, to show him how to hide the shame of his brother. "Woe is me!" said he;

"Was I not even able to be as this raven, and to hide the shame of my brother?" Then he became full of regrets.

The sons are not named, but Islamic literature knows them as Qābīl and Hābīl. The Qur'an's use of the story is similar to some of the New Testament uses of it, warning against jealousy and murder, and implying that believers should be like Abel and not like Cain. However, it sees Abel's blood only as pointing to the seriousness of murder, and does not mention the sacrifice of Jesus the Messiah.

The qur'anic account focuses on Cain's murderous thoughts and actions, and on his conversation with Abel before he slew him. It includes features which are found in pre-Islamic Christian and Jewish literature rather than in the Bible. For example, the dialogue between Cain and Abel has parallels in Syriac writings, including the late fifth-century *Life of Abel* by Symmachus. Cain's learning to bury his brother by observing a raven burying its mate can be compared to the following rabbinic account:

> Adam and his wife sat weeping and lamenting him, not knowing what to do with the body, as they were unacquainted with burying. Then a raven came whose fellow raven was dead; it took him and buried him before their eyes. Then said Adam, "I shall do like the raven, and taking Abel's corpse, he dug in the earth, and hid it. (Pirke Rabbi Eliezer,[44] 21; cf. al-Mā'ida 5:31)

Sūra *al-Mā'ida* is late Medinan. Islamic tradition sees the occasion of revelation for the Cain and Abel passage as a Jewish plot against The Islamic Prophet Muhammad's life, and the Qur'an follows the story with laws about killing people. The Mishnah, the central Jewish collection of the oral Torah, also uses the Cain and Abel story to discuss murder, and the Qur'an quotes directly from it:

> On that account: We ordained for the Children of Israel that if any one slew a person – unless it be for murder or for spreading mischief in the land – it would be as if he slew the whole people: and if any one saved a life, it would be as if he saved the life of the whole people. Then although there came to them Our apostles with clear signs, yet, even after that, many of them continued to commit excesses in the land. (Sūra al-Mā'ida 5:32; cf. Mishnah Sanhedrin 4:5)

---

44. This rabbinic source reached its present form after the time of the Islamic Prophet Muhammad, so it is not certain that this story pre-dates the Qur'an. However, the question of how Cain was buried is attested at least as far back as *Genesis Rabbah*.

This implies a warning for the Jews that, if they kill the Islamic Prophet Muhammad, then they will be punished by God as if they killed not only him but also his progeny.

The World of the Text
Structure and Genre

The overall structure and genre of Genesis 4 is that of genealogy. It begins the genealogy of humanity and follows a pattern which will occur several times in Genesis: the genealogy of the line which will not lead to the *Bani Isra'il* is recorded before the genealogy which will lead to the *Bani Isra'il*. So Genesis 4 gives the descendants of Cain, who will be wiped out in the flood, and prepares us for the following genealogy of the descendants of Seth in Genesis 5. Like so many of the Genesis genealogies, it includes narratives and poems – in this case, the narrative of the first two brothers, and the poem of Lamech:

> Genealogy: the first two sons of Adam and Eve (4:1–2a)
>> Narrative: the story of the sons and why Abel has no descendants (4:2b–16)
>>> Genealogy: the descendants of Cain (4:17–22)
>> Poem: Lamech and his wives (4:23–24)
> Genealogy: Seth, the third son of Adam and Eve, and his son Enosh (4:25–26)

The whole account of Cain and Abel (vv. 1–17) displays the Genesis author's use of the number seven. There are seven occurrences of "Abel" and of "brother," and fourteen of "Cain." In the account of Cain's descendants, it is the seventh descendant, Lamech, who gets the greatest attention.

COMMENTARY
Genesis 4:1–2a The Beginning of Genealogy

> *Now Adam knew Eve his wife, and she conceived and bore Cain, saying, "I have gotten a man with the help of the LORD." And again, she bore his brother Abel.*

Adam and Eve were still under God's loving care even outside Eden. "Knowing" here is not academic or intellectual. It conveys the personal sexual union of the first couple. The Lord blesses them by making their union fruitful.

Eve expresses her joy at the first birth, "with the Lord's help (Heb. *et-YHWH*, literally from or with YHWH) I have gotten (*qaniti*) a man (*ish*)" and names her son "Cain" (Heb. *qayin*), which sounds like Hebrew *qanah*, "to get or acquire." The sentence is strange and difficult to translate: *qanah* is mostly used for buying something, and *et* has a variety of meanings. But we can see that this first birth is special, and that Eve recognized the truth that children are gifts from the Lord alone (Ps 127:3; cf. Ps 128). The narrator refutes the idea that fertility gods like Baal could give children.

The name of the second son, Abel (Heb. *hebel*), means a breath, fleeting or meaningless. It probably indicates Abel's fleeting life, and points to the shortness and fragility of human life (cf. Ps 39:5).

We wonder how these two sons will turn out. Might one of them be the "seed" who will crush the serpent's head? What kind of parents will Adam and Eve be? Will they bring their children up to love and obey the Lord, or will they pass on their sinful rebellion? We will soon find out.

Genesis 4:2b–16 Narrative: The Story of the Sons and Why Abel Has No Descendants

The narrative of the two brothers has a chiastic form:

> **A.** Narrative of Cain and Abel, with God present (4:2b–5)
>> **B.** Dialogue between God and Cain (4:6–7)
>>> **C.** Cain and Abel alone: Murder! (4:8)
>> **B'.** Dialogue between God and Cain (4:9–14)
> **A'.** Narrative of God's acts which affect Cain (4:15–16)

The structure indicates the focus on the dreadful act of murder, the fact of God's involvement, and the importance of the dialogue between God and Cain. The story also has structural features which echo chapter 3, thus emphasizing that the sin of Cain is following on from the sin of his parents. The overall pattern of temptation, fall, dialogue between God and the sinner, punishment by exile, and mitigation by God's protection is repeated. We also note that, as God appears to be absent when Cain spoke with Abel and killed him, so he appears to be absent when Eve spoke with the serpent and with her husband ate the forbidden fruit. God gives the human beings all they need to resist temptation, but he then lets them make their own choices.

It is interesting to compare this with the Qur'an's narrative. The Qur'an has no dialogue with God at all – only a dialogue between Abel and Cain. We realise that, in Genesis, Abel says nothing: only his blood cries from the ground after he is dead. We could say that the Genesis story is not so much the story of Cain and Abel as the story of God and Cain, the sinner.

A. Narrative of Cain and Abel, with God present

> *Now Abel was a keeper of sheep, and Cain a worker of the ground. In the course of time Cain brought to the LORD an offering of the fruit of the ground, and Abel also brought of the firstborn of his flock and of their fat portions. And the LORD had regard for Abel and his offering, but for Cain and his offering he had no regard. So Cain was very angry, and his face fell. (4:2b–5)*

The first two professions were herding and agriculture. Cain cultivated the ground like his father, Adam, who had been commissioned to till the ground and then sentenced to painful toil in that work. In contrast, Abel was a shepherd. At that time, permission to eat meat had not yet been given, so why did he nurture sheep? Perhaps his parents had told him how God killed an animal and clothed them with its skin, and this made him want to care for animals.

The next thing that happens is sacrifice. Sacrifices have been an expression of religion from the beginning of recorded history. The text has no indication that God commanded Cain and Abel to bring a sacrifice; rather, they voluntarily offered sacrifices suitable to their vocations.

The sacrifices were *minchah*, gift offerings, a term generally meaning a gift offered to a superior. In the Torah, *minchah* denotes grain offerings as opposed to animal sacrifices (Lev 2), although elsewhere it can include animal sacrifice (e.g. 1 Sam 2:16–17, 29). In Genesis, it is used of gifts given to people as well as to God – for reconciliation between brothers in 32:13–19, and to win the favour of a ruler in 43:11. We can conclude that the purpose of the offerings was to win God's favour and to become reconciled with him after the expulsion from Eden.

We do not know from the text how God accepted Abel's offering. One possibility is that he answered by fire, as we read elsewhere (Gen 15:17; Lev 9:24; Judg 6:21; 1 Kgs 18:38; 1 Chr 21:26; 2 Chr 7:1). Some Islamic scholars assert this, and see the smoke from the fire as the sign of acceptance;[45] but Genesis simply does not tell us. What matters is not how God accepted the offering, but that he did accept it, and that he revealed his acceptance. What

---

45. *Kasasul Ambiya* says that a smokeless white flame came from the mountain and the meat of Abel's sacrifice was burned up (p. 61); and *Bayunul Qur'an* that smoke of Abel's sacrifice rose upward and Cain's sacrifice smoke fell downward indicating acceptance and respectively rejection.

is more, it is not only the sacrifice that is accepted, as the Mesopotamian gods might have accepted an offering of food: the person is accepted with his sacrifice. In fact, the text puts the person first: "The Lord had regard for Abel and his offering." This is indeed good news! Even outside Eden, it is possible for human beings to be acceptable to God.

But Cain and his offering were not accepted. What might his reaction be? We remember Adam and Eve's reaction when they were challenged about their disobedience – shame and denial of responsibility. Cain's reaction is similar. He is angry, which implies that he is blaming someone else for what has happened. His face falls, which implies shame.

WHY DID GOD ACCEPT ABEL'S SACRIFICE AND REJECT CAIN'S?

This is a question which everyone asks, and it is a question behind the Qur'an's narrative in Sūra 5. The Qur'an gives a simple answer: Abel's deeds were righteous and Cain's deeds were not. In Genesis, Cain's anger suggests that it was his question too – he thought that God was not being fair.

"Does God like shepherds and dislike cultivators?," we wonder. Does he prefer animal offerings to grain offerings? Under the Mosaic law, there are regulations for both meat and cereal offerings (e.g. Lev 1–7), so it seems unlikely that this is the solution. The Bible will later teach that bloodshed is necessary for purification from sin (Heb 9:1–22; Lev 4, 5 and 16; cf. 1 John 1:7), but how could Cain or Abel have known that?

Genesis 4:3–4 says that Cain offered some of his harvest and Abel offered a first-born lamb and its best parts. It appears that Abel offered the best of his produce, while Cain offered neither the first nor the best of his crop, but this is not certain from the text. It is only as the story continues that we see Cain's problem – he gets angry, he does not listen to God, and he tries to restore his status by killing his brother. We guess that something of those attitudes were there in his offering – that he was not really wanting to please God, but was trying to get a good name for himself, or maybe to show that he was better than his brother. It was not that he had the wrong ritual, but that he had the wrong attitude.

Jewish, Christian and Islamic tradition have all developed stories which affirm this idea. A typical version from Islamic tradition is that Cain and Abel both had a twin sister. Adam, by God's direction, told

Cain to marry Abel's twin, and Abel to marry Cain's, but Cain refused because Cain's twin, Aklima, was more beautiful. Adam advised his sons to make sacrifices to discover God's will. Cain offered a sheaf of his worst corn, while Abel offered his best lamb. Cain's motivation was to disobey his father and to challenge God's instructions, and his offering showed his proud disrespect. No wonder God rejected it! (See *Tofsirul Baizawi* on *Sūra al-Mā'ida* 5:27.)

The New Testament agrees that it was Cain's attitude that was wrong (1 John 3:12). Coming back to Genesis, we can see that this is in the text because, in each case the person is mentioned before the sacrifice (Gen 4:4–5). The implication is that God regards Abel and does not regard Cain, and that this is why he regards Abel's sacrifice and not Cain's sacrifice. He sees beyond the ritual to the faith in one heart and to the hatred in the other heart.

If this is the obvious answer from the text, why do people spend so many words discussing this question?

- Do we, like Cain, doubt God's justice? Do we think that perhaps YHWH is like the Mesopotamian gods who each have their favourite human beings? The rest of Genesis 1–11 assures us that the Creator God is not like them, but is holy and just.

- Do we want to know how to judge other people and their sacrifices? Genesis 4 shows us that we can only see outward actions: only God knows peoples' hearts. It is God who judges whether people are acceptable, and we should leave that judgement up to him.

- Do we want to know how we ourselves can be accepted by him? This is the important question. Genesis gives us some pointers, but we will have to read the rest of the Bible to find out which sacrifices are acceptable and why.

B. Dialogue between God and Cain

> The LORD said to Cain, "Why are you angry, and why has your face fallen? If you do well, will you not be accepted? And if you do not do well, sin is crouching at the door. Its desire is for you, but you must rule over it." (4:6–7)

As God spoke to Adam and Eve about their disobedience, he speaks to Cain about his problem. He gives him an opportunity to change his attitude and to be accepted. The loving Father God wants to accept Cain!

God begins by asking Cain to consider why he is angry, which is surely the first step in resisting the temptation to violence. The question echoes down the years to us, "Why are you angry?" Perhaps there was a sense of injustice, and certainly there was jealousy. The next question is why his face fell, that is, why he was ashamed. We can guess that this was due to fearing loss of prominence in the family. He was the elder, but his younger brother was getting preference. As we shall see, he was right to fear this loss.

Verse 7 implies that the anger was needless and useless. It was needless because there was a way for him to be accepted, and it was useless because he could not be accepted unless he "did well." The word for "accepted" has the root meaning of rising up, so it could imply that Cain could return to his elder brother status. Sadly, there is no indication that Cain heeded these questions.

Next, God warned Cain of his danger. This is the first use of the term "sin" (Heb. *chattah*). It is like a wild animal lying down outside a closed door. (The verb *rabats* [to lie down] is often used of animals.) God had commanded the humans to rule over animals (Gen 1:26, 28), and now he urges Cain to rule over sin.

There was a Mesopotamian myth about demons who linger around doorways waiting to ambush their victims. In the New Testament, similar imagery is used of *Shaytān* when we read, "Your adversary the devil prowls around like a roaring lion, seeking someone to devour" (1 Pet 5:8). So we imagine sin crouching outside Cain's heart, awaiting an opportunity to pounce on him. However, "sin" is not a demon but evil within a human being. The Qur'an's statement that it was Cain's *nafs* – his soul, an aspect of himself – is similar to the Genesis picture (Sūra *al-Mā'ida* 5:30). In Genesis 3, the temptation came from outside Adam and Eve: now, outside Eden, the sin comes from within the human being.

The vocabulary used for "desire" and "rule" is the same as in 3:16. There, the woman desires her husband and her husband rules over her. Here, sin desires Cain, and Cain has to rule over the sin. Together, these two verses give a vivid picture of the tragic fragmentation, between humans and within humans, that follows the first disobedience.

C. Cain and Abel alone: Murder!

> Cain spoke to Abel his brother. And when they were in the field, Cain rose up against his brother Abel and killed him. (4:8)

Cain did not respond to God. Instead, he spoke to his brother. He did not even try to bring his sin under his control. He opened his heart to it and, like a crouching beast, it pounced on him and defeated him. Prompted by shame, feeling insulted, with anger breeding jealous hatred, he attacked his brother Abel and killed him (compare this with Matt 5:21–26). It was God who had rejected his sacrifice, but he was angry at his brother. Maybe he thought that getting rid of his brother would return him to the place of first honour in his family. How wrong he was!

Verse 8 begins, literally, "Cain said to his brother"; but we do not know what he said. Jewish tradition discusses what might have been said, and some translations follow this by adding, "Let us go out into the field."

The Qur'an has no speech from God, but goes straight to Cain who says to his brother, "I will kill you." It is then Abel who talks to Cain, warning him that God will only accept from those who have *taqwā* (Sūras *al-Mā'ida* 5:27; cf. *al-Ḥajj* 22:34–37). *Taqwā* (often translated "piety") is a central theme in the Qur'an, and its meaning is much discussed in Islamic tradition. It means turning from idolatry of all kinds, keeping God in mind at all times, and obeying him completely. *Al-Bayḍāwī* says about this verse that it is not the flesh nor the blood of sacrifice that reaches God, but *taqwā* – the sincerity and intention of the heart.

B'. Dialogue between God and Cain

> Then the LORD said to Cain, "Where is Abel your brother?" He said, "I do not know; am I my brother's keeper?" And the LORD said, "What have you done? The voice of your brother's blood is crying to me from the ground. And now you are cursed from the ground, which has opened its mouth to receive your brother's blood from your hand." (4:9–11)

Cain has not responded to God, but God speaks again to Cain. As God put Adam and Eve on trial in Genesis 3, he puts Cain on trial here. As inside Eden, so outside Eden, God questions the sinner, the sinner answers, and God pronounces the sentence. God asked Adam, "Where are you?" (Gen 3:9). He asks Cain, "Where is your brother?" Like Adam, Cain did not confess his sin. He simply lied, "I do not know." He had no fear of God and thus sarcastically turned round and questioned God, "am I my brother's keeper?" (Gen 4:9). The first recorded lie is immediately followed by the first human question to God. Cain does not want to answer God – he thinks that God should answer him! And he denies any responsibility for his brother. Cain's sinful state is even worse than that of his father.

In Genesis 1–3, God, man, woman, and even the Serpent all have speaking roles. In Genesis 4, Abel says nothing until his blood cries out. It is a metaphor – a symbol of the soul crying for its right to live. The Torah plainly teaches that the life is in the blood (Lev 17:11). The verb used for cry (*tsa'aq*) is very strong. It expresses a feeling of desperate need, like a starving man crying for food or a girl crying out during rape. God does hear his people's desperate cries for help (Exod 22:22–23). "Blood" in verse 10 is plural in the Hebrew. It is from this that the rabbis took the idea cited in the Qur'an that killing one person is killing many. They point out that all the people who would have descended from Abel were also destroyed when he was killed.

The epistle to the Hebrews will compare the cry of Abel's blood to the cry of Jesus the Messiah's blood, which was shed for the pardon of all of our sins, even for murder (Heb 12:24). The cries of the bloods of the three million martyrs in the 1971 liberation struggle have inspired the patriotic freedom fighters of Bangladesh to continue the martyrs' unfinished task. Christ's blood cries out peace and forgiveness for the whole world!

> *"When you work the ground, it shall no longer yield to you its strength. You shall be a fugitive and a wanderer on the earth." (4:12)*

Cain did not regain his firstborn status in his family by killing his brother. Instead, he was sent far from the family, and Abel's place was taken by another son (Gen 4:25). This is the first instance of sibling rivalry and the displacement of the rights of the firstborn by a younger son which will be a repeated pattern in Genesis, seen in Isaac and Ishmael, Jacob and Esau, Joseph and his brothers, and Ephraim and Manasseh. The punishment was an intensification of Adam's sentence in Genesis 3:17–19. It would be even harder for Cain to grow crops. What a contrast to the abundance of Eden! Where Adam was not cursed, but the ground was cursed, Cain himself is now cursed. Where Adam and Eve were expelled from Eden, Cain is sent even farther away and will not be able to settle in any land.

WHOM DID CAIN MARRY?

Every Bengali who reads Genesis wants to know who Cain married. We know that Cain had a brother, but that brother is now dead; and, even if he had a sister, we know that marriage between brothers and sisters is forbidden. We are not the first to ask these questions.

The most popular solution is that Adam had sons and daughters other than those named (Gen 5:4), so Cain could have married a sister. Jewish, Christian and Muslim traditions all suggest that Eve bore many children. Tradition points out that, in the early years, intermarrying with relatives was the only way to establish the human race and that the laws against marrying close relatives had not yet been given. Further, inbreeding was not yet a problem, because the genetic line was still pure. Hence the prohibition against incestuous marriage was given later (Lev 18:6–18).

From the word translated "again" in Genesis 4:2, Jewish tradition suggests that both Cain and Abel were born with twin sisters, and that they married each other's twins so that the marriage relationships were as distantly related as possible. Islamic tradition has similar stories.

Another possibility is that Adam and Eve were not the only human beings whom God had created. However, we then have to ask more questions. How does the "fall" of Genesis 3 apply to all of humanity? Are Adam and Eve representative of all humanity, and, if so, in what way?

Early commentators are concerned about legal details and use the question of Cain's wife as an opportunity for thinking about why marriage to close relations is later forbidden, and under what circumstances it might have been permissible. Today's readers are more likely to be concerned with historical and scientific questions. Going back to the Bible, however, we find that the question is simply not answered – either in Genesis or anywhere else. Genesis here is not about such literal and legal details, but about the nature of human beings and of God. Yet the question about who might have been the mothers whose seed breeds the family line will become an important one as we read on in Genesis. Mothers remain unnamed through the genealogies of Genesis 5, 10 and 11, but, from the promise of children to Abram (12:1–3) onwards, the narrative will often be about making sure that the heirs to that promise have the right mothers.[1]

---

1. see commentary on Gen 11:30

As so often, there is an implied refutation of fertility religions. The ancient Baal worshipers, and even the worshipers of the goddess of Kali in the Indian sub-continent, believed that the sacrifice of human or animal blood could bring purification and could increase the fertility of the soil.[46] Far from Cain reaping any reward by pouring innocent blood into the ground, he himself and the ground are cursed by God.

> Cain said to the LORD, "My punishment is greater than I can bear. Behold, you have driven me today away from the ground, and from your face I shall be hidden. I shall be a fugitive and a wanderer on the earth, and whoever finds me will kill me." (4:13–14)

Cain did not repent of his sin; he was only concerned about his punishment. He did not understand that God is omnipresent and that it is not possible to hide from God. Away from God's presence, Cain feared the presence of other people. Henri Blocher quotes the Latin proverb, *homo homini lupus* (a man is wolf to another man). Cain has devoured his brother, and now he realizes that he has unleashed something terrible. Others may devour him, and he is terrified.

This indicates that there were other people on earth, and is the basis for the belief that Eve had other children than those mentioned in this chapter.

A'. Narrative of God's acts which affect Cain

Then the LORD said to him, "Not so! If anyone kills Cain, vengeance shall be taken on him sevenfold." And the LORD put a mark on Cain, lest any who found him should attack him. (4:15)

As would happen in the covenant with Noah's offspring in Genesis 9, God promises to preserve the sinner's life (cf. 3:21; 9:6, 11). This is the miraculous grace of YHWH, the covenant God. He loves not only the innocent victim but also the murderer. Whoever killed Cain would be punished sevenfold. The word for "punish" is used for retaliatory killing in Exodus 21:20–21. Seven is a perfect number, so the sevenfold punishment means a complete divine judgement (cf. Prov 6:31).

God gave Cain a mark (*ot*, also used of the signs of the covenants in Gen 9:13; 17:11) to verify his promise and to warn potential enemies. The parallel with the later covenant signs implies that this was not a mark of stigma, but a sign of God's gracious protection. We are reminded of God's provision of

---

46. https://www.britannia.com/topic/sacrifice-religion/ blood-offering, accessed 2 Feb 2020.

protective skins for Adam and Eve in 3:21. Even when Cain is wandering away from God, he bears the mark of God's lordship, as a branded slave bears the mark of his owner.

Cain does not understand that he deserves death, as the later law of Genesis 9:5 will explain. He does not understand that God is mercifully giving him time to repent. This is the last conversation between Cain and God, and Cain has woefully failed to understand what God is saying to him.

Then Cain went away from the presence of the LORD and settled in the land of Nod, east of Eden. (4:16)

Cain leaves God's presence (Heb. *pane* YHWH, "the Lord's face") for the land of Nod (meaning "wandering"). We wonder how far God is sending Cain away, and how far Cain is deliberately leaving God behind. We do not know the location of Nod, but the phrase "east of Eden" reminds us again of the loss of the garden. Cain will now build a life for himself apart from God. But the reader knows that God's safeguard extends even to the land of aimless wandering: there is no place in the world outside of his secure protection.

Genesis 4:17–24 Genealogy: Cain's Descendants and Extension of Civilization

Cain knew his wife, and she conceived and bore Enoch. When he built a city, he called the name of the city after the name of his son, Enoch. (4:17)

Cain had sexual relations with his wife. The Genesis writer does not name the wife, but focuses on Cain's descendants and their skills and occupations. Cain tried to compensate for his despair by building a civilization in Nod, the place away from God (the narrator implies that this was a civilization without God). Cain had God's protection, but he wanted to build his own security for himself and to escape from his wanderings. He named the new city after his son, Enoch.

The name "Enoch" (*Chanok*) could come from the Canaanite *ḥanaku* (vassal), from the Hebrew *ch-n-k* (to dedicate), or from the Egyptian *ḥnk* (alluding to an offering made when the foundation stone of a building was laid).[47] The latter two meanings suggest that it has to do with a new beginning. Cain was initiating a way of life apart from God, a security apart from God, and a sense of rootedness apart from God. This was against God's desire, as he wished to live with his people even outside of the garden!

---

47. Here and elsewhere, our interpretations of names are informed by Douglas, *New Bible Dictionary*; and by Hess, Wenham and Westermann.

> *To Enoch was born Irad, and Irad fathered Mehujael, and Mehujael*
> *fathered Methushael, and Methushael fathered Lamech. And Lamech took*
> *two wives. The name of the one was Adah, and the name of the other*
> *Zillah. (4:18–19)*

There will be another Enoch in the godly line of Seth, a contrasting Enoch who walked with God (5:21–24). The Enoch who is Cain's son had a son named Irad. Like all the names in these two verses, the meaning of "Irad" is uncertain. Some link it with Arabic words meaning "bird," "wild ass," "strength" or "reed hut," but others think it is the name of a place or that it comes from the Hebrew *'ir* (city). We get a picture of a growing and complex world, and the description of Lamech's family will confirm this.

The names open many possibilities about the languages from which they were derived as well as about their meanings, but it seems that the people were not entirely godless. The name of Irad's son ends in *el*, the name of a Canaanite god and of a Mesopotamian god. "El" was also used by Abraham and elsewhere in the Old Testament for the one true creator God, usually with an added description (e.g. Gen 14:22; 17:1; 33:20). Mehujael could have opposite meanings, either "god smites" or "god gives life." Methushael could mean "man of the god Shael" or "man of Sheol" (the place of the dead).[48] Lamech could come from the Sumerian word *lumga* (the god who was patron of music), from the Akkadian *lumakku* (a class of priests), or be cognate with Arabic *ylmk* (a strong youth).

Lamech was the seventh generation from Adam through Cain's line. This Lamech will be very different from Lamech, the son of Methuselah, who will name his son Noah in hope of God's mercy (5:28–31). The Lamech through Cain's line will be a killer and also the first polygamist mentioned in the Bible, taking two wives. Polygamy is against the norm of God's marriage plan.[49] So Lamech will violate God's rule about marriage and continue the legacy of his forefather by living apart from God.

> *Adah bore Jabal; he was the father of those who dwell in tents and have*
> *livestock. His brother's name was Jubal; he was the father of all those*
> *who play the lyre and pipe. Zillah also bore Tubal-cain; he was the*
> *forger of all instruments of bronze and iron. The sister of Tubal-cain was*
> *Naamah. (4:20–22)*

---

48. Cf. Methuselah; see comment on Genesis 5:21.
49. See commentary on Genesis 2:23–24.

Lamech's children begin arts and technology. "Father" here should be understood metaphorically, as "precursor," rather than as a literal ancestor. The narrator is silent about God's attitude to this creativity. However, although Cain's civilization would be wiped out during the flood, the development of arts and crafts and technology would continue. We remember that the humans had the jobs of ruling the earth and of naming the animals, and can conclude that creativity is part of being made in the image of God, although, of course, the results can be used for sinful purposes as well as for the glory of God.

The name Adah could mean "pleasure" or "ornament," and her sons were the precursors of nomadic herders and of musicians. The meanings of Jabal and Jubal are uncertain, but they could be related to Hebrew y-b-l (to bring), or to yobel (a ram's horn). The latter would refer to the sheep raised by nomadic peoples as well as the ram's horn as a musical instrument.

"Zillah" could come from words for "shade" or for "cymbal," and her son was the precursor of metal workers. "Tubal-cain" is unusual, being double barreled. "Cain" could simply be the preservation of his ancestor's name, but it could also mean "smith" or "craftsman." "Tubal" could refer to the people who became the metal traders mentioned in Ezekiel 27:13, so Tubal-cain would be a metal smith. Another interpretation is that Tubal comes from the Hebrew taval (to improve), so that Tubal-cain means that he improved on Cain – where Cain killed his brother with his bare hands, or maybe with a rock, Tubal-cain made metal weapons.

Genesis does not tell us what Tubal-cain made with the bronze and iron. He may have made weapons, but he would also have made tools. Some traditions see him as the first chemist and miner. Bronze and iron are seen today as important markers of human development, the Bronze Age having begun in different places between 4000 and 3500 BC, and the Iron Age around 1200 BC. The narrator may intend us to suppose that Tubal-cain worked with both these metals, and that working with iron was lost due to the flood; but it is more likely that we should read this as some early metal work which was the precursor of all future metal work.

Tubal-cain's sister was Naamah (v. 22). We learn nothing about her, but Jewish tradition says that she became Noah's wife. It records two opposite meanings for her name: that her deeds were pleasing (ne'emim) or that she sang (man'emeth) as part of idolatrous worship (Gen Rab XXIII:3). The Qur'an will pick up the idea that Noah's wife was an unbeliever (Sūra at-Taḥrīm 66:10), but Islamic tradition gives her name as Walīyah or Amzura and not Naamah. Amzura is also named in Jubilees (second century BC), where she is not Tubal-cain's sister but Noah's cousin.

Poem: Lamech and His Wives

> *Lamech said to his wives:*
>
> *"Adah and Zillah, hear my voice;*
> *   you wives of Lamech, listen to what I say:*
> *I have killed a man for wounding me,*
> *   a young man for striking me.*
> *If Cain's revenge is sevenfold,*
> *   then Lamech's is seventy-sevenfold." (4:23–24)*

Lamech's speech is sometimes called the "Song of the Sword."[50] It has just twenty-one words, and its brevity makes it both memorable and powerful. It is a tragic description of the heart of the new community of Cain's offspring. What a contrast it is with Adam's poem in 2:23!

Lamech is a man boasting to two wives. What a contrast to Adam's recognition of his one perfect partner! As if to underline the sadness of polygamy, Lamech is expressing superiority over his wives. As in Adam's poem, each of the two phrases in the first line ends with *-i* (my), but while Adam is recognizing that his wife is like him, Lamech emphasizes that his wives should attend to him. He wants to be seen to be better than them, and he wants them to know that he has power to be violent and will use that power. Did this make the wives happy because they belonged to a powerful man, or did it make them afraid of what he might do to them if they displeased him? We do not know, but, like all good poetry, this stirs our emotions as we read it, and we panic as we imagine a worldwide population of cruel husbands.

Lamech is proud that he is a murderer like his ancestor Cain. Again, each of the two parallel phrases in the second line ends with *-i* (me). Lamech's murder is thoroughly centred on himself, and there seems to have been no inner struggle. Someone hurt him, so he killed them. The implication is that he is worse than Cain, and that he thinks that being more violent is something to boast of. The final line makes it explicit that he wants to multiply Cain's sin.

Worst of all, it seems that Lamech is setting himself up as a judge in place of God, and even above God. Whereas God would bring a sevenfold vengeance on the slayer of Cain, Lamech says he will avenge himself seventy-sevenfold. Lamech is not only boasting of what he can do, he is saying that he can do over ten times what God can do!

In contrast to Lamech's terrorist-like boast, Jesus the Messiah told his disciple Peter that he should forgive an offender "seventy times seven" times

---

50. See also Introduction page 19.

(Matt 18:22). Peter would doubtless have remembered Lamech's seventy-sevenfold vengeance. In God's sight, forgiving seventy times seven is far better than killing even once. On the cross, Jesus the Messiah takes all our violence onto himself, so that even the cruel Lamechs of this world have the possibility of repentance and forgiveness.

Genesis 4:25–26 Genealogy: The Third Son of Adam and Eve, and His Son Enosh

> *And Adam knew his wife again, and she bore a son and called his name Seth, for she said, "God has appointed for me another offspring instead of Abel, for Cain killed him." (4:25)*

Adam's second son, Abel, had been killed. This verse is the only hint of what the loss meant to Eve. The first tfhing that happened outside Eden was the blessing of children, but the next thing that happened was the tragic loss of one of those children at the hand of the other child. Here in verse 25, Eve recognizes again that a child is God's gift, and the implication is that this third son is in some way a replacement for Abel. Seth's name (Heb. *Shet*) is similar to *shat* – the word translated "appointed." It can mean "to place" or "to replace" or "to be appointed." Seth was appointed as a replacement for the murdered son so that the plan of God could continue. At the same time, we can infer that his birth would have been a comfort to his bereaved parents. Cain will never regain his first-born status: it is given to Seth.

Seth is the only child of Adam other than Cain and Abel mentioned by name. The Qur'an does not mention him at all, but Genesis makes it clear that he is important. In Eden, God had promised one who would come to deliver humans from the serpent's power (Gen 3:15). Since Abel was dead, and Cain's line was corrupt, the Saviour would come through the line of Seth. God's plan for a Redeemer continues to advance.

> *To Seth also a son was born, and he called his name Enosh. At that time people began to call upon the name of the LORD. (4:26)*

This verse seems to be teaching that Seth was a godly man, and that, in contrast with Cain, he raised his son, Enosh, in the knowledge of God. The word *enosh* is translated "man" in many places, such as Psalm 8:5; but here it could come from the Hebrew root *anash*, meaning "weak" or "frail." Psalm 8:5 puts these two ideas together, as it implies that the man is weak, and that it is amazing that God cares about him at all. Cain's line felt no need for God, but perhaps Seth's son Enosh felt his weakness and knew his need for God.

It also seems that, at this time, people knew the personal divine name YHWH. How did they know this? Why was it unknown by the time of Moses so that it had to be revealed at the burning bush (Exod 3:14–15)? We are not told, but this verse gives us yet another glimpse of hope that these fallen human beings will be included in God's covenant love, and that Seth's birth will mark the beginning of a new humanity that will never end.

So, although Genesis tells us little about Seth, Jewish and Christian tradition have seen him as a true believer, like his older brother, Abel. Although Seth is not mentioned in the Qur'an, Islamic tradition generally regards him as the second prophet, following his father Adam, and it is said that he was given fifty pages of scripture.[51] He is said to have received wisdom, including knowledge of time, a vision of the future flood, and revelation about the practice of night prayer.

Seth has also played a role in Sufism. For example, for Ibn 'Arabī, his major characteristic is that he was given to Adam as a gift, to ease his grief after the loss of Abel. God's gifts are, says Ibn 'Arabī, revelatory, so Seth shows believers that they should ask God for knowledge and revelation. Neither Jewish nor Christian tradition sees Seth as a prophet, but, in the second to fourth centuries AD, there was an Egyptian Gnostic sect[52] which claimed to have special knowledge which had been revealed to Seth. This could be a source of the Islamic traditions.

What Genesis does tell us is that Seth, like all Adam's descendants, was born outside Eden because of Adam's sin; but he called out to God,[53] and others did so too. Genesis 1–11 is about beginnings, and here we have the beginning of the important idea of people "calling on the name of the Lord."

Until this point, the story has been about God taking the initiative in speaking to people. In the garden of Eden, human beings were in direct communication with God. Outside Eden, God is not limited, but the people do not know his close presence. He accepts Abel's sacrifice, and he comes to speak to Cain, but it seems difficult for people to approach him. Now we find

---

51. Seth is seen as being in the genealogical line with Adam, who is said to have received ten pages (ṣuḥuf), Enoch, who received thirty pages, and Abraham, who received ten pages.

52. The "Sethians." See *Neander's Church History*, vol. 2, 115.

53. This is the common Christian interpretation of this phrase. Some Jewish traditions have a more negative view, seeing the "calling out" not as positive prayer but as profaning the Name of the Lord. They see Enosh as a weak man, who turned people to idolatry.

people beginning the practice of speaking to him. We notice several things, all of which will be developed later in the Bible:

1. "Call" means "cry out loud," not silent prayer. It does not mean a ritual or a formal prayer, but rather it means a cry from the human heart to the covenant Lord. It may also mean that people began to tell others about the Lord, just like the church was to tell all nations the good news many years later.

2. It suggests that Seth's descendants started something which Cain's descendants did not do: the godly people were very different from the other people. Genesis will later tell us about the separation of God's community from other people, and this will be an important theme in the later parts of the Torah. For example, we may compare the separations of Seth and Cain, Abraham and Lot, Jacob and Esau, and the *Bani Isra'il* and pagan nations.

3. This suggests a move towards the communication with God which had been lost when Adam and Eve left Eden. This is good news! Later on, people "call on the name of the Lord" when they worship and acknowledge him (Gen 12:8; 13:4; 21:33; 26:25; 1 Kgs 18:24; Ps 116:17). The patriarchs worshipped God sincerely even before the laws and the sacrifices were given. They did not need priests and rituals (Acts 7:2–53). Similarly, since Jesus the Messiah's death on the cross, believers do not need priests or shrines. Through the Holy Spirit, they can worship God anywhere in Spirit and Truth (John 4:19–24). God is with them, as he was with the patriarchs, wherever they go.

Theological Reflection

Genesis 1 and 2 show us God's beautiful, harmonious creation: Genesis 4 shows us some of the ugly disharmony produced by human sin. Its place in the chiasm of Genesis 2–4 (see page 92) emphasizes the contrast between the worlds inside and outside Eden. Theologically, we might say that Genesis 4 is all about questions. It asks the really important questions which we should be asking in our fallen world. In some cases, it hints at the answer; in others, it leaves us longing to know more. In this way, *it plants the seeds of many themes which will grow in the rest of the Bible*. This theological reflection will explore some of the questions.

Will God continue to bless us outside Eden?

Yes! He continued the creation blessings by giving Adam and Eve children.

Is it possible to please God outside Eden?

Yes! He accepted Abel and his sacrifice.

What do we have to do to please God and to be accepted by him? What is an acceptable sacrifice?

Genesis 4 gives us hope, but does not give us a clear answer.

From the qur'anic story of Cain and Abel, the answer seems to be that we can please God by being good people – being *muttaqīn* (people who practice *taqwā*), whose sacrifices are accepted. But how can we be like good Abel and not wicked like Cain? The Bible has many stories of two brothers. Often the brothers fight with each other, but it is usually not so easy to see that one is "bad" and the other is "good." Jesus the Messiah's story of the two brothers in Luke 15:11–32 illustrates this: one brother appears to be bad and leaves home and wastes his inheritance, but he repents and comes home and is welcomed by his father. The other appears to be good, staying at home and working for his father, but then he defies his father and refuses to welcome his brother home. There is hope for the person who recognizes that they are "Cain," and there is danger for the person who thinks that they are "Abel." Yes, we should pray to be shown the right path, but the world is not simply divided into Cains and Abels, that is, good people and bad people.

How can we live in peace with our brothers outside Eden?

Genesis 4 tells us that this is a very important question: we have a responsibility toward our brothers. This is one way in which we can see whether we are good or bad people. We cannot always tell what God thinks of people, but we can observe how we treat each other. When we are not in fellowship with God, we will not be in fellowship with our brothers, and terrible conflict will arise. Genesis 4 also tells us that living together is difficult: the Cain and Abel story is our first glimpse of life outside Eden, and people have been fighting and killing each other ever since.

How do we understand our tendencies to do evil?

Genesis 4 tells us that something called sin (Heb. *chattah*) is very close to us, and that it wants to rule over us. It is waiting for us to give it the slightest opportunity, but we do not yet know exactly what it is. It seems to be different from the serpent which tempted Eve – that snake was outside her, talking to her, while "sin" is inside Cain, wanting to conquer him. The Qur'an also recognizes that it is something inside Cain which causes him to sin – his *nafs*. The root of the evil is in his human nature, in his very self. South Asian people list six enemies (Sanskrit *sarad ripu*) which bind us and prevent our good selves from shining. These are *kama* (lust/craving), *krodha* (anger), *lobha* (greed), *moha* (delusion), *mada* (arrogance), and *matsarya* (jealousy). All human beings can recognize this inner battle.

How does God deal with us when we sin?

Genesis 4 both shows us that sin has serious consequences and gives us hope. The consequences are punishment and, eventually, death. The hope is that God speaks to the sinner, offers him a way of repentance and gives him less punishment than he deserves even if he does not repent. This is one of the most obvious differences between the Qur'an and Genesis. In the Qur'an, Abel is the one who speaks to his brother and warns him against sin. In Genesis, God does not speak to good Abel but to sinful Cain. God cares so much about the sinner that he speaks directly to him!

Can sin be forgiven?

This question is raised by Cain's speech in 4:13, which is usually translated, "My punishment is greater than I can bear." The Hebrew is just three words *gadol 'avoni min-nsho*: literally "great my evil more than to bear." *'Avoni* could refer to Cain's punishment, but it could also refer to his guilt or to his sin. It could be that Cain cannot bear his guilt or sin, but can some other person bear the sin? Can God bear the sin? Is Cain asking whether or not God can bear his sin? *Genesis Rabbah* asks this question by having Cain ask whether, since God can carry the entire universe, he cannot also carry Cain's sin. Which leads us to the next question.

Must sin be punished?

The answer is, yes. In Genesis 4, God punishes Cain and protects him, but, like Adam and Eve, he is still sent away from his place and from God's close presence (Heb. *pane*, "face"). God can allow the sinful person to remain on the earth, but sin is so serious that he cannot allow that person to remain before his face. So could God in some way "carry" Cain's sin, so that Cain would not have to be punished for it? This takes us back to the question of what might be an acceptable sacrifice, and points us forward to the sacrifices set down in the rest of the Torah, to the tabernacle, to the temple, and finally to the sacrifice of Jesus the Messiah.

The qur'anic story does not deal with the question of whether sin might ever be left unpunished. Instead, it deals with judgement, both in this world and in the hereafter. In the hereafter, Cain will experience the fire of judgement (al-Mā'ida 5:29). For this world, there is the legislation about murder which follows the story (vv. 32–34). Murder is strictly forbidden, but there are wrongdoings which have to be punished by death. This raises the important question of how human beings should deal with the crimes which are done among them. Genesis will begin to address that question after the flood (Gen 9:5–6). How far God can bear our sins, and how far we should bear with sins committed in our societies, are related questions; but they are not the same question.

What about repentance?

Genesis 4 makes it clear that Cain did not repent of his anger against his brother. He regretted that he was punished, and recognized that he had sinned, but he does not seem to have changed his mind about his original anger and jealousy. The Qur'an describes Cain as regretting that he did not know how to bury his brother but, as in Genesis, there is no suggestion that he really repented of what he had done. This raises the question of how we repent, of what we should repent, and how our minds can be changed.

What are the long-term effects of sin and conflict?

Genesis 4 gives us a sad picture of Cain and his descendants. They may build cities and develop culture, but Cain is exiled, and his descendants continue to propagate violence. The first family conflict generates more family conflict, and violence produces more violence. God has patience for many generations but, eventually, Cain's line will be destroyed in the flood. But, despite this, there is hope. There will be the hope of laws to limit the effects of murderous wickedness in Genesis 9 and of God's commitment never again to destroy humankind.

Through Sūra al-Mā'ida 5:32–34, the Qur'an reports on one long-term effect of the story on Jewish law: the Cain and Abel story is the basis of the Mishnah's laws about murder. In addition, the Qur'an also uses the story to warn people who are hostile to the Islamic Prophet Muhammad and want to murder him. So the story becomes a paradigm example of jealousy and murder, and a warning for future generations.

The New Testament, too, uses the story as a warning and an example – we are not to be like murderous Cain (1 John 3:12). This verse is in the context of another kind of hope, which answers the question, "Can God bear our sins?"

"Yes!" says the Apostle John. How can God bear our sin? The answer is that Jesus the Messiah bears our sins on the cross:

> He [Jesus] is the propitiation [atoning sacrifice] for our sins, and not for ours only but also for the sins of the whole world. (1 John 2:2)

The other place where the New Testament refers explicitly to the story of Cain and Abel is in Hebrews, where we read that "the blood of Jesus speaks better than the blood of Abel" (Heb 12:24). Again, there is a link between the sacrifice and our salvation, and between our salvation and the way in which we act. That brings us to our final question.

What is the connection between sacrifice and the control of the sinful nafs (self)?

Does the control of the sinful *nafs* make a person good, so that he or she can offer an acceptable sacrifice, or does an acceptable sacrifice somehow make the person good so that he or she can control the sinful *nafs*? Is it even possible for the sinful *nafs* to change?

The Torah gives many details about what sacrifices God accepts, but the Bible also teaches us that sacrifices by themselves cannot solve the problem of our sin. It is not the blood of animals or ritual purity that makes us acceptable or holy (Heb. *qadosh*, Gk. *hagios*, Ar. *quddus*). Because God is holy, he wants us to be holy (Lev 11:44; 1 Pet 1:16). The sacrifices in the Torah all point to the perfect sacrifice of Jesus the Messiah by whom God himself bears our sins. According to 1 John, we do not receive forgiveness by trying to be like righteous Abel; rather, we become holy by accepting Jesus the Messiah's perfect sacrifice, and we will know who belongs to Jesus the Messiah by seeing who loves other people. The person who has truly accepted the atoning sacrifice will not be a slave of sin, of the jealous, murderous *nafs* within them.

All the sacrifices ordained in the Torah are, say the prophets, useless if they do not lead us to fellowship with God, and therefore make us merciful towards our fellow human beings.[54] God has shown us the straight path – it is the path of fellowship with God and with our brothers, doing justice and loving righteousness and walking humbly with God (Mic 6:8). In the Gospel of Matthew, Jesus the Messiah quoted from the book of Hosea: "I desire mercy, and not sacrifice" (Matt 9:13); and the Apostle Paul urges his readers to offer themselves as a living sacrifice, which is the true worship that pleases God (Rom 12:1–2).

---

54. See especially Amos 5:21–24 and Hosea 6:6.

The Bangladeshi national poet, Kazi Nazrul Islam, also recognizes that a right heart is what matters, and that God wants us, not our rituals. His poem, "Martyrs Eid," appeals to Muslims to abstain from animal sacrifice and, instead, to sacrifice their own sinful *nafs*. Here is what he writes to those who sacrifice animals as a ritual offering to commemorate the willingness of Abraham to follows God's command to sacrifice his son, during the Eid ul Azha, the sacrifice feast:

> You have gorged your food like pigs,
> You have grown fat, ugly and stupid.
> Now, please, offer yourselves as sacrifice, . . .
> please offer no animal to God as a sacrifice.
> That will go in vain,
> and you will remain viler
> than the beasts you kill.
> Rather put to death the beasts
> that lurk in your heart.
> It will give a respite to the animals,
> and will be a noble deed on your part.[55]

What About Us?

Inside the garden of Eden, the earth was fruitful; outside, even hard work produced few crops (v. 12). Inside, there was a secure home in the presence of God; outside, people become restless wanderers (v. 14). Inside, there was safety; outside, there was danger (vv. 8, 14).

We live in the Genesis 4 imperfect world, but we can accept Jesus the Messiah the Messiah as God's perfect sacrifice for our sins. But how shall we then live? Do we ask ourselves the questions which are raised by the story of Cain and Abel, or are we, like Cain's descendants, more interested in building cities, making tools, playing music and taking revenge on people? Cities, tools and music are not, of course, bad things; but, when they are our focus, and they are combined with the desire to boast and to make ourselves seem greater, they become idols. (We will see more of this danger in chapters 10 and 11.)

Inside the garden, there was a perfect relationship between humans and the rest of creation, as humans cared for the earth and lived in harmony with

---

55. Kazi Nazrul Islam, "The Martyr's Eid," Original: "Shohidi Eid"; Translation: Kabir Chowdhury https://www.poetrynook.com/poem/martyrs-eid.

the animals. Outside the garden, humans also tilled the ground and cared for the animals, but only Abel really understood what it meant to do his work for God. Will we recognize that all that we have and all we do are from God, and will we give back to him all the fruits of our work, for his glory alone?

Inside the garden, there was peace and blessing. Outside, there was jealously, anger, competition and vengeance. Will we seek to live in harmony with God and with our fellow human beings? Will we learn to rejoice when others are blessed, and to deal with our anger and shame when we feel slighted? Will we recognize that we are "our brother's keeper"?

Inside the garden, there was a perfect relationship between male and female: all was prepared for the blessings of family life. Outside, there was still the blessing of procreation, but there was also sibling murder, polygamy, and husbands boasting to their wives. Will those of us who are married live in faithful mutual respect with one spouse?

And what about our families? Can we bring up our children to love one another and to cooperate with one another and not to be jealous of one another and fight one another? Can we raise Seths rather than Cains? Many of us are living as minorities in our communities in Bangladesh. Sometimes we do not have the opportunity to live with other believers to worship our Lord together, so what we do in our families is a very important example for our children.[56]

Genesis 4 tells us that none of this will be easy outside Eden. Even as believers, we need to listen for God's challenge when we are tempted: "Why are you angry? Why has your face fallen?" Like Cain, we have to resist sin by controlling our *nafs*. That means believers see themselves as dead towards their wrong desires. Dead people cannot be tempted. We cannot do this by ourselves, but through the death and resurrection of the Messiah and by the power of the Holy Spirit (see Rom 6–8).

---

56. Daniel and his friends in Babylon (Dan 1–6) and Naaman the Syrian (2 Kgs 5:1–19) offer biblical examples of faithful discipleship in minority situations.

4

The Beginnings of Death and New Life – Genesis 5:1–6:8

The *Toledoth* of Adam

Genealogies have a tremendous influence on our worldview. "To the fourteenth generation" is a common phrase among Bengali people. It is believed that those who can memorize their lineage to fourteen generations will be blessed by their forefathers, and when a person utters a blessing or curse, they pronounce it to fourteen generations. On rainy days or moonlit nights, the elders of a village, be they Muslim or Hindu, tell the younger generation stories about their family heritage.

Genealogies not only tell us about our origins: they also affect our lives. The caste system in South Asia, which has been in place since the Vedic Age, is based on genealogy, and sometimes determines the profession of the next generation. Vocations are often determined by genealogical background, and villages are often named accordingly; for example, Jelepara (Fisherman's village), Boat Village, Blacksmith Village or Sayeed Barih (the house of the Sayeed family).

Our genealogies are not only lists of names: they include stories passed down through the generations and they guide our thinking about who we are and where we are going. Were our ancestors godly people and if so, are we godly people, and are we teaching this path to our children? Were our ancestors bandits? Then are we in danger of being bandits, and will our children follow this path? The Genesis genealogies, too, are much more than lists of names. They give us glimpses of some of the ancestors, and they lead on to narratives which deeply challenge their descendants and us today.

The *toledoth* of Adam begins with the names of chapter 5, and continues to the introduction to the flood story in chapter 6:1–8. Similarly, the *toledoth* of Noah will tell the reader the family story of Noah and his three sons, and finish with a challenging and sad story (Gen 9:18–29). The *toledoth* of the sons of Noah starts with the Table of Nations in Genesis 10, and then goes on to the challenging story of Babel in 11:1–9, which in turn leads into the record of the line of Shem.

We see that the Genesis genealogies are carefully linked together and related to each other, and that each raises questions for the following generations. Genesis 10 will be interrupted by some details about Nimrod and thus raises the question of what happens when peoples make their lands a power base for expansion. This is explored in the Babel story. Similarly, the Adam *toledoth* is interrupted by some details about Enoch who walked with God and was the only person not to die, and thus raises the question of whether eternal life might be possible on earth even outside Eden. Genesis 6:1–8 answers that question with a resounding "No!" The human line has become so corrupt that God is going to limit life spans even further, and, in fact, to destroy everyone and begin again.

Yet, as we have seen repeatedly, things are not hopeless. The Adam *toledoth* is full of signs that God will continue to find ways of graciously blessing his creation and his creatures. The dark story of Genesis 6:1–8 is illuminated by an awesome glimpse into the very heart of God, and finishes with the wonderful statement that "Noah found favour in the eyes of the Lord." The *toledoth* begins with blessing (*berakah*, 5:2), and ends with grace (*chen*, 6:8).

The Worlds Behind and in Front of the Text

Just as in the ancient world, people today like to tell stories about their parents, grandparents and ancestors. In Bangladesh, our names tell our stories. Some people have family names that tell the history of their father's family, or sometimes people take their father's given name as a sign of their origins. Among Muslims, Arabic names are given alongside Bengali names. In Arab cultures, names usually include *bin/ibn* (son of) or *bint* (daughter of). So the famous Qur'an commentator, popularly known as 'Ibn Kathīr,' had the full name of Abū al-Fiḍā' 'Imād ad-Dīn Ismā'īl bin 'Umar bin Kathīr al-Qurashī al-Buṣrāwī. In Bangladesh, a *pir* may add titles to his name to identify his *tariqa* (path). The full name and title of the Bangladesh *Pir* Khwaja Yunus Ali was Oli Allah Gauchol Azom, Pir of Pirs, Friend of Khaja Mohammed Yunus Ali, of Enayetpuri Nokshabondi Mujaddei (the Venerable).

Islamic histories and "stories of the prophets" include many alternative genealogical details; the *Sīrah* (stories of the life of the Islamic Prophet

Muhammad) include many genealogies, and people in many Muslim countries proudly bear the name Sayeed, meaning that they are descendants of the Islamic Prophet Muhammad.

But the Qur'an has no genealogies. Why could this be? Unlike the Bible, the Qur'an presents itself as a book straight from heaven, and it is mostly uninterested in how the various people it discusses are related to each other. It tells us that Abraham was the father of Isaac and Ishmael, and that Jacob and Joseph descended from Isaac, but it simply does not give a history of human beings and how they are related to each other. It does have lists of names, but they are lists of prophets.

From the ancient world "behind" Genesis, some lists of names have survived. At one time, scholars thought that these might be related to the Genesis genealogies, but further study indicated that this was not so. The ancient lists have the names of kings – a list of Mesopotamian kings before and after the flood is the best known[1] – and these are often not related. Further, the lists work backwards not forwards – that is, they start from a later person and work back to an earlier person. They were written to give legitimacy to the current ruler. It seems that the world then was not so different from today's world: people did history by recording the powerful rulers rather than by recording family relationships.

We learn, then, that it was not unusual for a people to keep a list of their predecessors, but that the Genesis genealogies have a different purpose than those lists, and a different purpose than the qur'anic prophet lists. This is, as we have said, Genesis's way of doing history, and it is the way of doing history in a number of other places in the Bible.

Biblical history is not a history of God sending a series of prophets, and neither is it a history of kings and rulers. It is a history of how human beings multiplied under the blessing of God. In every generation, it acknowledges the large number of human beings who came into existence, but it focuses on a particular line. God's plan was to increase and save Adam's descendants and to use a particular line of those descendants to bring Jesus the Messiah, who would be the saviour.

So as we approach the text of the Adam *toledoth*, let us look beyond the list of names and glimpse the history of the world from God's perspective.

---

1. Jacobsen, "Sumerian King List," *Assyriological Studies*, 11.

The World of the Text
Structure and Genre

The Adam *toledoth* can be seen as a sad chiasmus. It begins with God's good creation of humans and the blessing of Adam's children; it ends with the distortion of God's good creation, and with God's decision to destroy those children. In between there is a sad litany of death. Again and again it is repeated, eight times over, "and he died." Because no other biblical genealogy has this repeated emphasis, some have called this the genealogy of death. This chapter emphasizes that we all die, and that death is the result of sin. However, if we look at it as a chiasmus, we can see that, although this *toledoth* is leading to the judgement of the flood, death is not at its heart. There is hope and there is life at the chiasm's central turning point.

> **A.** Creation and blessing of male and female (5:1–2)
> Adam's first descendant will be like him (5:3)
> > **B.** Hope in Seth (5:3)
> > > **C.** Life and death of Seth, Enosh, Kenan, Mahalel, Jared (5:4–20)
> > > > **D.** Enoch walks with God and does not die (5:21–24)
> > > **C'.** Life and death of Methuselah, Lamech (5:25–27)
> > **B'.** Hope in Noah (5:28–32)
> **A'.** Relationships between Adam's good daughters and powerful men gone wrong (6:1–5)
> Adam's descendants to be destroyed (6:5–8)

Within this structure, there is a repetitive genealogical structure. Readers discover four things about each ancestor: his name, his age at the birth of his first son, the length of his remaining life and, with one exception, his age at death. Although the birth of only one child is recorded, we are told that there were many more sons and daughters. As we read this chapter and wonder about the individuals named, we note the importance of the regular pattern. This is the way that life was, and this is the pattern that we will expect for generations to come. We also note that in each generation, only one name is recorded. This is not, as Genesis 10 will be, a general list of all humanity, but the special history of Genesis. This genealogy is going somewhere. The un-named people matter to God, but they are not part of the particular history which Genesis is telling.

We know little even about the named people, and their names are difficult to understand, so most commentaries do not suggest their meanings. Some can be found in the ancient Mesopotamian languages. Some can be linked to Hebrew words, and we think that these are particularly interesting because the Hebrew writer would surely have been aware of those links. Some of the names are *theophoric* – from the Greek *theophoros*, bearing or carrying a god – that is, they include the name of a god. In the previous chapter, we read of Mehujael and Methushael, whose names are linked with El, the high god of the Canaanites, whose name was later used to refer to the one true creator God. Examples from later in Genesis include Eliezer, the servant of Abraham (15:2), Ishmael (16:11), Bethuel (22:22–23), etc. Arabic has many theophoric names, from both pre-Islamic and post-Islamic times; for example, 'Abd Allāh, Sayf Allāh, 'Ubayd Allāh, etc. Such names are common in Bangladesh and among Muslim communities worldwide. Because Bengali people are very interested in names, we will look at the possible meanings of the names in this chapter, but the reader should bear in mind that most of the interpretations are uncertain.[2]

COMMENTARY
A. Genesis 5:1a Creation and Blessing of Male and Female

This is the book of the generations of Adam.

We noted in the introduction that this is the only place where Genesis adds *seper* (book or page) to the word *toledoth*, and this raises some interesting questions about possible written sources for Genesis. This verse also raises historical and theological questions. For example, "Adam" here is the Hebrew word *'adam*, which means "human being" as well as being the name of the first human. Does this mean that Genesis 5 is presenting a third way of describing human origins? We had the broad overview of Genesis 1, which tells us about the place of human beings in God's creation. We then had the detailed story of Genesis 2–4, which tells us about relationships between God and humans, between the earth and humans, between animals and humans, and between humans and other humans. This third account describes how people are related to each other through family descent.

Another interesting discussion comes from ancient Jewish scholars who ask, "Does this mean that Adam had a book?"[3] Is this a book which belonged to Adam or even that was written by Adam rather than a book about Adam? Did God give Adam a list of his descendants? That idea would indicate God's knowledge of all the people who were to come from Adam. Or does the *seper* refer to the whole Torah and not just to Genesis 5:1–6:8? That would indicate

---

2. Here and elsewhere, our interpretations of names are informed by Hess, *Studies in the Personal Names of Genesis 1–11*; and Douglas, *New Bible Dictionary*; as well as by Wenham and Westermann.

3. Talmud, *Avodah Zarah* 5a.

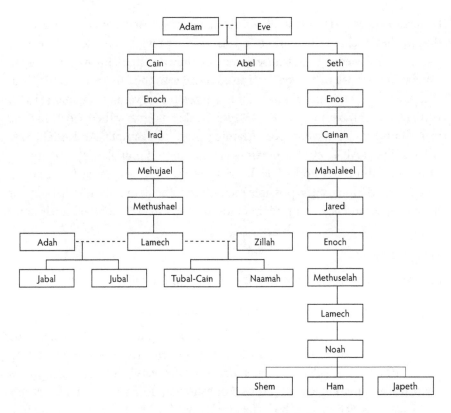

Figure 5 The Family Tree of Adam

that the Torah was in God's mind from the beginning of time. These questions are primarily theological, and it is interesting that they are picked up in some Islamic thinking. First, there is the Islamic tradition that Adam was a prophet. Some say that he received ten *ṣuḥūf*[4] from God, which could reflect this Jewish discussion. Second, there is the idea that Adam's descendants were already in his loins before he was put in the Eden garden (Sūra *al-A'rāf* 7:172). This could be linked with the Jewish idea of God knowing Adam's line beforehand. Third, there is the belief that the holy books came down from a pre-existing heavenly book (*umm al-kitāb*, mother of the book; Sūras *az-Zukhruf* 43:3–4; *ar-Ra'd*

---

4. Muslims believe that four heavenly books have been revealed – the Torah of Moses, the Psalms of David, the New Testament *(Injīl)* of Jesus the Messiah, and the Qur'an of the Islamic Prophet Muhammad. Besides these four books, traditions mention 100 *suhuf* (pages) revealed to four prophets – ten to Adam, fifty to Seth, ten to Abraham, and thirty to Enoch.

13:39, or *lawḥ al-maḥfūẓ*, the eternal tablet, *al-Burūj* 85:21–22), which could be linked with the Jewish idea of the pre-existent Torah.

> When God created man, he made him in the likeness of God. Male and
> female he created them, and he blessed them and named them Man when
> they were created. (5:1b–2)

Verses 1–2 set the scene by recalling the creation and blessing of human beings in Genesis 1 and 2. We are reminded of God's purposes and of his perfect creation of men and women in his image and likeness. We have now read chapters 3 and 4, so we know that things have gone wrong as people have used their godlike attributes in very un-godlike ways. Cain's descendants made things worse, but we remember that Abel's sacrifice was accepted, and now there is a new son in Abel's place. We wonder, "What will happen next to the image of God and to the original blessing?"

Name	Age at birth of first son	Remaining years	Total life span
Adam	130	800	930
Seth	105	807	912
Enosh	90	815	905
Kenan	70	840	910
Mahalalel	65	830	895
Jared	162	800	962
Enoch	65	300	365
Methuselah	187	782	969
Lamech	182	595	777
Noah	500	450	-

Figure 6 Genealogy from Genesis 5

> When Adam had lived 130 years, he fathered a son in his own likeness,
> after his image, and named him Seth. (5:3)

Adam's descendants will be like him. As God created man in his perfect image, so Adam has a son, Seth, in his own image. We know that Adam became a sinner, so we do not expect Adam's image to be perfect. However, as we have read, the birth of Seth was also the time when people began to call on the Name of the Lord. There is hope here of a godly line to replace Cain's ungodly line. This is another beginning, a second start outside Eden.

B. Genesis 5:4–5 Hope in Seth

> *The days of Adam after he fathered Seth were 800 years; and he had other sons and daughters. Thus all the days that Adam lived were 930 years, and he died.*

Chapter 5 traces ten generations from Adam, through Seth, to Noah. So the final chapter of Adam's biography is not the ungodly line of Cain, but the godly line of Seth. Islamic literature holds that Seth was born when Adam was over one hundred years old and that, before his death, Adam made Seth his heir as a prophet and guide.[5]

The passage finishes with Adam's physical death. We might have thought that the serpent got it right when he said that Adam and Eve would not die when they ate the forbidden fruit (Gen 3:4). The reader has watched them being banished from Eden and from God's presence and has realized that something went very wrong spiritually. But centuries have passed, and they seem to have escaped physical death. Now we find that, although God has given them so much time on earth and blessed them with godly as well as ungodly descendants, physical death comes to them, as it will to their descendants. As the Apostle Paul will later say, "In Adam, all die" (1 Cor 15:22). Only Enoch is an exception to the dismal refrain, "and he died" (Heb. *wa-yamot*), of this chapter.

C. Genesis 5:4–20 Life and Death of Seth, Enosh, Kenan, Mahalel, Jared

> *When Seth had lived 105 years, he fathered Enosh. Seth lived after he fathered Enosh 807 years and had other sons and daughters. Thus all the days of Seth were 912 years, and he died. (5:6–8)*

This verse sets the pattern for recording the following generations. There is life, and there are many children. Those children, we assume, will go out to populate the earth, but one is chosen whose name we are told and who carries the line of biblical history. Yet, despite very long lives, even those in that line eventually die.

We have already seen that Seth means "appointed" or "replacement," referring to his taking the place of Abel, and that *enosh* means "human being." In the Old Testament, *enosh* is often synonymous with *adam*, so the name Enosh here affirms the idea that this genealogy is a third account of human

---

5. See Ibn Kathir, *Stories of the Prophets*, 17–18.

origins. However, "Enosh" also reminds us of *anosh* (weak) and that the new line of human beings is going to be weak and subject to sin.

> *When Enosh had lived 90 years, he fathered Kenan. Enosh lived after he fathered Kenan 815 years and had other sons and daughters. Thus all the days of Enosh were 905 years, and he died. (5:9–11)*

In Hebrew, "Kenan" is the same as "Cain," but with an added "n," so it could have a similar meaning of being acquired. But it could also relate to *qinah*, the word for "lament" found in, for example, Jeremiah 7:29, 9:10 and 9:20. Does Kenan underline the pain and death in this world outside Eden?

> *When Kenan had lived 70 years, he fathered Mahalalel. Kenan lived after he fathered Mahalalel 840 years and had other sons and daughters. Thus all the days of Kenan were 910 years, and he died. (5:12–14)*

"Mahalalel" finishes with *el*, a name of God. The name is probably derived from the root *h-l-l*, from which we get hallelujah (the "Jah" part here is an abbreviation of YHWH). So Mahalalel probably means, "praise of God." This is a hopeful name!

> *When Mahalalel had lived 65 years, he fathered Jared. Mahalalel lived after he fathered Jared 830 years and had other sons and daughters. Thus all the days of Mahalalel were 895 years, and he died. (5:15–17)*

"Jared" probably means "descent," from the Hebrew root *y-r-d*, to go down. This could be a reminder of the deterioration of human beings – they have fallen, and now they are falling even further away from God. A sober name follows the hopeful name.

> *When Jared had lived 162 years, he fathered Enoch. Jared lived after he fathered Enoch 800 years and had other sons and daughters. Thus all the days of Jared were 962 years, and he died. (5:18–20)*

We have seen that Enoch (Heb. *chenok*) can be related to *ch-n-k*, to initiate or dedicate, from which comes *Channukah*, the Jewish feast celebrating the re-dedication of the temple during the time of the Maccabees. Perhaps Jared, whose name reminded him of the depths to which human beings had sunk, decided to dedicate his child to God.

D. Genesis 5:21–24 Enoch Walks with God and Does Not Die

When Enoch had lived 65 years, he fathered Methuselah. Enoch walked with God after he fathered Methuselah 300 years and had other sons and daughters. Thus all the days of Enoch were 365 years. Enoch walked with God, and he was not, for God took him.

Enoch was the seventh from Adam. There was fellowship between God and this "dedicated" man as he "walked" (lit. "walked about," that is, "lived") with God. We recall that fellowship with God is described as God "walking" in the Eden garden in Genesis 3:8. To "walk with God" is, then, a phrase that implies a manner of life in close relationship with God. Later in Genesis, similar phrases are used of Noah, Abraham, Eliezer and Jacob (Gen 6:9; 17:1; 24:40; 48:15).

Instead of letting him die, God "took" him (Heb. *laqah*, also translated "took" in Genesis 2:15, 21–23; 3:6, 19, 22–23; etc.), apparently both body and soul, without his experiencing death. We notice that Enoch's life was much shorter than the other lives in Genesis 5. The beloved novelist Humayun Ahmed echoes our grief over our short lifespans when he asks, "Why is human life so short?"; and Bengalis bless others when they say, "As the number of hairs on my head, so may your years be." Human beings today want long lives, but would we really wish to live for 700 or 900 years? Enoch's life was so much better than the lives of the other ancestors, and God took him to everlasting bliss at a younger age. This is all that Genesis tells us about him: no wonder that people have wanted to know more!

There is good news in this genealogy of Genesis – the terrible inevitability of death is challenged. It seems that it is possible to walk with God, to escape death, and to return directly to the presence of God which was lost because of Adam and Eve's disobedience. Much later, the great prophet Elijah would be "taken up" (2 Kgs 2:1–12; the same Hebrew word, *laqah*, is used in verses 3, 5, 9, 10). The door of Sheol[6] is not so strong, and Elijah bypasses it, going directly to heaven without death. The Old Testament gives little teaching about what happens after death, but the "taking up" of Enoch and of Elijah gave people hope and nourished a desire for life after death in the people of God, as can be seen in the examples of Psalms 49:15 and 73:24. When we get to the New Testament, we read that those who are alive at the second coming of Christ will ascend directly into God's presence (1 Thess 4:17).

---

6. In the Old Testament, *sheol* means dwelling place after death (Gen 42:38; Ps 139:8; Hos 13:14; Isa 14:9). Sometimes in the Bible, *sheol* is translated as the "underworld" or "grave".

But what about Enoch himself? The New Testament gives us a little further information about him. In Hebrews 11, he is one of the heroes rewarded for his faith. The author underlines how amazing his experience was by piling up the phrases: he "was taken up," "did not see death," "was not found," "was commended," and "pleased God" (Heb 11:5). Enoch is amazing, but Genesis says little about him, so it is not surprising that many stories have been told about him. Like Seth, people have attributed revelations to him. Jude quotes one of his sayings as prophecy (Jude 14–15). The quotation is not from the Bible but from 1 Enoch, one of the Jewish books attributed to him. Jude affirms the truth of that particular prophesy about the judgement of the ungodly, though this does not mean that all these extra books are true prophecy.

The tradition that Enoch was a prophet is continued in the Qur'an. The Qur'an describes a prophet called Idris, who was "trustworthy" and "patient" (Sūra al-Anbiyā' 21:85–86) and exalted to a high station (Sūra Maryam 19:56–57). Many of the early qur'anic commentators such as al-Bayḍāwī identify Idrīs with Enoch (Ar. Uhnukh) and link his name with the Arabic darasa (to study). As in Jewish and Christian tradition, many traditions have grown up about him which have no roots in the Bible or in the Qur'an. He is said to have been given thirty pages of revelation and to have been the initiator of many things, for example, astrology, weaving and writing.

C'. Genesis 5:25–27 Life and Death of Methuselah and Lamech

> When Methuselah had lived 187 years, he fathered Lamech. Methuselah lived after he fathered Lamech 782 years and had other sons and daughters. Thus all the days of Methuselah were 969 years, and he died.

Methuselah (Ar. Mitoshilah) was the son of Enoch and grandfather of Noah.[7] He lived for 969 years, longer than anyone else recorded. We note here the contrast with the Mesopotamian list of kings whose ten pre-flood kings lived for tens of thousands of years. In Genesis 5, we do not read about kings or god-like heroes: all are ordinary men who died before they reached 1,000 years. If we take the ages literally, Adam would have been alive for Methusalah's first 243 years. We can imagine the stories of Eden and of Cain and Abel being passed down the generations, as the Bangladeshi elders pass their stories on to their descendants.

---

7. Ibn Hisham and Ibn Ishaq said in their Sīrah that the Islamic Prophet Muhammad was a descendant of Methuselah. See Ishaq, Sīrah, 3.

The name Methuselah has two parts. Most scholars say that the first part comes from Akkadian *mutu* (a man), but, especially in this chapter of death, it also reminds us of the Hebrew *mut* (to die). The second part could be the name of a god, or it could mean "spear" (Heb. *shelach*, from *sh-l-ch*, to send). So possible meanings include "man of the spear" and "death before it is sent." Some people understand this to mean that he would die just before the flood;[8] and calculations from the numbers given indicate that he did so (Methuselah was 187 when Lamech was born; Lamech was 182 when Noah was born; Noah was 600 when the flood came. 600 + 187 + 182 = 969, the age at which Methuselah died).

As the Enoch of this chapter stands in stark contrast with the Enoch of Cain's line, so the Lamech of this chapter will stand in stark contrast with the Lamech of Cain's line. Seth's descendent Lamech lives by faith; Cain's descendent Lamech lives by instilling fear and murder; Lamech from Seth's side looks for future hope by naming his son "Comfort"; Lamech from Cain's side looks for future revenge on his enemies.

B'. Genesis 5:28–32 Hope in Noah

> When Lamech had lived 182 years, he fathered a son and called his name Noah, saying, "Out of the ground that the LORD has cursed, this one shall bring us relief from our work and from the painful toil of our hands." Lamech lived after he fathered Noah 595 years and had other sons and daughters. Thus all the days of Lamech were 777 years, and he died.
>
> After Noah was 500 years old, Noah fathered Shem, Ham, and Japheth.

Rabbinic tradition stresses that there are ten generations from Adam to Noah. The number 10 reminds us of God's perfect control over his world, so there is important symbolic meaning to this *toledoth*. These ten ancestors became well known, and their names are repeated in 1 Chronicles 1:1–4. In Genesis, the genealogy shows how Abraham fits into God's world. In Chronicles, the genealogy will be used to show how Abraham's descendants eventually produced David and his messianic line. In the gospels, Luke will use it to show how that line did indeed lead to the Messiah, Jesus (Luke 3:36–38).

The Hebrew name, Noach (Eng. Noah; Ar. Nūḥ), sounds like "relief" (Heb. *nacham*). Lamech hoped that his son would bring relief from the painful toil (*itzvon*, echoing the words in 3:16 and 17) resulting from the fall.

---

8. See Alfred Jones, *Dictionary of Old Testament Proper Names* (Grand Rapids: Kregel, 1990).

At the age of 500, Noah became the father of Shem, Ham and Japheth. Elsewhere in Genesis 5, the narrator mentions sons and daughters, and records how long the ancestor lived and his death; but, in the case of Noah, there is no mention of daughters, nor how long he lived, and his death is not reported until Genesis 9:28–29. There is more about Noah and his sons to come!

A'. Genesis 6:1–5 Relationships between Adam's Good Daughters and Powerful Men Gone Wrong

We have now read about the descendants of Cain and about the descendants of Seth, and we know that the number of human beings is rapidly increasing. We might wonder what they were like. How many were "calling on the name of the Lord"? How many were building cities and making tools? What was the result of the first Lamech's thirst for revenge? All the narrations were about men. What about the women? Here we get the answer – a sad answer.

The Adam *toledoth* began with a reminder of the creation blessings: God made the human beings male and female. He blessed them with children. It finishes with a picture of the relationships between Adam's attractive daughters and powerful men gone terribly wrong (6:1–5). It began with a godly son, and it finishes with an ungodly world (6:5). It began with the blessings of Adam's descendants multiplying, and it finishes with God's decision to destroy those very descendants (6:6–7). Yet, as we have so often seen, things are not quite so bleak. The last word of the *toledoth* is one of hope and grace (6:8).

> When man began to multiply on the face of the land and daughters were born to them, the sons of God saw that the daughters of man were attractive. And they took as their wives any they chose. (6:1–2)

The words of blessing, "be fruitful and multiply," have this outcome. A literal translation tells us that some unknown males called the *bene elohim* saw that the "daughters of the *adam*" (*banot ha-adam*) were good. The word translated "attractive" is actually "good" (Heb. *tov*) – the word used in Genesis 1 when God sees that his creation is good. The men saw the "good" things and they took them for themselves. We immediately remember chapter 3 verse 6, where the woman saw that the forbidden fruit was good, and took it for herself and for her husband.

Eve had grabbed the forbidden fruit, and she and Adam had become "like God" in knowing evil as well as good. This was so dangerous for God's creation that their fruitfulness had been limited by pain and their lives had been limited by being barred from the tree of life. Now males who wanted to be so "like God" that they called themselves his sons were grabbing not fruit but other human beings – women, whose humanity is stressed by their being called "daughters of Adam." This is so bad in God's eyes that he will not only further limit lifespans: he will send the flood to destroy them all.

There are three possible interpretations of the *bene elohim* which correspond to three different interpretations of the *banot ha-adam*. First, the *bene elohim* could be superior, powerful men, the sons of judges or rulers, and the *banot ha-adam* would then be ordinary women who did not have the power to refuse them.[9] The evil would be the exploitation of the weak women by the strong men. Second, the *bene elohim* could be godly men, the descendants of Seth, and the *banot ha-adam* would then be from the line of Cain, so the evil would be the mixing of the godly line with the ungodly line, which produced ungodly children.[10] Third, the *bene elohim* could be non-human beings like angels, demons, or spirits, and the *banot ha-adam* would be human women, descended from Adam. The evil would be a forbidden crossing over between the human world and the spiritual world. Whatever the case, the women were God's good creation, but they were being abused and the results were disastrous. As Genesis continues, we find that it really matters who marries who, and how the marriage partner is chosen. There are serious consequences when men see the beauty of a woman and decide to take her (Gen 12:10–20; 20:1–18; 34:1–31; 38:1–30) or when a woman tries to grab a handsome man for herself (Gen 39:6–23).

> *Then the LORD said, "My Spirit shall not abide in man forever, for he is flesh: his days shall be 120 years." (6:3)*

There are many puzzles in interpreting this verse, but its overall meaning is clear. God's life-giving breath, which created the first human beings in Genesis 2:7, will not tolerate the sin of the human beings forever. "Strive" here could mean "fight," or it could mean, "remain." "Flesh" has to do with the physical nature and reminds us of the dust into which God breathed life. Without breath, human beings die, and God is going to limit their life span.

"His days shall be 120 years" either means that the maximum human life span is 120 years or that the flood will come after 120 years. On the one hand, this would show the consequences of sin in the reduction of human

---

9. The Bible sometimes uses *elohim* in contexts where it could mean rulers or judges (e.g. Exod 22:8–9; Ps 82).

10. See commentary on 2:24 about believers marrying unbelievers (pages 111-112). This was the interpretation of Augustine, Luther and Calvin.

ARE THE *BENE ELOHIM* FALLEN ANGELS?

Human beings are fascinated by stories of spiritual powers, so it is not surprising that there is a long history of speculation about the *bene elohim*. The Book of Enoch (also called 1 Enoch and mentioned in Jude 14–15) presents itself as visions given to Enoch. In its version of the Genesis 6:1–2 story, the *bene elohim* are rebellious angels who fall in love with human women and make them pregnant, so God punishes them and imprisons them in the uttermost depths of the Earth.

A strong argument against this interpretation is that the only spiritual beings mentioned up to this point are the cherubim in 3:24. Genesis carefully omits the many spiritual beings of the ancient world. Genesis 6:3 emphasizes the point that men are flesh, and this could refer to the *bene elohim*; however, the interpretation that the *bene elohim* are spiritual beings also has some biblical warrant. There are several places in the book of Job which use the term *bene elohim* for spiritual beings (Job 1:6; 2:1; 38:7), and 2 Peter 2:4 and Jude 6–8 and 14–15 refer to fallen angels. However, there are no explicit links with Genesis 6, and the Bible is otherwise silent on the matter.

The idea of fallen angels is not in the Qur'an. Rather, the Qur'an explicitly states that angels have no free will (Sūra *an-Naḥl* 16:50), but are servants of God (Sūra *al-Anbiyā'* 21:26). As we have seen, *Shayṭān* is a rebellious jinn, not a rebellious angel. However, in Islamic tradition, there are stories similar to those in the Book of Enoch. The qur'anic starting point for these stories is the mention of Hārūt and Mārūt, two angels who taught magic in Babylon during the time of Solomon (Sūra *al-Baqara* 2:102–3). It is said that they followed the example of Iblīs and refused to bow to Adam. One story is that they were bound and put upside down in a well in Babylon until judgement day. Another says that they were given a human *nafs*, fell in love with a beautiful woman, Zahrā', and committed *zīna* (sexual sin) with her, like mortal men. (See *Kasasul Ambiya* and Al-Kisai, *Qisas al-Anbiya*.)

It is significant that Genesis does not tell us such stories, and neither does the rest of the Bible. We know that there are evil as well as good spiritual powers, but the Bible does not feed our curiosity. All we need to know about evil powers is that they will flee from us at the very name of Jesus the Messiah (Luke 10:17; Acts 16:18; James 4:7). We should conclude that it is not our business to tell these stories, or to use our minds to think about the possible sexual sins of angels. Instead, we should fill our minds with good things (Phil 4:8).

life span. On the other hand, it would show the grace of God in giving time for repentance. These two aspects, God's judgement of sin and God's mercy towards sinners, are seen again and again through Genesis 4–11, so perhaps both meanings are intended.

> *The Nephilim were on the earth in those days, and also afterward, when the sons of God came in to the daughters of man and they bore children to them. These were the mighty men who were of old, the men of renown. (6:4)*

Who were these Nephilim (sometimes translated, "giants")? Jewish tradition associates them with the root *n-ph-l* (to fall). They fell, they caused others to fall, and people fell down in front of them because of their size and strength. The name Nephilim is also used in reference to giants who inhabited Canaan at the time of the *Bani Isra'il* conquest of Canaan (Num 13:33). The Qur'an's references to the tall and mighty men of 'Ād and Thamūd could reflect these ideas:

> God says about them, "Have you not seen how your Lord dealt with 'Ad of Iram, known for their lofty columns, the like of whom no nation was ever created in the lands of the world?" (Sūra al-Fajr 89:6–8; cf. 41:15)

> Call in remembrance that He made you inheritors after the people of Nūḥ, and gave you a stature tall among the nations. (Sūra al-A'rāf 7:69)

Here in Genesis, the Nephilim are linked with the relationship between the "sons of gods" and the "daughters of men." They could be the same as the sons of gods, or they could be monstrous children born from the union of the sons of gods and the daughters of men. However, Genesis does not say that. It simply describes them as *gibborim* (mighty) and *anshe ha-shem* (men of name, so "renowned") and says that they were *me-'olam* (from ancient times). Some of the nations surrounding Israel had mythical stories of semi-divine heroes – people who were part god and part human. Here, we again see Genesis countering such myths – these were real human beings. They were flesh, not some kind of human-divine mixture.

Genesis 6:5–8 Adam's Descendants to Be Destroyed

> *The LORD saw that the wickedness of man was great in the earth, and that every intention of the thoughts of his heart was only evil continually. And*

> *the LORD regretted that he had made man on the earth, and it grieved*
> *him to his heart. So the LORD said, "I will blot out man whom I have*
> *created from the face of the land, man and animals and creeping things*
> *and birds of the heavens, for I am sorry that I have made them." (6:5–7)*

Eve saw something good . . . the *bene elohim* saw something good . . . the Lord saw the wickedness of humankind.

This passage is going to give us a glimpse into the very heart of God as he contemplates the evil which has grown in his beautiful world. Here begins Genesis's own treatment of the questions which the Jewish Midrash and the Qur'an put into the mouths of the angels when God announces his plan to create a human being with free will.[11] In today's world, the question is usually called "the problem of evil," and is expressed like this: "How can a good and just and almighty God allow evil in his world?" Many people think that even asking the question sheds doubt on God's existence, his goodness and his power. Genesis 6–9 turns the question upside down. The problem of evil is not about what we think of God – it is about what he thinks of us! It is because of his goodness and love that he has made a being who is free to love and to be good, but that being has chosen not to love and chooses instead to know evil as well as good. We are about to learn how God deals with this problem.

We note first the depths of human sinfulness as seen by God. People do not commit sin only outwardly, doing mischief and killing each other (cf. Sūra *al-Baqara* 2:30), but also in their minds. We can only see what people do and hear what they say, but the Lord looks at the heart, at the inner processes of our thoughts (1 Sam 16:7). And what he sees is terrible. The phrases pile up: great was the wickedness; every intent was evil; only evil all the time. As the prophets will later underline, sin is pervasive. The human heart is deceitful and incurable (Jer 17:9). Jesus the Messiah said that the evil thoughts come out of the heart, and it is this that makes people unclean (Matt 15:17–20).

What was God's response to such wickedness? Our translation has "he was sorry." The verb's root, *n-ch-m*, expresses a range of meanings, including to "repent," to "regret," to "reconsider" or to "be consoled." It is used in 5:29 for the relief for which Lamech longed. The common thread is that it means a change of mind or action – "reconsider" is a good translation. Elsewhere in the Bible, it is used when people repent and God changes his plan to judge them (e.g Jonah 4). In Genesis 5:29, Lamech wants a change from work to rest, but, when God sees what people are doing, the Creator decides to destroy

---

11. See commentary on Genesis 1:26–27.

his creation. God does not "regret" in the sense that he wishes he had never made the people – God's actions are always good and wise. God regrets that human beings made in his image have not walked in the kind of love that he has shown them, and so he decides on a new course of action.

We have to acknowledge that there is mystery here. God can see into the human heart, but how far can we humans understand why God acts as he does? The Qur'an agrees that God can see all hearts (*Ghāfir* 40:19; *al-Mulk* 67:13), but many Muslim theologians insist that humans cannot see into God's heart or mind. It is commonly said that if we say God acts out of, for example, mercy, that mercy does not mean the same as it would if it were attributed to a human being. Rather, God's actions are such that, were a human being to do them, we would say that they were being merciful.

Genesis has already given us glimpses of God's thoughts (1:26; 3:22); now, even more remarkably, it gives us a glimpse into the very heart of God. It adds to the idea of *n-ch-m* the idea that God was "grieved to his heart." The root of the Hebrew word for "grieved" is *'-ts-v*, which echoes the pain with which the woman would bear children and the man would till the ground in Genesis 3:16–17, and from which Lamech hoped that Noah would give them rest (5:29). The same word will be used of the sons of Jacob being grieved when the local ruler's son sees their sister Dinah and takes (the verb is the same as in Gen 6:1) her to do with her as he pleases (Gen 34:1–7).

It seems that human wickedness not only results in human pain, but also in divine pain, because God really cares about his creatures. The judgement of the flood is not only a mark of God's just anger, but also a mark of God's love. If Jacob's sons' grief was due to their love for their sister, how much more was God's grief due to his love for his creatures!

Sin not only harms the sinner, but also causes harm to the whole world and so it affects the Maker of the world. And this is not only true of unbelievers: the Apostle Paul says that the sin of the believer grieves the Holy Spirit (Eph 4:30).

But Noah found favour in the eyes of the LORD. (6:8)

What a relief! The Adam *toledoth* finishes on a note of hope and with the one occurrence in Genesis 1–11 of *chen* – the word translated "favour" or "grace."[12] Although God determines to destroy all the human beings, he makes an exception. We are not told how or why, but somehow, God offers his grace and love and mercy to just one person. Is this because that person was somehow better than everyone else? The Hebrew *chen* reverses the consonants

---

12. See also Introduction page 31.

of Noah (*noach*), so is it because of his father's prayers that he is chosen? We do not know. It seems to be God's sovereign choice.

Reading on, we will get a clue: as there is a contrast between people being destroyed and Noah finding grace, so the rest of chapter 6 will show us a contrast between the rebellion of Genesis 6:1–2 and the obedience of Noah (6:22; 7:5, 9, and 16). Whatever the reason for God's favour, the result was that Noah did just what God told him to do, and that, in chapter 9, God's grace would be extended to all his family and descendants – which includes us and every human being who has lived since then. In the New Testament, the word translated "grace" (*charis*) describes unmerited favour given to an inferior by a superior. That grace is not only for human beings, but for every living creature.

Theological Reflection

The *toledoth* of Adam may be a genealogy of human names, but it is held in *the unfolding bud of theology*. It is God who gave Seth, it is God who gave the blessing of descendants, it is God with whom Enoch walked, and it is God who will deal with the problem of human sinfulness.

Two bright petals begin to unfold as we glimpse God's thoughts in 6:6 – God's holiness and God's pain. This Creator will not forever permit the sinful distortion of his creation, but will wipe out the sin completely. But God can also change things in response to humankind – that is the force of the word translated "repent/regret" in 6:6. If he has planned judgement, he will change that plan when people repent. This is according to his holy character. And if he has planned blessing, he will re-plan that blessing when people rebel against him. This is according to his loving character, which, as we will see in Genesis 8:20–9:17, will always find a way of renewing the creation blessings.

At the heart of God's response to sin, there is not only holy anger but also loving pain. God is grieved by the pain which sin causes his creatures, and that is why he does not simply destroy them all, but saves some and will eventually offer salvation to all. The Lord Jesus the Messiah will bear all the pain and shame of sin, and so all peoples will be invited to find God's grace.

This third account of the "beginning" of humanity (see pages 180-181) builds *the seedbed for biblical history* as it establishes the centrality of relatedness and community to the biblical worldview. God is not only going to work through individuals, but through families. It is not surprising, then, that it is from the writings of a particular family which grew into a particular community that the Bible will emerge. The community of faith, first the *Bani Isra'il*, and then the body of Christ, will discern and accept the inspired scriptures. The history of the Bible is a history of people passing down the revelation through the generations. Examples in the Torah include the passing down of the story of the redemption from Egypt in the family circle during the Passover feast (Exod 13:3–10), and the passing down of the laws through repeated recitation and writing as well as through obedient example (Deut 6:7–9, 17–25).

A major seed planted in this seedbed is the theme of life and death. The message of the Adam *toledoth* is loud and clear: death is real, and sin brings death. As the Bengali proverb says, "If you are born, you will die, no one is immortal." Yet, somehow, in the midst of all the death of Genesis 5, there is a hope of life. We are not told how, but it is possible to "walk with God" and to be freed from death.

What About Us?

Genesis is a book of blessings, but what sort of blessing are we looking for? Genesis 5 shows us that God continues the blessing of giving children, but Genesis 6:1–2 shows us the tragedy of people taking for themselves what they think is good for them. Sometimes what we consider a good thing results in a curse, because it is against God and it hurts other people.

The hope offered in this *toledoth* is not the blessing of a longer and more comfortable earthly life. In fact, it seems as if the shortness of Enoch's time on earth is actually a reward for walking with God. We all have the instinct to fight to keep on living; we all want to live long enough to see our families secure; and we all grieve when people die. Death is the result of sin, and it is not a beautiful thing. The Apostle Paul describes it as "the last enemy" (1 Cor 15:26). But Enoch reminds us that the point of life is to walk with God, and that the goal is to be in God's presence after death. Living for God is more important than the length of our lives.

Enoch's grandson, Lamech, hoped for rest from the hard and painful work of living and so named his son *noach* (relief). But Noah could not give his people rest: only the Messiah can give us true rest. He comes through the line of Noah (Luke 3:23–38) to achieve salvation for humankind. As Lord of the Sabbath (Matt 12:8), Jesus the Messiah invites us: "Come to me . . . and I will give you rest" (Matt 11:28). This is not a rest from the ceaseless physical labour of this present world, but a release from the ceaseless labour of trying to win God's favour through religious activity. Religious activity will never give us life. We do not know how Noah gained God's favour (*chen*), but through the Messiah we can rest assured now in God's undeserved grace (*charis*), and can come to our final rest after death (see also Heb 4).

5

The Beginnings of Judgement and Covenant – Genesis 6:9–9:29

The *Toledoth* of Noah

What will be the result of God's anger and sorrow over human sin? How will he "blot out" the people and the creatures? What is the hope to which 6:8 is pointing? And can the human heart be changed? These are the questions which the end of the Adam *toledoth* provokes. These are the questions which the Noah *toledoth* will begin to answer.

Genesis 1–11 dedicates an entire five chapters to Noah and his sons, so we know that this is a very important story. In the Bible, he is one of the five main[1] people associated with a covenant (Noah, Abraham, Moses, David, Jesus). In Islamic thinking too, Noah is very important: he is one of the six most prominent prophets (Noah, Abraham, Moses, David, Jesus and Muhammad). The Qur'an mentions him in twenty-six sūras, and the seventy-first chapter, Sūra *Nūḥ*, is named after him. The Noah narrative sets the pattern for many of the subsequent prophetic stories, which tell of the prophet warning his people and then the community rejecting the message and facing punishment.

---

1. Note that some see Adam (Gen 1:26–30) and Ishmael (Gen 21:13–18) as having received covenants, and that God also makes a covenant with Phineas (Num 25:12).

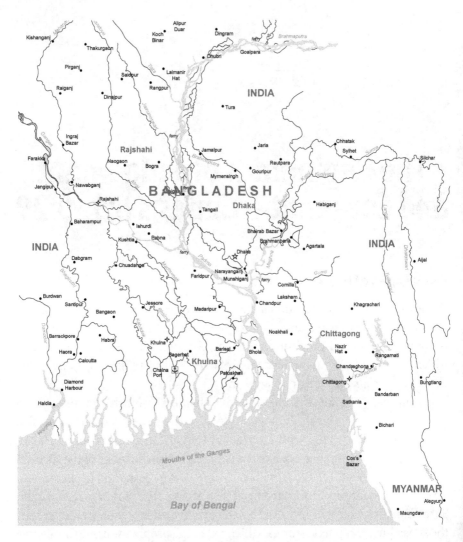

Figure 7 Map of Bangladesh and its Rivers

The Worlds Behind and in Front of the Text
Flood Stories

From ancient times, Bangladesh has been well acquainted with floods. Our elders tell stories of the floods of their childhood during lazy afternoons or on rainy nights, and we read stories about floods in today's newspapers. There are also flood stories from the subcontinent which have been transmitted to us in both oral and written literature.[2] Perhaps the best known is the story of Manu, which dates from at least the third century BC[3] and has remarkable similarities with the biblical Noah story. Manu is instructed by a fish which appears when he is washing his hands. He builds a ship in which he is saved from a flood, and afterwards offers sacrifices. The fish is regarded as an *avatar* of the Hindu deity, Vishnu, the Preserver.

Many peoples around the world have similar flood legends. T. H. Gaster recounts stories from all continents, many of which date from before people could have heard the biblical version.[4] In the biblical narrative, Noah and his descendants have a single language for one hundred years after the flood but are then scattered and have different languages. It would not be surprising, then, to find different versions of a common flood story in different languages and in different locations.

Mesopotamia Flood Stories

The Ancient Near East also had many stories of floods which covered the world. From Mesopotamia come the story of Ziusudra in the *Eridu Genesis*, and the epics of *Atrahasis* and *Gilgamesh*. The most famous and the most similar to Genesis 6–9 is the latter, written about the seventeenth century BC, perhaps the oldest written story on Earth. It was written on twelve clay tablets in cuneiform script, and the flood story is on the eleventh tablet. In it, the gods send a flood to destroy human beings, but one man, Ut-napishtim, and his family are preserved in a huge boat. Eventually, Utnapishtim and his wife are given immortality.

The following table summarizes the remarkable similarities and significant differences between Genesis and the *Epic of Gilgamesh* which we will discuss in the commentary:

---

2. For an overview of flood legends from India, see Gaster, *Myth, Legend and Custom*, 94–97.

3. Found in the ancient *Satapatha Brāhmana* 1.8.1, https://sacred-texts.com/hin/sbr/sbe12/sbe1234.htm, and elaborated in the *Mahabharatra*; see also Wilkins, *Hindu Mythology*, https://sacred-texts.com/ /hin/hmvp/hmvp19.htm.

4. Gaster, *Myth, Legend and Custom*, 82–131.

Theme	Bible (Genesis 6–9)	Sumerian Epic of Gilgamesh
Doctrine about God	Monotheism – belief that there is only one God.	Polytheism – belief in many gods.
Reason for Flood	Humanity became corrupt and violent.	Humans were noisy, and the gods could not sleep.
The Boat Builder	Noah built the ark with three decks, probably over many years. Noah and his seven family members survived.	Ut-napishtim built seven levels of the boat in seven days. He and his family survived.
Humans Saved by	YHWH, who created all humans.	The god Ea, who had superintended the creation of humans, in defiance of the other gods.
Water Sent by	YHWH, who controls all the creation.	Enlil, the wind and weather god, with the approval of the other gods.
Door Closed by	God closed the door.	Ut-napishtim closed the door.
Fellowship with God	Noah enjoyed God's close presence before the flood.	Ut-napishtim went to dwell with the god after the flood.
The Ark	Flat bottom, with a window under the roof, rectangular in shape (estimated 450x75x45 feet). Covered with pitch and made from the gopher wood.	Ziggurat-shaped (estimated 200x200x200 feet), nine windows. Sealed with bitumen and oil and a slate roof.
Navigation	Launched by the floodwater. No navigational equipment.	Pushed to the river. No navigational equipment.
Duration of Rain	Forty days, forty nights	Seven days
Duration of the Flood	Estimated 370 days	Seven days
Landing of the Ark / Boat	Mount Ararat	Mount Nisir, southeast of Ararat in Kurdistan.

Theme	Bible (Genesis 6–9)	Sumerian Epic of Gilgamesh
Sending of Birds	Ravens sent. Dove sent, and returns twice. The last dove sent does not return.	A dove and swallow return but the raven does not. Birds sent in opposite order: first the dove, then the swallow and finally the raven.
Lives Saved	Eight persons (Noah's family) and representatives of each animal in pairs.	Several families, craftsmen, representatives of all living things.
Offering after the Flood	Sacrifices of worship: one of clean animals and one of clean birds. God is never hungry.	Sacrifice of appeasement. Wine and sheep. The gods gathered around the offering "like flies," as they were hungry.
Post-Flood Blessings	Covenant with all creatures on earth.	Immortality for one couple, Ut-napishtim and his wife.

For thinking about the historical nature of the Genesis account, similarities between the stories are important. However, for understanding what Genesis is saying, it is the differences which matter. As in the creation narratives, Genesis gives a very different picture of the nature of God and of his relationship with humans and with the world. For example, in the Babylonian religion the waters were evil; but, in the Bible the waters were part of God's good creation, and it was the human beings who learned evil (Gen 3:22). The Mesopotamian stories have many gods, but Genesis has one God who has sovereign authority over all the aspects of life which other nations saw as gods, including the raging sea. God does not destroy people because they annoy him but because he is the righteous judge who punishes sinners.

The New Testament

There is surprisingly little mention of Noah in the Old Testament after Genesis. He is included in the genealogy of 1 Chronicles (1:4), and in Ezekiel 14:13–20 he is one of three exemplary men whose righteousness could not avert judgement on a wicked community (the other two are Daniel and Job). As the Old Testament has so much about God's covenant faithfulness, we might expect several references to the covenant of Genesis 9, but the only specific reference is in Isaiah 54:9, where God compares his faithfulness to Israel after the judgement of the exile to his promises at the time of Noah.

In the New Testament, Noah is a hero of faith who acted on the evidence of God's word alone (Heb 11:7). Jesus the Messiah uses the time of Noah as an example of a time of wickedness which resulted in judgement (Matt 24:37–39; Luke 17:26–27). He is warning here of the judgement which will occur at his second coming. We know from Genesis 9 that God will not repeat the universal flood judgement until the end of time: Jesus the Messiah's second coming marks that final judgement. In its vision of the end times, Revelation does not mention Noah, but it does twice mention a rainbow, reminding the reader of God's love for his world (Rev 4:3; 10:1).

The Apostle. Peter uses the Noah story in several ways. In his first letter, he encourages persecuted believers by citing God's patience in keeping back judgement at the time of Noah (1 Pet 3:20), and the safety of Noah and his family in the ark is a picture of security through baptism and salvation in Christ (1 Pet 3:20–22). In his second letter, he uses Noah's story together with the stories of Lot and of the rebellion of Satan to give assurance that God will both rescue believers and judge evil doers at the right time (2 Pet 2:4–9). This passage calls Noah a "herald of righteousness," but it is not clear what that means. It could mean that he preached, but it could also mean that he was a sign of God's righteousness to the people of his time, and to all of us right up to today.

More puzzling, the Apostle Peter says that the risen Jesus the Messiah preached to the "spirits in prison," that is, to the people who perished in the flood (1 Pet 3:18–20). This appears to have happened between his death on the cross and his resurrection appearances. We are not told whether this preaching affirmed the judgement or whether it was an opportunity for repentance; but it does assure us that God's justice extends to all.

The Qur'an and Islamic Literature

While 1 Peter has Jesus the Messiah preaching to those who were drowned centuries after the flood, the Qur'an has Noah preaching to his people for centuries before the flood. According to Islamic tradition, Noah was a prophet in the lineage of the first prophet, Adam. As Adam has the title shafī-Allāh (God's chosen one), Noah has the title najī-Allāh (God's saved one). In the Qur'an, he is also described as "messenger of God" (Sūras Rasūl-Allāh; ash-Shuʿarāʾ 26:107) and "grateful servant of God" (al-Isrāʾ 17:3). He is not said to have been given a book.

The Qur'an refers to Noah in twenty-six sūras. Ten of these have accounts of various lengths: the others include him in a list of prophets. The main passages are Sūras *Hūd* 11:25–48; *al-Aʿrāf* 7:59–64; *Yūnus* 10:71–73; *al-Muʾminūn* 23:23–28; *ash-Shuʿarāʾ* 26:105–21; *al-Qamar* 54:9–16; and all of *Nūḥ* 71, which is named after him. Except for Sūra *Nūḥ*, Noah's story always occurs in the context of a list of other prophets, and, in each case, the aspects of Noah's story dealt with are parallel to the emphases in the other prophets' stories. Most frequently, he is at the head of a list which includes Lot and the non-biblical prophets Hūd and Ṣāliḥ. Each story recounts the wickedness of the people, the preaching of the prophet, the peoples' rejection of the prophet, usually the prophet's prayer to God, and then a catastrophic judgement in which the prophet is saved with a few believers, while the unbelievers are destroyed.

From this, we can see several features of the qurʾanic Noah. First, he is a paradigm prophet, that is, the first of a series of similar prophets. Second, the Qurʾan never gives a full story of Noah in his historical context; rather, it uses different aspects of the story for different purposes, which in some ways is similar to the way in which the New Testament uses the stories. Third, the focus is on the time before the flood and on Noah's preaching and prayers: this is in contrast with Genesis where we learn very little about Noah before the flood, and there is no record of his preaching or praying.

In every case, these stories are from the mid-to-late Meccan period, and they are being used to encourage the Islamic Prophet Muhammad in his ministry, so it is not surprising that they focus on Noah as a prophet. Commentators agree that Sūra *Nūḥ*, which contains only the story of Noah, is a picture of the Islamic Prophet Muhammad's preaching in Mecca.

The Qurʾan omits the Genesis details about the ark, and about the rising and falling of the flood, although it does have some vivid description. It has no sacrifice after the flood and, although it agrees that God made a covenant with Noah just as he did with Abraham, Moses, and Jesus the Messiah (Sūra *al-Aḥzāb* 33:7), it gives no further details. Most strikingly, in Genesis, the judgement of the flood is a unique and unrepeatable event, but the Qurʾan sees the flood as but one in a series of similar judgements.

Another significant difference is that, while Genesis has Noah's whole family saved, the Qurʾan portrays one of his sons as an unbeliever who does not enter the ark (*Hūd* 11:43–47). Noah prays for him, but God tells him that he should not pray for the deliverance of someone who refuses to believe. It is not the whole family that is saved, but Noah and the believers, including some who were not of his family.

The following table summarizes the main points of similarity and difference between the Bible and the Qurʾan in the flood account. We should note that the Qur'an has few unique features. Many pre-Islamic Jewish and Christian writings also portray Noah as a preacher.

Noah	The Bible	The Qur'ān
Preaching	No dialogue. 2 Peter 2:5 could refer to his preaching.	Extensive dialogue between Noah and his people (Sūras al-A'rāf 7:59; Hūd 11:32–37; al-Mu'minūn 23:23).
Ark	Many details of measurements, materials and design of the ark given.	Noah built under God's supervision (Sūra Hūd 11:37), but no details are given, although Islamic tradition expands on this.
Who was in the ark?	Noah, his wife, his three sons and their wives.	Some of Noah's sons and other believers. Noah's wife and one of his sons refused to board the Ark (Sūras Hūd 11:42–46; at-Taḥrīm 66:10).
Resting place of the ark	Unspecified peak in the Mount Ararat range.	Mount Judi in the Ararat range.
Noah in the eyes of God	Noah was righteous, blameless, and obedient and walked with God.	Noah was God's righteous and grateful servant (Sūras at-Taḥrīm 66:10; al-A'rāf 7:3).
Animals in the ark	Seven pairs of clean animals and two pairs of other animals.	Two of every animal.
Cause of the flood	Humankind's sin and corruption.	People rejected Noah's warning and refused to turn from idolatry.

The World of the Text
Structure

The Noah *toledoth* is an extended chiasm. Many words and themes are repeated as the plan for the flood is announced and put into action, the waters rise and then fall, and the covenant plan for after the flood is announced.

> **A.** Noah and his sons (6:9–10)
>> **B.** God's plan and covenant announced (6:11–22)

> **C.** Entering the ark: clean and unclean animals (7:1–9)
>> **D.** The waters rise and cover the earth (7:10–24)
>>> **E.** GOD REMEMBERED NOAH (8:1)
>> **D'.** The waters recede and the earth reappears (8:2–14)
> **C'.** Leaving the ark: Sacrifice (8:15–22)
>> **B'.** God's plan and covenant announced (9:1–17)
> **A'.** Noah and his sons (9:18–28)

The story is shaped so that we can feel the rise of the waters and the blotting out of life. At the centre is the turning point, and then the waters recede and the living beings in the ark come out to re-populate the earth. At the heart of the chiasm is God and his covenant faithfulness: "God remembered Noah." The message of this structure is clear – Noah and his sons are God's way of establishing his covenant with all of sinful humanity.

But this is not all. The reader can find other structures in the text. The most striking is the way that the rise and fall of the waters is set out to reflect the creation narrative of chapter 1.

> 1:6–7 The waters are separated and boundaries set
>> 7:11 The water boundaries are broken and waters are rejoined
>>> 8:2 The boundaries are reset
> 1:9–10 The dry land emerges from the waters
>> 7:19–20 The dry land disappears
>>> 8:5–14 The dry land re-emerges
> 1:11–12 Creation of plants
>> 7:20 Depths of the water covers plants
>>> 8:11 Reappearance of plants
> 1:20–26 Creation of animals and humans
>> 7:21–23 Destruction of animals and humans
>>> 8:15–19 Reappearance of animals and humans

Again, the structure presents a clear message: God is unmaking and re-making his good creation. This is his response to his being "sorry" that he created human beings. His covenant is not given because human beings are good; far from it. It is given because human beings have become evil, but God still loves them. As we saw in Genesis 6:6, he is not only sorry, he is also grieved. The covenant will point to a way of dealing with both his holy anger and his loving grief.

COMMENTARY

A. Genesis 6:9–10 Noah and His Sons

> *These are the generations of Noah. Noah was a righteous man, blameless in his generation. Noah walked with God. And Noah had three sons, Shem, Ham, and Japheth.*

Genesis 6:9 begins the Noah *toledoth*. The genealogy mentions only one generation after Noah: his three sons, Shem, Ham and Japheth. The whole *toledoth* section will deal only with these two generations. Again and again, it will stress that Noah and his wife and his sons and their wives were the people who were saved in the ark. Four whole chapters are given to the story of the survival of this small family and the repetitions emphasize its importance (6:18; 7:7, 13, 23; 8:16, 18; 9:18).

The previous *toledoth* ended with God's grace in an evil generation (6:8). This *toledoth* begins with the good news of Noah's righteousness: he was different from the rest of his generation. Like Enoch, he walked with God.

It is important that the announcement of Noah's righteousness follows the announcement of God's grace. Commentators ask whether Noah found grace because he was righteous, or whether he became righteous through God's grace. By now, readers of Genesis have learned how thoroughly sinful humans have become outside Eden, so the latter seems most likely. The rest of the Bible will confirm this – in the fallen world, no one is righteous without God's grace and forgiveness.

The word translated "perfect" or "blameless" (Heb. *tamim*) means "whole" or "complete" rather than "without sin." In this case, it could mean that Noah was not involved in the violence of his time. Elsewhere in the Torah, it is used to describe the animals which are acceptable for sacrifice (Lev 1:3, 10; 3:1, 6; 4:3, etc.). When used of human beings, it is often associated with "righteousness"(Heb. *tsaddiq*) and with doing things God's way (Deut 18:13; Ps 15:2; Prov 11:05; Job 12:4). Later in Genesis, God tells Abraham, "Walk before me, and be *tamim*" (Gen 17:1).

In the Bible, neither Noah nor Abraham nor any other prophet is sinless: they all share in human fallenness, and the Bible records some of their sins. The only exception is Jesus the Messiah, who is so much more than a prophet. He is the one and only truly *tamim* sacrifice for the sins of the whole world.

The Qur'an agrees about the unique holiness of Jesus the Messiah. In Sūra *Maryam* 19:19, Mary is told that her son will be *zakiyyān* (pure). A well-known hadith explains the significance of this verse:

I heard the Messenger of God saying: "There is none born among the off-spring of Adam, but Shayṭān touches it. A child therefore, cries loudly at the time of birth because of the touch of Shayṭān, except Mary and her child." (Bukhārī Vol. 4, Book 55, Hadith 641 cf. Muslim, Book 30, Hadith 5838)

B. Genesis 6:11–22 God's Plan and Covenant Announced

> *Now the earth was corrupt in God's sight, and the earth was filled with violence. And God saw the earth, and behold, it was corrupt, for all flesh had corrupted their way on the earth. (6:11–12)*

Noah found grace in God's eyes, but the earth was corrupt, literally, "before the face" of God. The Hebrew word order of verse 11 begins with corruption and ends with violence, stressing the tragedy. God's good world was to have been filled with humans and animals. Now, instead of being filled with life, it was filled with violence. Violence can include social as well as physical malice, such as the exploitation of the weak by the strong described in verses 1–2 (see also Amos 6:1–3). The threefold repetition of "corrupt" and the fourfold "earth" stress that something which was good has gone wrong.

The corruption is universal. "All flesh" seems to include animals as well as humans, as is specified in verse 19. This raises the intriguing question of whether animals can have moral responsibility: neither Genesis nor any other part of the Bible addresses this question. The point here is that, although the humans are uniquely made in God's image, all creation has been ruined as a result of human sin.

> *And God said to Noah, "I have determined to make an end of all flesh, for the earth is filled with violence through them. Behold, I will destroy them with the earth." (6:13)*

This is one of the most sombre verses in the Bible. "God saw" (v. 12) and, now, "God said." In chapter 1, God said, something was created, then God looked, and saw that it was good. Now, the process is reversed, God looks again, and sees that it is corrupt, so he speaks again, but, this time, it is to destroy what he has made.

> *Make yourself an ark of gopher wood. Make rooms in the ark, and cover*
> *it inside and out with pitch. This is how you are to make it: the length of*
> *the ark 300 cubits, its breadth 50 cubits, and its height 30 cubits. Make a*
> *roof for the ark, and finish it to a cubit above, and set the door of the ark*
> *in its side. Make it with lower, second, and third decks. (6:14–16)*

But Noah, the man who has found grace, is not left to despair. He does not yet know how the judgement will come, so he cannot know how to protect his family; but the greatest of all engineers is the one who commands and supervises the building of the exact protection that he needs. There is hope!

The only other place that we read of an ark (Heb. *tebah*) in the Old Testament is in Exodus 2:3, where the word is used of the basket in which Moses was kept safe from drowning. Like Noah's ark, Moses's basket was kept safe by its covering of tar. The word for "cover" is from *k-f-r*, which is most often used for the covering of sin and translated "atone" (see Exod 29:33–37; 30:10–16; and throughout Leviticus). The ark will later become a symbol of the eternal safety of the believer in the Messiah (1 Pet 3:20–21). As the tar covered the wood and kept it from rotting, so the blood of the Messiah covers the believer's shame and protects us from spiritual rot.

The ark (Ar. *tabut*) is mentioned in the Qur'an in two places. Sūra *Hūd* 11:39 has the instructions, "build the ark under our eye, and our revelation," and in Sūra *al-Mu'minūn* 23:27 we read:

> *So We inspired him (with this message): "Construct the Ark within Our*
> *sight and under Our guidance: then when comes Our Command, and the*
> *fountains of the earth gush forth, take thou on board pairs of every species,*
> *male and female, and thy family – except those of them against whom the*
> *Word has already gone forth: And address Me not in favour of the wrong-*
> *doers; for they shall be drowned (in the Flood). (Yusuf Ali)*

Sūra *al-'Ankabūt* 29:14–15 tells readers that Noah was saved in a boat (Ar. *safina*), and that the boat was a sign for the worlds (*ayat li-l'alamīn*).

Nowhere does the Qur'an say how the ark should be built. We find the details here in Genesis. First, Noah is instructed about materials: the boat would be made with gopher wood (probably cypress or cedar) and covered inside and out with "tar" (the word could possibly mean tree resin). Next, Noah is given the ark's dimensions (6:14–16). We do not know the exact length of a cubit at Noah's time, but at later times it was about eighteen inches, comparable to the Bangladeshi measure "one hand" (from the elbow to the fingertips). According to that measure, the ark was about 450 feet long, 75 feet broad and

45 feet high, about half the size of a modern ocean vessel like the *Titanic*. We realise that the details recorded by Genesis do not only have a theological purpose: Noah needed them in order to build a boat which would survive the buffeting of the winds and waters for a whole year.[5]

There is also practical wisdom as well as theological symbolism in the instructions about doors and windows. There was an open space for light and air, which ran like a gallery around the top edge of the ark. The roof protected the inmates from rain and sun (6:14–8:19). There was one door, in the side: this is surprising, as boats usually have a hatch on deck. Another surprise is that there was no rudder or sail. We can see these surprises as signs that this boat would be entered and left only before and after the flood, and that the navigation would be solely in the hand of God.

> *For behold, I will bring a flood of waters upon the earth to destroy all flesh in which is the breath of life under heaven. Everything that is on the earth shall die. But I will establish my covenant with you, and you shall come into the ark, you, your sons, your wife, and your sons' wives with you. And of every living thing of all flesh, you shall bring two of every sort into the ark to keep them alive with you. They shall be male and female. Of the birds according to their kinds, and of the animals according to their kinds, of every creeping thing of the ground, according to its kind, two of every sort shall come in to you to keep them alive. Also take with you every sort of food that is eaten, and store it up. It shall serve as food for you and for them. (6:17–21)*

God now tells Noah how he is going to destroy everything: "all flesh" is repeated to emphasize the universality of the judgement. However, as a loving God, he also wants to preserve some of his creatures and continue his plans for his creation. Therefore, in his mercy, he will establish a covenant for all time with Noah and his family and their descendants (v. 18).

This is the first appearance in the Bible of the term "covenant" (Heb. *berit*, Ar. *'ahad/mithaq*). It is a highly significant word, which will appear again 253 times in the Old Testament and twenty times in the New Testament. It means a binding agreement between two or more parties, and covenants become the main basis of relationship between the Creator and the creatures throughout the Bible (see box on covenants page 224 below).

---

5. There has been much discussion about the seaworthiness of the ark. Some recent studies have indicated that it would, indeed, have floated (see Y. Bishop, 'Can Noah's Ark Float?' www.futurescienceleaders.com/blog/2020/06/can-noahs-ark-float/ accessed 20/8/21).

WHY ALL THE NUMBERS?

Most of the stories in Genesis 1–11 are told briefly, leaving the reader to imagine the details. Now, suddenly, the Noah *toledoth* tells us the exact dimensions of the ark, and it will go on to give details of days and dates as it describes the flood. Why is this?

This is not the only place where the Bible records exact times and measurements. The instructions on building and furnishing the tabernacle are given in such detail that we could build it again today (Exod 25–27, 30, 36–40), and the dates of many of the events at Sinai are recorded (e.g. Exod 19:1; 40:2, 17; Num 1:1; 7:1–78; 9:1; 10:11). Similarly, the dimensions of the temple and the times for building it are given in detail (1 Kgs 6; 2 Chr 3–4); in Ezekiel 40–43, the new temple is carefully measured in a vision; and the new Jerusalem is measured in Revelation 21:15–17. Practically, such detailed descriptions take the place of the architectural plans and beautiful pictures that we have in today's world. Theologically, they emphasize God's part in these special buildings and their importance. The careful student can also detect much symbolism in the dimensions and the symmetries.

In the Noah *toledoth*, the construction details suggest a parallel between the ark and the tabernacle, both being places built under God's direction, enabling selected people to be kept safe and to experience his presence in the midst of a chaotic world. As the *Bani Isra'il* needed sure guidance through the desert, Noah needed a seaworthy refuge from the cataclysmic flood. The time details include the symbolic numbers forty and seven, which emphasize the significance of each period of time, and we will note how the timings emphasize the chiastic symmetry of the narrative, with God's remembrance of Noah at the centre.

Further, in contrast with the *Enuma Elish*, which has the flood lasting only seven days, Genesis teaches that the flood lasted a very long time. This emphasizes the vastness of the flood and the seriousness of the judgement. Everything was destroyed – it was a very thorough cleaning job on the whole of creation.

Yet in the midst of this judgement, the times alert us to God's loving provision: imagine the provision of enough food and water for eight people and many animals for a whole year! We remember the repeated periods of 40 days (7:12, 17; 8:6). The number 40 will recur in Exodus (ref. Deut 8:4; 29:5), where the *Bani Isra'il* experience God's care for forty years in the desert, and in the gospels, where Jesus the Messiah spends 40 days fasting, and then refuses to yield to Satan's temptation to provide bread for himself (Matt 4:1–11; Mark 1:12–13; Luke 4:1–13).

Ancient Near Eastern covenants were two-sided and conditional. Both parties agreed to their own parts, and the covenant could be annulled should either party violate it. Thus the covenants did not guarantee permanent safety. In contrast, this first covenant is a promise of safety which is binding on God, but which requires nothing from Noah except that he should go into the ark as instructed.

God would renew this covenant after the flood with full acknowledgement that humans would continue to be sinful and undeserving (Gen 8:21–22). This time, the covenant would not only be with Noah but with all of his descendants and all other living beings until the end of time (9:8–17).

Noah did this; he did all that God commanded him. (6:22)

Noah bound himself to the covenant by obedience. That is all that Genesis tells us about the building of the ark. This is where readers want to ask questions. What relationships did Noah have with his neighbours? Did he tell them about what God had told them? Did he pray for them? How did people react when they saw him building the ark?

A rabbinic idea which has become widespread is that God chose to save Noah and his family in this way so that, during the construction of the ark, people would see and ask questions and have a chance to repent.[6] The New Testament does not add much to Genesis, saying only that Noah was a "herald of righteousness" (2 Pet 2:5), but there were plenty of stories in circulation by the time of the Qur'an about what Noah might have preached.[7] Genesis simply does not tell us whether Noah preached, whether he answered questions, or whether it was simply his action of building a huge boat in a dry place which "heralded righteousness" to the people of his time.

The Qur'an picks up the idea of Noah as a preacher, and sees him as a great prophet. It gives extensive details of what he said and of how people reacted to him. Most of them mocked him and his boat, but a few believed (e.g. Sūra Hūd 11:36–40). This becomes one of the stories which shows a pattern of God's rescue of believers and his judgement of unbelievers. There is a parallel here with 2 Peter.

The Qur'an does not say how long it took to build the ark. Genesis introduces Noah at the age of five hundred (5:32), and says that he entered into the ark at the age of six hundred (7:6). Some interpreters suggest that the

---

6. *Pirke De Rabbi Eliezer* 22:9; *Genesis Rabbah* 30:7.

7. For example, in the *Sibylline Oracles* (possibly from 2nd century, collected 6th century, 1:160–245).

120 years of Genesis 6:3 was the time from God's decision to destroy the earth to the flood. However we interpret these figures, it seems that it took many years to build the ark, so that the watching people would have had plenty of opportunity for repentance. The Qur'an implies that some did repent and enter the ark, but there is no indication of this in Genesis. Quite the opposite: it indicates that everyone outside of Noah's immediate family was drowned.

C. Genesis 7:1–9 Entering the Ark with Clean and Unclean Animals

Then the LORD said to Noah, "Go into the ark, you and all your household, for I have seen that you are righteous before me in this generation. Take with you seven pairs of all clean animals, the male and his mate, and a pair of the animals that are not clean, the male and his mate, and seven pairs of the birds of the heavens also, male and female, to keep their offspring alive on the face of all the earth. For in seven days I will send rain on the earth forty days and forty nights, and every living thing that I have made I will blot out from the face of the ground." And Noah did all that the LORD had commanded him.

Noah was six hundred years old when the flood of waters came upon the earth. And Noah and his sons and his wife and his sons' wives with him went into the ark to escape the waters of the flood. Of clean animals, and of animals that are not clean, and of birds, and of everything that creeps on the ground, two and two, male and female, went into the ark with Noah, as God had commanded Noah.

Chapters 7 and 8 give a detailed narrative of the flood. Again, Noah's difference from his contemporaries is underlined. Again, we see the emphasis on all of Noah's family being in the ark (vv. 1, 7). However, instead of the general "food" of 6:21, it is specified that extra pairs of "clean" animals should be taken on board. These animals could have been used for sacrifices as well as for food. The Qur'an has only a brief mention of the pairs of animals, and no mention of clean animals. Unbelieving family members, including one of Noah's sons and probably his wife, were drowned; and some believers who were not part of Noah's family were saved (Sūras *Hūd* 11:40; *al-Mu'minūn* 23:27; *ash-Shu'arā'* 26:105; *at-Tahrīm* 66:10).

It should be mentioned here that no animals are bad in themselves. God created all of them, and all were very good (Gen 1:31). Later on, under the Mosaic Law, animals called "clean" would serve both for food (Lev 11; Deut 14) and for sacrifice (cf. Gen 8:20). As believers, we do not need to sacrifice animals or to consider some animals unclean to eat, because the creator's original intention is restored through the Messiah. As God taught the Apostle Peter, "What God has made clean, do not call common" (Acts 10:15; cf. Rom 14:14).

D. Genesis 7:10–15 The Waters Rise and Cover the Earth

> And after seven days the waters of the flood came upon the earth.
>
> In the six hundredth year of Noah's life, in the second month, on the seventeenth day of the month, on that day all the fountains of the great deep burst forth, and the windows of the heavens were opened. And rain fell upon the earth forty days and forty nights. On the very same day Noah and his sons, Shem and Ham and Japheth, and Noah's wife and the three wives of his sons with them entered the ark, they and every beast, according to its kind, and all the livestock according to their kinds, and every creeping thing that creeps on the earth, according to its kind, and every bird, according to its kind, every winged creature. They went into the ark with Noah, two and two of all flesh in which there was the breath of life.

This was not a flood like we see every year, when monsoon rains bring floods to the riverine areas of Bangladesh. It was not a natural phenomenon, but a supernatural disaster. The vivid picture is of water coming from both directions: catastrophic rain for a whole forty days and forty nights, plus water bubbling up from the seas and maybe from the ground. Forty is a number often used to denote a complete long period of time, and the "fountains" and the "windows" may be poetic rather than literal, but we get a clear picture of an abnormal catastrophe lasting for far longer than any natural flood might do. It shows us that the earth was going back to the pre-creation *tohu wa bohu* "without form and void," when the water covered its face (Gen 1:2). As God had separated the waters above and the waters below in Genesis 1:6–7, so now those waters break the boundaries he had set.

The Qur'an also tells of waters falling from above and waters gushing from under the earth (Sūra al-Qamar 54:11–12). The waters below are said to come from *al-tannur*, which literally means "the oven." Some commentators think that there was a specific baker's oven which produced water as a sign to Noah that the flood was beginning (e.g. *Kasasul Ambiya*, 77), but this more likely refers to a hot water spring, following the Jewish tradition that the generation of the flood was punished with hot water (Talmud, *Sanhedrin* (108a–b); *Rosh Hashanah*, xi 42; xxiii, 27).

The first things to disappear from the world are the human beings and animals who are going to re-populate the earth: they all go into the ark.

> And those that entered, male and female of all flesh, went in as God had commanded him. And the LORD shut him in. (7:16)

In the *Gilgamesh Epic*, Ut-napishtim closed the door of the ship: in Genesis, the Lord shut the door. Perhaps this emphasizes that God alone had the authority over the only way into the ark, and that the opportunity for repentance was over. Noah might have tried to open the door when he saw the misery of drowning men, or perhaps some of them might have tried to come in. But, as it will be at the Messiah's second coming, God's time of waiting for their repentance was gone (Matt 24:36–42). Or perhaps the closed door emphasizes that God would keep the ark safe and watertight, so it would then point to the security of our salvation if we do repent and receive Jesus the Messiah. Either way, it reminds us of the pattern of God's fatherly mercy in the midst of judgement in the narratives of Adam and Eve, and of Cain. The Qur'an does not mention that God shut the door.

> The flood continued forty days on the earth. The waters increased and bore up the ark, and it rose high above the earth. The waters prevailed and increased greatly on the earth, and the ark floated on the face of the waters. And the waters prevailed so mightily on the earth that all the high mountains under the whole heaven were covered. The waters prevailed above the mountains, covering them fifteen cubits deep. And all flesh died that moved on the earth, birds, livestock, beasts, all swarming creatures that swarm on the earth, and all mankind. Everything on the dry land in whose nostrils was the breath of life died. He blotted out every living thing that was on the face of the ground, man and animals and creeping things and birds of the heavens. They were blotted out from the earth. Only Noah was left, and those who were with him in the ark. And the waters prevailed on the earth for 150 days. (7:17–24)

According to the *Epic of Gilgamesh* the flood lasted seven days: the Genesis narrative emphasizes the long forty-day period. The forty days of rainfall is probably included in the one hundred and fifty days of verse 24. As the water rose, it naturally lifted up the ark (Gen 7:17; cf. *Sūra Hūd* 11:42). The flood water covered the high hills and then the mountains for more than three months. The whole of "the earth" which God created had disappeared, and all is once again chaotic water.

The word "increased" (*yirbu*) is repeated twice – the waters increased (v. 17) and they greatly increased (v. 18). This emphasizes the huge amount of water. "Prevail" is repeated even more: the waters prevail (v. 18), they prevail exceedingly (v. 19), they prevail again (v. 20), and in verse 24 they prevail for 150 days. The verb translated "prevail" has the root *g-b-r*, which denotes strength, so this repetition emphasizes the power of the waters.

Everything died. Again, the repetitions emphasize the scale of the catastrophe. All flesh died (v. 21), all creatures who breathed died (v. 22), all living things were blotted out (v. 23). "Blotted out" translates the verb *machah*, which is used twice in this verse as well as once each in Genesis 6:7 and 7:4. A Jewish tradition suggests that the repetition, and the phrase "blotted out from the earth," means that there was absolutely no trace of them. Even their eggs were destroyed, so that never again could any of them reproduce. Only those in the ark survived, floating on waters which covered everything and every person that they had known. It is a bleak and lonely picture.

The Qur'an, too, paints a picture of terrible destruction, with only the people in the ark surviving, but it does not have the detail and repetition which emphasizes the destruction of all life. Rather, it emphasizes the judgement on wicked people. In accordance with Noah's prayer in Sūra *Nūḥ* 71:26–27, no evil doer was alive after the flood (see also Sūra *al-Mu'minūn* 23:27). Sūra *Hūd* makes the point very strongly with its story of Noah's unbelieving son, who refused to enter the ark and tried to escape by climbing a mountain (Sūra *Hūd* 11:40–47). The fact that he could not escape on top of a mountain is sometimes used as an argument that the Qur'an envisages a universal flood.

E. Genesis 8:1 God Remembered Noah

> *But God remembered Noah and all the beasts and all the livestock that were with him in the ark. And God made a wind blow over the earth, and the waters subsided.*

Here is the central and pivotal verse of the whole flood story: God in his mercy remembered Noah and all who were with him. When the Old Testament says that God remembered, it is combined with the idea of faithful love (cf. Jer 2:2; 31:20). The phrase, "God remembers" (from the verb *zakar*) occurs seventy-three times in the Old Testament. In the midst of the terrible destruction, we are to look at the faithful Lord.

The result of remembrance was that God sent his *rûach* across the earth, and the waters went down. The reader is reminded of the second verse of

WHAT WAS THE EXTENT OF THE FLOOD?

Traditionally, most Bible readers have supposed that the flood covered the whole of the created world, whereas most Qur'an readers have supposed that it was a local flood, affecting only Noah's community. However, both texts can be interpreted differently.

Genesis clearly teaches that all the humans and animals were drowned, but it has no indication that the creatures had yet spread out far from their place of origin. Further, although the word translated "the earth" (*ha-arets*) can mean the whole planet Earth, in modern Hebrew it often simply means "the land" and so could refer to the limited area which was inhabited at the time. As we have already seen in our study of worldviews (pages 39-40), people described the world as they saw it, and so the "whole earth" was the world that they knew. They did not know that the Earth was a planet!

We might also note that the famine of Genesis 41 is described as affecting "the whole *arets*" (41:57), but it is not understood as effecting the whole world. The covering of the mountains is a stronger indication of the coverage of a large area than is the use of universal language.

The Qur'an clearly teaches that Noah's people were destroyed, but Noah also prayed that no wicked person should be left on the earth, *al-arḍ* (Sūra *Nūḥ* 71:26) and the Qur'an, too, has the mountains covered (Sūra *Hūd* 11:40–47). If Noah's people were all the humans on earth at his time, the flood could have been universal.

As with some of our other inquiries, we therefore need to go outside the texts in order to discover the extent of the flood. The most obvious place to go is to geology, and most geologists would say that there is no evidence of a universal flood. As with other scientific questions (see earlier text box page 8), believers take a range of positions on this:

1. Giving priority to Genesis. The "flood geology" movement interprets all geological evidence on the assumption of a universal flood at the time of Noah.

2. Seeing Genesis and geology as two separate but complementary sources. Genesis is studied for its theological insights, and geology is studied for physical information, so we do not need to worry about how Genesis relates to historical events.

3. Giving priority to geology. This position argues that, since humans are created with the ability to do science, their scientific observations can tell them how to interpret Genesis. Since geology indicates no universal flood, we should interpret Genesis as teaching that only the world known to its writer was flooded.

Genesis, where, at the brink of creation, God's *rûach* hovers above the formless world. *Rûach* is usually translated "Spirit" in Genesis 1:2 and "wind" here, because 1:2 speaks of the *rûach* of God while this verse speaks of God causing a *rûach*, but it is significant that the word is the same. We are about to read of the re-creation of what has been destroyed.

Rûach is also used in 6:3, where God says that his spirit will not contend forever with human beings, and it has been repeated in verse 15 and 22 of chapter 7, where it describes what makes living beings. We are reminded of God's breathing the soul into the first man in 2:7 (although *rûach* is not used there). Human beings depend for every level of their lives on God's spirit, and that spirit is active in creation and in the new creation.

Curious readers may wonder how a wind could make the waters go down. One poetic suggestion is that the miraculous wind of God's faithful love evaporated the miraculous water of God's judgement.[8] In Islamic literature huge amounts of water were sucked up by the commands of God (Sūra *Hūd* 11:44; cf. Sūra *Kasasul Ambiya*, 79).

D'. Genesis 8:2–14 The Waters Recede and the Earth Appears

> *The fountains of the deep and the windows of the heavens were closed, the rain from the heavens was restrained, and the waters receded from the earth continually. At the end of 150 days the waters had abated, and in the seventh month, on the seventeenth day of the month, the ark came to rest on the mountains of Ararat. And the waters continued to abate until the tenth month; in the tenth month, on the first day of the month, the tops of the mountains were seen. (8:2–5)*

The flood began with the waters from above and the waters from below (7:11–12), reversing the separation of the waters and the making of the dry land in Genesis 1:6–7. So, when God remembers Noah, he again reverses the process by shutting off the water sources. Once again, the waters are separated. This is not a creative act as in Genesis 1 – after the flood, we see natural processes as the earth recovers from God's act of judgement.

Now, at last, the ark finishes its journey, an event so important as to merit another exact date. It has been exactly five months since the flood began, and, if Noah's home was in Mesopotamia, it has travelled perhaps five hundred miles. It stays in its place in the Ararat mountains for another three months.

---

8. Hamilton, *Book of Genesis, Chapter 1–17*, 300.

WHERE IS MOUNT ARARAT?

Figure 8 Location of Ararat

Ararat is a mountainous region in what was North Assyria, now shared between Turkey, Iran and Armenia. The Hebrew *Ararat* is cognate with the name of the ancient Armenian kingdom of Urartu, which is mentioned in inscriptions from the twelfth century BC and which stood up against Assyria in the 9th–6th centuries BC. It is mentioned in 2 Kings 19:37, Isaiah 37:38 and Jeremiah 51:27. The region covers tens of thousands of square miles and has hundreds of mountains.

Genesis does not mention a particular mountain, but there is one particular mountain in Eastern Turkey which the Persians call *Koh-i-Nuh* (mountain of Noah). This is a volcanic mountain, which could have been formed during and after the flood. The town *Lacuna* is there. Lacuna means "Noah settled here," so some say that is where the ark settled.

Others have different ideas. The *Gilgamesh Epic* specifies that the ark alighted on Mount Nimush, which is in southern Kurdistan. The Qur'an names the mountain Judi (Sūra *Hūd* 11:44), which, the commentators agree, is part of the Ararat Mountains.

Genesis arguably implies that the ark rested on a smaller mountain. Doves have limited ability for sustained flight, and olive trees do not grow on high mountains. If the dove plucked the olive leaf and returned to Noah in one day, this would mean that the ark was on a small mountain (Gen 8:11).

Many people have tried to find the remnants of the ark. Some have claimed that they have found it, but it then turns out that they were wrong. Given all the alternatives above, it is not surprising that their searches have, so far, been unsuccessful!

At the end of forty days Noah opened the window of the ark that he had made and sent forth a raven. It went to and fro until the waters were dried up from the earth. Then he sent forth a dove from him, to see if the waters had subsided from the face of the ground. But the dove found no place to set her foot, and she returned to him to the ark, for the waters were still on the face of the whole earth. So he put out his hand and took her and brought her into the ark with him. He waited another seven days, and again he sent forth the dove out of the ark. And the dove came back to him in the evening, and behold, in her mouth was a freshly plucked olive leaf. So Noah knew that the waters had subsided from the earth. Then he waited another seven days and sent forth the dove, and she did not return to him anymore. (8:6–12)

Noah opened not the main side door of the ark, but a window. He sent out birds to find out about outside conditions. We remember that the birds were among the first living beings created in chapter 1. The *Epic of Gilgamesh* features a similar use of the birds, but the Qur'an does not mention them.

Noah first sent a raven. Ravens can fly long distances, and can survive on muddy ground, so it went out and stayed away. Because it may feed on rotten flesh, the raven is considered "unclean" and unsuitable for human consumption (Lev 11:13–15; Deut 14:12–14). But this natural scavenger has its place in our ecosystem, and Noah kept it in the ark for the well-being of future generations! The raven (Heb. *'oreb*, Ar. *ghurab*) is mentioned twelve times in the Bible, but only once in the Qur'an, where it teaches Cain how to bury his brother (Sūra *al-Mā'ida* 5:31). However, as in Mosaic law, the raven is forbidden as food in Islamic law.

After seven days, Noah sent a dove, but it returned with nothing. After seven days, Noah again sent a dove. The olive trees were alive and their leaves grew rapidly, so this time the dove returned with a fresh olive leaf. Then, Noah waited another seven days and sent out the dove for the third time, but it did not return (8:12). Noah realized that the flood was definitely ended.

In Genesis 1, after the separation of waters and the appearance of dry land, the next things to appear were the plants (Gen 1:11–12). Here, the olive leaf symbolizes the first life in the re-made world as well as that fact that God's wrath is past. Thus, the dove holding an olive branch in its mouth has long been a universal symbol of peace. The qur'anic Noah narrative does not mention the olive, but the Qur'an seven times calls the olive a blessed tree, and, in Sūra *at-Tīn* 95:1, God takes an oath "by the olive."

> *In the six hundred and first year, in the first month, the first day of the month, the waters were dried from off the earth. And Noah removed the covering of the ark and looked, and behold, the face of the ground was dry. In the second month, on the twenty-seventh day of the month, the earth had dried out. (8:13–14)*

"Behold!" The Hebrew word *hinneh* is used to call the reader to attention and to wonder. In Genesis 1, it draws our attention to the wonder of creation, as God tells the first humans to "behold" the fruit-bearing plants for their food (1:29), and then himself beholds the great goodness of his creation (1:31). In Genesis 6, God beholds the great wickedness of fallen humanity (6:5) and then tells Noah to behold his judgement (6:13, 17). Here in Genesis 8 it draws our attention to the re-emergence of the good creation, as we see the fresh olive leaf (8:11) and now the dry land. We are drawn to imagine ourselves with Noah as he at last opens up the ark and fills his eyes with dry land instead of water!

Again we read of exact dates and times. The flood began on the seventeenth day of the second month of Noah's six-hundredth year (7:11) and lasted one year, one month and ten days. Here, many people try to calculate the exact duration of the flood, and to fit this into the various time periods recorded in the narrative. This is not easy, because there are uncertainties about the exact length of the years and months according to the ancient lunar calendar, about the intentions of the author in using symbolic numbers, and about whether some of the periods overlap with each other. Typical calculations would yield an exact solar year or a little more.

Looking back over the symbolic numbers, we notice yet another chiastic pattern:

7 days in the ark waiting for the flood (7:10)

    40 days of rainfall (7:12, 17)

        150 days the water prevailed (7:24)

            GOD REMEMBERED NOAH and the *rûach* turned the waters (8:1)

        150 days the water receded (8:3)

    40 days of waiting (8:6)

7 more days in the ark (8:12)

C.' Genesis 8:15–22 Leaving the Ark and the Sacrifice

Then God said to Noah, "Go out from the ark, you and your wife, and your sons and your sons' wives with you. Bring out with you every living thing that is with you of all flesh – birds and animals and every creeping thing that creeps on the earth – that they may swarm on the earth, and be fruitful and multiply on the earth." So Noah went out, and his sons and his wife and his sons' wives with him. Every beast, every creeping thing, and every bird, everything that moves on the earth, went out by families from the ark. (8:15–19)

In Genesis 1:20–30, God creates the animals and then the human beings. Here, there is no creative act but a new beginning, as the animals and the human beings together come out of the ark. However, there is a repetition of the blessing, "Be fruitful and multiply" (cf 1:22, 28). Creation is being given a second chance!

As they entered the ark at God's command in 7:1, so now they leave the ark at God's command. All aboard are safe. We notice the repetitions, emphasizing again who was in the ark – Noah and all his family and all sorts of animals. Noah's obedience is also emphasized: he did exactly what God had told him to do.

Then Noah built an altar to the LORD and took some of every clean animal and some of every clean bird and offered burnt offerings on the altar. And when the LORD smelled the pleasing aroma, the LORD said in his heart, "I will never again curse the ground because of man, for the intention of man's heart is evil from his youth. Neither will I ever again strike down

> *every living creature as I have done. While the earth remains, seedtime and harvest, cold and heat, summer and winter, day and night, shall not cease." (8:20–22)*

Here, we get another glimpse into God's heart, which we can compare to the glimpse into his heart before the flood in 6:6. This follows the third sacrifice found in Genesis: Abel's sacrifice was accepted, Cain's sacrifice was rejected, and now Noah's sacrifice is accepted.

Noah built an altar to YHWH and sacrificed some of the clean animals which he had been told to take with him (7:2–3). This is the first reference to an altar (Heb. *mizbeach*) in the Bible, and the text does not state what sort of altar it was, nor how Noah knew what to build. Neither does it specify the purpose of the sacrifice, only that it was a "burnt offering." The term translated "burnt offering" (Heb. *olah*) is different from the term *minchah* used of Abel's offering, and signifies something which goes up to God – here, the aroma "goes up." Burnt offerings are offerings of worship and thanksgiving, and are often described as "pleasing aromas" to the Lord (Lev 1:9, 13, 17; cf. Eph 5:2; Phil 4:18).

Here is another contrast to the *Gilgamesh Epic*. There, after the flood, Ut-napishtim offers wine and grain as well as meat in order to provide a feast for the gods. The gods swarm around Ut-napishtim's sacrifice like flies because they are hungry. Unlike the Mesopotamian gods, YHWH was not craving food, so he was pleased with only the aroma. As will be emphasized in the next passage, it is YHWH who provides food for human beings, not human beings who provide food for YHWH.[9]

And now comes the glimpse into God's heart. The earth has been renewed, but the human heart has not changed. In words very similar to those of 6:5, God sees that human hearts are still evil; and this is not something which is true only of adults – they are like that "from their youth." Yet in 8:21, God determines "in his heart" that he will never again curse the ground because of human sin. This is his decision to confirm the covenant which will be given in chapter 9.

Genesis 8:22 is like a brief poem, affirming that he will never again return the earth to the chaos of *tohu wa bohu*. This assurance from God gives hope. Climate change may affect Bangladesh and other countries, but God will

---

9. In Bangladesh's northern region of Sylhet, worshipers offer food – unboiled milk and various fruits – to gods and goddess. Many Muslims take part in this idol worship. Similar reports come from the Barak coastal area of Bengal people worshipping a local god, Broto parbon (Karimganj College newspaper 2013–14, representing the Karimgang student society, 23–29, 2014; https://www.barakbulletin.com/).

never destroy the earth by flood again. He has authority to control floods and tsunamis and the natural cycles of the seasons and harvests. As God set the pattern at the beginning of creation (Gen 1:14), so here, he promises that this pattern will continue. God recalls this great promise centuries later in the book of Isaiah:

> "This is like the days of Noah to me:
>> as I swore that the waters of Noah
>> should no more go over the earth,
> so I have sworn that I will not be angry with you,
>> and will not rebuke you.
> For the mountains may depart
>> and the hills be removed,
> but my steadfast love shall not depart from you,
>> and my covenant of peace shall not be removed,"
>> says the LORD, who has compassion on you. (Isa 54:9–10)

We may ask why God decides never to send another flood of judgement, even though humans are still wicked. How can he tolerate again the sort of violence and corruption described in Genesis 6? Will he let his world be so spoiled again? The text does not tell us, but God's decision is a response to the sacrifice. Once again, Genesis reveals that sacrifice is the way to please God in a fallen world but, once again, the reader will have to go on in the Bible to find out how and why that might be.

B'. Genesis 9:1–29 God's Plan and Covenant Announced

Genesis 9:1–17 is one of the most important passages in the Bible, as it recounts God's covenant with all humanity and with all that he has created. As God had told Noah about his plans for judgement and salvation in 6:11–22, here he tells Noah about his covenant plan for after the flood. In 6:18, God mentioned the first step of the covenant, which was to save Noah and his family. This chapter gives details of how this will apply to all living beings for all of time. This is the Bible's basis for understanding how God relates to his world and to everyone in it.

The Qur'an has only a few scattered echoes of this wonderful covenant. It mentions that there was a covenant with Noah, as there was with Abraham, Moses, David and Jesus the Messiah, but gives no details. After the flood, it mentions peace and blessings for the people in the ark, and provisions for other people. But these are conditional: they are limited in time and the people will eventually be punished. Far from the repeated "never again" of this chapter, the Qur'an sees the Noah story as the beginning of a pattern of judgement on unbelieving peoples who reject their prophets.

The passage we are going to look at is the very words of God, speaking to the little group of people who have survived the flood. We have seen a little of what was going on in God's heart: now he is going to tell them – and us – what is in his heart for his creation. Is it more judgement? No! It is his steadfast, loving commitment. The author introduces it, "And God blessed Noah and his sons." This covenant is a great blessing for all of us for all time. Verses 1–7 are about human responsibility, and verses 8–17 describe God's commitment. Sadly, the last part of the chapter describes an incident which shows us that families after the flood are not going to be any better than families before the flood.

Blessing and responsibility

And God blessed Noah and his sons and said to them, "Be fruitful and multiply and fill the earth. The fear of you and the dread of you shall be upon every beast of the earth and upon every bird of the heavens, upon everything that creeps on the ground and all the fish of the sea. Into your hand they are delivered. Every moving thing that lives shall be food for you. And as I gave you the green plants, I give you everything. But you shall not eat flesh with its life, that is, its blood. And for your lifeblood I will require a reckoning: from every beast I will require it and from man. From his fellow man I will require a reckoning for the life of man.

"Whoever sheds the blood of man, by man shall his blood be shed, for God made man in his own image.

And you, be fruitful and multiply, increase greatly on the earth and multiply in it." (9:1–7)

God's blessing here is both similar to and different from the original creation blessings in Genesis 1:28–30. At the beginning and the end comes *the blessing of fruitfulness*. God has already repeated this blessing on the animals (Gen 8:17; cf. 1:22), and now it is the turn of the humans. Verse 1 repeats exactly the "be fruitful and multiply and fill the earth" of 1:28. Verse 7 not only brings the number of times that humans are given this blessing to a perfect 3, but adds emphasis as it adds a second "multiply" and intervenes with *sh-r-ts* – "swarm" or "increase greatly" (cf. Gen 1:20–21; 7:21; 8:17). God's purpose for humankind is not altered: it is re-established and underlined.

Next comes *the blessing of responsibility*, but with a sad difference. Before the statement of responsibility, we hear that the animals will be afraid of the humans: the peaceful balance of Eden is upset. And the responsibility is stated in a very different way: this is not so much a joyful conferral of dominion, as a solemn conferral of answerability. "Into your (plural) hand they are delivered" (*bi-yedkem nittanu*). The word "hand" (*yad*) will be repeated three more times in the coming verses.

What about *the blessing of provision*? In 1:29–30, both humans and animals were given the bountiful provision of plants for food. Here, they get added permission to eat meat. The Torah will later introduce many other dietary laws for the *Bani Isra'il*, but here there is no restriction: as they were given all the plants, so now they are given "every moving thing," and it is repeated that this is a gift from God. Verse 3 ends emphatically: "I give you *EVERYTHING*." In the New Testament, as all peoples are called into the new creation in the Messiah, the dietary restrictions will be lifted and we can return to the blessing of these verses (Mark 7:14–23).

But, there are two very important provisions, both introduced by the emphatic Hebrew word *ak*, which appears at the beginning of verses 4 and 5. It can mean "but" or "however" or "surely," and it calls our attention to what is coming. Both prohibitions have to do with blood, and we remember the plural "bloods" of Abel crying from the ground in Genesis 4:10. This is serious!

In Hebrew, verse 4 begins "but flesh" (*ak basar*). It forbids eating flesh with its blood, which is equated with its life or soul (*nefesh*). This prohibition appears repeatedly in the Torah, and it was one of the few restrictions placed on Gentile believers by the early church (Lev 7:26–27; 17:10–14; Deut 12:15–16, 20–24; cf. Acts 15:29). The reason is also repeated: the *nefesh* is, in some unspecified way, associated with its blood (Lev 17:14; Deut 12:23). Creatures cannot live without their blood, and so the blood stands for the precious life which distinguishes animals from plants and from the rest of creation. Life belongs to God alone, so all blood belongs to him.

In Bangladesh, ethnic Christians and animists alike, especially the Garo, Robidas, and some other poor communities, eat meat with the blood still in it. In order to retain the blood, they do not slaughter the animal by slitting the throat with a sharp knife as do the Muslims: some pierce its heart with a bamboo stick or an iron spear so that the blood is retained. This is based on a traditional belief that the animal's blood contains its vital force, and some still see drinking blood as a mystical identification with the life of the animal. Genesis forbids such practices. The *nefesh* is not a soul which can somehow enter our souls, but life which is given by God. We cannot get an animal's power by drinking its blood.

Verse 5 begins "but your blood" (*w-ak et-dimkem*), and specifies that this is "of your lives" (*nefesh*). The great exception is human life, and verses 5 and 6 underline in the strongest possible way the prohibition not only of eating human flesh but also of spilling human blood. The repeated "your" of verse 5 implies that we are not even permitted to take our own lives, because they too belong to God. God has given responsibility into our hands, and he will require us to answer for what we have done with that responsibility.

Three times in verse 5, God says "I will require" (*edrosh*). Three times, the requirement is, in Hebrew, "from the hand" (*mi-yad*) – from the hand of every living being (*chayah*, translated "beast"); from the hand of the human (*adam*); from the hand of the brother of every man (*ish*). Even the animals have responsibility, and the Torah will give rules for what should be done with an animal which attacks a human being (Exod 21:28–32); but the more serious offence is the murder of a brother, reminding us again of Cain's killing of his brother, Abel. At the centre is the *adam* – the human being – and we wonder if there is a parallel here; whether all human beings are being described as "brothers."

The poem of verse 6 underlines these points, with its three-fold repetition of the word *adam*, finishing with the reminder of the reason for the whole passage: God made the *adam* in his own image. Even in translation, we see the memorable chiasm, which has only six words in Hebrew:

> *Shopek dam ha-adam, ba-adam damu yishshapek*

> Who sheds the blood of the man, by man his blood shall be shed.

We have previously been aware of the link between *adam* and *adamah* – the human and the ground for which and out of which he was made (Gen 2:5–8). Now we hear the similarity of *adam* and *dam* – the human and his God-given lifeblood.

The poem adds a further dimension. Where verse 5 declares that murderers will be answerable to God, verse 6 says that human beings will punish them. On the one hand, we have already seen that killing set in motion a cycle of retaliation (Gen 4:23–24). On the other hand, the Torah will lay down laws for dealing with murder and give human beings the responsibility for carrying them out in this life. These require the death penalty for deliberate murder, but not for unpremeditated killing[10] (Exod 21:12–14; 22:2; Num 35:6–34; Deut

---

10. Capital punishment was also specified as the punishment for rape (Deut 22:25–25) and for some cases of, for example, sexual misconduct (Lev 20:10–16; Deut 22:22–24); blasphemy (Lev 24:10–16); idolatry (Deut 17:2–7); Sabbath-breaking (Exod 31:14) and necromancy (Lev

19:1–13). In the New Testament, criminal judgement and punishment is the duty of state (Rom 13:3–4; 1 Pet 2:13–14).

The Qur'an, too, declares human life sacred, ". . . and do not kill the soul which God has forbidden [to be killed] except by [legal] right" (Sūra al-An'ām 6:151); and it, too, has capital punishment for murder. The sharī'a has capital punishment for both premeditated and unpremeditated murder, apostasy, fasād (mischief in the land) and zīna (adultery). Execution by stoning (rajm) is not supported by the Qur'an, but it is supported by several hadith (for example, Bukhari, Vol. 2, Book 23, Hadith 413; Vol. 9, Book 92, Hadith 432) and is practiced today in some Muslim majority countries in the Middle East and Africa. Bangladesh's penal code does not follow the sharī'a: it is based on the penal code of the British Indian Empire enacted in 1860, which allowed capital punishment for murder. Britain itself, like many other countries, has now abolished capital punishment.

In this solemn context of humans inflicting death on each other, the final repetition of "be fruitful and multiply" comes with new force. Far from killing each other so that there will be fewer human beings, God values us all and wants more of us.

God's universal covenant

> Then God said to Noah and to his sons with him, "Behold, I establish my covenant with you and your offspring after you, and with every living creature that is with you, the birds, the livestock, and every beast of the earth with you, as many as came out of the ark; it is for every beast of the earth. I establish my covenant with you, that never again shall all flesh be cut off by the waters of the flood, and never again shall there be a flood to destroy the earth." (9:8–11)

"Covenant" (Heb. berit; Gk. diathēkē) is one of the most significant words in the Bible (see text box on page 224). In this covenant, God establishes a public agreement not only with Noah's immediate family (cf. Gen 6:18) but also with his descendants – that is, with all human beings – and with all other living creatures (see also verses 16–17 and Isa 54:9).

The initiative is entirely from God. Verses 1–7 were introduced by "And God blessed" (wa-ybarek Elohim): here, we read, "And God said" (wa-yomer

---

20:27). In practice, the strict laws of witness have meant that capital punishment has seldom been practiced by the Jewish people; and most Christians understand the life and teaching of Jesus the Messiah as having revoked capital punishment for these crimes.

Elohim). Perhaps we expect God to give Noah some more instructions. But God's very first word tells us that this speech is not about Noah but about God – the Hebrew begins with the emphatic *ani* (I). Then comes *hinneh* – the word which emphatically draws our attention to what is about to be stated (see page 216). This is God telling not only Noah but also his sons what he is going to do. Readers have often noted that the coming speech of God includes no conditions – God's covenant here announces his commitment to his creatures, and he is promising that he will never change his mind on this (cf. Gen 6:6–7). We humans may ignore the prohibitions of verses 4–6, but God says, "Look, I will keep my part!"

Never again. Those two words have been said in 8:21–22, they are repeated twice here in 9:11, and they will be repeated again in 9:15. God promises that he will never wipe out a whole generation of human beings with a catastrophe like the flood. As we have seen, this is the opposite to the Qur'an's use of the Noah story: the Qur'an's repetition is of the pattern of judgement as it recounts the stories of *Hūd*, *Ṣāliḥ*, Lot, and Shuʻayb as parallels to the story of Noah (Sūras *al-Aʻrāf* 7:57–87; *Hūd* 11:25–95).

COVENANTS

Covenants were a common form of agreement in the ancient world. They were usually between a superior and an inferior party; for example, between a conquering king and the people whom he had conquered, there would be an agreement that they would obey him and pay tribute in exchange for peace and security, and there would be penalties for violating the agreement. There would be some sort of ceremony, often including invocation of the gods and blood sacrifice, and there would be a sign of the agreement, such as a stone tablet.

Bangladeshis today know the importance of agreements of different kinds. We have binding legal contracts, but we also have personal relationships which carry obligations. For example, eating together in a home implies a binding contract of loyalty on both parties. If someone "shared salt" (Bn. *nimok*) with a person and then betrayed him, he is disgraced, and people call him *nimok haram*. This unthankful treachery is called "biting the hand that feeds one." In the Bible, too, we read about covenants of salt with the priests and with David (Num 18:19;

2 Chr 13:5). This emphasizes that God's covenants are faithful forever, because salt is a preservative.

Biblical covenants (Heb. *berit*) are usually agreements between God and humans, although the term is also used of agreement between humans (e.g. Josh 9:15; 2 Sam 3:12–13). Every covenant between God and humans includes a sign, and a promise from God. Some, but not all, include something that God requires the humans to do. The obvious big difference with other ancient covenants is that it is the superior party who is making most of the promises, and sometimes, as here, God commits himself to something which requires no human agreement, or which he will do even if the humans do not exercise their responsibilities! Individuals may lose their blessings, but God will carry out his promises to humanity and to peoples. The other major biblical covenants are given through Abraham (Gen 12:1–3; 15; 17), Moses (Exod 19; Deut 29–30), David (2 Sam 7; 1 Chr 17), and Jesus the Messiah (Matt 26:26–28; Heb 9:11–22).

The Qur'an uses two words which are translated "covenant": *'ahd* (pledge or obligation) and *mithāq* (firm agreement). They are used many times and describe agreements between people as well as with God. It mentions covenants with Adam (Sūra *Ṭā Hā* 20:115), and with Noah, Abraham, Moses, David, Jesus, and Muhammad (Sūras *Āl 'Imrān* 3:81; *al-Aḥzāb* 33:7). There are also covenants with all humanity, in which they agree to the rightness of the commandment to worship only God (pre-creation, Sūras *al-Aʿrāf* 7:172; and to all the *banī adam* (children of Adam), *Yā Sīn* 36:60–61).

These covenants are generally conditional. Thus, the covenant between God and Muslims is based on the pledge of allegiance to their prophet (Sūras *al-Fatḥ* 48:10). The Muslims are obligated to keep their covenant (*an-Naḥl* 16:91), and those who break it forfeit its benefits (*ar-Raʿd* 13:20–25). God will remember those who remember (*dh-k-r*) him (*al-Baqara* 2:152). Abraham's descendants will be excluded from the covenant if they do wrong (*al-Baqara* 2:124). God declares that he can only keep his side of the covenant if the *Bani Isra'il* keep their side (*al-Baqara* 2:40), and most direct references to the Mosaic covenant are about its being broken (*al-Baqara* 2:63–66, 83–85, 93; *an-Nisā'* 4:154–55; *al-Māʾida* 5:12–13, 70–71; *Ṭā Hā* 20:86). The Christians, too, have a covenant which they broke (*al-Māʾida* 5:14). In most cases, the Arabic is literally "taking a covenant" rather than "giving a covenant," which implies that the emphasis is on what God requires of people in order that he might bless them.

And God said, "This is the sign of the covenant that I make between me and you and every living creature that is with you, for all future generations: I have set my bow in the cloud, and it shall be a sign of the covenant between me and the earth. When I bring clouds over the earth and the bow is seen in the clouds, I will remember my covenant that is between me and you and every living creature of all flesh. And the waters shall never again become a flood to destroy all flesh. When the bow is in the clouds, I will see it and remember the everlasting covenant between God and every living creature of all flesh that is on the earth." God said to Noah, "This is the sign of the covenant that I have established between me and all flesh that is on the earth." (9:12–17)

As binding agreements today have signatures, biblical covenants always have signs. The sign of this covenant is a rainbow – it is as if God himself signs the agreement, but needs no signature from humanity. The Hebrew word (*qeshet*) means simply "bow" but, as it is in the clouds, it evidently means a rainbow. Rainbows often appear after rains, so we do not suppose that this was the first rainbow, but that God gave this natural phenomenon a special meaning. Thus God used his creation for fulfilling his purpose (cf. Gen 7:11; 8:1). A rainbow is produced when the sun shines onto rain drops, so it is an appropriate reminder of God's love and faithfulness shining through his judgement into all the clouds which are produced by our sin.

Of course, the ancient Hebrews did not know the science of rainbow formation. Some other ancient peoples thought of rainbows as signs of coming storms, rains and disasters, and they had expert diviners who would read the meanings of particular rainbows. Genesis says, "No." You don't need an expert to tell you what the rainbow means. God has already told you what it means. You don't need to worry about disasters – God is in control and he cares about you.

Bows were the major weapons in Mesopotamia. In *Enuma Elish*, after the god Marduk triumphs over Tiamat (the sea), he hangs his bow in the sky, thus declaring his victory. We can therefore see the rainbow as the One God declaring victory over evil. As one ancient Jewish commentator points out, the shape of the bow points any arrows away from the earth. It was, he says, the custom of triumphant warriors to hold their bows upside down as a symbol of peace, so the rainbow is God's declaration of peace to his world.[11]

---

11. See Ronald Hendel, "The Rainbow in Ancient Context," The Torah, https://thetorah.com/the-rainbow-in-ancient-context/.

Rainbows have their places in many traditions. In Arabic, "rainbow" is *qaus quzaḥ*, literally, "the bow of many colours." It can also be interpreted as meaning the war bow of the pre-Islamic rain god *Quzaḥ*. There is a tradition that the Islamic Prophet Muhammad forbade calling the rainbow *qaus quzaḥ* – bow of *Quzaḥ* – and replaced the term with *qaus Allāh* – God's bow, linking it to a promise to preserve the world after the flood.[12] In this way, the rainbow serves its purpose of retaining the memory of the covenant despite the Qur'an not recording its details. In Bangla, the terms *ramdhonu* (bow of Ram, the incarnate of god *Bishnu*) and *rongdhunu* (bow of colour) respectively reflect Hindu and monotheistic views of the universe.

Here in Genesis 9, the rainbow is a constant reminder of the oath that God will not again wipe out the earth with floodwater. However, it is not only a reminder to us but a reminder to God! God repeats in verses 15 and 16 that, when he looks at the rainbow, he will remember this covenant. There are many rainbows which we do not see, but God sees all. We may forget this covenant, but God will not forget it, no matter how sinful we are. We recall that the centre or turning point of this *toledoth* is Genesis 8:1 – at the height of the flood, God remembered Noah, and the floodgates were closed. We can be sure that, whatever is happening to us, God will not forget us or any other of his creatures.

The rainbow appears to the Prophet Ezekiel, surrounding the divine chariot, the "appearance of the likeness of the glory of the LORD" (Ezek 1:28). It appears again in Revelation 4:3 surrounding the throne of God, and in Revelation 10:1 surrounding the angel who announces the thunders and the end of the world. In the first two cases, we see the sovereign Lord who will judge surrounded by the reminder of his faithful love and mercy. In the third case, we are coming to the end of this world when there will be the final judgement which will cleanse not only present sin but all the hearts of those who have accepted God's covenants and who worship the Lord Jesus the Messiah. Right up to the end, God will remember his covenant.

---

12. *Majma'u 'l-Bihar*, vol. ii., 142, cited in T. P. Hughes, *Dictionary of Islam* (London: W. H. Allen, 1885), 533.

A'. Genesis 9:18–29 Noah and His Descendants: Cursing and Blessing

> *The sons of Noah who went forth from the ark were Shem, Ham, and Japheth. (Ham was the father of Canaan.) These three were the sons of Noah, and from these the people of the whole earth were dispersed. (9:18–19)*

Chapter 10 is going to tell us about how the descendants of Noah's three sons were scattered across the earth, but first the Genesis author tells a story that warns of the implications of the divisions of chapter 10 and also prepares us for the confusion that will mark the character of future generations in chapter 11:1–9.

> *Noah began to be a man of the soil, and he planted a vineyard. He drank of the wine and became drunk and lay uncovered in his tent. And Ham, the father of Canaan, saw the nakedness of his father and told his two brothers outside. Then Shem and Japheth took a garment, laid it on both their shoulders, and walked backward and covered the nakedness of their father. Their faces were turned backward, and they did not see their father's nakedness. (9:20–23)*

The Noah *toledoth* began by introducing righteous Noah and his three sons, who were lights in the darkness of the violent generation of the flood (6:9–10). It nearly ends sadly, in the new world after the flood, with an unsavoury incident and with Noah cursing one of his sons; but the final word is one of blessing before the inevitable death of Noah. We remember that Adam also had three sons. Adam, too, fell into abusing the fruit of a tree, and one of Adam's sons was killed, one was a killer, and the third was a sign of hope.

Noah is a "man of the earth/soil" (Heb. *ish ha-adamah*): this emphasizes his relationship to the ground, but also tells us that he was a farmer like his father Lamech (5:29). He planted a vineyard, and seems to have grown plenty of fruit, because he had enough wine to become drunk. This is the first incident in the Scriptures linking wine to drunkenness and shame: it is a picture of the abuse of the good fruits in God's creation.

Perhaps it was because he became warm that Noah "uncovered" himself; but this is more likely to be a euphemism for some kind of sexual misconduct.[13] The text is deliberately not explicit, so we will not speculate further. His son Ham saw, and instead of covering his father's nakedness, went and told his

---

13. The Torah often uses "uncovering nakedness" to describe sexual activity. See Leviticus 18.

HOW COULD A "RIGHTEOUS" PERSON DRINK WINE?

Noah's mistake was not that he drank wine but that he drank too much of it, and that led to drunkenness and impropriety. In the Bible, wine is not forbidden, and people drank it regularly, partly because the water was not pure. They did not have the efficient filters that we have in Bangladesh today! The Bible also affirms wine as God's gift to gladden the heart (Ps 104:15) and as having medicinal use (1 Tim 5:23). Jesus the Messiah himself provided wine for a wedding (John 2:1–11), and wine is part of the Passover celebration and represents Jesus the Messiah's redeeming blood in the Holy Communion.

However, the Bible also strongly warns against intoxication (Prov 20:1; 21:17; 23:29–35; 31:4–7) and against the sort of drinking which is associated with carousing and immorality (Luke 21:34; Rom 13:13; Gal 5:21; 1 Pet 4:3). Further, the priests were strictly forbidden to drink alcohol when they went into the tabernacle (Lev 10:9), and abstaining from alcohol was part of the Nazirite purity vow which devotees could take (Num 6). As with so many other things in God's good creation, wine has its place, but it is dangerous when misused and there are times when it should be avoided.

Like the Bible, the Qur'an does not see wine as necessarily bad. Sūra al-Baqara 2:219 states that there is both sin *(ithm)* and profit in gambling and wine *(al-khamr)*, but the potential for sin is greater than the potential for profit. Later, an-Nisā' 4:43 warns against praying while drunk, and, later still, al-Mā'ida 5:90–92 describes alcohol and gambling as works of Satan and forbids them. It seems that warning against the dangers was not sufficient. To guard against the evils of drunkenness, the early Muslim community needed complete prohibition, and Islam has continued that prohibition until today. Similarly, people who suffer from alcoholism have to abstain from all alcohol even after they have stopped their drinking, or they will fall back into their old habits.

Some Christians abstain completely from alcohol because they want to avoid any temptation to abuse it, or because they want to avoid tempting other, weaker brothers and sisters. However, this is a choice and not a law.

brothers about the matter. Thus he disrespected his father. In contrast, Shem and Japheth did not talk but acted. They walked backwards and carefully averted their faces as they covered their father, thus showing their respect (v. 23).

The reader is reminded of Adam and Eve's discovery of their nakedness, of their futile attempts at covering it, and of God's provision of cover (Gen 3). But we also note that this is the first account of the relationship between a father and his sons in the Bible, and demonstrates the huge importance of respect for parents.

The Qur'an does not mention this incident, perhaps because it could dishonour Noah, whom the Qur'an sees as a righteous prophet. However, as we have seen previously, it does acknowledge that Noah had an unbelieving son (Sūra *Hūd* 11:42–47), and Islamic literature, while omitting Noah's drunkenness, gives accounts of his nakedness and his sons' respect and disrespect (*Kasasul Ambiya*, 81).

> When Noah awoke from his wine and knew what his youngest
>   son had done to him, he said,
>
> "Cursed be Canaan;
>   a servant of servants shall he be to his brothers."
>
> He also said,
>
> "Blessed be the LORD, the God of Shem;
>   and let Canaan be his servant.
> May God enlarge Japheth,
>   and let him dwell in the tents of Shem,
>   and let Canaan be his servant." (9:24–27)

Here is the first human "curse" (Heb. *ārûr*), surprisingly not of Ham, but of Ham's youngest son, Canaan (10:6). Perhaps the boy was involved in the sin along with his father, or perhaps this strengthens the idea that the consequences of sins affect future generations.

But here, too, is the first human blessing on future generations. We note that this is not Noah giving his own blessing, but Noah praising God and praying for God's blessings. The curse on Canaan came from Noah, but the blessings would come from God alone.

This is important, because some people have used the curse on Canaan, the idea that he would serve his brothers, as a justification for slavery. It has even been said that the "curse" was blackness, so that black people were inferior and could be badly treated. Sadly, some Muslim literature reflects the idea that dark skin is a result of the curse on Ham,[14] and subcontinental cultures

---

14. *Kasasul Ambiya* says that the curse on Ham resulted in his descendants being black (p. 81).

prefer light-coloured skin. Parents seek fair-skinned brides for their sons, and dark-skinned girls use whitening creams which are actually harmful to their skin and health.

This is in complete contradiction to the teaching of Genesis, which is that all people are made in the image of God, that God has put his rainbow over all of Noah's descendants, and that God blesses all peoples through the seed of Abraham. There is no suggestion here that skin colour can be a result of a curse. Anything which treats some humans as inferior is a result of sin. The New Testament reminds its readers that even slaves and masters have equal status in the eyes of God (Col 3:11). In the words of the Bangladeshi poet Shattendranath in his famous poem, "Humankind," "Black and white is merely outward; inside, we are of the same hue."

The curse on Canaan and the blessing on Shem point towards the future, when the land of Canaan would be given to the descendants of Abraham, who was a descendant of Shem (Deut 9:3). The Canaanites came under God's judgement because they had become very wicked, so they were first subjected by Joshua and later by King Solomon (cf. 1 Kgs 9:20–21).

It is worth repeating that this is not teaching a form of racism. On the contrary, the whole world would be blessed through the descendants of Abraham (Gen 12:3), and Jesus the Messiah, the descendent of Abraham, would eventually fulfil this promise. This is underlined by the blessing on Japheth, whose name means "enlargement." His descendants (see Gen 10:2–5) seem to have included all the peoples other than the Middle Easterners; for example, the Caucasians, who came to know the Messiah and then took the good news to bless many people, even in Bangladesh (Luke 2:32; Eph 3:6; Gal 3:26–29).

The middle part of verse 27 is intriguing: grammatically, it could be the sons of Japheth who would "dwell in the tents of Shem," or it could be God. Both meanings are wonderful. If the sons of Japheth dwell in Shem's tents, the Gentiles are equal with the *Bani Isra'il* and share all their blessings. If God himself dwells in Shem's tents, this is pointing towards the presence of God in the tabernacle and in the temple. Yet the verse ends with a repetition of Canaan's servitude. As this *toledoth* began with righteous Noah in the midst of a wicked generation, so it ends with facing the long-term results of sin in the midst of God's covenant promises. There will be future judgement as well as future blessing.

Genesis 9:28–29 The Death of Noah

> After the flood Noah lived 350 years. All the days of Noah were 950 years, and he died. (9:28–29)

According to this verse, two-thirds of Noah's life was pre-flood and one third post-flood. Noah was the last of the long-lived pre-flood generation. After that, the lifespan of humankind reduced (cf. Gen 6:3). The Qur'an also mentions Noah's age as 950 years (Sūra al-'Ankabūt 29:14). Those who believe that the age of the ancestors described in the geological list is literally true make an interesting observation: Abraham was fifty-eight years old at the time of Noah's death, so he could have heard about the flood from Noah himself.

The Bible is silent about the burial place of Noah. Because of this, several sites are claimed as his tomb. Shi'a Muslims believe that he is buried next to Imam Ali within the Imam Ali Mosque in Najaf, Iraq. Others believe that he is buried in the sacred mosque of Mecca, or in Baalbak in Lebanon or in Jordan or in Turkey.

Theological Reflection

Creation and re-creation, community and covenant – these great themes will blossom throughout the Bible from the bud of the Noah *toledoth*. Underlying them all is the "regret" and pain in the heart of God which we saw in Genesis 6:6, and which are echoed in the holy judgement of the flood and the loving commitment of the covenant. We get here only a glimpse of how this will be resolved in the sacrifice. But we are warned that even the most righteous person who was saved can get drunk, and can have sons who will cause chaos. The judgement waters may have swept the whole earth clean of blood and violence, but they have not cleansed the human heart (Gen 8:21).

A beautiful aroma rises from *the theological bud* as, at the centre of it all, God remembers Noah (8:1). Indeed, if the Noah story is at the centre of Genesis 1–11,[15] this sentence is at the heart of the whole of Genesis 1–11. God remembers. God is faithful. God is determined to bless humankind, despite their sinfulness (8:21–22; 9:1, 7). So God accepts the sacrifice, and God declares his covenant: God will remember (9:15), and God will still remember (9:16). Of this we can be sure – there is here a mountain top more than high enough to match the depths of the abyss of human rebellion at the centre of the *toledoth* of the heavens and the earth (see page 92).

---

15. See analysis of the Genesis structure in the Introduction, page 24.

Even more vividly than the expulsion from Eden, Genesis 6–9's description of the un-making and re-making of the world shows us that every aspect of creation has been affected by that abyss. But every aspect of creation is also under God's care. He not only remembers human beings, but also the animals; his commitment is not only to living beings, but to guarding the seasons, and his sign is the physical phenomenon of the rainbow. As in Genesis 1–2, humans have their place and have unique responsibility within this creation, but they also have unique ability to spoil it and to cause its destruction.

Such an understanding is crucial to *the DNA of any science* which respects both the Creator and the creation. Those who use the sciences need to be aware of how human beings can use their knowledge for good or for evil. There is another way in which the Noah story has been a "grandmother" contributing to the historical development of science: the measurement and building of the ark inspired interest in accurate measurement and in engineering, and the collection of animals inspired early zoological collections.[16]

We might see the qur'anic Noah stories as forming *the seedbed of the qur'anic view of revelation*: Noah is a paradigm prophet and the Qur'an presents the history of God's interaction with his world as the sending of a series of similar prophets, culminating in the Islamic Prophet Muhammad. Indeed, the qur'anic Noah can be regarded as a picture of the Islamic Prophet Muhammad's preaching and experience in Mecca. Some of the lessons which it draws from the story are similar to those drawn by the New Testament; for example, both the Qur'an and 2 Peter use it to encourage people towards steadfastness under persecution, and, like the Qur'an, the Messiah uses the pre-flood people as an example of wickedness (Matt 24:38) – but the Qur'an misses the context and the main thrust of the Genesis narrative.

If we miss the context and thrust of the Noah *toledoth*, we miss the whole shape of biblical history. The New Testament writers understood that history. Jesus the Messiah knew that the primeval judgement would not be repeated until the end of time, so he used the Noah story as a picture of the last days (Matt 24:38). The writer of Revelation knew that the rainbow signified God's covenant commitment to all humanity, so he tells of the rainbow around the throne which reminds us of God's love and mercy which will triumph even through the last judgement. The Apostle Paul knew that the whole creation had been affected by human sin, and that there would eventually be a new creation (Rom 8:22–27). And, of course, the New Testament knows of the acceptable sacrifices in the Old Testament, of which Noah's was the second. This history

---

16. See Mandelbrote and Bennet, *The Garden, the Ark, the Tower.*

of the unique judgement in the flood, God's covenant commitment to sinful humankind, and the sacrifices which lead towards the new creation forms *the seedbed in which all the seeds revealed in Genesis 1–11 will grow.*

In contrast, the Qur'an seems not to know how the Noah story fits into the history of humankind. It does not know that the world has been un-made and re-made because of sin, or that a judgement like the flood will never be repeated until the end. It has no details of the covenant of God's unconditional commitment to his creation, and it has no sacrifices except the enigmatic ram given to Abraham as a substitute for his son (Sūra aṣ-Ṣāffāt 37:98–113). Most poignantly, the Qur'an portrays the anger but not the pain in the heart of God which is his response to human evil.

A key to understanding the difference is realizing that in the Qur'an, it is the believers who are saved, whereas in Genesis, it is a family that is saved. The peoples descended from them will all be sinful as well as being made in the image of God; so biblical history will be about God's working through a family and its descendants in order to bring about a new creation of people who will love him. At the heart of the history will be Jesus the Messiah, as God remembers his people and their need, and takes upon himself all their sin and pain. We can understand the Bible as a record of that history and of the relationship between God and his people. It does not only include messages given to the prophets by God, it also includes the peoples' words to God and about God, and his interactions with them.

A key for understanding this history can be found in *two seeds planted after the flood*: the sacrifice which changed the divine response to evil from judgement to covenant (8:20–22), and the sacredness of the lifeblood (9:5–6). Genesis leaves us wondering how a sacrifice can make such a difference, and why eating the blood is banned. The Torah will bring together the two seeds in the sacrifices which are at the centre of the worship system given to the *Bani Isra'il*. A large part of the Torah describes the holy tent which symbolized God's presence, and the ways in which the tent and the people could be kept holy, that is, worthy of the presence of the pure, holy and transcendent One God. At the heart of holiness grew a tree of life – a system of sacrifices which dealt with the spiritual death which results from sin, and at the heart of this was the shedding of blood.

The sacrificial meat was sometimes burned and sometimes eaten, but the blood was never to be eaten; rather, it could be poured on the ground or sprinkled on and around the altar. Leviticus 17:10–14 lays out the prohibition, not only within the holy tent, but for all the *Bani Isra'il* and anyone staying with them (see also Lev 7:26). Its reason is the same as that given in Genesis 9:5 –

the blood is associated with the life (*nefesh*) (Lev 17:14), and the life belongs to God alone. But there is an added dimension: this passage follows descriptions of sacrifices which atone for unintentional sins (Lev 4:1–6:7; 6:24–7:21) and the chapter which describes the day of atonement on which sacrifices were offered to deal with all sins (Lev 16:1–34). So here we read that God gives the lifeblood to the people "to make atonement (*k-f-r*) for your souls (*nefesh*)" (Lev 17:11). The root idea of *k-f-r* is "to cover up," and it describes God's way of covering the shame of sin and averting the spiritual death which would otherwise engulf the soul.

As the tree of life reaches its fruition, we get a terrible shock as the prohibition against eating human flesh and drinking any blood is broken by Jesus the Messiah himself. "Truly, truly, I say to you, unless you eat the flesh of the Son of Man and drink his blood," he says, "you have no life in you" (John 6:53), and he then repeats these ideas three times more in the next three verses. No wonder we read that "many of his disciples turned back and no longer walked with him" (John 6:66). How could this be the Messiah if he violated such basic laws? The Messiah was not breaking the laws but fulfilling them. He himself was the sacrifice which God was giving to cover our sins. "Eating his flesh" means that we are invited to accept him as the sacrifice that God has given us for our own sins, as the ancient Jews were invited to share in eating the meat of some of their sacrifices.[17]

The ethnic Bangladeshis are wrong in thinking that they can get the power of animals by drinking their blood, but they are right in thinking that the blood represents something very important. "Drinking" Jesus the Messiah's blood means sharing in his resurrected life and power. How do we do this? Obviously it can't mean physically eating flesh and blood, because we do not have Jesus the Messiah's flesh and blood. It is first and foremost a spiritual eating and drinking, as we believe in the Messiah and offer our lives to him. But he also gave us a physical way of expressing this faith in "the Lord's Supper," when he took bread and said, "This is my body" and poured wine and said, "This is my blood." Some people think that the bread and wine mystically become the actual flesh and blood of Jesus the Messiah, but the writers of this book think that they are merely symbolic. However we understand it, eating this bread and drinking this wine is a way in which we experience fellowship with the Messiah and receive all the benefits of his death and resurrection.

---

17. Notably the Passover sacrifice (Deut 16:1–8) and the fellowship offerings (Lev 7:11–18).

What About Us?

There are many challenges for us in the Noah narrative. We will choose just three.

First, we are challenged by Noah's obedience, even when he did not understand what God was doing. God instructed him, and he did exactly what he had been told to do. Then he spent months inside the ark, with no means of steering it and not knowing where he was going or what was going on outside. If Genesis 6:13–21 records all that God said to Noah before the flood, he did not even know that, eventually, the waters would go down! He had God's word that he was going to establish a covenant (6:18), but he did not know what would be in it. When the storms of life surround us, and when we seem to be flooded by difficulties and we wonder what God is doing, can we also trust and obey him (see Prov 3:5–6; 16:3; Phil 2:13)? Romans 8:28 promises that God always acts for our benefit. We may not understand it immediately, but in the future, we will recognize God's wisdom.

Second, how should we understand our own floods in Bangladesh? Are they caused by God's judgement on us? Some people say that the communities which are worst affected by the floods must be particularly wicked, and that God is punishing them as at the time of Noah. But we must realise that this is not what Genesis is teaching. In fact, it teaches the opposite: God has given us a wonderful promise that he will never again judge the earth in the way that he did at the time of Noah. God is with us during natural disasters as he was with Noah. It is not his intention to destroy us. We can trust him. He has promised to protect his people when they pass through seas of trouble (Isa 43:2; Zech 10:11).

Later, God did destroy the wicked communities of Sodom and Gomorrah (Gen 19), so we cannot say that God will never punish a whole group of sinful people. The main point in Genesis 9 is that he will never again destroy the whole world, so never again can we assume that any natural disaster must be a punishment sent by God. Rather, the whole world has been affected by human sinfulness, and so human beings will suffer from that sin.

Perhaps the worst aspect of Bangladesh's floods are the famines that follow them. There was the Great Famine of 1770 AD when ten million people died after the harvest was destroyed by a flood: it was exacerbated by war and by taxation from the East India Company. In 1943, 2.1 million died when problems were compounded by a ban on rice imports from Myanmar as ships bearing rice were diverted to Europe.[18] Today, there are many man-made causes behind our devastating floods – global warming, deforestation and dam-building upstream from our rivers, and unplanned barrages, bridges and roads in the riverine areas in Bangladesh. We have learned that a natural phenomenon which brought fertility to our land can turn into a disaster when exacerbated by human actions.

As Creator, God is able to control natural calamities (Ps 107:23–30), but he has given free will to humanity, and he will not overrule this. We have our part to play. Noah was to protect the flood-affected animals by providing food and shelter to keep the biodiversity (Gen 6:20; 7:13), and we can follow his example by seeking ways of protecting all living beings, including ourselves.

We have an example in the work of Dr. David MacKill, who developed a strain of rice which can survive salt-water flooding, and thus has greatly reduced the impact of flooding on our food supplies.[19] We are not helpless. We have God's blessing on his creation and his mandate to have dominion over it, and we can develop science and work towards sustainable development.

Third, we notice the importance of family. The Qur'an's view, that it was the believers rather than the family who were saved, has alerted us to the Noah *toledoth*'s emphasis on the salvation of a family. Looking over Genesis 1–11 as a whole, we notice an emphasis on family throughout. God's first blessing was "Be fruitful and multiply" (1:28), and a man was to leave his parents to form a family with his wife (2:24). Genesis 4 describes a disastrous sibling relationship which led to a violent family, and Genesis 5 follows the line of a new family. In Genesis 12, we will find that God will choose to bless the whole sinful world through another family.

We also notice an alternation between the goodness of family life and its spoiling due to sin. The first marriage was spoiled, the first siblings fought, and the murderer's family became polygamous and violent. Now the story of Noah's sons adds a glimpse of the parent-child relationship, and shows us what can happen to the family and to future generations when parents are not respected.

Family has always been the basic structure of society in South Asia. We should not be surprised to find that our families display both the fallen nature and the image of God. Problems reflecting Genesis 1–11 include polygamy,

---

18. See M. Mukherji, "Bengal Famine of 1943: An Appraisal of the Famine Inquiry Commission," *Economic and Political Weekly,* vol. 49, no. 11 (2014): 71–75 and https://bn.wikipedia.org/wiki/famine.

19. See Gene Hettel, "A Rice Breeder's Odyssey from Surfer to Scientist – and Onward to 'Mars'," *Rice Today,* July 1, 2011, accessed Aug 21, 2021, https://ricetoday.irri.org/a-rice-breeders-odyssey-from-surfer-to-scientist-and-onward-to-mars-2.

divorce and patriarchal systems which consider male children more important than females and discriminate against women and girls. In theory we love our siblings and respect our parents, but, in practice, we can be guilty of rivalry and disrespect.

Believers in Jesus the Messiah are at the same time members of this sinful society and members of God's family (John 1:12–13). Jesus the Messiah is the master of the believers' families, so he can enable them to follow his pattern of mutual love (Matt 15:4; Eph 6:1–2, 4). Like Noah, they seek to live obediently in the midst of a corrupt society. Like Noah, and unlike the first Lamech, they have one wife. Like Noah, they should understand the importance of saving females as well as males. They should turn from discriminating between their children, because all are made in the image of God – not only male and female children but also those of the third gender (Bn. *Hijra*).[20] Children are a gift from God (Ps 127:3), so a girl child is not a source of sorrow, shame, and poverty, but a blessing from the heavenly Father.

In the midst of the problems of life, a God-fearing family can provide a safe haven for its members. Bangladeshi parents, like Noah's father, always hope that their children will give them comfort (Gen 5:28–29). There is a Bengali proverb, *Songsar Sukher hoi Romonir Gune* (Eng. "The happiness of domestic life depends solely on the wife"). In our male-dominated society, people blame the women for any unhappy family situation, but it is not only the children's or the wife's duty to make the home a place of comfort. Every family member has a role to play.

God rescued Noah and his family and commissioned them to accomplish his will to be "fruitful and multiply in the earth" (9:7). Under the new covenant, God also commissions his adopted children to preach his gospel in this earth. This is the new way of "being fruitful and multiplying," but it does not cancel out God's creation plans for families. On the contrary, it helps believers to build godly families and societies free from discrimination, nepotism, polygamy and divorce.

---

20. In Bangla, the term *Hijra* refers to people who are considered to be neither entirely male nor entirely female. They have long had their place as what is understood as the "third gender" in much of the Indian sub-continent. The term does not have an exact translation into English.

6

The Beginnings of Nations –
Genesis 10:1–11:9

The *Toledoth* of Noah's Children

> The floods have lifted up, O LORD,
>> the floods have lifted up their voice;
>> the floods lift up their roaring.
> Mightier than the thunders of many waters,
>> mightier than the waves of the sea,
>> the LORD on high is mighty! (Psalm 93:3–4)

The Lord who is mightier than the floodwaters is also the Lord of all the clashing voices of the fallen human nations. When the one who said, "Let there be" speaks, it will be so.[1]

This *toledoth* will tell us about the sons of Noah, from whom all the peoples of all the earth spread out (9:19), and about the beginnings of the results of the group tensions of 9:25–27. It does this by describing the origins and nature of ethnic and political communities. Genesis 2–4 opened up the nature of individual humans and their families as creatures made in God's image but tragically fallen. Genesis 4:17–24 described the beginnings of urban civilization. Genesis 6–9 revealed God's holy but loving responses to human sin, destroying those very cities but preserving one family. Now, we are going to see the development of larger communities which will not be destroyed.

This *toledoth* shows two aspects of this new world. On the one hand, Genesis 10 is organized to demonstrate that the different communities are under God's providential blessings as they grow into tribes and nations with

---

1. Cf. Sūra *Maryam* 19:35; *an-Naḥl* 16:40.

territories and languages. On the other hand, Genesis 11:1–9 shows how such communities can, like the community of Lamech in 4:23–24, become centres for self-aggrandizement where human beings dare to challenge God.

At the heart of Genesis 10 is a "beginning" (*reshit*) which contrasts with the "beginning" of the heavens and the earth in Genesis 1:1 – the beginning of the kingdom of Nimrod, which is Babel (10:10). Chapter 11:1–9 will tell us about the building of that beginning, with a tower raising its head (*rosh*, from the same root as *reshit*) to the heavens. We will find that, as the Lord ruled over the flood (*mabul*) and saved Noah's family to begin a fruitful and ordered world (10:1, 32), so he ruled over the beginning of Babel and saved Abraham's family to begin the plan of salvation for all. He confused (*balal*) language to limit wickedness rather than sending a flood to destroy wickedness.

It is helpful here to recall the chiastic structure of Genesis 1–11 (page 24)

  A. God creates the universe and blesses humans (Gen 1)
  　B. Man's beginning, his sin and expulsion from the garden (Gen 2–3)
  　　C. The rise of man's hatred, scattering and the first city (Gen 4)
  　　　D. The genealogy of Adam (Gen 5)
  　　　　E. The degradation and oppression in the world (Gen 6:1–6)
  　　　　　F. Noah and the flood (Gen 6:7–8:22)
  　　　　E'. The covenant with Noah (Gen 9)
  　　　D'. The generations of the nations (Gen 10)
  　　C'. The establishment of a city and the scattering of people (Gen 11:1–9)
  　B'. The children of Israel are brought out of the evil city by the call of Abraham (Gen 11:10–32)
  A'. The plan of God to bless the nations (Gen 12:1–3)

The *toledoth* of the sons of Noah comprises elements D' and C': the Table of Nations of Genesis 10, which parallels the genealogy of Genesis 5; and the sin and dispersion of the Babel story, which parallels the sin and dispersion at the time of Cain and also echoes the expulsion from Eden.

In both the Cain story and the Babel story, the growing community builds a city (*'ir*). In the Table of Nations, Nimrod builds cities (10:10–11). In element B', Abram is called to leave a city – the name of that city is Ur (11:28, 31). Yet Abram will never build a city or a temple – he will always be a nomad – but he will build altars for worship in many places. It will be centuries before God gives to the *Bani Isra'il* the city of Jerusalem, and then, eventually, permits a temple to be built there. Centuries later still, Jesus the Messiah would enter that city on a donkey and would cleanse the temple of his time, but he would be crucified outside the city walls. Both the city and the temple would be destroyed a short time later.

In contrast, the Qur'an asserts that Abraham did build a permanent house for the worship of God: he re-built the Ka'ba in the place which became the "secure city" (*balad imana*) of Mecca (*al-Baqara* 2:125–26). The Islamic Prophet Muhammad eventually conquered that city, and re-established the Ka'ba. In order to do that, he first established a political base in the city of Yathrib, which became known simply as Madīnat an-Nabī, The City of the Prophet.[2]

The question that arises from this *toledoth* is how religious people make use of cities, buildings and political systems. This question challenges our life today, and calls us to examine our past history as well as our present policies and the histories of other nations and language groups.

The Worlds Behind and in Front of the Text
Today's World and the Ancient World

A century ago, Bangladesh was under British rule. In 1947, India and Pakistan separated and Bengal was divided into East Bengal (under Pakistan) and West Bengal (under India). Finally, in 1971, through a great, armed struggle, the people of East Bengal won their freedom and became the country of Bangladesh. At present, we suffer huge losses at the hands of richer and more powerful countries. The news of political conflict over Bangladesh and other countries is reported by the media and the internet. At the same time, we are scattering our own citizens as immigrants all over the world to find work, and these expatriates are supplying us with foreign currency. Many Bangladeshi immigrants have established themselves in these other countries and they and their children have become citizens there.

The ancient world had fewer people and fewer communications, but they were not so different from us. They did not have nation states like we have, but they had different people groups and great power blocks. The people groups sometimes moved or divided, and the power blocks clashed and changed and made a big difference to the lives of the peoples over whom they ruled.

---

2. The comparison between the political dimensions of the lives of the Messiah and the Prophet of Islam is very important for the comparison of Islam and Christianity. For some introductory analysis, see Glaser and Kay, *Thinking Biblically about Islam*, 231–246.

To understand Genesis 10–11, we need to imagine what life was like for the *Bani Isra'il* as a growing people group among other peoples, surrounded by the huge powers of Egypt, Assyria and, especially, Babylon. The Table of Nations in chapter 10 would help them to make sense of the variety of different peoples whom they met and heard about, and the Babel story of chapter 11:1–9 would help them to understand God's view of people who try to build power for themselves.

There is no good parallel to either the Table of Nations or the Babel story in other ancient texts. As we have seen, the other creation accounts are about the origins of the particular groups that produced them. Genesis 1–11 is unique in that it gives the histories of all peoples, even though it will then focus in on one particular people.

Genesis 10 underlines the point that *all* the peoples are descended from a single origin, so that *all* are under the covenant with Noah. Genesis 11:1–9 echoes some of the Mesopotamian sources but, as we have so often observed, the differences are far greater than the similarities. The Babylonian creation story climaxes with the gods building the great temple in Babylon, and the god Marduk and his companions coming down to live there and to be served by human beings. This establishes Babylon as a power centre. In Genesis, the tower of Babel is built in defiance of the One True God, and that God comes down not to live in the temple but to stop the building, to scatter the people, and thus to destroy their power. There is also a Sumerian epic which tells of a time when there was a single language, and of how competition between the gods led to one of them changing this situation. However, there is nothing which links temple building and language change.

The New Testament

The New Testament has a number of allusions to both the Table of Nations and Babel/Babylon, because it is about God's blessing going to all the nations, and because it was written in a world dominated by an imperial power.

At Pentecost, the Holy Spirit reversed the Babel confusion by enabling people from many different nations to hear the gospel in their own languages (Acts 2:1–11), and the Apostle Paul's speech in Athens is based on the idea that God is the creator of all the nations with their territories (Acts 17:26). Now, at last, all these peoples are receiving God's great plan of blessing!

The link with Genesis becomes explicit in the visions of Revelation, where the Genesis 10 phrase, "languages, tribes and peoples" (10:5, 20, 31) becomes a refrain, although without the "lands." The whole purpose of Jesus the Messiah's death was to ransom people from every tribe and language and nation, and people from all tribes and languages and nations are seen worshipping around God's throne (Rev 7:9). Alongside the description of glory for the peoples, there is also judgement. The awesome prophecies of judgement are addressed to all the tribes and languages and nations (Rev 10:11), and all will be affected by the terrifying Beast (Rev 13:7), and by the destructive "prostitute" (Rev 17:15). The good news is that there will be people from all nations who resist the Beast and worship God (Rev 15:4), and who are citizens of the final, perfect, heavenly city (Rev 21:24).

Of all the evil powers revealed in Revelation, the greatest is called "Babylon." In its immediate context, it refers to the Roman empire, but the name "Babylon" reminds the reader that this is but one of many similar empires which began at Babel, which God has limited, and which eventually come under his judgement. The perfect heavenly city of the new creation in Revelation 21 and 22 stands in contrast to the corrupt idolatrous city of Babylon in Revelation 18, just as the corruption of the flood generation and the Babel generation stand in contrast to the creation beauty of Eden in Genesis 1–2.

The Qur'an

The Qur'an does not have direct parallels either to the Table of Nations or to the Babel story, but it does present the one God as over all the nations (Sūra al-Ḥujurāt 49:13). It also mentions the variation of languages as a divine sign (ar-Rūm 30:22), and it does have passages with elements similar to those of Genesis 11:1–9. Like Genesis 11:1–9, the Qur'an exposes idolatrous imperial powers. Two major imperial figures who defy God are Nimrod and Pharoah, and both of their stories have some parallels with Genesis 10–11. Islamic tradition expands on all of this and also offers versions of how different peoples descended from the sons of Noah.

The Qur'an mentions Babel/Babylon once, in Sūra al-Baqara 2:102, where it is a city of sorcery at the time of Solomon. In Sūra an-Naḥl 16:26, there is a very short story from "those before them" – that is, from an unspecified time in the past – of people who plotted. God shook their building and it fell on them. Commentators like Ibn Kathīr and the Jalālayn say that the building was built by Nimrod, although it could also refer to the buildings which were destroyed in Thamud at the time of Salih (Sūra an-Naml 27:50–52). Readers of the Bible are reminded of Samson causing a roof to fall and destroy the Philistines (Judg 16:30).

Nimrod (Ar. *Namrūd*) is not named in the Qur'an, but it is generally agreed that he is the king who tried to silence Abraham by putting him in the fire (Sūras *al-Baqara* 2:258; *al-Anbiyā'* 21:67–69; *Kasasul Ambiya*, 112; and see the commentary below on Gen 11:28). Islamic tradition has many tales of his defiance of God,[3] and it is even said that he climbed a tower and fired an arrow upwards to attack God, but that the arrow miraculously came back and injured him. Another story tells of his making a flying machine powered by vultures and going up in it to attack God. He fires an arrow upwards but, in this case, an angel catches it, dips its head in fish blood, and drops it back to him. Nimrod then boasts that he has killed God. If we put this together with Genesis 10:10 and Jewish and Christian traditions that Nimrod was the builder of the Babel tower, we can see Sūra *an-Naḥl* 16:28 as a reference to Genesis 11. Islamic tradition sees the tower of this verse not only as selfish disobedience to God, but as deliberate plotting against him or even attacking him.

In Sūras *al-Qiṣaṣ* 28 and *Ghāfir* 40, Pharoah's defiance of God includes building a tower. Pharoah made himself great (literally, "raised himself") in the land or earth ('*arḍ*, cognate with the Heb. *erets*), divided people into groups and oppressed one group (Sūra *al-Qiṣaṣ* 28:2–3). Both the sūras introduce a character called Haman who appears to be Pharoah's right-hand man (Sūra *al-Qiṣaṣ* 28:6, 8; *Ghāfir* 40:24). When Moses challenges Pharoah's idolatry, Pharoah declares himself god and instructs Haman to bake bricks and build a tower so that he can climb up to look for Moses's god. The idea seems to be that he wants to disprove the existence of God (Sūras *al-Qiṣaṣ* 28:38; *Ghāfir* 40:36–37). Whether or not the tower was built we are not told, but Pharoah is fearfully judged. Some interpreters suggest that the tower was never built, but Ibn Kathīr says that this was the highest tower ever built. Al-Kisā'ī agrees, and adds that God sent Gabriel to destroy the tower.

The World of the Text

Commentators usually deal with the Table of Nations and the Babel story separately, but it is important that they are in a single *toledoth*. They give two different ways of looking at the descendants of the sons of Noah. Each section has its own structure and genre, so we, too, will deal with them separately, but then consider them together in our theological reflection.

But first, why does the Babel story come after the Table of Nations? The Babel story seems to be telling of the origins of the different languages

---

3. Those cited here can be found in at-Ṭabarī's *History* and al-Kisā'ī's *Qiṣaṣ al-Anbiyā'*.

mentioned in the Table of Nations, so one would think that it should come first. There are two possible reasons. First, this position fits better into the structures of Genesis 1–11 which we noted in our introduction (pages 22-24) In terms of the creation/fall/judgement/hope pattern, the creation blessings of chapter 10 should come before the fall and judgement of Babel. In terms of the chiastic structure, this position brings to our attention the parallels between Babel and the story of Cain and his descendants.

Second, since Babel is clearly what we now call Babylon, the position of the story could indicate that it is more about Babylonian power and religion than about the origin of languages. The "single language" could be an allusion to an imperial language used by all the empire's conquered peoples. If this is so, the position of the story is entirely appropriate. It picks up on the concern about cities signalled in the Nimrod section of chapter 10, and leads straight into the world of Mesopotamian powers which Abraham will be called to leave.

The Table of Nations
Structure and Genre

Genesis 10 is a genealogy which affirms that the blessing of human multiplication will resume after the flood, as promised in 9:1; but is a very different genealogy than Genesis 5. Rather than following a particular line, it follows the lines of all three of Noah's sons, so that it is giving a picture of the whole post-flood world. Another unique feature is that it not only deals with individuals but also with peoples, and it functions more as a classification of the peoples with whom the *Bani Isra'il* will deal than as a family tree. We could call it their map of their world; but this is not like our modern maps, which divide the world into geographical territories. It is a map of human groups and how they are related to each other.

The pattern of the chapter is as follows:

A. Descendants born after the *mabul* (flood) (10:1)

B. Sons of Japheth (10:2–5)

    Sons of Gomer (3)

    Sons of Javan (4)

C. Sons of Ham (10:6–20)

    Sons of Cush (7–12)

        Nimrod and the *reshit* (beginning) of his kingdom: Babel (8–12)

    Sons of Egypt (13–14)

    Sons of Canaan (15–19)

D. Sons of Shem (10:21–31)

    Sons of Aram (23)

    Sons of Arpachshad (24–30)

A. Nations spread after the *mabul* (flood) (10:32)

We immediately see that the lines of 7 of Noah's grandsons are chosen, laid out in a pattern of two, three and two. The chapter is carefully structured in groups of three and seven and ten – all important numbers which tell of peace and perfection and completion. The total number of peoples mentioned is 70[4] – 7 x 10.

> From Japheth, fourteen (7x2) peoples – seven sons and seven grandsons.

> From Ham, thirty (3x10) peoples – four sons and three groups of their descendants (eight from Cush, seven from Egypt, eleven from Canaan).

> From Shem, twenty-six ([10+3] x2) peoples – five sons and five grandsons (total of ten); twenty-one (7x3) descendants from the sons.

A and A' repeat that this is the world after the flood, and there is a refrain at the end of each of the three main sections, telling us that the people are all organized to live in different places according to their languages, lands and nations (v 5, 20, 31). This structure shows us that the different peoples are all under God's blessed and providential ordering. But, in the centre, there is the *babel* that echoes the *mabul* at the beginning and *mabul* at the end of the chapter. This signals the human rebellion that will yet again mar God's good world. The length and centrality of the genealogy of Ham alerts the reader to the enmity that began in 9:18–29.

While the order of Noah's sons is given as "Shem, Ham and Japheth" in verse 1, as it was in 5:32, the genealogy is ordered in the opposite direction. It moves from the Japhethites to the Hammites to the Shemmites. A closer examination of the names indicates that this is a move from peoples who will have little or no relationship with the *Bani Isra'il*, to peoples who will often be their enemies, to their own ancestors and peoples who will be their friends. It is noticeable that each section mentions a list of Noah's grandsons, but follows

---

4. There are seventy-one names in the chapter, but it is usual to omit the Philistines from the total (see commentary on verse 14). An alternative is to include the Philistines and omit Nimrod.

only some of them further. Some of these are then selected for augmentation with extra information.

We can see that all this is preparing the reader for the story of Babel and then the genealogy leading to Abraham. It reinforces the message of the whole of Genesis 1–11, which is that all human beings, in all their diversity, are under one creator God, and that the story of the children of Israel is to be read as pertaining to the history of the whole world. At the same time, it is, through its focus on Shem, signalling that the history of the whole world will be read in relation to what God will be doing through Abraham and his descendants.

COMMENTARY
A. Genesis 10:1 Descendants Born after the Flood

> *These are the generations of the sons of Noah: Shem, Ham, and Japheth. Sons were born to them after the flood.*

This verse, together with 9:18 and 10:32, emphasizes the unity of all humans as descendants of Noah. All the peoples of the world, including Bangladeshi people, are not only created in the image of God, but also included in the rainbow covenant of Genesis 9:1–24 and dwelling amidst the sinful power imbalances instigated in Genesis 9:25–27.

The Qur'an does not mention the names or the number of Noah's sons, but tradition agrees that there were four of them: Shem, Ham, Yam and Yafeth. Yam was, they say, the rebel who died in the flood (*Hūd* 11:42–47), and some identify him with Kanan. Sūras *al-Anbiyā'* 21:76 and *aṣ-Ṣāffāt* 37:77 state that God saved Noah and his family, and *Hūd* 11:40 and *ash-Shu'arā'* 26:118 say that Noah and the believers were saved. There is much discussion among commentators about how many people were saved, and whether there were other believers who joined Noah's family in the ark, but the Qur'an has no further mention of the descendants of Noah or of other flood survivors. This is partly because, as we have seen, the Qur'an's flood seems to have been local rather than universal, so Noah's descendants have no particular significance.

However, Islamic tradition is very interested in the origins of the nations, and especially of those in Arabia and in the regions which were occupied by the early Islamic empires. At-Ṭabarī's *History* gives several pages to alternative reports of the relationships between the peoples described in Genesis 10 and the peoples known in his time.[5] Much of at-Ṭabarī's information comes from

---

5. At-Ṭabarī, *History*, vol. 2, 10–27 of the English translation (SUNY Press, 1987).

the biblical, Jewish and Christian material which was in the first part of Ibn Isḥāq's *Sīrah* (Life of Muhammad). This first part was omitted in Ibn Hishām's edition of the *Sīra*, so we can only know about it through at-Ṭabarī's reports. They are important evidence of the ways in which the Bible has influenced Islamic tradition.[6]

Al-Ṭabarī reports a saying of the Islamic Prophet Muhammad which can be seen as summarizing Genesis 10:

> Noah begat three, each of whom begat three: Shem, Ham and Japheth. Shem begat the Arabs, Persians and Byzantines, in all of whom is good. Japheth begat the Turks, Slavs, Gog and Magog, in none of whom is good. Ham begat Copts, Sudanese and Berbers.[7]

He cites other reports which have Shem the father of the Arabs, Japheth of the Byzantines and Ham of the Abyssinians, or Shem the father of handsome people with beautiful hair, Japheth the father of those with full faces and small eyes, and Ham the father of those with black faces and curly hair. At-Ṭabarī's careful recording of conflicting reports on this and on Noah's grandsons and their offspring indicate the range of genealogical tradition in his community. In contrast, it looks as if the Genesis author's attention to accuracy has led him in the opposite direction: to include only those details of which he knows, and to omit names about which he knows nothing. The gaps in the record make us curious. Like at-Ṭabarī, we will explore some of the traditions about the names in this chapter, but, like the Genesis author, we will refrain from going beyond what we know.[8]

B. Genesis 10:2–5 The Sons of Japheth

> *The sons of Japheth: Gomer, Magog, Madai, Javan, Tubal, Meshech, and Tiras. The sons of Gomer: Ashkenaz, Riphath, and Togarmah. The sons of Javan: Elishah, Tarshish, Kittim, and Dodanim. From these the coastland peoples spread in their lands, each with his own language, by their clans, in their nations.*

---

6. See Whittingham, *History of Muslim Views*, 62–64, 70–71. For an English translation of the extant *Sīra* of Ibn Ishaq, see Guillaume (1955).

7. At-Ṭabarī, *History*, vol. 2, 223 (p. 21 in the English translation).

8. As in our study of Genesis 5, we have mainly relied for our information on Hess, Westermann, Wenham, and the *Illustrated Bible Dictionary*.

Japheth had seven sons and seven grandsons. Following Noah's blessing of Genesis 9:27, we are not surprised at these sevens of perfection, or that Japheth's people will spread across a very large area.

Only Gomer and Javan are selected for further attention, and little is said about any of Japheth's descendants in the rest of the Old Testament. Gomer, Magog, Meshech and Tubal are all mentioned in Ezekiel 38:2–6, along with Cush and Put who will appear among the descendants of Ham. This is the description of the allied army of "Gog from the land of Magog", which will attack the *Bani Isra'il* but eventually come under God's judgement. Most of these peoples originate from north or west of Mesopotamia and of the promised land, Canaan.

Gomer was probably a people known as *kimmeroi* in Greek, who came from what is now south Russia and eventually settled in what is now mid-Turkey. Meshech and Tubal appear in ancient texts as peoples from what is now mid- and East-Turkey and, in history, are sometimes seen as enemies of Assyria and sometimes as its allies. They are also mentioned in Ezekiel 27:13; 32:26 and 39:1. The "Madai" are the Medes, who lived between the upper Tigris river and the Caspian Sea, and are mentioned in 2 Kings 17:6 and 18:11 and in Isaiah 13:17 and 21:2.

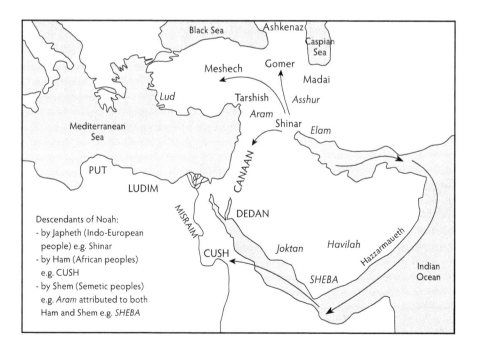

Figure 9 Table of Nations: Descendants of Noah

The people of Javan are Greeks.[9] In ancient times, the word referred to a business community known as the Ionian Greeks, who lived on the coast of Turkey (Ezek 27:13; Isa 66:19), but by the time of Daniel it refers to all Greeks (Dan 8:21; 10:20). The other names are of uncertain origin, but are mostly associated with areas around Greece – Tiras with Thrace, Elishah and Kittim with Cyprus, and the Dodanim with the coastal area.

The overall picture of the Japhethites in verse 5a is that they include many peoples either unknown to the *Bani Isra'il* or of little interest to them, and who were widely scattered. The Jewish historian Josephus describes them as spreading out eastwards through Asia, northward to the river Don, and westward through Europe to Cadiz (*Antiquities of the Jews*, I. 6). Islamic tradition reports that thirty-six languages of the world go back to the Japhethites.[10]

Verse 5b is the first refrain of "lands, languages, families and nations." "Land" is *erets*, the word so often used for the earth in previous chapters. "Language" is *lashon*, literally, "tongue." "Family" is *mishpachah*, a family or clan of related people. "Nation" is *goy*, what we would probably call now an ethnic group or a people group. It is not a nation in the sense that Bangladesh is a nation, that is, an entity with physical boundaries and with a structured government and laws and citizens with identity cards. Most of the world did not exist in what we now call "nation-states" before the nineteenth century. In Hebrew, *goy* came to mean any people group except the *Bani Israi'l*. Genesis 10 reminds the *Bani Isra'il* that they, too, are a *goy* – one of the many people groups which descended from Noah.

C. Genesis 10:6–20 The Sons of Ham

The sons of Ham: Cush, Egypt, Put, and Canaan. (10:6)

The sons of Ham take the centre place and the most space in the Table of Nations, so we know that they will be important in the Bible's history. All four are referred to in other parts of the Old Testament, and their levels of importance are indicated by the attention paid to them here. Following Noah's

---

9. In nineteenth-century Bengali literature, "Jaban" indicated Muslims, but some Muslims objected to this. See *Bengali Practical Dictionary*, Bangla Academy, 1006.

10. *Encyclopaedia of Islam*, "Yaphith," 236.

curse of chapter 9:25–27, we are not surprised to find that they include future enemies of the *Bani Isra'il*.

All are peoples living in what is now North and East Africa and Southwestern Asia. Cush is the most southerly group, and is often understood as Ethiopia. "Egypt" translates the Hebrew *Mitsraim*, to which the Bible also refers as "the land of Ham" (Pss 78:51; 105:23, 27; 106:22; 1 Chr 4:40). Egypt is called *Miṣr* in Arabic today. Put is mentioned only in Nahum 3:9 as an ally of Egypt, and could be Libya. It was not of great importance in relation to the *Bani Isra'il*, so Genesis 10 does not follow Put's line. It is Canaan who will become the best-known among Ham's sons, as the land of Canaan is the place which God gave to the *Bani Isra'il*.

Anyone who reads Genesis 10 wants to know where their own people fit into it, and Bangladeshis are no exception. There is a long tradition that we are Hammites, perhaps coming from the ancient Jatt people of Persia, descendants of Ham who spread to the Punjab and elsewhere in the Indian subcontinent. There are other traditions. At-Ṭabarī reports, "It is said that Put journeyed to the land of Sind and Hind, where he settled; the inhabitants there are said to be his descendants," although he also cites another tradition that has the Indians and Sindis descending from Shem through the line of Arpachshad, Shelah, Eber, and Yaqtan through a son of Yoktan called Buqayin, who is not mentioned in Genesis 10.[11]

An interesting tradition is recorded by the Bangladesh historian Mohammad Hannan, who uses a well-known eighteenth-century book to argue that one of Ham's sons was Hind, and that he had a son called Bong who travelled to East India.[12] The place where his descendants lived was called Bongodesh (Land of Bong), and that is present-day Bangladesh.

> *The sons of Cush: Seba, Havilah, Sabtah, Raamah, and Sabteca. The sons of Raamah: Sheba and Dedan. (10:7)*

Cush seems to have settled around ancient Babylon (Gen 10:8–10) and thence spread far and wide. Seven of his descendants are mentioned, the names implying that some went to southern Arabia, some into Asia, and some to East Africa. East Africa south of Syene was called "Kushu" or "Kosh" by the Egyptians, the Chaldeans and the Assyrians.

---

11. At-Ṭabarī, *History*, vol. 2, 16; cf. 11–17.

12. Mohammad Hannan, *Bangalir Itihas (Bengali History)*, 29, using Salim, *Riyazu-s-Salātīn: A History of Bengal*. For the "Bong" tradition, see *Kasasul Ambiya*, 82.

The people of southern India and Ceylon are also considered by some to be descendants of Cush through Seba. Historians call them Dravidians, but other ancient peoples called them Sibae. The Jewish historian Josephus recognized an eastern and a western Cush – one in Asia, the other in Africa (*Ant*, Book 1, VI, 2). The Greek historian Herodotus (BC 484–425), too, mentions Ethiopians from Asia (*Thalia*, Section 94).

Dedan was a north Arabian tribe whose territory bordered on Edom (Jer 49:8; Ezek 25:13). They had trading relations with Tyre (Ezek 27:15). Seba, Havilah, Sabtah, Raamah, and Sabteca were probably in areas on either side of the Red Sea, in East Africa and Southwest Arabia.

The names Havilah and Sheba will appear again as Shemites in verse 26, and Sheba and Dedan as descendants of Abraham in Genesis 25:3; so there is discussion about who these peoples were. There could have been separate peoples with the same names, but it is more likely that the repeated names are acknowledging a mixed African-Arab ancestry of these peoples. There was much trading between East Africa and South Arabia. Sheba was the place whose queen visited King Solomon (1 Kgs 10:1–13; 2 Chr 9:1). The Ethiopians have a strong tradition that she was from Ethiopia, but most identify Sheba with part of today's Yemen (see below, on Gen 10:26).

> *Cush fathered Nimrod; he was the first on earth to be a mighty man. He was a mighty hunter before the LORD. Therefore it is said, "Like Nimrod a mighty hunter before the LORD." The beginning of his kingdom was Babel, Erech, Accad, and Calneh, in the land of Shinar. From that land he went into Assyria and built Nineveh, Rehoboth-Ir, Calah, and Resen between Nineveh and Calah; that is the great city. (10:8–12)*

Nimrod is singled out for attention. He was "mighty" (*gibbor*). The word is repeated three times to emphasize the point. It is not immediately obvious whether this is a good thing or a bad thing, but closer study suggests the latter, in that his might is set up against God's might. There are Jewish and Muslim traditions about his rebellion (see above pages 243-244).

First, his name is probably from the Hebrew *marad*, "to rebel."[13] Second, he was a hunter "before the Lord." He could simply have been a notable hunter of animals, but interpreters have suggested that he also hunted human beings to conquer and enslave them, and that "before the Lord" implies that he was

---

13. Scholars have looked for figures in the ancient world who might have been Nimrod. For example, his name is similar to that of Ninurta, a Sumerian and Babylonian god of war and hunting. See Hess, *Studies in the Personal Names of Genesis 1–11*, 73–74.

trying to be better than God himself. But the greatest indication of his rebellion is the kingdom which he founded – headed by Babylon, the rebel city about which we will read in the next chapter.

The other cities named are all in Mesopotamia. Erech, ancient Uruk, was an important Sumerian city 160 miles southeast of present-day Baghdad. Accad was in northern Babylonia, but the location of Calneh is uncertain.

From Nimrod also came the Assyrians who, like the Babylonians, would have a huge empire which would attack the *Bani Isra'il* and take them into exile. Assyria is called "the land of Nimrod" in Micah 5:6. Nineveh is the great and wicked city to which the prophet Jonah was called, and on which God had mercy (Jonah 1–4; *aṣ-Ṣāffāt* 37:147). The location of Rehoboth-Ir is unknown, but it could have been a suburb of Nineveh. Calah, south of Nineveh, indeed became a great city, and was the home of the Assyrian kings before Nineveh took that role.

> *Egypt fathered Ludim, Anamim, Lehabim, Naphtuhim, Pathrusim, Casluhim (from whom the Philistines came), and Caphtorim. (10:13–14)*

Egypt (*Mitsraim*) also has seven sons. Egypt was a great power in the ancient world, and has an important place in the Bible. It appears many times in Genesis itself (e.g. 12:10–13:1; 13:10; 16:1), the story of Joseph and his brothers in the last eleven chapters of Genesis will be situated in Egypt, and Egypt is the place from which God would free Abraham's descendants and lead them into the promised land.

All the sons of Egypt are peoples rather than individuals, as we can see from the plural endings of the names, *-im*. The Philistines will become well-known as competitors for territory with the *Bani Isra'il* (e.g. 1 Sam 4:1–10; 14; 17; 31; 2 Chr 28:18). Grammatically, it could be that the Philistines come from Casluhim, or that they come from interbreeding of the Pathrusim with the Casluhim, or that the Philistines and the Caphtorim both come from Casluhim. Rabbinic commentary favours one of the former, concluding that the reference to the Philistines is a note on the genealogy and not part of the genealogy itself. It therefore excludes the Philistines from the counting of the nations: there are, then, seventy nations despite there being seventy-one names.

We have little information about the other groups, either from the Bible or from history or archaeology. Ludim are mentioned in Jeremiah 46:9, where they are linked with people from Egypt, Cush and Put more generally. The Targum Pseudo-Jonathan suggests that the Anamim were in the west of Egypt, near Cyrene. Lehabim were perhaps the Lubim, or Libyans (Nah 3:9; 2 Chr

12:3), and Naphtuhim perhaps from the Nile delta region. Patrusim lived in Pathros, or Upper Egypt, and Caphtorim either in Crete or some other islands in the Aegean Sea. In short, as far as we can ascertain, the sons of *Mitsraim* are the peoples in and around Egypt. They were probably among the peoples who came to Joseph for food (Gen 41:56–57), and we can suppose that the *Bani Isra'il* who left Egypt with Moses would have known who they were.

> *Canaan fathered Sidon his firstborn and Heth, and the Jebusites, the Amorites, the Girgashites, the Hivites, the Arkites, the Sinites, the Arvadites, the Zemarites, and the Hamathites. Afterward the clans of the Canaanites dispersed. And the territory of the Canaanites extended from Sidon in the direction of Gerar as far as Gaza, and in the direction of Sodom, Gomorrah, Admah, and Zeboiim, as far as Lasha. These are the sons of Ham, by their clans, their languages, their lands, and their nations. (10:15–20)*

The Canaanites are important in biblical history because they are the peoples living in and around the land which God promised to Abraham and his descendants in Genesis 12:1–6. Several appear frequently in the Bible, and some in Genesis itself. We note the break with the sevenfold pattern – there are eleven Canaanite peoples. They do not merit a perfect number.

Sidon is an important Phoenician commercial city on the Mediterranean coast northwest of Canaan, mentioned in Genesis 49:13. "Heth" refers to the Hittites, a people of Asia Minor who dominated Canaan from 1800–1200 BC. They are mentioned in Genesis 23:3–20; 25:10; 27:46 and 49:32.

The Jebusites were the original inhabitants of Jerusalem (Josh 15:63; 2 Sam 5:6). They appear alongside the Hittites and the Amorites in the list of peoples whose land will be given to Abraham's descendants in Genesis 15:21. The Amorites are particularly mentioned as being under judgement by God for their wickedness (15:16). The Girgashites are not mentioned again in Genesis, but they appear with the Hittites, the Amorites, the Jebusites and the Hivites in several lists of the Canaanites who are to be conquered by the *Bani Isra'il* (Deut 7:1; Josh 3:10; 24:11; cf. Josh 9:1–2 and 11:3 where they are omitted).

Little is known about the Hivites as a people group, but there are some interesting references to particular Hivites in the Bible. The Gibeonites who make a treaty with Joshua are Hivites (Josh 9:7). In Genesis, the man who violated Jacob's daughter, Dinah, was a Hivite (Gen 34:2), and Esau married a Hivite as well as a Hittite (Gen 36:20). The "entrance to Hamath" (today's Hama in Syria) was sometimes referred to as the northern boundary of the promised land (Num 34:8; Josh 13:5; 1 Kgs 8:65), but exactly where this entrance might be is unknown, and Hamath was usually outside the territory of the *Bani Isra'il* (e.g. 2 Sam 8:9; 2 Kgs 14:28; 17:24).

The other sons of Canaan do not appear again in the Bible except in the genealogy of 1 Chronicles 1:13–16. However, the geographical places of verse 19 are well-known and imply that they were inhabitants in and around what became known as the land of Canaan (see also Num 34:2–12). Sidon was on the northwest coast and Gaza and Gerar in the south; and Sodom, Gomorrah, Admah and Zeboiim are to the east. The location of "Lashar" is uncertain. Sodom and Gomorrah were the towns destroyed at the time of Lot (Gen 13:8–13; 19:1–29), and are believed to have been where the Dead Sea is now. Admah and Zeboiim were among their allies (Gen 14:2). In short, these verses about the sons of Canaan are the *Bani Israi'il's* map of the peoples of the promised land.

D. Genesis 10:21–31 The Sons of Shem

> To Shem also, the father of all the children of Eber, the elder brother of Japheth, children were born. The sons of Shem: Elam, Asshur, Arpachshad, Lud, and Aram. The sons of Aram: Uz, Hul, Gether, and Mash. Arpachshad fathered Shelah; and Shelah fathered Eber. To Eber were born two sons: the name of the one was Peleg, for in his days the earth was divided, and his brother's name was Joktan. Joktan fathered Almodad, Sheleph, Hazarmaveth, Jerah, Hadoram, Uzal, Diklah, Obal, Abimael, Sheba, Ophir, Havilah, and Jobab; all these were the sons of Joktan. The territory in which they lived extended from Mesha in the direction of Sephar to the hill country of the east. These are the sons of Shem, by their clans, their languages, their lands, and their nations.

Shem's line will be followed from Genesis 11, as it is he who is the ancestor of Abraham. The descendants of Shem are called "Semitic peoples" and include Jews, Assyrians, Syrians and Edomites. There are some significant differences here in the genealogical pattern, as Shem's great-grandson Eber is mentioned before his sons, and it is pointed out that Shem is the older brother despite being mentioned last in this map of nations. We understand that the whole map is leading us forward towards the line of Eber. The numbers also differ, but still display patterns of perfection, with ten sons and grandsons, seven descendants from the sons to Peleg, and a group of fourteen which includes Joktan and his descendants.

From Genesis, all we know about Shem can be found in Genesis 9:23–28, but, because he was blessed by Noah and became the ancestor of Abraham, Jewish tradition has made much of him. With Eber, he is said to have founded a Torah school at which he passed on teaching which God had given to Adam, and the patriarchs and matriarchs studied there (for example, Isaac, *Gen Rab* 56:11). He is also said to have been so righteous that he was born circumcised (*Gen Rab* 26:3), and some identify him with the mysterious king and priest of Genesis 14:18–20, Melchizedek (e.g. Talmud *Nedarim* 32b; *Gen Rab* 46:7). It is not surprising, then, that some Islamic literature describes Shem as a believer and a prophet (*Kasasul Ambiya*, 81).

Of Shem's five sons, four will appear later in the Bible. The fifth, Lud, is unknown, but could be the Lydians of Asia Minor. Elam and Asshur will become well known, the Elamites living in what is now Iran and being present at Pentecost (Acts 2:9), and Asshur referring to the Assyrians.

Genesis 10 follows only the lines of Aram and Arphaxad. Aram's descendants, the Arameans, will become important as biblical history develops. They will include the Syrians, who develop the Aramaic language. The common people of Palestine and Jesus the Messiah and his disciples probably spoke that language. A variation of this language is Syriac, the language used by many Christians at the time of the development of Islam. Little is known about the sons of Aram named here; only Uz appears elsewhere in the Bible where Scripture tells us that Job lived in the area of Uz (Job 1:1). There is a tomb said to be Job's tomb in Oman, but there are also traditions of his coming from Turkey, Syria, Lebanon and Uzbekistan.

The line of Arphaxad is going to take us through Eber and Peleg to Abraham in the next *toledoth*. Here, we read that the earth was "divided" during the time of Eber's two sons, Peleg and Joktan (v. 25). This probably refers to the scattering of peoples in 11:9.

"Joktan" (Heb. *yaqtan*) is related to *q-t-n*, a root meaning "small" in ancient Semitic languages, so perhaps means "younger son" here. Joktan's descendants are probably all in the South Arabian region. Sheba here is probably in the Yemen area, the home of the Sabaeans. Archaeology indicates that they were a powerful centre for trade and religion from the seventh century BC, and the Old Testament knows them as raiders (Job 1:15) and as traders in precious goods (Ps 72:15; Isa 60:6; Jer 6:20; Ezek 27:22) but also in slaves (Joel 3:8). It was Sheba's queen who made the memorable visit to the kingdom of Solomon (1 Kgs 10:1–3; *an-Naml* 27:20–44); but there is also a tradition that she came from Ethiopia (see above, on Gen 10:7). Solomon procured gold from Ophir, but, like Havilah (see above on Gen 2:11), its location is uncertain (1 Kgs 9:28; 10:11; 1 Chr 29:4; Job 22:24; 28:16; Ps 45:9).

The other sons of Joktan are unknown elsewhere in the Bible, but some are discussed in Islamic tradition, as the ancestors of the Arab tribes. At-Ṭabarī's *History* records that Joktan was the first king of Yemen (vol. 2, pp. 15, 20) and that, as a result of the confusion of languages, the Semites had eighteen languages. The children of Joktan were, he says, among those who spoke Arabic (vol. 2, p. 18).

A'. Genesis 10:32 Nations Spread after the Flood

> *These are the clans of the sons of Noah, according to their genealogies, in their nations, and from these the nations spread abroad on the earth after the flood.*

This verse mirrors verse 1 of the chapter, and so completes the structure of the Table of Nations. Verse 1 announced the list of families born after the flood, and this verse concludes that these are the very people who populated the earth after the flood. The nations are "spread" – the word used in 2:10 and 10:5 – not the word translated "dispersed" in 9:19, 11:4 and 11:9, implying that this is a positive division under God's providence whereby each people has its own place. They also have their own histories – "genealogies" here is *toledoth*. Chapter 11 will begin the specific account of Abraham's family; but others, too, have their stories.

Looking back over the chapter, the reader can reflect on the ordering of the peoples in God's world. The "earth after the flood" has not only been re-ordered from the *tohu wa bohu* of the waters: it has also been re-ordered from the *tohu wa bohu* of the violent pre-flood peoples. But that is not the end of the story . . .

The City and the Tower of Babel
Structure and Genre

The Babel story adds the final touch to Genesis's description of the world which God plans to bless through Abraham and his descendants. Unlike most of the Genesis narratives, it is not presented as an elaboration of a particular genealogy. Although it is part of the *toledoth* of Noah's sons, it mentions none of those sons, but is about "the whole earth." It stands as a separate narrative between the genealogies of 10:1–32 and 11:10–26. This is somewhat similar to Genesis 6:1–7, which stands at the end of the genealogy of Genesis 5. That, too, is about people in general who spoil God's good world, and that, too, leads towards a person who brings hope. Genesis 11's place in the chiasmic structure of Genesis 1–11 encourages us to compare its story of the development of civilization with that in Genesis 4.

Genesis 11:1–9 is one of the most carefully constructed Hebrew narratives in the Bible, with multiple patterns in its words and structure.[14] Even in translation, we can see structural patterns. The story falls into two parts (verses 1–4 and verses 6–9) and has a central pivot in verse 5 where the Lord comes down. The two parts are so cleverly constructed that the second part mirrors the first part in two different ways.

First, both parts follow a similar pattern:

> Human unity: One speech and language (11:1). One people and language (11:6).
>
> The place: They settle "there" (11:2). They are confused "there" (11:7).
>
> Communication: "Said to each other" (11:3). Not understanding "each other" (11:7).
>
> Building: Let us build a city (11:4). They stopped building the city (11:8).
>
> The name: "A name for ourselves" (11:4). The city's name (11:8).
>
> Purpose: "Lest we be scattered" (11:4). The Lord scattered them (11:8–9).

At the same time, the second part mirrors the first part in the opposite direction, forming a chiasm:

> **A.** The whole earth had one language (11:1)
> > **B.** They settled "there" (11:2)
> > > **C.** They speak "to each other" (11:3)
> > > > **D.** "Come let us make bricks" (11:3)
> > > > > **E.** "Let us build for ourselves" (11:4)
> > > > > > **F.** A city and a tower (11:4)
> > > > > > > **G.** The Lord comes down (11:5)
> > > > > > **F'.** The city and the tower (11:5)

---

14. Our analysis follows Wenham, *Genesis 1–15*, 234–36.

E' "which the sons of men had built" (11:5)

D'. "Come let us mix up" (11:7)

C'. They cannot understand "each other's speech" (11:7)

B'. They are scattered "from there" (11:8)

A'. The language of the whole earth is confused (11:9)

We can immediately see that the story is about God reversing the plans of the human beings. The pattern is emphasized by plays on the Hebrew words. "Let us make" is *nilbenah*, "let us build" is *nibneh*, and "let us mix up" is *nabelah*. "Confused" in verse 9 is *balal*, obviously a play on the word Babel. The very words used demonstrate the "mixing up" of just three consonants (*n-b-l*) to give different meanings!

The shortness of this narrative, its memorable construction and its place by itself between two genealogies all draw the reader's attention. This narrative is not difficult to understand, but it is of huge importance. It gathers up a remarkable number of ideas from the previous chapters.

COMMENTARY

Now the whole earth had one language and the same words. And as people migrated from the east, they found a plain in the land of Shinar and settled there. (11:1–2)

The scene is set. We are going back to the time before there were many languages. This is emphasized by the repetitive parallel of "one language" and "one words" (*devarim ahadim*, usually translated "the same words" or "one speech"). The phrase "the whole earth" (Heb. *kal ha-arets*) is clearly important, as it occurs five times in the nine verses of the Babel story. As in Genesis 9:19, it means all the inhabitants of the world.

We are not told who the ones who migrated are, but we can suppose that these are some of Noah's descendants spreading out from the Ararat area. "From the east" or "in the east" (*mi-qedem*) reminds the reader of Adam and Eve leaving Eden which was *mi-qedem* (Gen 2:8), of the cherubim guarding the return *mi-qedem* of Eden (Gen 3:24), and of Cain's moving eastwards (4:16). "Shinar" has been explained in 10:10 as the Mesopotamian area where Nimrod reigned. There, the group finds a place where they want to stay.

And they said to one another, "Come, let us make bricks, and burn them thoroughly." And they had brick for stone, and bitumen for mortar. Then

> *they said, "Come, let us build ourselves a city and a tower with its top in the heavens, and let us make a name for ourselves, lest we be dispersed over the face of the whole earth." (11:3–4)*

God is absent from these verses. The people have convened their own consultation, and are discussing their future with each other and not with God. They start by making bricks. "Why?" we wonder. Then, quickly, we discover that they have a purpose – to build a city and a tower. We remember the first city, built by Cain (4:17). That was a place of music and crafts, but also of violence and vengeance. This city is going to be marked by something else: a huge tower.

The city is for themselves, so that they can have a name for themselves and a home for themselves. The motivation is that they are afraid of being scattered. Why is this? We remember that God had told them to "fill the earth" (9:1–7 confirms 1:28), so spreading out across the earth is part of God's blessing. "Scattering" implies something negative – a loss of power and of group identity, which is often associated with God's judgement (Num 10:35; Deut 4:27; 28:64). The people want security.

The tower is part of this security. They settled "there" (Heb. *sham*). The tower has its top in the heavens (Heb. *shamayim*). The people will make a "name" (Heb. *shem*) for themselves. The tower was almost certainly a ziggurat, that is, a four-sided brick building in the shape of a tall pyramid, probably imitating the shape of mountains. These were common in ancient Mesopotamia; they were temples which were described as having their tops in the sky. The tower reaches up to the *shamayim*, but has its foundations in the earth, and so makes a meeting place for the gods of a particular people with a particular *shem* (name) in a particular *sham* (place).

The details of the building underline the location of the city. Elsewhere, in Egypt and in the promised land, stone was used for building foundations, and sun-dried mud-brick for super structure. As in the alluvial land of Bangladesh, so in the alluvial land of Mesopotamia, stone was not available; so people used kiln-baked bricks with tar to hold them together.

> *And the LORD came down to see the city and the tower, which the children of man had built. (11:5)*

Outside Eden, we have seen God coming to speak to Cain, and walking with Enoch and with Noah. Here, we have a very deliberate "coming down" of God, using his covenant name, YHWH. The experience of Babel is going to be more like that of Cain than of Enoch or Noah.

This verse is the centre and the pivot of the story. It would remind the ancient readers of the story of the gods coming to live in the temple in Babylon, to be served by the human beings. Later Jewish readers would remember the glorious coming of the *shekinah* into the tabernacle and the temple (Exod 40:34; 2 Chr 7:1), and the promise of God's return after the exile (Mal 3:1). Christian readers would remember the coming of God in the Messiah (John 1:14) and in the Holy Spirit (Acts 2:2–4). Muslim readers may find the whole idea of God's "coming down" incomprehensible. Orthodox Sunnis might ask how a transcendent God could come down, and Sufis might ask how an immanent God could ever have been absent. The Bible does not see this as a problem: the creator God who is above all and sees all is also the personal covenant God who comes to his creatures at particular times and in particular places.

In this verse, God comes down to see the tower. There is ironical humour here, emphasizing the greatness of God and the smallness of the tower. The people were trying to build high enough to reach him, but their best technology produced something so small that it was invisible in comparison to God's greatness.

We also note that the people who built the tower are called "sons of *adam*" (*bene ha-adam*, translated above as "children of men"). This may be in contrast to the *Enuma Elish* idea that gods built the Babylonian temple. Genesis is saying, "Of course they did not build it: it was not a divine building with its top in the sky, but a human building that did not reach very high." But the phrase "sons of adam" also reminds us of Adam's sin. The Babel incident shows that the tragic tale of humanity's desire to rival the glory of God through self-sustained autonomy continues even after a judgement as catastrophic as the flood.

> And the LORD said, "Behold, they are one people, and they have all one language, and this is only the beginning of what they will do. And nothing that they propose to do will now be impossible for them. Come, let us go down and there confuse their language, so that they may not understand one another's speech." So the LORD dispersed them from there over the face of all the earth, and they left off building the city. (11:6–8)

Verses 3 and 4 begin, "and they said." This second part of the story begins, "and the Lord said." As in Genesis 1:26 and 3:22, we see the plural of majesty or of trinity;[15] and as in Genesis 2:18, 6:6–7 and 8:21–22 we see something of God's decision making. These awesome glimpses into the divine thought take us on a

---

15. See commentary on Gen 1:26, p. page 72.

journey. First, God chooses to make humans "in his own image," with language and moral choice, and to give them dominion in his beautiful world (1:26). Next, he reflects on the need for companionship and community, and creates the woman from the man (2:18). When she, and then he, use their choice to rebel against God, he puts a limit on their lifespan and their power by excluding them from the tree of life (3:22–24). Next, he sees the terrible mess which has resulted from the humans abusing their God-given nature and status, so he decides to give them a new start and to further limit their lifespan (6:1–8). As the new start opens, he recognizes that there will be continued sin, but he makes an unconditional commitment to bear with them (8:20–22) – he loves these problematic beings! Now, he has again looked at the abuse of dominion (11:5), and he is recognizing that this will continue.

How will he deal with this? Will he bring down the tower on their heads, as in the story in Sūra an-Naḥl 16:26? Will he destroy them and save only a few as in the time of the flood?But he has promised that he will never do that again! So he identifies a way of limiting the evil that they can do, of stopping their building project, but at the same time of letting them go on living so that he can keep on blessing them. His solution is brilliant. If they all have one language, they can work together as one people and use their creative abilities to do terrible things. So he will do something which will put an end to their unity.

"Come, let us build up," said the people. "Come, let us go down," said God. "You want to build up to me? You can never do that! I will come down to you!" But God did not come down to build them up into a great people with a great name. He came down to stop them building by confusing the very facet of their nature which had enabled Adam to give names – their language. As mentioned earlier in this chapter, the irony is underlined by the word plays: *nilbenah* (let us make), *nibneh* (let us build), and *nabelah* (let us mix up).

The result is that they stopped building the city. The end is surprising: there is no mention of the tower! Perhaps we can conclude that the whole purpose of the tower was to establish the city in its proud self-reliance with its own anti-YHWH religion: if they abandoned the city-building project, the tower was irrelevant and would eventually fall down. But the last word of this verse, *ha-'ir* (the city), is leading us to the final denouement – we are going to find out what city this is!

> *Therefore its name was called Babel, because there the LORD confused the language of all the earth. And from there the LORD dispersed them over the face of all the earth. (11:9)*

This city is what we call "Babylon," the place built by Nimrod, and the place which would become a symbol of proud idolatrous power throughout the Bible, right up to the final judgement. In Akkadian, the Babylonian language, *bab-ilu* means "gate of the god." The tower is evidently the temple of Marduk, which was known as Esagila, literally meaning, "the building with a high head." The Babylonians believed that their tower was the gate between their gods and themselves. Not so, says Genesis. Babel means *balal*, "the place of confusion."

Some of the ancient Mesopotamians shared the *Bani Isra'il*'s tradition that humanity had once had one language which had been confused, but they gave different reasons for the confusion. A Sumerian epic claims that it resulted from fighting between gods. Not so, says Genesis. It was the result of the One God's righteous commitment to his creation.

The final irony is that the very thing the people feared happened to them. They were building to keep themselves anchored to one place in the earth so that they would not be scattered (11:4), but the result of their building is that God himself scatters them over all the earth (11:9). God put them into the places where he wanted them, whether they liked it or not. He was their creator, their Lord and their master, and they needed to acknowledge him if they were ever to have the blessing of a permanent home.

Theological Reflection

The one God who created and ordered the world is also the one God who created and ordered the nations. If Genesis 1:1–2:3 assures us of God's ordering of the *tohu wa bohu* chaos of the waters, and Genesis 6–9 assures us of his control of the chaotic violence of human beings, Genesis 10 assures us that he orders the confusing mixture of peoples and languages in our world, and Genesis 11:1–9 assures us of his control over even the greatest imperial powers. This is a key part of *the theological bud* – perhaps even the *stem* – without which the rest of the bud cannot be understood. This is the international God of all nations and languages, not the tribal god of Babylon or even of Israel!

The Genesis 10:1–11:9 *contribution to the DNA of science* is a warning. As human beings made in the image of God, we have amazing creative and technological capacity; so we can build things for the good of the communities in which God has put us, and for the good of all the descendants of Noah. But we can also use knowledge idolatrously, to serve our own people, our own ends and even our own religion. The people of Babel were surely proud of the height of their tower, as today we are proud of the scientific progress which enables us to control so much of the natural world. Babel warns us that, if we work together to use this power to build for ourselves rather than for God, God will surely bring our work down and confuse us!

Some early scientists were fascinated by the technology of the Babel story. They did not think that there was anything wrong in building things, as long as their attitudes were right. The Babel story inspired them, and some even went to look for the remains of the tower of Babel so that they could learn about the ancient technology.[16] But how tempting it is to listen to Shayṭān, who says, "you will be like God" (Gen 3:4). Today, people build taller and yet taller buildings. Sometimes, Muslims build a mosque near a church, and make it higher than the church. Then the Christians want to build a higher church!

Sadly, people often use buildings to make a name for themselves. The tallest building in the world today is the Burj Khalifa in Dubai. Its website boasts: "Burj Khalifa stands as an anchor to the world's most prestigious square kilometer – Downtown Dubai which is also described as 'The Centre of Now.'"[17]

This huge symbol of wealth was built through the labor of migrant workers, many from south Asia, who were paid as little as three dollars a day and housed in miserable conditions.[18] We must remember that if we want to build something just for our own name and if we do not care for the lives of the oppressed workers who are doing the building, God will not be pleased!

As part of *the seedbed of the Bible*, the *toledoth* of the sons of Noah introduces us to the various peoples among whom the *Bani Isra'il* will live. It also introduces us to the two sides of all human communities. On the one hand, the very existence of a people group is a mark of God's blessing, and their culture and language are part of his multifaceted creation. On the other hand, people will strive for security and power and wealth for their own group. The nations surrounding Israel associated their gods with their own people and their own place, and thought that their gods fought for them against everyone else. So, throughout the Bible, we will see peoples who set themselves up in opposition to the One True God and his people; but we will also see the *Bani Isra'il* fall into the same Babel-like ways. They demanded to have their own king, like the other nations (1 Sam 8:6), and then, again and again, the kings used their powers wrongly. Again and again, we see that God's kingship is different from earthly kingship. This will be supremely seen in Jesus the Messiah, the perfect anointed king. He will challenge the kingdoms of Caesar

---

16. See Sadway, "Fortunes of Babel," 191–214.

17. https://www.burjkhalifa.ae/en/downtown-dubai/, accessed 21 April 2019.

18. L. Allen, "The Dark Side of the Dubai Dream," *BBC News Magazine*, 6 April 2009, http://news.bbc.co.uk/2/hi/uk_news/magazine/7985361.stm, accessed 3 October 2018.

and the religious rulers of his time, but he will not do it in their way. As he says to Pilate, his is a different kind of kingdom (John 18:36).

The Qur'an, too, challenges ungodly political powers, not least through its portrayal of Abraham and the king who is identified as Nimrod (Ar. Namrūd) in Islamic tradtion (see pages 284-285). However, its challenge is different, because the Islamic Prophet Muhammad was more like some of the leaders of the *Bani Isra'il* than like Jesus the Messiah. He established a political kingdom, which fought its competitors, and which rapidly conquered many other kingdoms after his death.

The Islamic empire which grew up was, in many ways, like the Christian Byzantine Empire, known as *ar-Rūm* in the Qur'an. The Byzantines thought that their earthly empire was also the kingdom of God on earth. They were wrong. Like the people of Babel, their power was limited, and, as the Qur'an expected (Sūra *ar-Rūm* 30:2–5), their empire came to an end. The Babel story assures us that no earthly kingdom will ever be permitted to expand beyond the limits set by God.

After his return to heaven, Jesus the Messiah sent the Holy Spirit who reversed the Babel story. He inspired the apostles to preach the gospel in different languages, so that all could share the blessings and work together to build God's kingdom of peace and humility (Acts 2:1–11). The New Testament was written in the language best understood by people across the Mediterranean area, using Greek translations of the Old Testament and of the Aramaic words of Jesus the Messiah. This understanding of language is important for understanding the nature of the Bible and especially why so many believers read the translations of the Bible in their own language rather than trying to learn Hebrew and Greek.

It is helpful to compare the Greek New Testament to the Arabic Qur'an. The Qur'an is believed to be the words dictated to the Islamic Prophet Muhammad in the Arabic language (Sūra *ash-Shūra* 42:7), and Muslims have therefore always read it in Arabic, and have argued that a translation is no longer "The Qur'an" but an interpretation of the Qur'an. Had the apostles understood the Scriptures in a similar way, they would not have accepted the Greek translation of the Hebrew Scriptures (the Septuagint – signified by letters LXX) as the words of God. However, the New Testament writers quote from the Septuagint, and it seems that Jesus the Messiah himself used it. The implication is that the same Holy Spirit who inspired the writers of the Old Testament also helped the Septuagint translators. The same Holy Spirit inspired the apostles to write the New Testament in Greek. Today the same Holy Spirit leads the followers of Jesus the Messiah to translate the Scriptures into different languages, so that everyone, from all the world's 7,000 language groups,[19] can read the good news.

What About Us?

The reasonable response to all this is worship. Today's world, in its amazing array of nations and peoples, refugees and migrant workers, tourists and business people, is a result of the Creator's blessing, "Be fruitful and multiply." And today's "Babels" are all minute in comparison to that mighty Creator. He can and will limit their wickedness, yet he will do it in a merciful way which will give them the chance to repent and to accept his blessed rule of their lives.

And there are many "Babels" today. In our media, every day, we see the great nations of the world each trying to build a name for themselves. Within nations, there are political parties and huge corporations and sports teams and celebrities, all trying to build something which will make them rich and powerful and famous. We feel like very small people, but that is not a bad thing. The Babel story tells us that all human beings and all their buildings are very small: the important thing is that we remember our smallness and humbly bow before the only Being who is worthy of worship, the Name above all Names (Ps 148:13; Mal 1:11; Phil 2:9–10).

So, let us ask ourselves whether we see the world through the eyes of Babel, from ground level; or do we see it from the heavenly perspective of God?

Of Whom Are We Afraid?

We can imagine the *Bani Isra'il* hearing the Babel story as they sat in exile in Babylon, looking at its huge buildings and the towering temple. They would have understood the Genesis 11 message: these buildings do not reach God, and this great imperial power is nothing next to the One True God who created it all. In a moment, he can come and confuse them all, so that they will never again be able to conquer and oppress other peoples. So, whatever powers we may be under, whatever human arrogance surrounds us, we too, can be sure that the Lord God, the Almighty Creator and Loving Covenant Keeper, has control over wickedness, and will set the limits on the growth of any evil.

---

19. https://www.ethnologue.com/guides/how-many-languages.

What Are We Building?

Are we building for ourselves, for our own families and for our own communities, or are we building for God? Do we think that we need buildings or fame or honour or status in order to establish our faith? We need to think seriously here, to avoid pride and godless unity. Human effort apart from God will not succeed. Humans have their own plans, but in Bangladesh it has often been observed that human plans evaporate when pursued. (The Bangla word for "plan" is a compound of two words: *pari-kalpana – pari* meaning "fairy" and *kalpana* meaning "to imagine.") But God's plans stand firm forever (Ps 33:11 NIV).

Do We Think That We Can Somehow Climb Up to Reach God?

We cannot. If we are outside Eden, we cannot get back there by building upwards or by climbing some sort of spiritual ladder – keeping the law, prayers and devotions, *dhikr* or anything else – to reach it. Only God can restore what has been lost through the fall. The good news, as we shall see in chapter 12:1–3, is that he has a plan for redemption and re-creation for all the peoples through the people of Abraham.

If we accept the invitation to join the *millate Ibrahim*, we are part of God's great redemption plan; but his plan is not only that we should receive blessing but that we should bring blessing to others.

Do We Want God's Blessing for All Peoples, or Only for Ourselves?

If we thank God for those who translated the Bible into Bangla, are we also praying for those who are translating it into the languages of those who do not yet have a Bible? Is God calling some of us to translate the Bible? Are we willing to learn new languages so that we can share the good news with people who come to Bangladesh from different countries, and with people in the many countries throughout which our Bengali brothers and sisters now live, including Dubai?

7

The Beginnings of Abraham – Genesis 11:10–12:1

Up to now, Genesis has been telling us about all the peoples in the whole world. We have read about the creation of everything, about Adam and Eve and their sons who show us what all people are like, about the judgement on everyone, and about Noah, who is the ancestor of all peoples. It has been a journey of ups and downs, of blessings and sins, of judgements and mercies. We have travelled from the glories of Eden in Genesis 2 to the abyss of sin in Genesis 3–4; through the slow climb of the blessings of birth and the judgement of death in Genesis 5 to the downward plunge into universal wickedness in Genesis 6:1–7. We travelled on to the soaring heights of God's remembrance of Noah at the heart of Genesis 6–9 to the undeserved promises for all living beings in the rainbow covenant.

But Genesis 1–11's account of all the peoples has left us with a dismal picture. The last part of the *toledoth* of Noah has notice of coming blessing as well as coming servitude (9:25–27), and the Table of Nations brings hope that God is ordering all the peoples (10:1–32). But the final story of the origins of the whole world is one of defiance against God, of confusion of the human beings, and of cessation of their project (11:1–9). It is a tragic ending to the Bible's introduction to God's world.

But it is not the end of the story! From 11:10, Genesis narrows down to focus on one particular line: the line of Shem. From that line, Genesis 11:27 selects another, the line of Terah, whose descendants will be the subject of the following thirty-nine chapters. As the book of beginnings, Genesis thus begins the salvation history of humankind through one family, whose line will bring to the confused nations the promised blessing which has been glimpsed since Genesis 3:15, and enable them to join the Creator's holy Sabbath rest of Genesis

2:1–3. The Qur'an also speaks of the beginning of this blessing, calling it "the religion of Abraham" or *millate Ibrahim* (community of Abraham).

Abraham's influence is so great that Jews, Christians and Muslims revere him every day throughout the world. Each faith considers Abraham the father of their own community, and their religion the true flower from the bud of his religion. Many peoples have also claimed descent from Abraham through Keturah, whose sons settled in Arabia (Gen 25:1–6). Some people also trace the origins of Hinduism or of African groups to Keturah.[1] In Bangladesh, people are proud to call themselves *millate Ibrahim*.

In the Qur'an, Abraham is known as a man of truth and a prominent prophet (Sūra *Maryam* 19:41). He is mentioned sixty-nine times, including nine references to the *millate Ibrahim* (Sūras *al-Baqara* 2:130, 135; *Āl 'Imrān* 3:95; *an-Nisā'* 4:125; *al-An'ām* 6:161; *Yūsuf* 12:37, 38; *an-Naḥl* 16:123; *al-Ḥajj* 22:78). Abraham is described by the word *ḥanīf* (*al-Baqara* 2:135; *Āl 'Imrān* 3:95; *an-Nisā'* 4:125; *al-An'ām* 6:161; *an-Naḥl* 16:123); that is, he followed a form of monotheism which pre-dated both Judaism and Christianity[2] (*Āl 'Imrān* 3:67; *an-Naḥl* 16:120). It is foolish, says the Qur'an, to turn away from the *millate Ibrahim* (*al-Baqara* 2:130). The *millate Ibrahim* is the *sīrat al-mustaqīm* (the straight path) which the Islamic Prophet Muhammad preaches (*al-An'ām* 6:161; *an-Naḥl* 16:121–23; *al-Ḥajj* 22:78), it is the *millate Ibrahim* that Muslims are to follow (*al-Baqara* 2:135; *Āl 'Imrān* 3:95; *an-Nisā'* 4:125). Isaac, Jacob and Joseph, too, followed the *millate Ibrahim* (*Yūsuf* 12:38). No wonder that we want to be part of this!

So, then, who was Abraham? Who are his people? What was his faith? The Torah's answer is in Genesis, and 11:10–12:1 is the Bible's introduction to Abraham, his family and his journey of faith. The two genealogies in verses 11–26 and 27–30 take us from the accounts of the beginnings of the cosmos and of the nations to the history of a specific nation, the *Bani Isra'il*, and its ancestor, Abraham. They tell us how Abraham fits into God's world, which means that they are an important step towards understanding what it might mean to have Abraham as a "father."

---

1. See "Keturah" in James Orr, ed. *International Standard Bible Encyclopedia* (Chicago: Eerdmans.1939), https://www.internationalstandardbible.com/K/keturah.html retrieved September 2018; Olaudah Equiano, *The Interesting Narrative and Other Writings* (Penguin Books, 1995), 44.

2. There seem to have been monotheists called *Hanif* in Arabia before the coming of Islam. See Hans Köchler, ed. *Concept of Monotheism in Islam and Christianity* (International Progress Organization, 1982), 29.

The Worlds Behind and in Front of the Text
The Ancient World and Today's World

In the ancient world, the Jewish people were few, and they were surrounded by greater nations, so those nations attached small importance to the Jews' claim to be the people of Abraham. But, for themselves, they needed to know who they were, and they needed to be glad of the heritage which God had given them. One of the Ten Commandments was, "Honour your father and your mother" (Exod 20:12; Deut 5:16). They needed to know who their foremothers and forefathers were in order to honour them. We have already discussed the importance of genealogies in the ancient world and in today's world (page 173), so we can understand that the genealogy of Abraham was an important part of establishing their identity.

In today's world, emigrant peoples not only want to know about their families; they also want to know about the places from which their families came. Bangladeshis around the world tell their children stories about Bangladesh, and send them back to visit their hometowns and villages whenever possible. In the ancient world, travelling and communication were much more difficult, but people could still remember the places and tell the stories. So we can understand that the geography of Genesis 11 was important to the ancient Jewish readers.

But there is an important difference between the ancient Jews and today's scattered Bangladeshis. While Bangladeshis in Britain tell their children, "The people in that village are our people," the ancient Jews told their children, "The people in those areas are not of our religion and are no longer our people." The places mentioned were to become the centres of the Assyrian and Babylonian empires which would often be the enemies of the *Bani Isra'il* and would take them into exile. It was from these areas that Abraham was called out by God. Joshua said:

> Thus says the LORD, the God of Israel, "Long ago, your fathers lived beyond the Euphrates, Terah, the father of Abraham and of Nahor; and they served other gods. Then I took your father Abraham from beyond the River and led him through all the land of Canaan, and made his offspring many." (Josh 24:2–3)

Stories would grow up about the idolatry of the region, about how Abraham came to understand the One True God, and about how he challenged the idolaters. We can imagine how all this would have helped people to keep their faith when they had to live in exile among idolaters in that very region.

Geography and religion

The most probable period for Abraham's life is the Middle Bronze Age, between 2000 and 1600 BC. We need to know about Mesopotamia at that time in order to understand Genesis 11. The map below (figure 10) shows the main places through which Abraham journeyed:

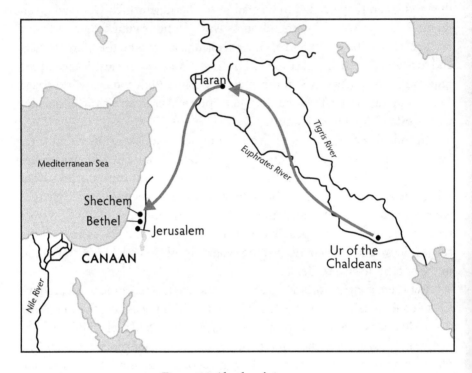

Figure 10 Abraham's journey

The most likely location of Ur of the Chaldeans (Heb. *Ur kasdim*) was beside the Euphrates, in what is now south Iraq. There has also been a tradition that Ur was what is now Urfa or Edessa, or elsewhere near Ḥaran in Upper Mesopotamia; but these would not have been places identified with the Chaldeans.

The Ur on the Euphrates began as a small village, but became a significant port and the largest and wealthiest city of southern Mesopotamia. There is archaeological evidence of the growth of writing, arts and sciences there. At the time of Abraham, it had a huge temple to the Sumerian moon god, Sin. He was the lord of wisdom and of the calendar, and his temple was a ziggurat tower like the temple of Marduk in Babylon. His symbol was the crescent moon, which can be seen on ancient coins as well as on the chest of ancient moon-god statues.

Ḥaran was also a centre for the worship of the moon god, Sin. The Akkadian *harran* means "cross-roads" or "highways," and the city had a strategic position at a river crossing on the main route from Nineveh to Allepo, about 30 kilometres south of what is now Edessa in Turkey. It was a trade centre and would become the capital of Assyria before being taken over by the Babylonians in 609 BC.

Names

Readers will notice that in Genesis 11 we have the names Abram and Sarai, not Abraham and Sarah. The names will be changed to Abraham and Sarai by God himself in Genesis 17. As we have seen throughout our study, names were at least as important in the ancient world as they are in our world today. We do not change our names unless we have a very good reason to do so. For example, in some cultures, people change their names when they get married; or someone might change their name if they have been in prison and wish to hide their identity. In the case of Abram and Sarai, God will give them new names which declare their very special roles in his plan to bless the world. From here on, we will use Abram and Sarai only when we refer to what Genesis says about them before their name changes. Otherwise, we will use Abraham and Sarah.

In studying the names in Genesis 11, we will see that some have meanings in both Hebrew and the ancient Mesopotamian language of Akkadian, which would have been spoken by Abram and his family. Many people in Bangladesh mistakenly think that Hebrews referred to Abraham with the Arabic word *Ibrāhīm* and therefore, that he spoke Arabic. Arabic did not develop until perhaps 1500 years after the time of Abraham.[3]

The New Testament

There are many references to Abraham in the New Testament, but only a few to Genesis 11:26–32. The genealogy is cited in Luke 3:34–36: Matthew's genealogy (Matt 1:1–17) begins with Abraham, so does not include this information about his ancestors. The only other clear reference is in Stephen's speech in Acts 7, which begins by emphasizing that the reason for Abraham leaving Ur was that God spoke to him there. In contrast, Genesis 12:1–3 is referred to many times in the New Testament, and, indeed, in the Old Testament. The Apostle

---

3. The earliest Arabic writing dates to the fourth century BC.

Paul even calls it "the gospel preached to Abraham," and gives two chapters to discussing it (Gal 3 and 4).

The Qur'an

In contrast to the New Testament, the Qur'an has very little about Abraham's life in Canaan, but a great deal about his life in Ur. It speaks of the idolatry of his birthplace, of how he came to believe in the One True God through observing the heavens and through rational analysis, of the beginnings of his preaching, and of his confrontations with his family and with Nimrod, the ruler of Ur. All this is similar to Jewish stories about the idolatry of Abraham's family in Ur. The Qur'an declares that he was not a *mushrik*, idol worshipper (Sūras *al-Baqara* 2:135; *Āl 'Imrān* 3:95; *al-An'ām* 6:161; *an-Naḥl* 16:123), and these stories underline his stand for monotheism.

The qur'anic Abraham was not only a *nabī* (prophet) and *rasūl* (apostle) in the line of prophecy from Adam to the Islamic Prophet Muhammad, but also the founder of the Ka'ba, and Muslims believe that he established the ḥajj, the pilgrimage to Mecca (Sūras *al-Baqara* 2:122–28; *Āl 'Imrān* 3:96–97). When Muslims perform the ḥajj, they believe that they are following the actions of Abraham, of his son Ishmael, and of Ishmael's mother, Hagar.

With the exception of the material about the Ka'ba, Islamic views of Abraham have similarities either with the Bible or with Jewish tradition. For example, Genesis uses the term "prophet" (*navi*) for Abraham, although this is in the speech of a pagan king (Gen 20:7). Midrash and other Jewish traditions describe him reasoning about the stars and other aspects of creation, and confronting his idolatrous family and king.[4]

There are other Islamic beliefs about Abraham which can be compared to Genesis and to Jewish and Christian beliefs about him, and they will be explored in the forthcoming commentary on Genesis 12–50 in this series. He is seen as fulfilling all the commandments and passing all the tests with which God tried him, including the command to sacrifice his son (Sūra *aṣ-Ṣāffāt* 37:102–7; cf. Gen 22). Jewish tradition, too, has much to say about the ten trials of Abraham. The Qur'an tells us that it was because of his unwavering faith that he passed the tests and that God promised that he would be an *imam* to all the nations (Sūra *al-Baqara* 2:124). The New Testament also stresses the importance of Abraham's faith (e.g. Rom 4:1–25; Heb 11:8–19). He has the title *Khalil Allāh* (Friend of God, Sūra *an-Nisā'* 4:125): this title was used 1,000

---

4. See commentary on Gen 11:26–28 below.

years earlier in the book of Isaiah and again in the New Testament epistle of James (Isa 41:8; Jas 2:23).

The World of the Text
Genesis 11:10–26 The Toledoth of Shem: From the Family of Noah to the Father of Abraham

This is a short *toledoth*. We might think it unimportant, but shortness does not mean that it does not matter. Rather, giving a whole section to one short genealogy tells us that something special is happening. It is this genealogy that provides the link between the origins of the world and the nations in the distant past, and the specific history of the patriarchs in known times and places.

Structure and Genre

The *toledoth* of Shem is a straightforward genealogy. It has both similarities to and differences from the genealogies we have encountered so far. Genesis 5 noted the many children born, but recorded only one name from each generation. That is, it was at the same time recording the multiplication of humanity and following the line leading to Noah. Genesis 10 recorded the spreading out of humanity, naming several people in each generation, but not focusing on any one line. Genesis 11:10–26 follows one line from the Genesis 10 genealogy. It reiterates the relevant names from Shem to Peleg (Gen 10:21–22, 24–25) and then adds another five generations. In each generation, we know that there were other sons and daughters, but only one name is recorded. The pattern is similar to that of Genesis 5, but without the repeated phrase, "and he died." We know, now, that everyone is going to die! We note again the numbers pattern: there are five generations from Shem to Peleg and five more from Peleg to Abraham; that is, ten generations from Shem to Abraham.

In short, as we have seen in Genesis 5, and as the general *toledoth* pattern in Genesis, we narrow down at every stage. This is the *toledoth* which is, at last, going to get us to the person to which the line has been leading – Abraham.

COMMENTARY

These are the generations of Shem. When Shem was 100 years old, he fathered Arpachshad two years after the flood. And Shem lived after he fathered Arpachshad 500 years and had other sons and daughters.

When Arpachshad had lived 35 years, he fathered Shelah. And Arpachshad lived after he fathered Shelah 403 years and had other sons and daughters.

When Shelah had lived 30 years, he fathered Eber. And Shelah lived after he fathered Eber 403 years and had other sons and daughters.

When Eber had lived 34 years, he fathered Peleg. And Eber lived after he fathered Peleg 430 years and had other sons and daughters.

When Peleg had lived 30 years, he fathered Reu. And Peleg lived after he fathered Reu 209 years and had other sons and daughters.

When Reu had lived 32 years, he fathered Serug. And Reu lived after he fathered Serug 207 years and had other sons and daughters.

When Serug had lived 30 years, he fathered Nahor. And Serug lived after he fathered Nahor 200 years and had other sons and daughters. (11:10–23)

This passage follows the descendants of Shem through Eber, to whom attention was drawn in 10:21, and the list is repeated in the genealogy of the *Bani Isra'il* in 1 Chronicles 1:24–26 and the genealogy of Jesus the Messiah in Luke 3:34–36.

It is not always possible to be sure about the meanings of the various names.[5] As in Genesis 10, some can be interpreted as referring to places or to people groups, some to individuals, and some to both. As in other biblical genealogies, "fathered" could mean that the person was the direct father of the next named person, but it could also mean that he was a grandfather or a more distant ancestor. We will think first about what we can learn from the names and, second, about what we can learn from the numbers in these verses.

The Names

The names tell a story. We move from five names listed in Genesis 10 towards two names which refer to known places in the patriarchal story. That is, the *toledoth* begins in the history of how the nations came into being, and takes us towards the exact place from which Abraham would set out towards the promised land.

The names Arphaxad, Shelah, Eber and Peleg, all mentioned in Genesis 10:24–25, could signify a story of people spreading out. The meaning of "Arphaxad" is uncertain, but the fact that the names of his brothers in Genesis 10 are all names of places has led people to link "Arphaxad" with a place; for

---

5. Most of the interpretations here are from Douglas, *New Bible Dictionary*, with added insights from Hess, Keil and Delitzsch, Wenham and Westermann.

example, "Arraphu" in what is now Kirkuk, or with the Chaldeans of southern Mesopotamia.

The next three names could have various origins, but all have possible Hebrew roots which contribute to the story. Shelah means "sent" or "going out" or even "a missile" – something that is thrown (as in the second part of "Methuselah," see comment on Gen 5:21). Eber means "someone who crosses over," or "emigrant," and is similar to *'ibri*, which is translated "Hebrew." Peleg shares letters with the word describing the "dividing" (*niplegah*) of the world at his time (Gen 10:25). Together, these names describe the migration and formation of a new people – the Hebrews who so often lived as landless foreigners.

The meaning of Reu is uncertain, although it could mean "shepherd" or "friend," as in the name of Moses's father-in-law Reuel, "God is a friend" (Exod 2:18). He is an individual whose life leads on to people whose names will be attached to particular places. Serug is probably "Sarug" in Mesopotamia, just north of Ḥaran. Nahor's name would later be associated with a city, also near Ḥaran (Gen 24:10).

It is interesting to note that the central name, Peleg, is the only name about which we had extra information in chapter 10. Peleg, we were told, lived at the time of the division of the earth (10:25), which probably refers to the scattering of the peoples from Babel. This underlines the Babel story as a key "bridge" between ancient times and patriarchal history.

The Numbers

The numbers in this genealogy are interesting and have been the subject of much debate. As they stand in the Hebrew text, they would mean that Shem was still alive when Abram set out for Canaan! So we are not surprised to find that ancient translations such as the Samaritan Pentateuch and the Septuagint add one hundred years to the age of each father at the birth of his first son, thereby lengthening the gap between Shem and Abraham by one thousand years. Modern readers are more likely to point out that, as so often in the Bible, the names may not represent all the generations that existed, one evidence for that being that the Septuagint adds the name "Kainan" between Arpachshad and Shelah. The implication is that we cannot simply add up the numbers to find the age of Shem when Abram was born, for example.

We can, however, clearly learn that human lifespans decreased, and this is probably the main lesson from the numbers. The average lifespan of the ten generations from Adam to Noah was 857 years. The average life span of the next ten generations, after the flood, was only 357 years. There was a dramatic decrease immediately after the flood, followed by a steady decrease in the next generations. It seems that God is slowly executing his plan of limiting humans to 120 years on earth (Gen 6:3), as we see the increasing impact of death in a world cut off from the tree of life in the garden of Eden.

> *When Nahor had lived 29 years, he fathered Terah. And Nahor lived after he fathered Terah 119 years and had other sons and daughters.*
>
> *When Terah had lived 70 years, he fathered Abram, Nahor, and Haran. (11:24–26)*

Terah was the ninth generation after Noah. The name Terah probably comes from *yareach* (moon) which is similar in Hebrew and other ancient Semitic languages. It would then indicate that Terah's family were moon worshipers. It could also be linked with *Til sha Turahi*, an ancient site near Ḥaran, the place to which Terah would emigrate (Gen 11:31).

The sons of Terah were Abram (meaning "exalted father" or "father of Aram"), Nahor (meaning "blow" or "snort," and therefore implying strength), and Haran (meaning "caravan," "road" or "route"). Abram is the person we know as Abraham. It is not until Genesis 17 that God changes his name to Abraham, which means "father of a great number." The Qur'an uses only Abraham (*Ibrāhīm*), and Islamic literature makes no reference to a name change. In Genesis, the change of name is highly significant, as it confirms God's promise that, against all logic, Abram would indeed become Abraham, the father of a great number of people.

The order of the names does not mean that Abram was the oldest of Terah's sons. On the contrary, tradition interprets the details about the sons' marriages as implying that Haran was the eldest (Gen 11:27–29). However, as the father of the chosen family and the messianic line, his name is mentioned first. We noted the same pattern in Genesis 5:32, where Shem is mentioned first although he was not Noah's eldest son.

Islamic tradition calls Abraham's father Azar on the basis of Sūra al-Anʿām 6:74: "Abraham said to his father, Azar, 'Do you take idols as gods?'" Most commentators say that Azar is another name for Terah,[6] but some suggest that Azar was the name of an idol and interpret the verse, "Abraham said to

---

6. For example, Maulana Faridpuri, a distinguished Islamic teacher, asserts that most commentators are agreed that his original name was Terah (Ar. *Tarikh*) and his nickname was Azar (*Bukhārī Sharif*, vol. 4, 75).

his father, 'Do you take Azar as an idol of the gods?'"[7] In current internet discussion, some Muslims suggest that Azar was Abraham's uncle or guardian, while Terah was his biological father.[8] There are several theories about the origins of the name Azar; for example, it could come from *atar*, an ancient Persian demon, or from Eliezer, Abraham's servant (Gen 15:2).

The idea that Terah was an idolator comes from Joshua 24:2, and there is a long tradition of Jewish and Christian thinking about how Abram came to reject his father's religion. The New Testament says that God appeared to him and spoke to him (Acts 7:2–3). In contrast, Jewish tradition has Abram using observation of the universe and rational analysis to show the truth of monotheism to himself and then to others, and then demonstrating that truth by smashing his father's idols.[9] For both traditions, God's showing Abram the stars in Genesis 15:5–6 is important. Jewish tradition discusses the role of looking at the stars in directing Abraham's faith, perhaps from the idolatrous astrology of Ur to the One True God. The New Testament and Christian tradition emphasize Abram's response of faith, which was "counted to him as righteousness" (Gen 15:6; cf. Rom 4:9, 22; Gal 3:6; Jas 2:23).

Islamic tradition, too, recounts that Abraham rejected idolatry through logical reasoning, and sees him as one of the first Muslims (*Āl 'Imrān* 3:67). It emphasizes the difference between Abraham and other people in his family and community. Genesis will stress this difference in chapter 12 verse 1, where God tells him to leave his home and to break with his father's household.

Theological Reflection

As we consider this genealogy, we are filled with budding hope that God is going to bless the fallen world by planting *the seed of Abram*. He will not, as the Qur'an portrays, send a series of different individual prophets to individual peoples. He will plant and grow one people through whom he will bless the whole earth.

These ideas are another key basis of the whole Bible. Without them, the rest of the Old Testament may seem as if it is teaching that God is racist, that he loves the *Bani Isra'il* and does not care about anyone else. But that cannot be

---

7. Translations here are from Reuven Firestone's article on Azar, in *The Encyclopaedia of the Qur'an*, vol. 1, 192–93.

8. E.g. https://salafiaqeedah.blogspot.com/2012/01/was-azar-father-of-prophet-abraham.html, accessed 1 Nov 2019.

9. Reynolds, *Qur'an and Its Biblical Subtext*, 77–84, explores the relevant Jewish and Christian texts. See also the commentary on Genesis 11:28 below.

so. We have already learned from chapters 1–10 that the One God is the God of all peoples, that every one of us is made in his image, that he is committed to all his creatures, and that he is the one who orders all the nations. The *toledoth* of Shem does not introduce us to a racist God, but to God who is the master planner, and who executes his plan through a whole community. If we read the Old Testament with this *bud of theology* in mind, we can discern the unfolding petals of God's concern for the whole world, which will come into full bloom through Jesus the Messiah.[10] God called Abram because God loves the Bangladeshi people!

What About Us?
How Do We See Our Families?

This *toledoth* reminds us again of the importance of human families. Unlike many of our current genealogies, it does not begin with the person we want to know about: it starts ten generations earlier and leads up to him. It does not say, "Abram is important because he had such and such ancestry." It says, "God gave children to these people, and this is the way in which he prepared the person whom he would call." The fact that there are ten generations from Noah to Abram, as there were ten from Adam to Noah, underlines that this is God's perfect plan.

Bengalis, like many other people, want to know about their ancestors. But why do we want to know? Do we judge people on the basis of who their parents and grandparents are? Do we think there is no value in a family with no influential ancestors? Or that we are important because our family is important? Or do we look back at God's amazing love and providence in bringing us into his world, and at the line of human beings without whom we would not exist? Without God's word, we cannot truly discern what is important and what is unimportant.

How Do We Think about the Length of Our Lives?

It is natural for living beings to want to stay alive. As Rabindranath Tagore write is his poem "*Pran*" (Life):[11]

---

10. There are many Old Testament examples here: the best known include Gen 12:3; 26:4; Exod 19:5–6; 1 Kgs 17:8–24; 2 Kgs 5:1–14; Ps 96; Jonah. See also Glaser, *Bible and Other Faiths*.

11. From his *Poems on Love*. English translation available at http://nkganesha.blogspot.com/2019/08/poems-on-love-by-rabindranath-tagore.html?m=1.

I don't want to die in this beautiful world,
I want to live among human beings.

Some people even have their bodies preserved in the hope that one day science will be able to revive them! How do we react to this chapter, which records the steady reduction in human lifespans over ten generations? Perhaps we see this as a tragedy. However, Genesis 6:3 gave a reason for limiting lifespans – on the one hand, death is God's judgement on sinful human beings but, on the other hand, this is God's mercy in restricting evil. We remember that Enoch's lifespan was shorter than the other lives in Genesis 5. What is important is not how long our lives are, but a life walking with God on earth and then onward forever.

Genesis 11:27–12:1 Abram and His Family
The Beginning of the Toledoth of Terah

The *toledoth* of Terah stretches right up to Genesis 25:11. In this commentary, we look only at its beginning. A new beginning often starts with a journey. The *Bani Isra'il* journeyed from Egypt to the Promised Land; the Islamic Prophet Muhammad and the first Muslims journeyed from Mecca to Medina; and Bangladeshis journey from Bangladesh to many parts of the world. This section deals with the beginnings of Abram's journey from Ur to Canaan, and tells us about the family from which he came. It is not until chapter 12 that we discover that God is involved and learn about the purpose of the journey.

We cannot overemphasize the importance of this introduction to Abraham. Not only does it give us the family background needed to understand the later chapters of Genesis, it is also in this short passage that we can find the background to much of the qur'anic material on Abraham.

Structure and Genre

The first part (11:27–30) has the familiar pattern of genealogy with additional explanation. However, unlike previous genealogies, it records only one generation, it includes the names of the women, and it ends with a shock. Instead of the familiar, Abram "had sons and daughters," we read that his wife was barren – "she had no child."

Genesis 11:31 begins a narrative section which will go on for nearly fourteen chapters. It opens a new stage of history. We are now in the realm of the ancestors who were remembered by the *Bani Isra'il*, rather than in the primeval stage of the background to all humanity. The style changes to a real-life narrative of Abram and his descendants. God, the controller of all history, will appear as a character in the story. People of the Abrahamic faiths see this as an essential part of their history as well as the beginning of their faith. We note the difference here with the genre of the qur'anic Abraham narratives: while the Qur'an refers to several incidents in Abraham's life in many different places, Genesis has a continuous history.

Structurally, the first section of the Terah *toledoth* is a chiasm which finishes at Genesis 12:9.

> **A.** Terah and family in the idolatrous city of Ur with its temple (11:27–30)
>> **B.** Terah leaves with Abram, Lot and Sarai (11:31)
>>> **C.** Settlement in Ḥaran: death of Terah at age 205 (11:31–32)
>>>> **D.** The Lord says, "Go!" (12:1)
>>>>> **E.** The sevenfold blessing (12:2–3)
>>>> **D'.** Abram went, as the Lord told him (12:4)
>>> **C'.** Setting out from Ḥaran at age 75 (12:4)
>> **B'.** Abram takes Lot and Sarai: they arrive but do not settle (12:5)
> **A'.** Abram and family travel through Canaan and set up altars to the Lord (12:6–9)

Our commentary will finish with the central blessing of 12:2–3, but we will not understand the passage from 11:27–12:1 unless we see it as the first half of a chiasm, and of a combined genealogy and itinerary. The genealogy tells of the father's household from which Abram was called to "Go!" (12:1) as well as introducing some of the people in Abram's household who would go with him. The itinerary tells of the places from which Abram went and the places to which he would go. There is remarkable contrast here, between Ur and Ḥaran, the settled cities of the moon god Sin which Abram left; and the nomadic life of a shepherd setting up small places of worship to the one creator God in Canaan. The key to the change is the Lord's command (D) and Abram's obedience to it (D'). This opens the way to the ongoing relationship with God that will be seen again and again as Abram travels through the promised land.

> *Now these are the generations of Terah. Terah fathered Abram, Nahor, and Haran; and Haran fathered Lot. (11:27)*

We notice first that this is the *toledoth* of Terah, and not the *toledoth* of Abraham. Indeed, Genesis has no "*toledoth* of Abraham." This is surprising, as Abraham is such an important figure, and Genesis has great emphasis on Abraham as father. Perhaps Genesis is emphasizing that Abraham, too, is part of a family.

Perhaps it is also signalling that the coming story is not just about Abraham and his immediate descendants, but also about his siblings and their families.

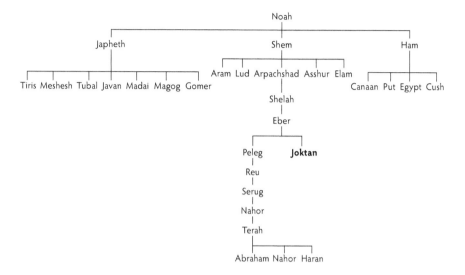

Figure 11 Abraham's Family Tree

The three brothers have already been named in 11:26: Abram, Nahor and Haran. We have already noted that this is not necessarily the order of their ages. We could see it as the order of their importance as ancestors in the coming narrative.

Abram is the most important, and it is his story which will be followed from chapter 12 onwards.

Nahor is important because it is from his line that the mothers of the *Bani Isra'il* will come. These include Rebekah, the wife of Isaac, and Leah and Rachel and their maidservants, the mothers of the twelve sons of Jacob. In Genesis, it is just as important that the chosen people have the right mothers as that they have the right fathers. Indeed, a great deal of space is given to the choice of mothers. We are reminded of the promise to Eve that it would be through her seed that the serpent's head would be crushed (Gen 3:15).

Haran was the father of Lot (11:27), about whom we will read much in Genesis. Lot is also mentioned numerous times in the Qur'an, as a prophet sent to the people of Sodom (Sūras *al-Aʻrāf* 7:80–84; *Hūd* 11:74–83; *al-Ḥijr* 15:59–74; *ash-Shuʻarā'* 26:160–75; *an-Naml* 27:54–58; cf. Gen 19). In biblical history, his descendants, the Moabites and the Ammonites, would often be the enemies of the *Bani Isra'il*, but God would give them land (Deut 2:9, 19) and the seeds of an Ammonite woman and of a Moabite woman would be in the line of the Messiah (1 Kgs 14:31; 2 Chr 12:13; Ruth 4:13–22; Matt 1:5–7).

> *Haran died in the presence of his father Terah in the land of his kindred, in Ur of the Chaldeans. (11:28)*

The *toledoth* of Shem did not mention any deaths; it only mentioned the length of peoples' lives. In this *toledoth* of Terah, we read again about a death – Haran, a son of Terah, died before his father. This is a premature death and no reason for it is given.

Genesis 10 mentioned that each people had their land, and the story of Babel showed how much importance the people gave to their lands. Here, we are told about the particular place which was home to Terah and his family. It seems important to the Genesis author that this is not just any city called Ur, such as the various cities near Ḥaran that some scholars suggest: it is Ur of the Chaldeans (Heb. *kasdim*). Later in the history of the *Bani Isra'il*, "*kasdim*" referred to Babylon or to the whole area of Babylonia (e.g. Isa 13:19; 47:1–5; Ezek 23:23; Dan 3:8). So the use of the term here emphasizes that the place Abram would leave was in the region of Babel, about which we have just read. As Babel would become known for its tower-like temple to Marduk, so Ur was known for its tower-like temple to the moon god, Sin.

This short verse is very important for understanding the Qur'an's account of Abraham. It apparently simply tells us the place of Abram's family home, and that his brother died an unexplained early death. But on the basis of a close study of the Hebrew and the context of the verse, the *Genesis Rabbah* rabbis asked several questions. We can see their answers echoed in the Qur'an and, to a lesser extent, in the New Testament.

First, the word *ur* can mean "flame" or "fire." What might the "fire of the Chaldeans" have been? Second, why does the text tell us that Haran died "before his father"? The Hebrew *'al pene*, translated "before," literally means, "before (the) face." So, did Haran die while his father was actually present? If so, why? The rabbis took back to this text the question of why God chose Abram which arises from the next chapter; and they answered all these questions by telling a story (*Gen Rab* 38:13):

Abram's father was not only a worshipper of idols but also a maker of idols (this is suggested by Josh 24:2). Abram realized that he should not worship the moon (or the sun or the stars), and he also challenged his father and his people. For example, he put a stick into the hand of the biggest idol and smashed the other idols. When his father saw what had happened, Abram told him that the idols had fought over an offering that had been brought for them. Terah was so angry that he took Abram to the king, Nimrod, who told him to worship fire. Abram argued with him until Nimrod became frustrated, and ordered that Abram be thrown into a furnace. His father and his brother, Haran, were there watching. Haran thought to himself, "If Abram dies, I'll be on Nimrod's side. If Abram is saved, I'll be on his side." Miraculously, Abram was not harmed by the fire, so Haran announced that he believed in Abram's god. Nimrod punished him by putting him into the furnace and, because he was not sincere in his faith, Haran died – as the verse says, it was in front of his father, in the fire of the Chaldeans.

The story of Abraham confronting idolatry appears eight times in the Qur'an (Sūras *al-Anʿām* 6:74–82; *Maryam* 19:41–50; *al-Anbiyā'* 21:51–73; *ash-Shuʿarā'* 26:69–86; *al-ʿAnkabūt* 29:16–27; *aṣ-Ṣāffāt* 37:83–98; *az-Zukhruf* 43:26–27; *al-Mumtaḥina* 60:4). It includes Abraham reasoning about monotheism from observation of the universe (*al-Anʿām* 6:75–79; *al-ʿAnkabūt* 29:19–20), the smashing of his father's idols (*al-Anbiyā'* 21:57–58; *aṣ-Ṣāffāt* 37:93), his confronting a king (*al-Baqara* 2:258), and then being thrown into the fire and rescued from it by God (*al-Anbiyā'* 21:68–69; *al-ʿAnkabūt* 29:24; *aṣ-Ṣāffāt* 37:97–98). None of this is recorded in the Bible, but some parallels can be found in the stories of Gideon (Judg 6:25–32) and of the three friends of the prophet Daniel (Dan 3:19–26).

The repetition of this story in the Qur'an emphasizes Abraham's confrontation of idolatry. Commentaries and prophet stories affirm this emphasis, elaborating on the idea that Abraham's people worshipped heavenly bodies.[12] The Qur'an does not name Abram's birthplace, but it is understood that the king who put him in the fire was Nimrod (Ar. *Namrūd*).

Although these stories about Abram's family and people are not in Genesis, they do alert us to the fact that God called Abram out of an idol-worshipping city and family. Genesis generally deals with the idolatry of its time by focusing on the One True God, while the Qur'an takes the opposite strategy, and deliberately argues against the idols. The Bible does not make Terah's idol worship explicit until Joshua 24:2; but, as the ancient readers would have recognized the allusions to Babylonian stories in the creation and flood narratives, they would also have known that Ur and Ḥaran were centres of

---

12. For example, Ibn Kathīr wrote: "At this time people worshipped idols of stone and wood and many worshipped the planets, stars, sun and moon; and others worshipped their rulers and kings (*Stories of the Prophets*, 38). For more details, see Reynolds, *Qur'an and Its Biblical Subtext*, 74–78.

idolatrous worship. As they understood from Genesis 1:14–19 that the heavenly lights were part of God's creation, they understood from this chapter that God's people were to abandon the worship of those lights.

> *And Abram and Nahor took wives. The name of Abram's wife was Sarai, and the name of Nahor's wife, Milcah, the daughter of Haran the father of Milcah and Iscah. (11:29)*

This is the first record of people "taking wives" since the disastrous "taking of wives" by the powerful male figures of Genesis 6:2. Terah's sons are continuing God's initiative of marriage which began with Adam and Eve (Gen 2:23–24). It is important that the women are named. In contrast, the Qur'an does not record the name even of Abraham's wife. The only woman it names is Mary, the mother of the Messiah, Jesus.

Abram's wife was Sarai, his half-sister (see Gen 20:12). In Hebrew, her name means "princess." Nahor married his niece Milcah, the daughter of Haran (11:29). In Hebrew, her name could be related to "counsel" or to "queen." She has a vital role as the grandmother of Rebekah, Isaac's wife (Gen 22:20–23) and the foremother of Leah and Rachel, Jacob's wives (Gen 29–30). In Akkadian, Sarratu was the consort of Sin, the moon god, and Malkatu was Sin's daughter, so these names may add to the evidence for the influence of moon religion on Terah and his family.

As in the case of Naamah, Tubal-Cain's sister (Gen 4:22), the Bible will have nothing more to say about Milcah's sister, Iscah, and we wonder why she is mentioned. As some Jewish tradition sees Naamah as the wife of Noah, Jewish tradition suggests that "Iscah" is another name for Sarah, but there is no indication of this in the text, and Sarah is later described as the daughter of Terah (Gen 20:12). The Qur'an has no mention of Nahor, Haran, Milcah or Iscah.

In the eyes of modern human beings, this looks like a very complicated family. Abram married his half-sister, Sarai, a daughter of his father Terah through another wife (Gen 20:12). Nahor married his niece, his brother Haran's daughter. Such marriages were common practice in the ancient world even to the point that people married this way as a part of their religion (Gen 24:3–4; 28:1–2). Later, God prohibited marriages to close relations, explicitly forbidding marriage between aunt and nephew (Lev 18:14; 20:19) and to "the daughter of a father" (Lev 18:9). However, it does not explicitly forbid marriage between uncle and niece. The prohibition of these types of marriage continues among the *millate Ibrahim*.[13]

> *Now Sarai was barren; she had no child. (11:30)*

The final sentence of this description of the marriages strikes a painful blow to the mind of the reader. Until this point, no matter how corrupt people had become, God had never removed the blessing of fruitfulness from them. Suddenly, we read of a barren woman. The word "barren" (Heb. *'aqar*) is not enough: it is explained that she had no child. It is as if the shock is too great, and the reader needs to be told the meaning of this strange new word.

> *Terah took Abram his son and Lot the son of Haran, his grandson, and Sarai his daughter-in-law, his son Abram's wife, and they went forth together from Ur of the Chaldeans to go into the land of Canaan, but when they came to Haran, they settled there. (11:31)*

Here begins the narrative of the migration from Ur to the land promised by God. Terah and his family move from "Ur of the Chaldeans" to Ḥaran.[14] They were planning to go to Canaan, but they stop on the way. The orphan, Lot, and the barren wife, Sarai, are included.

They went to Ḥaran,[15] about nine hundred kilometres away from Ur and settled there. Ḥaran had, like Ur, a temple to the moon god, Sin, so perhaps that is why Terah stopped there. We might even guess that he found work again there, in idol-making. From the map, it seems surprising that they should travel to Ḥaran if they wanted to go to Canaan, but, in fact, it was much easier than using the more direct route through the Arabian Desert, where there would have been no water.

Genesis does not mention the reason for the travel, but the New Testament will tell us that God called Abram when he was in Ur (Acts 7:2–4), and the tense of the verb in Genesis 12:1 suggests that Abram had heard God's call earlier. Perhaps Terah decided to move, and God reassured Abram that he should go with his father; perhaps God told Abram to go, and he persuaded his father to

---

13. Marrying a maternal or paternal uncle ("avunculate marriage") is forbidden in Islam (Sūras *al-Nisā'* 4:23; *al-Aḥzāb* 33:50). These marriages are also deemed sinful in several Christian traditions.

14. There is no mention here of Nahor, but we learn later that his family did eventually settle in Paddam-Aram, the area around Ḥaran (Gen 24:10; 28:1–10).

15. Note that the place name Ḥaran is different from the personal name, Haran, as they have different initial letters.

go with him; or perhaps Abram did, in fact, challenge the idolatry of Ur, and Terah wanted to move away because it became unsafe for his whole family. All we know is that they moved away from a wealthy place which had plenty of work for a maker of idols; and that this was God's plan for Abram and Sarai.

We recall the beginning of the chapter, where the migrant people found a place and "settled there" – *yeshbu sham* – the same Hebrew phrase as at the end of this verse (Gen 11:2). Terah's family have left the Babel area and its towered temple, but they have again settled. The reader's mind is filled with questions: What will happen next? Will they build more idolatry? Will they try to build themselves a name and again be scattered? Or is something quite different going to happen?

> *The days of Terah were 205 years, and Terah died in Ḥaran. (11:32)*

The only thing we know about what happened to Terah is that he died.

In Genesis 12:4, we will read that Abram was seventy-five years old when he left Ḥaran. If Terah died immediately before that, Abram would have been born when Terah was 130, which would mean a very large gap – sixty years – between the births of Haran and Abram. So it is probable that Terah was still alive when Abram left, and the Genesis writer records his death here to complete the genealogy before going on to Abram's story.[16] The main point is that Terah was still in Ḥaran when he died: he had set out to go to Canaan, but he never got there. He would have no more part in Abram's story.

The problem is that we would not expect Abram, a godly man, to abandon his elderly father. Jewish tradition solves this by saying that, as an idolator, Terah was effectively dead already. The Midrash has Abram asking God whether he should really leave his father behind, and God replying that he was exempted from his filial duty. That is why, say the rabbis, Terah's death is recorded before Abram's journey is recorded (*Gen Rab* 39:7).

Going, Go!

> *Now the LORD said to Abram, "Go from your country and your kindred and your father's house to the land that I will show you. (12:1)*

---

16. Compare this with Gen 25:17, which completes a genealogical section by recording the death of Ishmael, and goes on to narrate events which would have occurred during Ishmael's lifetime.

Genesis 12:1 begins the section of the Torah[17] known to Jewish people as *lek leka*, the emphatic phrase translated here "Go!" It literally means, "going, go" or "walking, walk." The Hebrew grammatical construction is similar to that found in Genesis 2:17 and 3:4, where "you shall surely die" translates *mot tamut*, "dying, die." The "dying death" meant that Adam and Eve had to leave the garden: now Abram is to "going, go" into a new and unknown place. The text does not tell us when God spoke these words, but, as noted above, the tense implies that God had originally spoken to Abram earlier, and this is confirmed in Acts 7:2–3.

There is a two-fold command to "Go." First, Abram is to leave his home. The Hebrew word translated "country" is *erets* – "land." The *erets* is God's good creation, and the beautiful place which he has prepared as our home. Each people has its God-given *erets* (Gen 10:5, 20, 31). Up to now, people have only lost their land as punishment for sin: Adam and Eve were expelled from Eden, Cain was banished from his home, all the *erets* was covered by the waters of the flood, and the Babel generation were scattered from their chosen place. It shocks the reader that God's chosen person should have to leave his land.

Second, Abram must leave his family and relatives and so lose them. Undoubtedly, Asians feel the heart-wrenching impact of this command. Surely God would not want to destroy the family ties! Is not "Honor your father and mother" central in the Ten Commandments (Exod 20:12; Deut 5:16)? Did not Jesus the Messiah chide religious leaders for failing to serve their parents (Matt 15:4–6; Mark 7:10–13)? The Qur'an, too, upholds the importance of filial responsibility (Sūras *an-Nisā'* 4:1; *al-Isrā'* 17:26). This may be why the Qur'an does not refer to Abram being told to leave his family but rather to go to a land which will benefit all (Sūra *al-Anbiyā'* 21:71).

It seems that, after God spoke to Abram in Ur, he left his home and his wider kin, but he did not leave his father's household (cf. Acts 7:2). On the contrary, Genesis 11:31 implies that his father was leading the party. Now, because Terah has either died or refused to continue the journey, God explicitly tells Abram to leave his father's house, to set off again and to leave behind anyone who does not want to come with him. God's plan for the new family to grow from Abram and Sarai is even more important than the honouring of parents.

No wonder Jewish tradition sees this call as one of great tests of Abram's faith. The Qur'an affirms that Abraham was tested through various commands

---

17. The whole Torah is divided into weekly portions (Heb. *parashat*), each named after a prominent word or phrase from the first verse of the portion.

(*kalimāt*, literally "words"; Sūra *al-Baqara* 2:124), and Islamic tradition echoes Jewish tradition that there were several tests.[18] Hebrews 11:8–10 uses his faithfulness as an example for us to follow, focusing on the fact that this verse does not tell Abram where to go. He may know that the general area is Canaan (Gen 11:31), but the exact land which God will give him is unknown. He needs to depend entirely on God's direction!

We note that there is no mention of God giving the new land to Abram either here or in the blessings of verses 2 and 3. It is not until Abram has stepped out in obedient faith and has travelled all the way to Canaan (12:4–5) that God speaks to him again and promises to give him the land (12:6–7). At that time, there were other people living there, and it would be centuries later, in the time of Joshua, that the *Bani Isra'il* would begin to have that land as their own place.

The *bud of the promise of the land* will underline the whole story of the Torah and will open into a blooming flower as the story of God's plan of salvation proceeds. In Exodus, the promise to the family of Abraham is a vast territory from the Red Sea to the Euphrates (Exod 23:31). In the New Testament, the gospel goes out into all the lands of the earth, as all peoples are invited to join Abraham's family through the Messiah, Jesus. For the future, we are encouraged to look forward to the new earth, to the final fruit from the flower in the new creation (Rev 21–22). During Abram's lifetime, his family would own only one field as a burial ground. Yet Abram would believe God's promise and continue to obey his instructions because, the writer of Hebrews tells us, he "looked forward to a better country" (Heb 11:10). He was looking towards his home and family with all believers in the new creation!

Theological Reflection

Genesis 11:27–32 has no mention of God, but it is deeply theological because it introduces God's plan for blessing the fallen world which we have read about in Genesis 1:1–11:9. Reading forward, we will realise that God has been at work through all the events of this passage. Genesis 12:1 implies that God had called Abram some time before he actually left Haran; and in Genesis 15:7, God tells Abram that it was he who brought him out of Ur. Stephen, in Acts 7:4, goes further, telling us that "the God of glory" actually appeared to Abram in Ur.

If we read this passage as the first part of the chiasm of Genesis 11:27–12:9 (see page 282), we realise that *it is cultivating an important theology* of family

---

18. Different commentaries on *al-Baqara* 2:124 enumerate the tests in different ways. Jewish tradition counts 10 tests; see Maimonides, *Mishnah Avot* 5:3

and of place, the seedlings of which have been planted in chapters 1–10. God's creation blessings included the marriage of male and female, the multiplication of humanity, and a beautiful place within which they lived and worked. We have seen themes of family and of land throughout the stories of the fall and judgement and God's gracious commitment to humankind. Again and again, human sin breaks families and they lose their places. Now, God himself is going to work through a disruption of family and place.

We might think of this as the beginning of a new creation – the start of a new family in a new place. As Noah and his family lost their land and all their relations and started again, so Abram will leave his land and his relations so that God can start a new community in a new land. The difference is that, at the time of Noah, God destroyed all the sinful people; but now, God will work among the sinful people, dealing with sin in a different way by separating Abram's family from others. *The bud of God's grace and remembrance* which is at the heart of Genesis 1–11 (Gen 6:8; 8:1) will bloom into and open the door of salvation for all peoples.

But we cannot have a new creation without a disruption of the old order. The most shocking disruption in this passage is the barrenness of Sarai. We have been following the "seed of women" since God's promise to Eve in Genesis 3:15, wondering how and when the serpent's head will be crushed. Now when we get to witness God's plan being fulfilled in this new couple, we are dumbfounded to hear that the woman is barren.

There are many possible reasons for barrenness. Sometimes God prevents conception because of sin (e.g. Gen 20:18), but he is also the one who opens barren wombs (Gen 20:17; 25:21; 29:31), and there are notable instances of righteous women being barren for much of their lives (e.g. Hannah, 1 Sam 1:5–20; Elizabeth, Luke 1:6–7). In this case, we do not know why Sarai was childless, and we can only guess what she felt about it. When, eventually, God declared that she would bear a child, she expressed her doubt and fear with sarcastic laughter (Gen 18:12; 21:1–8). The Qur'an, too, tells of her barrenness and her laughter, and agrees that the birth of Isaac shows God's mighty power (Sūra Hūd 11:71). Nothing is impossible for the omnipotent Lord of the universe! This gives hope to all barren women. YHWH is the covenant God who shows his power through human weakness, and he will reveal his glory through a barren couple.

What About Us?

Like Noah, Abram shows extraordinary loyalty to the One True God. His response to God's call was to sacrifice his wealth, his father's home, and the city he lived in. Abram's story is like the story of many Muslim-heritage followers of Jesus the Messiah in Bangladesh. Bangladesh does not have any law against changing religion, but social pressures often force them to leave their homes, and they may lose their property and their inheritance. In recent years, despite government protection, there have been ongoing threats from several Jihadist groups, and people have had to flee their communities and even the country to avoid facing false legal cases or even illegal execution by radical Islamist groups. Like Abram, we must literally live as sojourners in this world. Like Abram, we are called to seek the heavenly city built by God (Heb 11:10). We may not see it now, but we know that it is not a useless tower which will fall down, but an everlasting dwelling place with foundations which will never collapse.

In this life, like Abram, we have a job to do. Like him, some of our family will work with us, but some we might have to leave behind. This raises many questions in our minds. Is it too difficult for God to work through our family? Would it be possible for God to implement his plan if we had an orphan and a barren wife to care for? Do we think that this would ruin God's plan? If God told us to go wherever he wanted us to go, what would our response be? If God selected us to start a "settlement" somewhere, what would our responsibility be as "head of the family"? How far do we think we could go in obeying God if our parents are unbelievers? What happens when our father dies?

These questions were no easier for Abram than they would be for us today. These characteristics of the ancient world – family, marriage, land, relatives – all held the same importance then as they do now for us in South Asia. Society would have viewed the surrender of these things with fear and trepidation, and so also today, many people are hesitant to answer the call of Jesus the Messiah. We need to meditate on the way Abram accepted the promises given to him if we want to be included in his family – to be part of the *millate Ibrahim*.

We remember the words of Jesus the Messiah:

> Truly, I say to you, there is no one who has left house or brothers or sisters or mother or father or children or lands, for my sake and for the gospel, who will not receive a hundredfold now in this time, houses and brothers and sisters and mothers and children and lands, with persecutions, and in the age to come eternal life. (Mark 10:29–30)

8

God's Blessing on Abram – Genesis 12:2–3

Genesis is a book of beginnings and a book of blessings. Genesis 1 and 2 told of creation: of the blessings in the beginnings of the world. Genesis 3:1–11:9 told of the beginnings of human rebellion against God and of the resulting loss of blessings. At the centre of it all was the story of the flood and of the rainbow covenant in which God announced his commitment to continue his blessings despite human sin. Here, in Genesis 12:2–3, we read about the beginnings of God's plan to bless his world through Abraham. Abraham's family would be the vehicle of blessing which would bring all the divided peoples of Peleg's generation into one community, the people of the true *millate Ibrahim*. Every family of the earth would be blessed through Abraham's family.

We All Want Abraham's Blessing

Jews understand that Abraham was their ancestor, and that they are the people who were promised to him as his descendants. The Apostle Paul insists that the roots of Christian faith go behind Moses and his law to Abraham and his faith (Gal 3:6–14; Rom 4:9–17). The Qur'an, too, claims to follow the religion of Abraham (Sūras *al-Baqara* 2:135; *an-Naḥl* 16:120–23), and points out that he was neither a Jew nor a Christian, because he came before Jesus the Messiah and before Moses.

Devout Jewish people pray the "*Amidah*" (standing prayer) every day, beginning with,

> Blessed are You, Lord our God and God of our fathers, God of Abraham, God of Isaac and God of Jacob; the great, the mighty and awesome God, God Most High, who bestows acts of

lovingkindness and creates all, who remembers the lovingkindness of the Patriarchs and will bring a Redeemer to their children's children, for the sake of His name, in love. King, Helper, Saviour, Shield. Blessed are You, Lord, Shield of Abraham.[1]

Many Christians regularly recite the prayers of Mary (the "*Magnificat*") and of Zechariah (the "*Benedictus*") which rejoice that Jesus the Messiah will fulfil God's promise to Abraham:

> He has helped his servant Israel,
>   in remembrance of his mercy,
> as he spoke to our fathers,
>   to Abraham and to his offspring forever.[2]
> To show the mercy promised to our fathers
>   and to remember his holy covenant,
> the oath that he swore to our father Abraham, to grant us
>   that we, being delivered from the hand of our enemies,
> might serve him without fear,
>   in holiness and righteousness before him all our days.[3]

Muslims, too, remember the blessing of Abraham and request the same blessing for the Islamic Prophet Muhammad and his family in the prayer known as *durūd-e-Ibrāhīm*, which is part of the salah prayer. They say it 27 times a day if they perform them all!

> O God, bestow Your favor on Muhammad and on the family of Muhammad as You have bestowed Your favor on Ibrahim and on the family of Ibrahim, You are Praiseworthy, Most Glorious. O God, bless Muhammad and the family of Muhammad as You have blessed Ibrahim and the family of Ibrahim, You are Praiseworthy, Most Glorious. (Bukhārī, Vol. 4, Book 55, Hadith 589)

The Qur'an summarizes the importance given to Abraham in receiving God's blessing:

---

1. Translated by J. Sacks, *Authorised Daily Prayer Book*, 4th ed. (London: Collins, 2006), 75–76.

2. Luke 1:54–55. The "Magnificat" (Luke 1:46–55), Mary's prayer of praise after the angel told her about the birth of Jesus the Messiah, is part of the daily evening prayer of many churches.

3. Luke 1:72–75. The "Benedictus" (Luke 1:68–79), Zechariah's prayer of praise after the birth of John the Baptist, is part of the daily morning prayer of many churches.

And who has a better religion than him who submits his will to God, being virtuous, and follows the millate Ibrahim, a hanif? And God took Abraham for a dedicated friend. (Sūra an-Nisā'4:125)

In a world parted from fellowship with God in Eden, what could be a greater blessing than being chosen by God as his friend? (cf. Isa 41:8; Jas 2:23)

COMMENTARY
Genesis 12:2–3 The Seven Blessings

> *And I will make of you a great nation, and I will bless you and make your name great, so that you will be a blessing. I will bless those who bless you, and him who dishonours you I will curse, and in you all the families of the earth shall be blessed.*

Genesis tells us that there is not only one blessing for Abram: there are seven specific, precious promises which will follow Abram's "going." Grammatically, we could understand this as God saying, "Go so that I can bring all these blessings!"

We are reminded of another great commandment with a promise:

> Honour your father and your mother, that your days may be long in the land that the Lord your God is giving you. (Exod 20:12)

If Abram does not leave his home and his father's idolatrous household, God cannot begin the new people in the new land which will bring the blessings. But that does not mean that he, or any of his *millat*, should dishonour his parents. Later, Abram would honour his father's family by choosing a wife for his son from among his father's grandchildren.

The people of Babel had said, "Come . . ." because they wanted to stay together securely in one place and to make a name for themselves. Abram would obey God by "going" (Gen 12:4). He would lose his community and his security, but God would give him not only a name but a great name. He would not only gain blessing for himself but be a blessing to others. God himself would give him security and honour, and through his family God would bring blessing to all other families.

The First Blessing: "I will make of you a great nation"
How will a childless couple become parents of a great nation? To the human mind, it seems impossible and makes us laugh like Abram and Sarai (Gen 17:17; 18:13). Sarai's barrenness, announced in Genesis 11:30, was a shocking

loss of the creation blessing of fruitfulness of Genesis 1:26–27. Now, the reader who lives in our fallen world where so many marriages are barren is shocked again – this time, at God's ability to restore the blessing. More than twenty years later, under his name God Almighty (Heb. *El Shadday*), the creator will fulfil this promise and change Abram's name from "exalted father," to Abraham, "father of many nations" (Gen 17:5).

Today the people who want to be part of Abraham's family are indeed like the stars in the sky (Gen 15:5). Jews speak of "our father Abraham" (Heb. *Avraham Avinu*) as both their biological ancestor and the father of their faith. Christians see Abraham as the spiritual father of all believers, Gentiles as well as Jews (Rom 4:13–15). The Qur'an claims him as the spiritual father of Muslims (Sūra *al-Ḥajj* 22:78). The Qur'an also knows that the *Bani Isra'il* is the blessed nation, from which came not only the Messiah, but many other prophets, including the Islamic Prophet Muhammad, who descended from Abraham through his son Ishmael (Sūra *al-Mā'ida* 5:20).

The Second Blessing: "I will bless you"

We remember how God blessed human beings with relationships, with fertility, with an abundance of food, with a beautiful home, and with the responsibility of governing the earth in Genesis 1 and 2. We remember the results of disobedience in Genesis 3:14–19, and how Adam and Eve were expelled from their home in the Eden garden. All these blessings became distorted through sin, and humanity lives in a strange land. Now, the blessings lost by Adam and his family will be restored to Abram and his family, and it will happen through God leading Abram to a new land.

The Third Blessing: "I will make your name great"

The people of Babel tried to make their own name great. Would Abram's name become great because of his own efforts? No! It would become great because of God's blessing. Or would it be by his own piety and his ability to pass God's tests? Again, no! It would be God and God alone who, through his mercy and grace, would give him a new name, Abraham, and that name would be venerated by countless millions of people. His name would not be magnified through force or violence, nor through armies or skyscrapers or abundant resources, but by means of the Spirit and love of God (cf. Zech 4:6).

The Fourth Blessing: "You will be a blessing"

God blessed Abram in order that he might bring blessing to others; but, if we read on in Genesis, we will find that Abram does not always bring blessing on those whom he meets. In the very next section, he brings disaster to someone who tries to treat him well (Gen 12:10–20). How and when would he become a blessing? In Genesis 22:18, we will find that it is specifically through Sarai's promised son that the blessings will come to other people, so we can see that this promise is pointing to the seed of the woman who will bruise Satan's head (Gen 3:15). Jesus the Messiah, the descendant of Abraham (Matt 1:1), would leave his home and his Father's house in heaven to bring the blessing. He would not seek a great name, but would make himself nothing (Phil 2:7). God would raise him from the dead, and give him the name above all names, far greater than the name of Abraham (Eph 1:20–21; Phil 2:9–11). Now, every believer in every family can share in the power of that name, and can receive the spiritual blessings of redemption, sanctification, remission of sin, adoption and eternal life (Eph 1:3, 15–21).

The Fifth Blessing: "I will bless those who bless you"

Abram will be a channel of God's blessing to those who bless him. Although the main blessings will be spiritual, God does sometimes bring material blessings to those who bless Abraham's descendants. In Genesis, the major example is the blessing that comes to the people of Egypt through Joseph, Abraham's great-grandson, during seven years of famine (Gen 41).

We have seen that it is not only Jews and Christians but also Muslims who want to share the blessing received by Abram and his family. The principle of the *durūd-e-Ibrāhīm* prayer is that, as people bless Abraham, they hope that God will bless them. From Genesis 12:2, we can imagine how much God wants to answer these prayers.

The Sixth Blessing: "Him who dishonours you I will curse"

Not everyone will be blessed through Abram. This next promise tells us that God himself will guard Abram's honour. Two different verbs are used here: *qalal*, with the root meaning of "belittle" or "despise," and *arar*, the common word for "curse." If any individual humiliates Abram or his seed, God will punish him. The Quran implicitly affirms this biblical promise when it narrates Nimrod's attempt to burn Abram in the fiery furnace and records that "those who wished to do him harm, God harmed them" (Sūra *al-Anbiyā'* 21:69–70). The prophets of the *Bani Isra'il* often warned that, although God might use other nations to punish his chosen people, anyone who mocked them and mistreated them would eventually be judged (e.g. Isa 47:6; 49:24–26; Jer 2:3; 30:10–17; 50–51; Ezek 25–26; Amos 1; Obad; Zeph 2:8–11).

The Seventh Blessing: "In you all the families of the earth shall be blessed"

The Hebrew of this blessing can be interpreted in three ways.[4] It could mean that the peoples will bless themselves by Abram, that they would be blessed through him, or that they will find blessing through him. All these meanings tell us that God plans for his blessing on Abram's family to be the source of blessing for all other families. All peoples of the earth described in Genesis 10 were made in his image and likeness and were under the rainbow covenant. It is because the faithful God remembered them that he called Abram.

We are amazed at the thought that the people of all the nations spoken of in Genesis 10 could be blessed through Abram and wonder what this can mean. Centuries later, the Apostle Paul will give an answer, as he calls this blessing the gospel preached to Abraham (Gal 3:8).

Theological Reflection

The blessing of Abram reflects all of the three facets of theology that we have followed through this commentary.

The Bud of Theology

In these seven blessings, we glimpse many petals of *the bud of theology* which has been opening in Genesis 1–11. The one who blesses is the God who, in spite of the rebellious and violent nature of humankind, promised Noah that he would never again wipe out his creatures. We see a God who loves his world, the faithful covenant Lord who will not only preserve us but also bless us. This is a God who chooses to work through particular humans: as he chose Noah and his family, he now chooses one barren couple as his vehicle of blessing to every family on this earth. This is a God who shows his power of reproduction. As so often in Genesis 1–11, we see that it is the One Creator God, and not any deity such as the Canaanite fertility god Baal, who has full power over what he has made.

The God who created light in the darkness and made a beautifully ordered world from the chaos of *tohu wa bohu* is the only one who can banish the darkness of sin and bring the blessings of truth, obedience, fruitfulness and just dominion to illuminate and order our fallen world.

---

4. Grammatically, the verb is in the *niphal* form, which can be translated as passive, middle or reflexive. See Wenham, *Genesis 1–11*, 277–78 for a thorough discussion.

The Grandmother of the Sciences

There are aspects of the story of Abram which have deeply affected the attitudes of Jews, Christians and Muslims to the natural world. We noted Jewish and Christian discussions of God's exhortation to Abram to "look at the stars" (Gen 15:5), and the stories which grew up about Abram's rejection of the worship of heavenly bodies. This means that astrology – the idea that the heavenly bodies somehow rule our destinies – was rejected. These bodies are ruled by their Creator and have no power over us;[5] however, we can learn by looking at them. In Genesis 15, the stars taught Abram about God's infinite power and faithfulness. This plants a seed which becomes a theme in the Bible (e.g. Job 38–41; Pss 19; 104; Isa 40:12–26; Rom 1:19–20). Much later, the Qur'an will call humanity to study the *ayāt* (signs) of God in creation (e.g. Sūras *adh-Dhāriyāt* 51:20–21; *Yūnus* 10:5–9; *ar-Ra'd* 13:2–4; *an-Naḥl* 16:65–69; *ar-Rūm* 30:8–11, 18–26).

So, those who wish to share in the blessings of Abram have, down the centuries, learned about the Creator as they have observed the creation, and this has fed the growth of the sciences. They have studied the natural world alongside their Bible, what they called the "book of God's works" alongside the "book of God's words." Charles Darwin placed this quotation at the beginning of *The Origin of Species*, the book which launched the theory of evolution:

> In conclusion, let no man upon a weak conceit of sobriety or an ill-applied moderation think or maintain that a man can search too far, or be too well studied in the book of God's word, or the book of God's works, divinity or philosophy (i.e. science); but rather let men endeavour an endless progress or proficiency in both.[6]

Darwin's book did not reject the idea of God as Creator; rather, it argued that understanding what God created can best be achieved through observation and reason, and that his observations challenge traditional understandings.

It is important that the blessing of Abram also reminds us of the limitations of science: of human knowledge based on observation and reason. Even today, despite all our advances, medical science cannot always enable a barren couple to have children. This blessing tells us that the Creator has greater control of his creation that we can ever have, and that is an essential basis for all our discussion of medical and scientific ethics.

---

5. See commentary on Gen 1:14–19.

6. Quoting Francis Bacon's *The Advancement of Learning* (1605), a book which was very influential in the beginnings of modern science.

The Seedbed of the Bible

These blessings are the beginning of the *Bani Isra'il*, the people formed by God to bring blessing to the world. The Bible contains the books given by God to this special people and, through them, to the people of all nations. Most of the books were written by descendants of Abraham as they were guided by the Holy Spirit. They include prayers, praises and questions which the *Bani Isra'il* used in their relationship with God, as well as narratives of how God was at work in their history, and prophetic messages through which God spoke to them.

Through the various books of the Bible, therefore, we learn how God fulfilled the plan of blessing which he announced to Abram. The books of history and of the prophets tell us that the *Bani Isra'il* often failed in their mission just as Adam and Eve failed in theirs; but they also tell us that God's plan did not fail. God loves the world so much that he continued his faithfulness to the *Bani Isra'il*.

In the Qur'an, God's promise to Abraham came only after he had proved his faith through certain commands and trials, and God's covenant with Abraham's family excluded evil-doers:

> And when his Lord tested Abraham with certain words, and he fulfilled them, He said, "I am making you the Imam [leader] of mankind." Said he, "And from among my descendants?" He said, "My pledge does not extend to the Ẓalimūn (unjust)." (Sūra al-Baqara 2:124)

Before this verse, the Qur'an reminds the Jews of seventh-century Medina about God's favour in making them a special nation and urges them to fulfil their covenant. It then reminds them of the many times when their ancestors disobeyed God and broke that covenant (Sūra *al-Baqara* 2:40–103). This is clearly teaching that if the *Bani Isra'il* are disobedient, they lose the blessing of Abraham.

In contrast, although the Bible teaches that many individuals who rebelled against God came under his judgement, his promise to bless the world through Abraham's children was unconditional. Throughout biblical history, we see that God preserved the *Bani Isra'il*, and that there were always some who were of the true *millate Ibrahim* who faithfully carried the blessings. Eventually, through the descendants of Abraham's promised son, God sent his own Son, Jesus the Messiah, into the world (Gal 3:19). All the seedlings that we have seen of God's love and mercy are gathered in him, and it is through him that all nations receive the promised blessing.

According to the New Testament, every person who receives Jesus the Messiah by faith is a true child of God and an inheritor of Abraham's blessings. The Messiah sacrificed his life on the cross. There is no need for us to be wiped out by a flood of judgement, because he has wiped out our sin through his blood. He offers us release from all cursing, because he became a curse for us. This gospel is for all nations, including the descendants of the son who was cursed by Noah (Gal 3:13–14). Jesus the Messiah, the seed of Abraham, has already begun to deliver God's grace and mercy to all families of the world; however, the Abrahamic blessings will not be fulfilled completely until he returns (Matt 24:30–31). Until then, God continues to call individuals and particular families to accomplish his plan.

Jesus the Messiah is the redeemer hoped for in the Jewish "*Amidah*" prayer, the fulfilment of the promise recalled by Mary in the *Magnificat*, and the answer to the *durūd-e-Ibrāhīm* prayer that we be blessed "as You have blessed Abraham and the family of Abraham."

The Beginning and the End

At the beginning of Genesis 1–11 is Adam, whose disobedience led to the loss of so much of God's blessing. At the end is Abram, whose obedience would be the seed for the blessing of many peoples. At the centre is Noah, and at the centre of the Noah narrative, the centre of the whole of Genesis 1–11, is the single verse, "God remembered Noah."

As Abram was the tenth generation from Shem, Noah was the tenth generation from Adam. Noah and Abram were both selected by God to form a new community. Both of them were commissioned to accomplish God's plan to form a God-fearing community. With both, God made a covenant which would bless all humanity. Both journeyed towards an unknown land, dependent on the faithful God for their direction. God remembered them both, before, during and even after their journeys.

Many Muslims cite the qur'anic idea that, if anyone remembers God, then God remembers him (Sūra *al-Baqara* 2:122). Biblical remembrance is not conditional like this; rather, God will remember his promises to all peoples. As the psalmist wrote, "He remembers his covenant forever, the word that he commanded, for a thousand generations" (Ps 105:8).

God's blessing to Abraham streams over the earth like rays from the sun and encompasses the whole earth. On the cross, the seed of Abraham, Jesus the Messiah, blessed his enemies and thus opened a way to bless every family on earth. But our world today has lost the beautiful blessings of Eden. There remain conflicts between people of the Abrahamic faiths, even in the *Shat al-Arab* area where Eden seems to have been situated. The Promised Land and its adjacent areas are constantly polluted with blood. Like Abel's blood, these bloods are crying out for peace and justice!

Such battles are seldom over who are the true *millate Ibrahim*: disputes are due to selfishness and pride, to the desires for power and domination which we have observed throughout Genesis 3–11. We replace God's loving rule with a worship of our own interests which is as bad as any worship of stone idols. As God called Noah and Abram and Sarai in their violent, idolatrous times, so he calls believers in the Messiah as peacemakers among all peoples today. We do not bring God's peace by trying to make a name for ourselves, but through God's chosen way of blessing and of dealing with the sin within us which waits to pounce on us (Gen 4:7).

We will not find the peace for which we long until the promise to Abram in Genesis 12:3 reaches its fulfilment when Jesus the Messiah comes again. In the book of Revelation 7:9–10, we read:

> After this I looked, and behold, a great multitude that no one could number, from every nation, from all tribes and peoples and languages, standing before the throne and before the Lamb, clothed in white robes, with palm branches in their hands, and crying out with a loud voice, "Salvation belongs to our God who sits on the throne, and to the Lamb!"

Here is the full blossoming from *the bud of theology* of Genesis 1–11, as believers see God in his glory. Here is the harvest from all the seedlings in the seedbed of the Bible. How wonderful is this vision of every blessed family which believes in Jesus the Messiah, the son of Abraham, worshipping together! It is the reverse of the curse of language confusion in Genesis 11, which began on the day of Pentecost, when people from different nations and languages gathered together and understood the good news (Acts 2:6–8). From Genesis 3 onwards, humanity has lived amidst sin, cursing, tears, corruption and death, but in the new heaven and earth at the end of time, these will disappear:

> And I heard a loud voice from the throne saying, "Behold, the dwelling place of God is with man. He will dwell with them, and they will be his people, and God himself will be with them as their God. He will wipe away every tear from their eyes, and death shall be no more, neither shall there be mourning, nor crying, nor pain any more, for the former things have passed away." (Rev 21:3–4)

Bibliography

Bangla Books

Al-Kisai, *Qisas al-Anbiya*, Dhaka: Taj Company Ltd, 6th edition, 1410 A.H.

Dawn, Deproshad, ed. *Baul Sangeeter Nondontotto* [Aesthetics of Baul Music]. Dhaka: M. Mohsin Rubel, 2012.

Faridpuri, Shamsul Haque (Trans), *Bhokhari Sharif*, Dhaka: Hamidia Library Ltd, 17th Edition, 2014.

Fordabadi, Amirul Islam, Shapori, Abdul Gaffar Shapori, and Habibur Rahman Hobigonji (trans and ed), *Tofsir Jalalin*, Dhaka: Moulana Mohammad Mustafa, undated.

Hannan, Mohammad. *Banglir Itihas* [Bengali History]. Dhaka: Agami Prokashoni, 2012

Ibn Hanbal, Ahmad, *Musnad-e-Ahmad*, translated, edited and published by Dhaka: Islamic Foundation, 2008

Ibn Kathir. *Tofsir Ibn Kasir*. Bangla translation by Muhammad Muzibur Rahman. Dhaka: Husain Al Madani Publications, 1406 AH/1986 CE.

Imdadullah, M. N. M. *Kasasul Ambiya*. Dhaka: Bangladesh Taj Co. Ltd., 1410 AH.

Khan, Mohammed Akram, ed. *Quran Sharif*. Kolkata: Mohammadi Publishing Co., 1919.

Khan, Muhiuddin. *Tofsir-e-Ma'reful Qur'an*. Bangla version of Muhammad Shafi's Urdu *Tafsir-e-Maareful Qur'an*. Dhaka: Islamic Foundation, 2011.

Kitabul Mokaddos. Dhaka: Manjile Kitabul Mukaddos, 1982.

Mishkaat ul Masaabeeh. Dhaka: Hadith Academy, 2013.

Mishkat Sharif. Dhaka: Solemania Book House, 2004.

Rahman, Musadir (trans), *Tofsirul Baizawi*, Dhaka: Islamia Kutubkhana

Sihah Sittah Editorial Board, trans. and ed., *Muslim Sharif*. Dhaka: Islamic Foundation, 2010.

Thanvi, Ashraf Ali, *Boyanul Qur'an*, Dhaka: Embodia Library, 2011

Texts Translated into English

At-Ṭabarī. *The History of Al-Ṭabarī, Volume 1: General Introduction and from the Creation to the Flood*, translated by Franz Rosenthal. Albany: State University of New York Press, 1987.

———. *The History of Al-Ṭabarī, Volume 2: Prophets and Patriarchs*, translated by William Brinner. Albany: State University of New York Press, 1989.

Ibn Ishaq. *The Life of Muhammad (Ibn Ishaq's Sirāt Rasūl Allāh)*. Translated by A. Guillaume. Oxford University Press, 1955.

Ibn Kathir. *Stories of the Prophet*. Translated by Muhammad Mustapha Geme'ah. Cairo: Al Azhar, date?

Khan, Syed Ahmad (his own translation). *The Mohammedan Commentary on the Holy Bible: Genesis 1–11*. Aligarh, 1965.

Origen. *Homilies on Genesis and Exodus*. Translated by R. E. Heine. Washington, DC: Catholic University of America Press, 1982.

Salim, Ghulam Husain. *Riyazu-s-Salatin: A History of Bengal*, 1787/8. Forgotten Books, 2011. (The 1912 English translation is reprinted by Forgotten Books, 2011.)

Satapatha Brāhmana 1.8.1. https://sacred-texts.com/hin/sbr/sbe12/sbe1234.htm. Accessed 22 April 2021.

Unless otherwise stated, references to the hadith collections of Bukhārī and Muslim use the USC-MSC numbering system from https://www.sunnah.com.

General bibliography

Aitken, James K., Hector M. Patmore, and Ishay Rosen-Zvi, eds. *The Evil Inclination in Early Judaism and Christianity*. New York: Cambridge University Press, 2021.

Alexander, Denis R. "Models for Relating Science and Religion." Faraday Paper 3, available at www.faraday.cam.ac.uk/resources/faraday-papers/.

Ali, Kecia. *Sexual Ethics and Islam*. London: OneWorld, 2006.

Anderson, Gary. "The Exaltation of Adam and the Fall of Satan." *The Journal of Jewish Thought and Philosophy* 6, no. 1 (1997): 105–134. https://doi.org/10.1163/147728597794761754.

Armour, Robert. *Gods and Myths of Ancient Egypt*. Cairo: American University in Cairo Press, 1986.

Bennett, Jim, and Scott Mandelbrote. *The Garden, the Ark, the Tower, the Temple: Biblical Metaphors of Knowledge in Early Modern Europe*. Oxford: Museum of the History of Science, 1998.

Berry, R. J. "Creation and Evolution, Not Creation or Evolution," Faraday Paper no. 12, www.faraday.cam.ac.uk/resources/faraday-papers/.

———, ed. *The Lion Handbook of Science and Christianity*. Oxford: Lion Hudson, 2012.

Blocher, Henri. *In the Beginning: The Opening Chapters of Genesis*. Downers Grove: InterVarsity Press, 1984.

Burke, John G. *Cosmic Debris: Meteorites in History*. Berkeley: University of California Press, 1991.

Campbell, William. *The Qur'an and the Bible in the Light of History and Science*. 2nd ed. Upper Darby: Middle East Resources, 2002.

Carman, Jon. "The Falling Star and the Rising Son: Luke 10:17–24 and Second Temple 'Satan' Traditions." *Stone-Campbell Journal* 17, no. 2 (2014): 221–231.

Cuypers, Michel. *The Composition of the Qur'an: Rhetorical Analysis*. London: Bloomsbury Press, 2015.

Douglas, J. D., et al (eds), *The New Bible Dictionary*. Leicester: Inter-Varsity Press, 1982.

Elliott, Jeri. *Your Door to Arabia*. Invercargill, NZ: Craig Printing, 1992.

Equiano, Olaudah. *The Interesting Narrative and Other Writings*. New York: Penguin Books, 1995 [1789].

Ernst, Carl W. *How to Read the Qur'an: A New Guide with Selected Translations*. Chapel Hill: University of North Carolina Press, 2011.

Evans, Mary J. *Women in the Bible*. Downers Grove: InterVarsity, 1984.

Gaster, Theodor Herzl, and James George Frazer. *Myth, Legend and Custom in the Old Testament*. New York: Harper & Row, 1969.

Geisinger, Alex. "Sustainable Development and the Domination of Nature: Spreading the Seed of the Western Ideology of Nature." *Boston College Environmental Affairs Law Review* 27, no. 1 (1999): 43–73. https://lawdigitalcommons.bc.edu/ealr/vol27/iss1/3/.

Gillingham, Susan E. *The Poems and Psalms of the Hebrew Bible*. Oxford: Oxford University Press, 1994.

Glaser, Ida. "An Experiment in Contextualized Comparative Hermeneutics: Reading Genesis 1–11 in the Context of Parallel Qur'anic Material and Christian Mission amongst Muslims in Elswick, Newcastle Upon Tyne." PhD Thesis from University of Durham, 1994. http://etheses.dur.ac.uk/968/1/968_v1.pdf.

———, and Hannah Kay. *Thinking Biblically about Islam: Genesis, Transfiguration and Transformation*. Carlisle: Langham Global Library, 2016.

———, and Napoleon John. *Partners or Prisoners?: Christians Thinking about Women and Islam*. Carlisle: Paternoster, 1998.

Goldingay, John. *Genesis*. Baker Commentary of the Old Testament: Pentateuch. Grand Rapids: Baker Academic, 2020.

Hamilton, Victor P. *The Book of Genesis: Chapter 1–17*. Grand Rapids: Eerdmans, 1990.

Harrison, Peter. *The Bible, Protestantism, and the Rise of Natural Science*. Cambridge: Cambridge University Press, 2001

———. *The Fall of Man and the Foundations of Science*. Cambridge: Cambridge University Press, 2007.

Hess, Richard S. *Studies in the Personal Names of Genesis 1–11*. Winona Lake: Eisenbrauns, 2009.

Hill, Carol A. "Making Sense of the Numbers of Genesis." *Perspectives on Science and Christian Faith* 55, no. 4 (2003): 239–251. https://www.asa3.org/ASA/PSCF/2003/PSCF12-03Hill.pdf.

Institute of Medicine, et al. *Science, Evolution, and Creationism: A View from the National Academy of Sciences and the Institute of Medicine*. National Academies Press, 2008.

Jacobsen, Thorkild. "The Sumerian King List." *Assyriological Studies* 11. The Oriental Institute, University of Chicago, 1939. https://oi.uchicago.edu/research/publications/as/11-sumerian-king-list.

Johnson, David L. *Earth, Empire and Sacred Text: Muslims and Christians as Trustees of Creation*. London: Equinox, 2010.

Keil, Carl F., and Franz Delitzsch. *Commentary on the Old Testament: The Pentateuch, Volume 1*. Peabody: Hendrickson, 1986.

Killeen, Kevin, and Peter J. Forshaw, eds. *The Word and the World: Biblical Exegesis and Early Modern Science*. New York: Palgrave Macmillan, 2007.

Köchler, Hans, ed. *The Concept of Monotheism in Islam and Christianity*. Wein: Wilhelm Braumüller, 1982.

Mathews, Kenneth A. *The New American Commentary: Genesis 1:11–26*. Nashville: Broadman & Holman, 1996.

Mir, Mustansir. "The Qur'an as Literature." *Religion & Literature* 20, no 1 (1988): 49–64. https://www.jstor.org/stable/40059366.

———. "The Qur'anic Story of Joseph: Plot, Themes and Characters." *The Muslim World* 76, no. 1 (1986): 1–15. https://doi.org/10.1111/j.1478-1913.1986.tb02766.x.

Moreland, James Porter. *Theistic Evolution: A Scientific, Philosophical, and Theological Critique*. Wheaton: Crossway, 2017.

Patmore, Hector M. *Adam, Satan, and the King of Tyre: The Interpretation of Ezekiel 28:11–19 in Late Antiquity*. Leiden: Brill, 2012.

Reynolds, Gabriel Said. *The Qur'an and Its Biblical Subtext*. London: Routledge, 2010.

Sawday, Jonathan. "The Fortunes of Babel: Technology, History, and Genesis 11:1–9." In *The Word and the World*, edited by Killeen and Forshaw, 191–214. New York: Palgrave Macmillan, 2007.

Schimmel, Annemarie. *Deciphering the Signs of God: A Phenomenological Approach to Islam*. Albany: State University of New York Press, 1994.

Seawright, Caroline. "Khnum, Potter God of the Inundation Silt and Creation." http://www.touregypt.net/featurestories/khnum.htm.

Wadud, Amina. *Qur'an and Woman: Rereading the Sacred Text from a Woman's Perspective*. New York: Oxford University Press, 1999.

Walton, John H. *The Lost World of Genesis One: Ancient Cosmology and the Origins Debate*. Downers Grove: InterVarsity, 2010.

Walton, John. *Genesis*. The NIV Application Commentary. Grand Rapids: Zondervan, 2001.

Wenham, Gordon J. *Genesis 1–15*. Word Biblical Commentary 1. Waco: Word, 1987.

———. *Rethinking Genesis 1–11: Gateway to the Bible*. Eugene: Wipf & Stock, 2015.

Westermann, Claus. *Genesis 1–11: A Commentary*. Minneapolis: Augsburg, 1984.

Whittingham, Martin. *A History of Muslim Views of the Bible: The First 400 Years*. Studies of the Bible and Its Reception (SBR). Berlin: De Gruyter, 2020.

Wilkins, W. J. *Hindu Mythology, Vedic and Purānic*. Calcutta: Thacker, Spink, & Co., 1901.

Wiseman, P. J., and D. J. Wiseman. *Ancient Records and the Structure of Genesis: A Case for Literary Unity*. Nashville: Thomas Nelson, 1985.

Subject Index

Qur'an Index

Langham
PARTNERSHIP

Langham Literature and its imprints are a ministry of Langham Partnership.

Langham Partnership is a global fellowship working in pursuit of the vision God entrusted to its founder John Stott –

to facilitate the growth of the church in maturity and Christ-likeness through raising the standards of biblical preaching and teaching.

Our vision is to see churches in the Majority World equipped for mission and growing to maturity in Christ through the ministry of pastors and leaders who believe, teach and live by the word of God.

Our mission is to strengthen the ministry of the word of God through:
- nurturing national movements for biblical preaching
- fostering the creation and distribution of evangelical literature
- enhancing evangelical theological education

especially in countries where churches are under-resourced.

Our ministry

Langham Preaching partners with national leaders to nurture indigenous biblical preaching movements for pastors and lay preachers all around the world. With the support of a team of trainers from many countries, a multi-level programme of seminars provides practical training, and is followed by a programme for training local facilitators. Local preachers' groups and national and regional networks ensure continuity and ongoing development, seeking to build vigorous movements committed to Bible exposition.

Langham Literature provides Majority World preachers, scholars and seminary libraries with evangelical books and electronic resources through publishing and distribution, grants and discounts. The programme also fosters the creation of indigenous evangelical books in many languages, through writer's grants, strengthening local evangelical publishing houses, and investment in major regional literature projects, such as one volume Bible commentaries like *The Africa Bible Commentary* and *The South Asia Bible Commentary.*

Langham Scholars provides financial support for evangelical doctoral students from the Majority World so that, when they return home, they may train pastors and other Christian leaders with sound, biblical and theological teaching. This programme equips those who equip others. Langham Scholars also works in partnership with Majority World seminaries in strengthening evangelical theological education. A growing number of Langham Scholars study in high quality doctoral programmes in the Majority World itself. As well as teaching the next generation of pastors, graduated Langham Scholars exercise significant influence through their writing and leadership.

To learn more about Langham Partnership and the work we do visit **langham.org**